WACO

David Koresh,
the Branch Davidians,
and a Legacy of Rage

JEFF GUINN

Simon & Schuster

NEW YORK · LONDON · TORONTO
SYDNEY · NEW DELHI

Simon & Schuster
1230 Avenue of the Americas
New York, NY 10020

First Simon & Schuster hardcover edition January 2023

SIMON & SCHUSTER and colophon are registered trademarks
of Simon & Schuster, Inc.

For information about special discounts for bulk purchases,
please contact Simon & Schuster Special Sales at 1-866-506-1949
or business@simonandschuster.com.

The Simon & Schuster Speakers Bureau can bring authors to your
live event. For more information, or to book an event, contact
the Simon & Schuster Speakers Bureau at 1-866-248-3049
or visit our website at www.simonspeakers.com.

Interior design by Paul Dippolito

Manufactured in the United States of America

1   3   5   7   9   10   8   6   4   2

Library of Congress Cataloging-in-Publication Data

ISBN 978-1-9821-8610-4
ISBN 978-1-9821-8612-8 (ebook)

In memory of Iris Chang:
Historian and Hero

"A fog of crosscutting motives and narratives,
a complexity that defies storybook simplicity:
that is usually the way history happens."

—RICK PERLSTEIN, *THE INVISIBLE BRIDGE*

Contents

A Note on Nomenclature

Victor Houteff founded the organization originally known as the Shepherd's Rod, then later as the Davidians. The proper term for the group subsequently led by Ben Roden is Branch Davidians. When Lois Roden moved into the leadership, for a time she called her followers the Living Waters, but they ultimately remained the Branch Davidians. David Koresh did not emphasize a group name. Most followers led by Koresh identified themselves as Bible students, or, less frequently, as Students of the Seven Seals. In 1993, the name on the deed to Mount Carmel was General Association of the Branch Davidian Seventh-day Adventists, so members of the media covering the initial ATF raid and subsequent fifty-one-day FBI siege identified the besieged as Branch Davidians in their reports. Since this is the name ingrained in public consciousness, it's the one I use most frequently in this book.

WACO

ATF, Morning, February 28, 1993

Just before dawn on Sunday, February 28, 1993, an eighty-vehicle caravan departed Fort Hood Army base outside Killeen, Texas, heading northeast toward Waco, sixty-five miles away. Cattle trailers pulled by pickup trucks took the lead and brought up the rear. In between was a hodgepodge of sports cars, station wagons, and non-descript government-issue sedans sporting telltale extended antennas. All had their headlights on—it was that early morning time when darkness and daylight weave together, and a brisk, chilly breeze blew about puffs of ground fog. Rain seemed certain sooner rather than later. The less-than-perfect weather was irritating, but the drivers in the mile-long procession had other things on their minds. They were all agents of the Bureau of Alcohol, Tobacco and Firearms, better known as ATF and tasked with enforcing often unpopular federal laws. For the last two days, they'd been receiving special training at Fort Hood. In another few hours, they were scheduled to participate in the largest and, hopefully, best-publicized raid in agency history, one that might improve perception of their controversial organization.

Since late June 1992, ATF had investigated prophet David Koresh and his followers, collectively known as the Branch Davidians and living in a sprawling, makeshift building (ATF reports described it as a "compound") called Mount Carmel on seventy-seven hardscrabble acres about eight miles outside Waco. ATF planners believed approximately seventy-five men, women, and children occupied the fire-ant-infested property; it was hard to get an accurate count because they milled in and around their building so incessantly. After eight months, accumulated evidence indicated that the group was illegally altering guns from semi- to fully automatic, with the intent of either selling them or else using the fearsome weapons as part of a plot to bring about the end of the world. This, ATF tactical planners speculated, might involve anything from an assault on outsiders to gory group suicide.

Though specifically what the Branch Davidians believed, and exactly what they intended, wasn't clear to the ATF, it was still obvious that they at least had illegal guns in their possession, and illegal homemade "improvised explosive devices" (hand grenades), too. This made them lawbreakers, and appropriate targets of agency action. Two days earlier, on Friday, February 26, a U.S. district judge signed off on an ATF search warrant for Mount Carmel; a criminal complaint against, and an arrest warrant for, Vernon Wayne Howell (David Koresh's given name); and, critically, an order to immediately seal the warrants from public view. ATF organizers feared above all else losing the element of surprise; every possible step to catch the suspects off guard was built into the raid plan.

Traditionally, ATF raids took one of two forms: "surround and call out," giving suspects a chance to give up peacefully, and "dynamic entry," bursting into the suspects' lair before they had time to take up arms and resist. After many meetings and drawn-out discussions, dynamic entry became the plan for Mount Carmel, avoiding any potential for the Branch Davidians fighting back, destroying evidence, or committing mass suicide before arriving agents could stop them. The ATF's intent was to swoop in, arrest Koresh, find and confiscate critical evidence, and close the raid without a shot fired by either side, with at least some of this efficient, bloodless action captured on film for the benefit of the media and members of Congress. ATF budgetary hearings were scheduled in March.

There were obvious impediments to the plan. The Branch Davidian property was located off a narrow country road, at the end of a long driveway winding up a barren slope with no cover for anyone approaching the front door. The suspects were up at dawn every day, and believed to be handy with their arsenal. But ATF officials based their plan on two factors vouched for by informants, former Branch Davidians who'd turned against Koresh. First, Koresh kept tight control on weapons; all guns were kept in a locked storage room and taken out only on the leader's personal command. Second, Mount Carmel residents adhered to a rigid daily schedule. Each morning after breakfast there was "the daily," a gathering for communion (grape juice and crackers rather than wine and wafers) and scripture-based discussion. After that, certainly by 10 a.m., all able-bodied men on the property came outside to continue excavation of a massive pit that surviving Branch Davidians later described as a tornado shelter. The ATF believed it was intended as a bunker to provide cover during firefights.

So, in just a few hours on this damp Sunday morning, the Branch Davidian men would be working outside, their guns would be locked away inside, and seventy-six ATF agents, concealed in two cattle trailers, a common sight on Central Texas country back roads, would rumble up the Mount Carmel driveway, emerge from the trailers on the double, get between the Branch Davidian men and their guns, and gain control of the property. From there, it would be easy. Everything hinged on taking the suspects by surprise. Raid planners were so confident of succeeding that there was not a fully formed Plan B if things didn't go as anticipated. During their special training at Fort Hood, ATF agent Mike Duncan recalls, someone asked a supervisor, "What happens if things go to shit? There's no place to take cover." The response was vague—get out of the trailers, move away from the compound, return any fire. Agent Dave DiBetta remembers, "That sounded like something out of *Monty Python and the Holy Grail*; our [backup] plan is to get out of the trailers and run away, and then surround the place?" But the agents bought into the basic premise; the Branch Davidians would do as expected, and total surprise would be achieved.

The ATF caravan reached the Bellmead Civic Center around 7:45 a.m. (Six agents arrived several hours earlier, and had already departed to secure the muddy, wooded area behind Mount Carmel and prevent escape in that direction.) This collection of squat public buildings just off Texas State Highway 84 was chosen as the raid staging area for its convenient location—the tiny town of Bellmead was a few miles northeast of Waco and nine miles from Mount Carmel. Despite planners' fixation on surprising the Branch Davidians, no thought was apparently given to concealing ATF's presence from Bellmead locals—an ATF official, wearing a jacket emblazoned with the agency's emblem, and several Bellmead cops stood in the street, directing caravan cars into the parking lot. Bill Buford, leader of an ATF Special Response Team (SRT) from the agency's New Orleans division, was appalled when he went inside and found "some sweet ladies, ten or twelve of them," serving coffee and doughnuts. The refreshments were welcome, but, at least to Buford, the civilians weren't: "It was obvious we were about to do something. [The women] could have told people about it."

The agents had about ninety minutes to go over raid plans with team leaders, change into combat gear, and prepare to board the cattle trailers for what would be another fifteen- or twenty-minute ride to Mount Carmel. Stacked in three abreast, thirty-seven agents would ride in Trailer #1 and thirty-nine in Trailer #2. Two ladders would also be crammed into the second trailer; some of the agents were expected to scale their way up to a roof just beneath an upper floor on a side of the compound where Koresh supposedly kept the guns locked away in a room.

The atmosphere as agents sipped coffee and chatted was energized rather than nervous. Most were either veterans of the U.S. military with considerable combat experience, or else had previously worked as police officers or members of the Border Patrol. There were elements about this operation that were unique, that made it, in the opinion of agent Rory Heisch, "a BFD, Big Fucking Deal." For the first time in agency history, agents from multiple divisions—Houston,

Dallas, and New Orleans—would combine in a joint operation. Typical ATF raids might involve up to twenty participants: an entry team, a perimeter team, and perhaps one or two members of the local sheriff's department. But those raids usually took place at houses or apartments no larger than a few thousand square feet.

The Mount Carmel facility, so far as ATF planners could tell, sprawled approximately 43,000 square feet, and there were questions about the actual floor plan inside. Because the Branch Davidians had built the place haphazardly and without outside contractors, there was no blueprint on file for the ATF to study. During training at Fort Hood, masking tape and rope were used to indicate approximate room locations. Beyond the certainty about the group's daily schedule and that all guns were locked away in an upstairs room, most of the rest of the raid plan for taking control of Mount Carmel's interior was based on guesswork. One hundred and thirty-seven ATF agents, including support personnel, were on hand that morning to participate in the raid. It was impossible to be certain if that was the right number, too many, or too few.

About half of the seventy-six agents assigned to the dynamic entry were members of ATF Special Response Teams, the agency's elite tactical units. SRTs were still relatively new; especially with the proliferation of hostage situations occurring across all of law enforcement, ATF agents had badgered their superiors for additional training equivalent to that undertaken by police department SWAT teams. Selection for SRT training didn't mean more money—it was voluntary—but it brought considerable status within the agency. With that status came risk: SRTs led the way into every major, potentially volatile encounter. Even so, agents' training and ability to remain cool under extreme pressure was reflected in an astonishing statistic: in the three years previous, ATF's crack emergency teams executed 603 warrants and gunfire occurred only twice, with a total of three fatalities, all suspects. No one at ATF ever set out intending to injure, let alone kill, anyone.

This was apparent as agents prepared for the Mount Carmel raid.

They armed themselves to gain and retain control rather than engage in a firefight. A half dozen agents carried AR-15 semiautomatic rifles, but most of the rest had lower-powered semiautomatic MP5s out of concern that Mount Carmel's walls, floors, and ceilings were apparently constructed of flimsy materials. If any shooting did occur, agents didn't want their bullets plowing into adjacent rooms where women and children might be sheltering. A few agents had shotguns. Almost everyone had a holstered handgun, and, particularly among the most veteran agents, a backup handgun. Agent Robert Champion was assigned to lug a fire extinguisher. The Branch Davidians had lots of dogs, some known to be aggressive. If any dogs attacked the raiders, Champion was to spray them with the extinguisher, in hopes that this would subdue the animals without making it necessary to shoot them.

Everyone donned protective vests, though the protective plates in them would not necessarily stop bullets fired from the high-powered guns that ATF believed the Branch Davidians had. Some of the agents who would lead the way through Mount Carmel's front door even removed these plates from their vests, anticipating that, since the Branch Davidian men wouldn't have access to guns, there might be some hand-to-hand fighting instead. A front vest plate alone weighed twelve pounds. Removing the plates gave these agents more mobility. Agents' headgear ranged from a variety of helmets to woolen caps; ATF's limited budget did not allow for providing much equipment beyond guns, ammunition, and vests. Penny-pinching was a fact of ATF life. Agents had to scrounge their helmets from military surplus outlets (frequently substituted wool caps were cheaper), and most bought their own combat boots, too. But despite forced frugality limiting their gear, the agents knew that, when they swarmed Mount Carmel, they'd still be an intimidating sight. Even the most apparently hard-bitten suspects usually surrendered abjectly when faced with the unexpected appearance of trained, combat-ready professionals. Agent Blake Boteler recalls, "We didn't think much about them [the Branch Davidians] fighting to the death. A lot of people claim they'll do that. If ten do, then when we kick down that door, four wet their pants and the other six may curl up like a ball on the floor. Sometimes, there's one ready to fight. The element of surprise helps. It gets people on their heels. They intend to fight, but self-preservation takes over and overrules whatever doctrine they have in their heads."

Far from actually fighting, ATF hoped to create a family-friendly atmosphere. Several females were among the seventy-six agents about to participate in the raid. They would enter Mount Carmel after the SRTs secured the building, then separate the Branch Davidian women and children from the men, gently escorting them to another area, where they'd soothe the kids by offering them candy. It was understood that Branch Davidian offspring rarely enjoyed such treats. When things were more settled, one or two agents were assigned to drive to a nearby McDonald's and bring back sacks of Happy Meals for the youngsters. ATF support staff planned to bring tents to keep the Branch Davidian women and children out of the cold, wet weather, and to set up Port-o-Lets so that they could relieve themselves in privacy, undoubtedly a welcome alternative to the ubiquitous buckets that comprised plumbing-free Mount Carmel's facilities. At the Bellmead Civic Center, all the women agents stuffed their pockets with candy, and so did some of the male agents. They hoped that the Mount Carmel kids, and perhaps their mothers, too, would feel less panicked thanks to all this bounty.

Even the final go-word signaling agents to exit the trailers and rush the compound was selected to be as nonaggressive as possible. The raid itself had the code name "Trojan Horse." ATF's traditional call to action was "Execute," but the term seemed risky: if that portion of the raid was recorded for public replay, irresponsible members of the media and Congress might cite "Execute" as an indicator of lethal intention. So, for the Mount Carmel raid, the go-word would be "Showtime!"

The raid leaders were Phil Chojnacki and Chuck Sarabyn, the special agent in charge (SAC) and assistant special agent in charge (ASAC) from ATF's Houston office. They were assigned these roles because Waco was part of their larger Houston region. There was some concern, especially among the more veteran agents, about Chojnacki and Sarabyn as raid leaders. Neither was considered to have much field experience. On this day, Chojnacki was scheduled to observe the raid from above in one of three helicopters provided to the ATF as support by the Texas National Guard, and Sarabyn planned to ride into Mount Carmel in Cattle Trailer #1. For the moment, both were out at ATF's field headquarters on the campus of Texas State Technical College (TSTC), a site several miles away from the Bellmead Civic Center and Mount Carmel, but handy for an adjacent landing strip that could accommodate the National Guard helicopters.

In early January, ATF had also established what the agency termed an "undercover house" in a rental property directly across the road from Mount Carmel, and staffed it with eight male agents pretending to be TSTC students. One of these agents managed to visit Koresh at Mount Carmel several times. This morning, he was supposed to go into the compound one final time, to ensure that the Branch Davidian day was on its anticipated schedule, and that the suspects still had no inkling of ATF's imminent arrival. Once the agent confirmed these facts to Sarabyn at the TSTC command post, the second-in-command would come to the Bellmead Civic Center and the raid would commence.

A point of unexpected concern was the first in a series of investigative articles about Koresh that was published on Saturday, February 27, by the Waco Tribune-Herald. Titled "The Sinful Messiah," the initial stories indicated that Koresh maintained a harem of Mount Carmel women, including underage girls, and that Branch Davidian children were so savagely disciplined that Texas Child Protective Services had investigated, though not enough evidence had been found for CPS staff to bring a case. Learning of the series in advance, ATF officials worried that its publication might goad the Branch Davidians into high alert and thwart the agency's plans for a surprise raid. At Fort Hood, the ATF agents were informed that the newspaper's editors had refused the agency's request to briefly postpone the series. Originally, ATF scheduled its raid for Monday, March 1. After being rebuffed by the *Tribune-Herald*, agency officials moved the date up one day to Sunday, February 28—Fort Hood training was cut from three full days to two. About the same time on Sunday morning that the ATF convoy left Fort Hood, Koresh and the Branch Davidians were reading a second installment of accusatory stories. The undercover ATF agent's morning visit to Mount Carmel was especially critical; he was to observe whether the newspaper's series was in any way disrupting the Branch Davidians' usual daily schedule.

Just after 9 a.m., operation second-in-command Chuck Sarabyn rushed into the room where agents continued making their preparations for the Mount Carmel raid. He was clearly upset, shouting, "Get geared up, we've got to go now," and several agents remember Sarabyn adding, "They know we're coming." To SRT team leaders Bill Buford and Jerry Petrilli, yelling out this news to the room at large was a breach of protocol. As raid tactical leader, Sarabyn should have first quietly summoned the more experienced team leaders to his side and elicited their advice before making and announcing the decision to carry on, even though the critical element of surprise was lost. They tried to calm Sarabyn and get more details. Both Petrilli and Buford recall that he kept repeating, "We've got to go right now."

Sarabyn did share more information: the undercover agent in the Branch Davidian building had said Koresh got a phone call and immediately afterward told his followers that the ATF and National Guard were coming. But Koresh didn't send the Branch Davidian men to the gun room to arm themselves. Instead, according to Sarabyn, the undercover agent reported that Koresh was sitting and holding a Bible. There was no sign of any weapons. There was still time to get to Mount Carmel before the suspects could prepare themselves to resist, if they planned to at all. All seventy-six participating agents scrambled to complete gearing up. SRT tactical medics used Magic Markers to note blood types on the agents' necks. This was a new precautionary measure adopted during training at Fort Hood.

Most of the agents in the room felt some degree of skepticism. The plan had been to call off the raid if surprise was lost. The Branch Davidians held the high ground and had higher-powered weapons than the federal agents. If they were ready to fight, then the arriving ATF would face a head-on barrage with limited access to even minimal cover. But a chain-of-command mentality was imbued in them: when orders were given, they must be followed. If, as Sarabyn indicated, Koresh really was reading the Bible instead of rallying his followers to fight, maybe the mission could still be successfully completed. A few agents, mostly younger ones craving the opportunity to be in on some action, remained unabashedly gung ho. There was a general rush to the cattle trailers. Order of trailer entry had been rehearsed to the point of tedium at Fort Hood. Now, everyone hustled into proper position. Light rain began falling. It was still quite chilly. The back gates of the trailers snapped shut, and the pickup trucks pulling the trailers lurched out of the civic center parking lot.

"We were sardined in, bumping up against the next guy," Mike Russell remembers. "Those trailers didn't have springs." The narrow county roads between Bellmead Civic Center and Mount Carmel were roughly paved, "and we were all bouncing around, trying to find something to hang on to, maybe the iron bar overhead or bracing against the side." Plywood slabs were tacked to the sides of the trailers, and plastic tarp stretched across the roofs, to prevent anyone from seeing in. But it also prevented the agents seeing much on the outside—the only interior light on this drab morning came between sections of plywood, or else seeped through the thin tarp taped overhead. But they could see each other, and most appeared worried. Champion says, "It was pucker time." They all had radios, and listened for any additional information. But there was nothing until they were almost to Mount Carmel, when word crackled through: "There's nobody outside." That chilled everyone. Boteler thought,

They're either inside destroying evidence, or else they're arming up and we'll run into a buzz saw.

In Trailer #1, SRT team leader Petrilli wished he could tell Sarabyn one more time "how bad I think this is," but Petrilli was wedged tight in the middle of the trailer itself, while Sarabyn rode with the driver in the cab of the pickup truck. So Petrilli, bowing to the inevitable, passed the word to his squad: "It's showtime; goggles down and fingers off the triggers." In Trailer #2, the driver shouted back to his passengers, "When I stop, you go."

Russell, struggling to keep his balance like everyone else in Trailer #2 as it made a wide right turn onto Mount Carmel's driveway, had a final, hopeful thought: *Well, maybe Koresh heard we were investigating, and would probably be coming after him. But maybe he doesn't know that we're coming right now.*

He did.

CHAPTER ONE

The Shepherd's Rod

The religious origin of what happened in 1993 in Waco extended back over 170 years to upstate New York. Farmer and Baptist lay minister William Miller, based on intense study and personal interpretation of the Bible, determined that the return of Christ and the destruction of the world by fire was imminent. Miller declared that Jesus would arrive, and the flames follow, sometime in late 1843 or early 1844, according to the biblical prophecies of Daniel and keyed to a certain span of time after a Persian king commanded the rebuilding of Jerusalem in 457 BC. Miller spread his message through lectures and published articles that were widely disseminated throughout the northeast U.S. and Canada. The concept that God would immolate the sinful earth and, with the long-awaited return of Jesus, bring about a fresh, spiritually pure kingdom was not unique, but Miller's specificity struck a powerful chord with many who took every word in the Bible literally. If the "Second Advent" was coming, they would welcome it in the hopes that their sincere beliefs would gain them admission to a new, better world.

Some estimates suggest hundreds of thousands awaited the great event, but by the end of 1843, nothing had happened. Miller suggested a new deadline of March 21, 1844, and, when Christ and the flames didn't appear, announced that he would watch and preach until the glorious day finally arrived. Loyal followers believed that Miller must have inadvertently made some miscalculation. There was a groundswell of support for October 22, 1844, as the correct date, but when that passed without incident—this was dubbed "the Great

Disappointment"—Millerites were left to ponder what went wrong, and how to correct whatever human failings might prevent them from being properly prepared when Jesus did come again, as the Bible promised, and only the pure would be spared.

Some concluded that William Miller's calculations of time were correct, but his biblical interpretation was flawed. Christ did return as predicted, but in Heaven rather than on earth. The significance of 1844 was that this was the time when Christ began judging individual mortals to determine their eligibility for salvation. To qualify, it was crucial to rigidly adhere to all holy strictures as they appeared in the Bible, with enlightened believers separating themselves entirely from the sinful ways of the world. These splinter Millerites formed the basis of the fledgling Seventh-day Adventist (SDA) Church, perhaps best known today for observing the Sabbath on Saturdays. The faith's appeal to generations of like-minded biblical literalists was such that it eventually became one of the fastest-growing denominations in the world.

SDA tenets included that resolutely correct faith alone saves souls; the dead are unconscious and will eventually be subject to judgment; and Christ will return to the earth after a time of trouble. The Bible must be constantly studied; all truth is written there for those wise and industrious enough to discern it. In particular, there was certainty that God occasionally utilizes humans as messengers or prophets. These individuals offer new theological insights and interpretations that must be honored. Ellen G. White emerged as the most prominent among them. White was raised in a Millerite family, and, beginning in 1844, experienced a series of visions that collectively supported and expanded SDA doctrine. Before her death in 1915, White wrote innumerable articles and dozens of books, which became treasured study guides among the Adventists.

By the early 1920s, Seventh-day Adventist fellowships extended across America from coast to coast (more SDA communities flourished overseas), with members striving each day to follow biblical admonitions, endeavoring all the while to study scriptural nuance and avoid worldly temptations, positive that in their rigorous piety they would be eligible for salvation above all errant others when Jesus returned to judge mankind. SDAs did not indulge in William Miller–like prediction of specific dates, only that the Second Advent, the End Time, could occur any day and they must be ready. But it was this sense of being perfectly right while everyone else was completely wrong—no lukewarm piety impressed the Lord—that lent itself, one devout Adventist concluded, to a dangerous sense of self-satisfaction, of having already done all that was necessary to please God, with favorable judgment at the Second Coming assured.

Adventist Victor Houteff feared that his beloved church had grown too comfortable and spiritually lax. Unless its members returned to the biblically mandated constant state of vigilant piety, they were in just as much danger as outsiders of Jesus's eventual negative judgment. Houteff, a Bulgarian immigrant born in 1885, moved to America as a young man. By the 1920s, he had made his way to Los Angeles, earning his temporal living as a washing machine salesman and expressing his spiritual piety by teaching in an SDA Sabbath school. Physically, there was nothing notable about him; Houteff was of average height, 5'9", and his most distinguishing feature was a thick pair of eyeglasses. But his mind was nimble, and his determination to understand and obey God's laws was unflagging.

In every available minute, Houteff pored over scripture and found himself increasingly drawn to the apocalyptic scenes of the Book of Revelation, and to Ezekiel 9:1–9, which depicts one angel coming to earth and marking the foreheads of 144,000 fortunate believers who would be spared in the End Time, with five other angels killing everyone who is unmarked. Houteff had long assumed, in company with his fellow Seventh-day Adventists, that all 144,000 elect would come from among their church's membership, which by 1929 numbered about 300,000. But now Houteff feared that too many SDAs were lazy in their study of, and adherence to, biblical law. He made a helpful list of damning errors, including selling church merchandise, lack of reverence, disbelief in prophecy, following the fashions of the world, and "insisting that we have all the truth and have need of nothing." Houteff began discussing these perceived flaws in his classes and other Adventist gatherings. Church leaders were alerted, and ordered him to desist. When he refused, it was decided that Houteff should have an opportunity to make his case before a group of SDA elders, and they would offer appropriate rebuttal. Afterward the elders weighed both sides, and announced that Houteff was proven wrong, and must recant. He did not agree, and escalated his efforts.

In 1930, using his own funds and contributions from supporters gleaned from SDA ranks, Houteff published *The Shepherd's Rod: The 144,000 of Revelation 7—Call for Reformation, Vol. 1.* In it, he repeated his stern warnings, all of them citing specific biblical scripture, and wrote, "The truth here is of great importance to the church just now because of the foretold danger which God's people soon are to meet. It calls for decided action on the part of the believers to separate themselves from all worldlings and worldliness; to anchor themselves on the Solid Rock by obedience to *all* the truth known to this denomination, if we must escape the great ruin." Houteff, utilizing italics, concluded with a key biblical verse: *"The Lord's voice crieth unto the city, and the man of wisdom shall see thy name: Hear ye the rod, and who hath appointed it.* Micah 6:9." But Houteff was also at pains to stress that he was not calling for a new church, only a recommitment by all current Seventh-day Adventists to shape up: "This publication does not advocate a new movement, and it absolutely opposes such moves. It brings out a positive proof which cannot be contradicted that the Seventh-day Adventist church has been used by God to carry on His work since 1844."

Houteff and his followers, all proclaiming themselves still loyal to the Adventists, continued arguing their case, often in parking lots of SDA churches after they were denied permission to speak to congregants inside. Houteff described himself as the rod sent by God; if only Adventists would listen and mend their ways, they could still comprise the surviving "End Time remnant."

Houteff decided that he needed room to build a following

sufficient for preparing the way for Christ's return, space where even the 144,000 elect might initially gather, if God so chose, in the beginning of the Second Advent. He studied the U.S. map as intently as he did the Bible, seeking out the perfect locale combining available, cheap land and a religion-friendly culture. Houteff didn't intend for his flock to mingle freely with new neighbors; these unfortunates, who might claim faith but lived in worldly ways, would have to face Final Judgment on their own flawed merits. Rather, he wanted a home where his people—"the Shepherd's Rod"—would be respected for their rigorous, Bible-based beliefs, and left alone to practice them.

In 1935, Houteff believed he'd found the perfect spot, and purchased almost two hundred acres just northwest of Waco, Texas.

Waco, home in 1935 to perhaps sixty thousand hardy souls, is perched in McLennan County, below the banks of the Brazos River, some seventy-five miles south of Fort Worth and Dallas and ninety miles north of Austin. The town's low-slung silhouette reflected its flat, unremarkable surroundings. Visually, there was nothing memorable about it. Waco's two claims to fame were as the place where popular soft drink Dr Pepper was invented, and as the home of Baylor University, a Baptist stronghold where rules for students were considered shining examples of conservative Christianity. Baylor students were expected to abstain from liquor, tobacco, and premarital sex; most notoriously, the school effectively banned dancing. Though there was no written policy forbidding this blatantly lascivious activity, the administration always denied requests by campus groups to hold dances. Students enrolling at Baylor were understood to be making a declaration of lifestyle choice as well as pursuing an education.

Even in Texas, Waco's religious fervor and conservative atmosphere were considered excessive: within state lines, its nickname was "Jerusalem on the Brazos," or, sometimes, "the buckle of the Bible Belt." Most residents took these appellations as compliments. Rod Aydelotte, a photographer for the *Waco Tribune-Herald* who was raised in the city, recalls that "we knew all about religion because we had every church in the world."

By luck or godly inspiration, Victor Houteff selected the perfect home for his transplanted Shepherd's Rod. He and his followers took possession of rocky land seven miles northwest of Waco city limits. The property abutted the pebbly shores of Lake Waco, whose 7,270-acre surface area was fed by the North Bosque and Bosque Rivers. Christ and Judgment Day were coming. In anticipation, the new settlement was named Mount Carmel, honoring the biblical passage Micah 7:13–14—"Not withstanding the land shall be desolate because of them that dwell therein, for the fruit of their doings, feed thy people with thy rod, the flock of thine heritage, which dwell solitarily in the wood, in the midst of Carmel."

Houteff's Mount Carmel eventually had some 120 denizens. Everyone who came, worked, either on the property or else in the outside community, where contact was cordial on both sides. Completely dependent on Houteff's leadership, the newly gathered Shepherd's Rod flourished. Though he claimed no special status beyond dedication to God's service, most followers believed Houteff to be the holy, modern-day equivalent of Elijah, a biblical prophet who proclaimed the imminent coming of the Messiah. Houteff ruled his rugged kingdom with a gentle, but firm, hand, constantly cautioning that even the most faithful faced eventual baptism by fire, as prophesized by John the Baptist in Matthew 3:11. Additionally, he stressed that this prophecy would be fulfilled not by Jesus, but by some as yet unidentified later figure as its instigator. Deserving God's favor after the Second Coming was going to be hard, and it was not only incumbent on true believers to welcome the challenge, it was their obligation to continue pleading with recalcitrant Seventh-day Adventists to mend their errant ways. A printing press was acquired at Mount Carmel, and all of Houteff's sermons and teachings were recorded in pamphlets, which then were sent to every SDA member in the nation whose home address was available.

As years passed, Houteff acquired more land along Lake Waco, until Mount Carmel encompassed about 375 acres. He sent out two-man preaching teams to visit Seventh-day Adventist congregations around the country and sway them toward the teachings of Shepherd's Rod. Houteff follower Dudley Goff remembers "going to [these] churches and getting pushed out, but they couldn't push us off the sidewalks in front because that was public property. We'd stand there and hand out leaflets. Sometimes people would spit at us." Houteff's messengers proudly flaunted their identity: "We had 'Hear Thee the Rod' signs on top of the car."

Two other notable events occurred in the era of Victor Houteff presiding over Mount Carmel. The first came in 1937, just two years after Shepherd's Rod arrived in Central Texas. Houteff was always scrupulously circumspect in appearance—modestly priced suits and ties—and behavior. No hint of scandal touched his ministry up to the moment when, at age fifty-two, he was finally married—to Florence Hermanson, the seventeen-year-old daughter of devoted followers. The age discrepancy disturbed some loyalists, especially when the new Mrs. Houteff immediately assumed the role of her husband's primary assistant, most notably during his Saturday Sabbath sermons, when she sat in the first row and took down all his remarks in shorthand for transcription immediately afterward. The couple lived in a second-floor apartment in the Mount Carmel administration building. No children were born to the Houteffs; Florence's youthful vigor was expended on behalf of her husband's ministry rather than birthing and raising progeny.

And in 1942, with American entry into the Second World War, Mount Carmel's young men were eligible for military draft. This conflicted with Houteff's role for them, the spreading of his message and the ongoing building of Mount Carmel into a spiritual haven where, if necessary, at the dawn of the Second Advent, the 144,000 elect could congregate before they (presumably including the Shepherd's Rod faithful) would be transported to Israel. Shepherd's Rod was not legally certified as a church, where young, pious male members could claim draft exemption on religious grounds. Houteff reorganized his flock as the Davidian Seventh-day Adventist Association, claiming both a connection to an established church and to King David's throne, which would be occupied by Christ following His return. The first word in the new name became how the group was commonly known in Waco: Davidians.

CHAPTER TWO

The Davidians

For two decades after their arrival in Waco, the Davidians couldn't imagine life without the leadership of Victor Houteff. The group had an executive committee ostensibly overseeing daily Mount Carmel affairs, but actual control remained in the hands of the founder. The focus at Mount Carmel remained what Houteff defined as the Davidians' main, really only, mission: win over as many recalcitrant Seventh-day Adventists as possible, and please the Lord with the presence of a truly righteous community, so that the End Time might commence and Christ make His return. Everyone at Mount Carmel believed this would eventually happen because Houteff was not only a godly man, but one of the Lord's rare human messengers, whether the modest Davidian leader admitted it or not.

But late in 1954, Houteff's health suddenly failed. The Davidians traditionally cared for their own, but this was clearly beyond any home medical care. Houteff was taken to a Waco hospital, where, for a few days, he rallied, and was able to have conversations with his wife, Florence, who shared this glad news with everyone else back at Mount Carmel. Then, on February 5, just a few weeks before his seventieth birthday, Victor Houteff died. The death certificate listed heart failure as the cause. His followers were staggered. No specific plan had ever been made regarding who might replace him as Davidian leader in the event of his death. No one wanted to abandon preparing the way for the Second Advent—they believed in that just as devoutly as they did in Victor Houteff's holiness.

Most assumed that the executive committee would prayerfully ponder and announce a new leader, but one committee member declared that Victor Houteff's successor as president of the Davidian executive committee was already decided. According to Florence Houteff, her beloved late husband had, with almost his final breath, bestowed on her both a pressing task and a deadline. Lying in his hospital bed, and for some time even before that, Florence explained, Houteff studied certain passages of Revelation and Daniel regarding a span of time that might—did!—indicate an actual date for the commencement of Second Advent. In their last conversation before his passing, "Brother" Houteff shared this with Florence, who now was divinely inspired to announce it: the End Time would arrive on Wednesday, April 22, 1959. In anticipation of this longed-for event, the Davidians, under Florence's leadership, must redouble recruitment efforts.

The fateful date was only a few years away. Their vital admonition to demonstrate appropriate Christian discipline and behavior must be as widely spread as possible, primarily to Seventh-day Adventists but also to anyone else willing to listen and obey. This was the task assigned to them by God Himself. Recruitment teams were not sufficient. Radio would be more effective—regular broadcasts of Davidian tenets would surely touch many more hearts than proselytizing on sidewalks outside SDA churches. Airtime was available for purchase, but the money to do so had to be raised. The means were obvious.

As Waco's city limits gradually extended northwest toward the town's namesake lake, property in the area gained steadily in value. Mount Carmel's acreage was worth a great deal more than it had been in 1935. The Davidians had no intention of leaving Waco—all the details of moving anywhere else would squander precious time—but if they sold their present property, the proceeds could not only finance radio broadcasts, but pay for another chunk of Waco-adjacent land, probably somewhere in the sprawling, less-pricey patch of scrub brush just northeast of town. The Lake Waco property was put on the market, and various parcels were sold until all 375 acres were spoken for. New property was purchased, 941 relatively desolate acres off Double Ee Ranch Road, the quirky capital-E-lowercase-e name that would in time become painfully familiar throughout the world. The Davidians called the land "New Mount Carmel." They built a main building, a chapel, and simple shacks where members lived. These amenities were constructed as cheaply as possible; every possible cent was required for mission outreach, radio especially. The Davidians purchased a weekly time slot on ABC Radio: *The 11th Hour Call* emanated from a studio built onto the chapel on the New Mount Carmel grounds. "A lot of money went into that," Dudley Goff recalls.

As Wednesday, April 22, 1959, loomed, the Davidians sent out a message, over radio airwaves and in pamphlet form, for the faithful to make their way to New Mount Carmel. There they would gather to await Jesus and holy, cleansing fire, certain that they would be among the 144,000 elect who would joyfully emerge afterward in a new, godly kingdom. Many came; local news reports indicated that, besides the Waco Davidians themselves, as many as one thousand more believers grouped in and outside the property's chapel, anticipating the arrival of Jesus and the End Time.

As Wednesday's final minutes ticked over into Thursday, disillusioned visitors made a mass exodus from the Davidian property. The Davidians themselves were stunned. No true prophet could make such an error. For many, Florence's failure shook even their longtime faith in Victor Houteff—if she was wrong, and based her prophecy on her husband's teachings, then he must have been wrong, too. SDA leaders, sensing opportunity, hosted a group of their errant brothers and sisters on an Adventist-subsidized visit to SDA headquarters in Washington, D.C., where Adventist theologians disparaged the Houteffs' teachings and invited the prodigals to return to the true church. Some did.

Others simply left Waco, many to return to former hometowns and adjust to existing without the imminent hope of Second Advent and new life beyond. Only about fifty troubled Davidians remained at New Mount Carmel. Then, without admitting any intentional miscalculation, Florence Houteff announced that she had been mistaken. Over the next two years, she sold off most of the New Mount Carmel property, until only a smallish parcel remained. That accomplished, Florence moved to San Jose, California, where she took an accounting job with IBM. She remarried to an investment manager, and died in September 2008.

Florence's departure from New Mount Carmel seemed to mark the end. But another husband-and-wife team stepped up, announcing that God now spoke through them—and God wanted the remaining Davidians to make certain adjustments, then carry on with their holy mission.

When Florence Houteff assumed the executive committee presidency in 1955 following the death of her husband, one opposing Davidian launched a lengthy campaign to unseat her. Ben Roden wrote in one of his frequent letters to the Davidians remaining at New Mount Carmel that the group's executive committee lacked authority to appoint a board president to succeed its founder. "Only God appoints a president," Roden insisted, and claimed that, while the board usurped that power, the Lord had already indicated His choice—He wanted Ben Roden presiding over the group preparing the way for the End Time.

Roden discovered the Davidians after a lengthy search for religious truth. Born in 1902 to a Jewish family in Oklahoma, Roden was raised in a region where Jews were few and regarded with considerable suspicion. Though he attended a teacher's college and briefly taught in a country school, Roden soon changed professions, working in the oil fields of Oklahoma and Texas. At age thirty-five, he married Montana native Lois Scott, a Christian of considerable zeal who apparently converted her husband. They joined the Seventh-day Adventists and became active church members. But in the mid-1940s, they learned of Victor Houteff and the Davidians in Waco. After several visits, they embraced the Davidians' strenuous adherence to biblical stricture.

Ben and Lois Roden greatly respected Victor Houteff, but held his wife in considerably lower esteem. Houteff's death, and Florence's subsequent board-approved ascension to Davidian leadership, coincided with Roden's announcement that he had received a message from God: Ben Roden was called to succeed Victor Houteff; he must lead the Davidians on their holy task. His predecessor was an honorable prophet, whom God directed to begin this great work, but the Lord intended another to complete it. As Florence Houteff called for renewed vigor in preparation for the commencement of Armageddon on April 22, 1959, Ben Roden insisted that she was in error, and that the Davidians, under his leadership, must evolve into a new entity—*Branch* Davidians. Just as Victor Houteff had done, Roden cited scripture: Zechariah 6:12 ("Thus speaketh the Lord of hosts, saying, Behold the man whose name is The Branch, and he shall grow up out of his place, and he shall build the temple of the Lord") and also John 15:1–3 (where Jesus tells his followers, "I am the true vine, and you are the branches").

Roden made his case energetically, but in vain, until Florence's specified date passed without anything happening and the disappointed Davidians at New Mount Carmel began splintering. Some were intrigued by Roden's description of what God wanted them to do next—embrace not just Israel, but Hebraic customs. Christmas and Easter were pagan holidays. The Branch Davidians should celebrate Passover and the Feast of the Tabernacle. At the beginning of the End Time, the Bible describes the elect as already present in Israel. Roden and his followers must establish a community there, to be in place when the longed-for event—not linked to a specific date, but still coming soon—occurred. (Roden declared that, as described in Revelation, Jesus had already completed his judgment of the dead, and was beginning to consider the individual cases of the living.)

Enough were persuaded that Roden's newly dubbed Branch Davidians soon numbered about forty. As Florence Houteff began selling off New Mount Carmel lots, squabbling broke out among those who still lived there—who was entitled to the money from the sales, and who retained ownership of the remaining seventy-seven acres? By mid-1965, Ben Roden and his Branch Davidians occupied the property. Lawsuits continued through 1973, when Roden legally acquired what remained of New Mount Carmel for $25,000, with the payment disbursed among former Davidians who originally contributed when Florence Houteff purchased the land.

Energetically assisted by Lois, Ben Roden worked to fulfill the mission he believed had been assigned him by God. Both Rodens traveled to Israel. In the name of the Branch Davidians, they acquired property there, in the town of Amirim and later in Jerusalem. Recruitment from among Adventists was now solicited on the premise of joining the group in Waco, then moving overseas to Israel as part of the Branch Davidian community there, preparing a place for the 144,000 elect. For several years, Ben Roden commuted between Waco and Israel, while Lois Roden lived on the Amirim property with the first few Branch Davidians resettling there. Where her husband focused on obeying the instructions he'd received from the Lord, Lois Roden was greatly inquisitive about outside beliefs and religious practices. She studied other faith-based groups, reading their literature and sometimes, when stateside, traveling to see places and organizations for herself. Lois supported her husband without accepting a subservient role. Far from feeling threatened, he appreciated her.

But neither felt the same way about George, their eldest son. Unlike his parents, who were strong-willed but generally welcoming of discussion or even debate, George Roden, born in 1938, was uninterested in any opinion other than his own, and prone to verbal aggression, and sometimes physical violence, toward anyone who dared disagree. In their early years of seeking, then gaining, control of the group, Ben and Lois Roden assigned George fine-sounding responsibilities; in particular, when the Branch Davidians eventually found themselves tasked with rebuilding the great temple in Jerusalem (the details of how this would come about remained vague), George would be in charge of the project. He took this critical assignment to mean

that he would also succeed his father as leader of the Branch Davidians. That lofty post was perhaps the least prestigious that George
envisioned for himself. At one point, he ran for United States president, declaring himself a Democratic Party candidate. His surviving
campaign literature, apparently printed on the press at New Mount
Carmel, pledges to immediately eradicate inflation upon his taking
office by permanently lowering both wages and prices by 40 percent.
There is no record of George Roden receiving even a single vote in
primary or national elections. Undaunted, he identified himself in
pamphlets and letters as "the king of Israel, the scourge of nations,
and the deliverer of saints."

His bumptious manner became well known locally beyond
New Mount Carmel's seventy-seven acres. At one point, George
attempted to change the name of the Branch Davidian property to
"Rodenville." Some locals started using the name. Decades later,
asked about his occasional contact with the Rodens' eldest son (who
constantly badgered authorities to do something about the schemes,
and even murder plots, that he claimed enemies engaged in against
him), former McLennan County district attorney Vic Feazell sighs,
ponders, and declares, "George Roden was, well, crazy."

While Ben Roden still led the Branch Davidians, George's parents
considered their son more of a nuisance than a threat. His attitude
was bothersome, but his passion was often useful. Some of their
followers actually enjoyed George's energetic exhortations to work
hard and keep preparing the way. But in 1977, Ben's health failed,
and George openly declared himself as leader-in-waiting. His father's
physical fading was gradual. Perry Jones, an outgoing man who'd
originally followed Victor Houteff from California to Waco, took on
some of the daily, on-site supervisory tasks. Lois Roden moved permanently back to New Mount Carmel; for the time being, she and
her husband effectively became co-presidents. Lois believed that she
must succeed Ben. Now in her early sixties, she understood that, for
many followers, a Branch Davidian leader best proved himself or herself deserving of primacy by receiving, then sharing, some significant

message from God, information that could only be revealed to a legitimate prophet. If Lois did so, that would negate George's constant claims that he had been designated as "the Branch" when his father appointed him to lead the rebuilding of the Jerusalem temple.

Sometime in 1977, Lois summoned everyone at New Mount Carmel to hear thrilling news: she'd received communication from the Lord, an insight that upended accepted, but errant, belief. The previous night, as she habitually did after fulfilling her daily duties, Lois retired to her bedroom to pore over the Bible. At about 2 a.m., as she pondered Revelation 18:1 ("I saw another angel come down from heaven"), she looked out the window and saw an actual "shining, silver angel flying by. Nothing was said, but I knew right there [that] the angel represented the Holy Spirit Mother. It was feminine in form. Until that moment, I had always thought that the Holy Spirit was masculine." The angel was sent to Lois by God, as proof that the Holy Spirit was female. This meant that the Father, Son, and Holy Ghost or Spirit were feminine as well as masculine.

Reaction was mixed. A few Branch Davidians left, believing that Lois's declaration was blasphemous. Others stayed, studying their Bibles, seeking out additional indications of this proposed new truth. Some were convinced by Genesis 1:27: "So God created man in his own image, in the image of God created he him, male and female created he them." Lois said this scripture proved that women, every bit as much as men, reflected the image of God. The remaining Branch Davidians either believed, or else waited to see what would happen next. George Roden did not declare that his mother was mistaken, but he continued to insist that he should still assume leadership whenever his father passed away. Ben Roden, weakened by what was probably progressive heart disease, fully supported his wife's claim. But his own ascension to leadership emphasized that only God could choose the group's leader. Lois's vision indicated she was a true prophet; it did not guarantee that she would automatically succeed her husband. It was the trust that her fellow Branch Davidians put in her special communication with God that qualified her for the role.

Ben Roden died on October 22, 1978. Afterward, Lois Roden had enough support to be recognized as president. She used her new station to aggressively proclaim that, in the eyes of God, women were equal to men, and she was particularly critical of denominations that refused to ordain women. Lois began publishing a newsletter called *Shekinah*, a Hebrew term for the manifestation or presence of God. The printed title emphasized *She*. Contents were mostly reprinted newspaper and magazine articles about women taking leading roles in religious practices, or else editorials criticizing various faiths for limiting leadership opportunities for females. Many reprinted articles involved interviews with Lois herself—she eagerly sought opportunities to speak with the media about her discovery of the Holy Spirit's distaff aspect. Lois also traveled extensively, addressing both religious conferences and secular gatherings. She frequently identified herself as "Bishop Lois Roden," giving the impression she was part of some substantial church hierarchy rather than leader of the relatively small New Mount Carmel community. Almost immediately, Lois stopped identifying her flock as Branch Davidians. Instead, she said that she represented the "Living Waters," alluding to several biblical passages, notably Revelation 7:17 ("For the Lamb which is in the midst of the throne shall feed them, and shall lead them unto living fountains of waters; and God shall wipe away all tears from their eyes"). The name on the deed to New Mount Carmel remained "General Association of the Branch Davidian Seventh-day Adventists." Such secular things were inconsequential. Lois had something more pressing on her mind.

George Roden continued agitating at New Mount Carmel, insisting that his mother wrongly denied him his rightful place as leader. Ignoring completely his father's declaration that only God could choose the Branch Davidian president, George insisted that the members of the group must do so instead, in a formal, binding vote. In 1979, he called for a leadership election, certain that he'd be comfortably in the majority. Such a thing was unprecedented at New Mount Carmel, but Lois, certain that her supporters far outnumbered those of her son, agreed. After she won in a landslide, she hoped the issue was settled. Instead, George continued arguing that he, rather than his mother, was rightful leader. Eventually, Lois lost patience and successfully sought a restraining order. George was ordered by the court to leave New Mount Carmel and not return. He departed, staying mostly in Texas but sometimes California, and defied the court order with occasional visits to New Mount Carmel, when he'd argue his case in person, then resort to a deluge of grammatically challenged letters to Lois's followers after departing.

Lois carried on, doing her best to compartmentalize George's ceaseless attempts to usurp her place. When in residence at Mount Carmel, she led "the daily," periods of prayer and study in the morning and late afternoon. Ben Roden, faithful to Hebrew traditions in all other things, eliminated animal sacrifice from New Mount Carmel practice, but Lois added daily consumption of grape juice and unleavened crackers as communion emblematic of Jesus symbolically sharing body and blood with His disciples. She continued tirelessly addressing almost any group willing to host her, often in and around McLennan County, but sometimes as far away as Canada and California. It was exhausting work, and, as Lois approached her mid-sixties, she was uncomfortably aware that, like her husband, Ben, she would not live forever. George lurked constantly; the moment his mother expired, he was certain to rush back to New Mount Carmel, and with his combination of verbal bluster and physical aggression, he might intimidate a majority there into accepting him as the new leader. That, assuredly, would be disastrous, not only to the community itself, but to its holy cause. Lois needed God to send her a suitable successor, someone she could teach and nurture, with a spirit worthy to rise to the leadership, and a temperament sufficiently resolute to withstand the inevitable challenge from George.

Lois prayed. In 1981, she believed her prayer was answered.

CHAPTER THREE

Vernon Wayne Howell

By secular standards, twenty-one-year-old Vernon Wayne Howell wasn't qualified to lead a one-man parade when he presented himself at New Mount Carmel during the summer of 1981. His life so far exemplified futility, with a likely future of continuing to flounder purposelessly.

The circumstances of Vernon's birth were only the first among many blighted childhood moments. In 1958, seventh-grader Bonnie Clark, daughter of an alcoholic ex-G.I. and his English wife, lived with her family in Houston, where she attended Seventh-day Adventist schools, sometimes earning tuition for herself and a sister by working in the school kitchen at lunchtime and cleaning bathrooms there at night. Bonnie had a friend named Roxie who lived in public housing, and often visited her chum's apartment there. Roxie knew an exciting older boy named Bobby Howell, who was eighteen and had his own pickup truck. Bobby chivalrously offered Bonnie a ride home, and kissed her when he dropped her off. Bonnie finished out the seventh grade and began eighth in public school, but education became irrelevant when Bobby proposed. Bonnie's father refused to sign the necessary papers for his underage daughter, then relented when she became pregnant. But the girl's pregnancy scared off Bobby. Though he remained occasionally in touch, he was no longer willing to marry fourteen-year-old Bonnie, making her an unwed mother when she gave birth to Vernon Wayne Howell on August 17, 1959.

Bobby never came to see his newborn son; Bonnie and the baby moved in with her parents, but infant Vernon was colicky and cried a lot. Things grew tense, and for a while Bonnie took her child to San Antonio, where they lived with her aunt and uncle. Out of the blue, Bobby decided he wanted them back, so Bonnie, feeling hopeful, returned to Houston with her baby. Within days, Bobby changed his mind again, and Bonnie reluctantly decided that "God had a plan for my life and Vernon's life, which didn't include Bobby Howell." Bobby's mother, though, befriended her, and Bonnie would periodically stay at her house with Vernon when things at her own parents' home grew too uncomfortable.

When toddler Vernon was about two, Bonnie met a man named Joe who was just out of prison for some crime she never specified. They felt mutual attraction, and Bonnie married him. The marriage lasted eighteen months. Vernon still cried frequently, irritating his stepfather, and Joe reacted by spanking him. Corporal punishment was common among working-class Texas families, but Bonnie felt Joe's physical discipline was excessive. It was a relief when Joe violated parole and was returned to prison. Bonnie divorced him, and later wrote in her memoir, "You make a lot of mistakes when you're young . . . I never saw him [Joe] again."

Now about to turn eighteen, she needed work to support herself and her child. A Houston acquaintance worked in a bar, and introduced Bonnie to Roy Haldeman, the thirty-four-year-old owner. The new employee eventually married the boss, recalling later that during their early days together, they had a lot of fun. When the wedding took place, the bride was six months pregnant. After baby Roger arrived, his father sold the bar and took up carpentry in Richardson, a Dallas suburb. Vernon started public school there, and immediately floundered. Much later, he described difficulty writing and spelling, even though his reading skills were adequate. By third grade, he was assigned to "special classes," and was taunted on the playground by cruel kids, who called him "retarded." His mother remembered the boy being diagnosed with a learning disability that she couldn't recall, except that "it was not dyslexia." The probable condition was attention deficit disorder (ADD), but that was not usually diagnosed until decades after the mid-1960s.

The upshot was that Vernon struggled in school. His mother felt he might do better in the same kind of church schools she once attended, and, when the boy was thirteen and the Howells moved to Sachse, another Dallas suburb, Bonnie enrolled Vernon and younger brother Roger in a Seventh-day Adventist school. Her husband didn't like it, but Bonnie insisted and got her way. Bonnie earned the money for tuition by cleaning houses for realtors before the homes were shown to prospective buyers. For a change, Vernon did respectably in school. All aspects of church enthralled him. He eagerly accompanied his mother, or, more often, his maternal grandmother, to SDA services. To Bonnie's astonishment, her book-adverse oldest son seemed to effortlessly memorize pages or even whole sections of the Bible, then endlessly dissect their meanings. He also enjoyed watching the ubiquitous Christian television broadcasts on local stations and cable networks, mocking the colorful preachers' spectacularly coiffed hair, but listening intently as they gave sermons and parsed lines of scripture. School contemporaries read comic books; Vernon closed himself in his bedroom with the King James Bible. He would later say that he felt the presence of God, not all the time, but he sensed Him.

In other ways, Vernon had the same interests as most ordinary blue-collar teenage boys growing up in Texas. He liked hunting small game with a rifle or shotgun (by his own account, "rabbits, doves and squirrels"), playing guitar (his mother offered to pay for lessons, but Vernon preferred teaching himself), and pulling apart and rebuilding anything mechanical. And, like countless other hormonal teens, Vernon was consumed by thoughts of sex. This brought him to the next unlucky phase of his life.

In 1976, Vernon dropped out of school before completing the eleventh grade. He'd met a girl, and was in love. Vernon supported himself by working carpentry jobs with his stepfather. Roy and Bonnie were going through a rough period in their marriage, and Bonnie

later admitted that, at this time when her son was making questionable decisions and could have used parental guidance, "my own life
was in so much turmoil that maybe I didn't notice." Vernon considered himself a full-fledged grown-up; besides his sixteen-year-old girlfriend, he was making decent money as a carpenter and even bought
a pickup truck. Then a familiar cycle repeated itself; the girlfriend got
pregnant, and, though Vernon proposed marriage, her father refused
permission.

Even as nineteen-year-old Vernon struggled with what to do next,
Roy and Bonnie Haldeman moved to Tyler in East Texas. For a short
time, Vernon stayed there with them, but soon felt compelled to
return to Dallas and take responsibility for his expected child. But
his girlfriend had an abortion. Nonetheless, she and Vernon still felt
deep attraction.

Unaccountably, her father allowed Vernon to move in with their
family and share a room with his daughter. Since Vernon believed
that God forbade birth control, she was soon pregnant again. Her
father threw Vernon out. Denied contact with the girl he loved, for
a time Vernon hung around Dallas and lived in his pickup. There
seemed no solution to this daunting impasse until, he believed, God
came to him and declared His displeasure: "For 19 years, I've loved
you, and for 19 years you've turned your back and rejected Me." But if
Vernon spiritually shaped up, he believed that God promised him he
might eventually get the girl back for good.

Feeling broken, mourning one child who'd been aborted and
a yet-unborn daughter he would never meet, Vernon rejoined his
mother, stepfather, and little brother in Tyler. In this time of trouble,
he looked for both solace and guidance in religion, attending a local
SDA church. His participation there was energetic, in a sense too
much so. Sabbath school teachers and ministers soon resented Vernon's constant interruptions. In particular, they were aggravated by
his criticism that Bible studies focused on what prophets had been
saying long ago. What about prophets who were alive today? There
must be some—did anybody know of one?

Vernon became friends with a young woman in the congregation—in her memoir, Bonnie Haldeman identifies her as "Harriet." While church elders strongly urged him to stop talking so much and listen instead, Harriet told Vernon that she knew of a woman who was reputedly a prophet, someone who led an especially spiritual group mostly comprised of former Adventists someplace around Waco. During the summer of 1981, Harriet and Vernon drove down to take a look. Harriet's mother had been part of Shepherd's Rod in California, and her family knew Perry Jones. That paved the way when the two visitors from Tyler located New Mount Carmel just northeast of Waco, and, for a few hours, Vernon found himself in the presence of people who believed the Bible was talking about things happening right now as well as long ago. He was enthralled. Either then or on a subsequent visit soon afterward, Lois Roden invited Vernon to stay and study with her Living Waters followers.

If the twenty-one-year-old expected to be welcomed warmly by everyone, he was quickly disabused of the notion. There were always visitors who wanted to explore life at New Mount Carmel, and residents generally paid them little mind, because almost all of the newcomers soon tired of the bare-bones lifestyle and constant Bible study. If anything, Vernon seemed among the least promising. Clive Doyle recalls, "When he showed up, he had this long hair; he didn't look like the rest of us did. He was considered pretty strange. He'd be in his room with his door closed, and he'd be praying so loudly that you could hear him outside. Some made fun of him. He was also of a sort of different age, very in between. Almost everyone else was older or younger. I felt sorry for him." Catherine Matteson, an older woman and one of the longest-tenured people there, described her first impression of Vernon as someone so befuddled that he constantly stammered, and mumbled rather than enunciated. When he did manage to coherently express himself, the topics he chose were off-putting: his habit of masturbating too much, and his dreams of becoming a rock star.

Doyle pitied the young man, and invited him to dinner at the small house on the property that Doyle and his family shared: "Later,

[Vernon] would tell stories about how he came to eat at my house, and all he ever got was macaroni and cheese. I hate macaroni and cheese. I would never have given him that. But this was the way that he remembered it." Even to Bible students who eagerly anticipated the End Time, Vernon seemed significantly separated from reality.

The only positive thing most at New Mount Carmel saw in Vernon was his skill as a handyman. All the ramshackle buildings on the windswept, barren hill were in constant need of repair, and Vernon cheerfully fixed everything. His knack for repairing engines kept cars in good working order, too. He didn't consider any chore beneath him.

After a few months, Lois Roden began asking Vernon to drive her when she had local speaking engagements or other appointments. This wasn't out of the ordinary—rather than taking the wheel herself, Lois, now sixty-five, liked using time in the car to think through whatever presentation she was about to give, or else quietly ponder some aspect of biblical significance. Followers serving as chauffeurs were used to drives passing in comfortable silence. When Vernon drove, though, apparently there was conversation, and Lois sensed such previously undetected potential in the young man that she began summoning him for private Bible studies in her quarters. Everyone else at New Mount Carmel was astonished. It wasn't just Lois providing such a priceless privilege to someone, but that she chose inarticulate, socially inept Vernon Howell. It seemed extremely odd.

They had no idea.

CHAPTER FOUR

Lois, Vernon, and George

Proximity to Lois Roden exhilarated Vernon Howell. He'd hungered for contact with a modern-day prophet, someone who could guide him to new spiritual places that involved things happening *now*. Through her, Vernon learned more about Adventist prophet Ellen G. White's writings, and, for the first time, Victor Houteff's rejection of Adventist self-satisfaction, Ben Roden's adherence to Hebrew customs and the certainty that Jesus, having judged the dead, was now examining the worthiness of the living, and Lois's own pronouncement of the Holy Spirit as feminine. On rare occasions, God was pleased to appoint prophets by favoring them with messages to convey to everyone wise enough to hear and believe. White–Houteff–Ben Roden–Lois Roden; Vernon, who'd believed for years that God was present in his life and in occasional communication, certainly felt it was the Lord's Will that there be a succession of prophets. Lois's tutoring indicated that she believed Vernon might be next in line. Considerable effort was required; Vernon felt blessed, and was willing to work hard to prove that he was deserving of that blessing.

Bonnie Haldeman was curious how her son was faring at New Mount Carmel, and drove down to visit. She arrived on a Saturday; people were leaving the chapel, which stood near the front of the grounds, following Sabbath services. Clive Doyle's mother, Edna, took an apparent liking to Bonnie and chattered away to her. Bonnie's ears were plugged from allergies, and Edna's unfamiliar accent (the Doyles came to Texas from Australia after hearing tapes of Ben Roden preaching) was also a problem. But Bonnie thought Edna and most everybody else seemed nice, and she was thrilled by how happy Vernon seemed to be. It was a welcome change from the depression he'd suffered in Tyler. After a potluck lunch in the administration building, Vernon insisted on showing his mother around Lois Roden's house. The leader wasn't present—she was away from New Mount Carmel that day—but Vernon wanted Bonnie to see all the repairs he'd made to his beloved teacher's abode. He urged his mother to come back again soon and, when she did, Bonnie met Lois and was impressed by her explanation of the Holy Spirit's femininity, recalling, "It hit me like a ton of bricks; it made so much sense, I grasped it."

Lois's private sessions with Vernon continued into 1982, then 1983. Some at New Mount Carmel began suspecting that, despite the age difference between them, something beyond spiritual instruction was going on. Vernon later confirmed that he and Lois had become lovers, not out of lust, but sincere desire to fulfill Isaiah 8:3 in the Old Testament: "And I went unto the prophetess; and she conceived, and bare a son." Lois was long past menopause, and no pregnancy apparently resulted. They did not take this as a sign of God's disfavor. In this, as in all things, they believed that they were doing what God commanded.

But someone else was outraged. George Roden kept visiting from California. Lois, preoccupied with grooming her chosen successor, or else feeling a sense of maternal guilt for pursuing the restraining order, didn't object as these visits grew more frequent and longer. Though there were now pockets of Branch Davidians around the country and in Israel, only about one hundred lived at New Mount Carmel. It wasn't long before George heard rumors that his mother and that weird guy Vernon were fornicating. He rushed back to New Mount Carmel, and this time he stayed. Rather than risk a full-on confrontation—George couldn't be certain that a majority of the people there would support him in any attack on Lois—he attempted a slightly more oblique approach. Anyone at New Mount Carmel, if so moved, could initiate a Bible study or pontificate at length. One day George, wearing a holstered gun, called everyone willing into the chapel and declared that Vernon Howell was raping Lois. Lois and Vernon chose not to dignify the allegation by responding, and George didn't make the accusation directly to them. His mother and her pupil continued their private lessons.

In Waco itself, the group that locals still called Branch Davidians had long since been accepted as an odd, but permanent, part of the community. A few Branch Davidian kids were enrolled in local schools. Some of the adults worked in town, as roofers or landscapers or grocery store cashiers. In turn, the Branch Davidians assumed that everyone in Waco knew about them. In October 1982, when word reached town that the group's printing press had caught on fire, an editor at the *Waco Tribune-Herald* ordered recently hired reporter Tommy Witherspoon to "go out to the Branch Davidian place" and write a story for the next edition. Witherspoon, who'd just moved to Waco, had to ask what and where that was. He remembers, "When I finally got there, they'd put the fire out, but there were still all these women and children running around. A guy came up to me, Perry Jones, who often acted as their public face or spokesman. I asked him, 'What is this place?' and he said, 'Go talk to your [newspaper's] religion writer.' Then he loaded me down with these little pamphlets about what they believed. Later on, I'd hear people occasionally talk about them. The general theory was, 'They're out there minding their own business. Leave them alone.'"

Though Lois Roden was the acknowledged leader, Perry Jones gradually assumed a place as the group's second-in-command. But in 1983, Lois began occasionally using Vernon Howell as her public representative. Vic Feazell remembers that not long after he took office as McLennan County district attorney, Vernon dropped by for an impromptu meeting.

"He showed up at the courthouse and wanted to see me," Feazell says. "He just wanted to talk and tell me that they didn't want any trouble, and also to talk about the Bible. I'm an ordained Baptist preacher, which I guess he knew. He was wearing dungarees and a shirt." By this point, acting considerably more self-assured thanks to Lois's mentoring, Vernon didn't have difficulty expressing himself. Feazell liked him: "He reminded me of young preachers I'd known in my life, energetic and charismatic. I didn't see him as a charlatan. He knew the Bible, though I wouldn't necessarily agree with his interpretations." Howell invited Feazell out to visit New Mount Carmel, and though the county D.A. never did, Howell continued dropping by his office. After a few years, he began bringing along Wayne Martin, an attorney whose law degree had been earned at Harvard. Martin, like more than two dozen other Branch Davidians, was Black. He practiced law in Waco, mostly working from New Mount Carmel. Martin's intellect and professional skills impressed Feazell—he thought the Branch Davidians must have a lot going for them to attract someone of such quality. Howell also made courthouse visits to chat with county sheriff Jack Harwell; as with Vernon and Feazell, they developed a casual, friendly relationship.

Lois extended Vernon's travel experiences beyond the McLennan County Courthouse. In 1983, she brought her protégé along on a trip to Israel, where she visited a handful of followers there and Vernon gaped at all the places he'd read about in the Bible. Back at New Mount Carmel, Lois called everyone together and said, "Vernon's been talking about something I think everyone should hear," and he began a series of Bible studies that later were collectively recalled as "The Serpent's Root." Not everyone came—it wasn't mandatory—and a lot of people at New Mount Carmel still thought of Vernon as a bumbler. But those who came to hear him were, for the first time, exposed to Vernon's unique way of teaching.

He began with the basics, God creating the serpent in Genesis; the snake tempts Eve to eat the apple, and man falls from perfect grace. God curses the serpent (Genesis 3:14—"Upon thy belly shalt thou go, and dust shalt thou eat all the days of thy life"), and orders

Adam and Eve out of the Garden of Eden. This was familiar scripture; what could Vernon possibly bring to it that was new?

No recording of this talk apparently exists, but based on numerous tapes of later Bible studies, Vernon used the serpent in Genesis only as a starting point. From there, he referenced other places and passages in the Bible where serpents were mentioned, many of them obscure even to an audience for whom reading the Bible was as ingrained a part of daily existence as breathing or eating. Serpents have evil intentions or represent evil in Proverbs 23:31–32 and Matthew 23:33.

But sometimes, Vernon could point out, the Bible says that it's not wrong to be a serpent. In fact, it's righteous, if you're acting like a serpent in service of the Lord. And, as became his hallmark, Vernon must have made all his references to mentions of serpents in the Bible not in the lofty tones of a highbrow lecturer, but in the folksy, friendly manner of someone sharing interesting information. Then, and ever afterward when he offered Bible study, he prefaced examples with low-key phrases like, "Now, where else in the Bible do we see this?" or, "As we already know." Whenever he sensed some or all of his listeners didn't understand a crucial point, he'd patiently go over it again, as many times as necessary. Vernon didn't allow anyone to take notes. He wanted them to listen, not write. Amazingly, Vernon never needed to pause and consult a King James Bible (the only version accepted among the Branch Davidians) to refresh his memory. He knew every passage by heart, and, further, he could talk endlessly about any of them, not only dissecting individual meanings, but linking everything to something else in the Bible. Vernon emphasized that the Bible was written about things happening today as well as in the past. It was just a matter of figuring it all out, updating some terminology. For instance, the Bible might mention a sword; in modern times, Vernon explained, that meant a gun.

Vernon's teaching skills would only grow over the next years, but even in this first attempt, most of his listeners were flabbergasted. Clive Doyle, who'd once pitied Vernon's ineptitude, remembers that during the "Serpent's Root" discussion, "I felt I was hearing new, true things." Vernon's early lectures, and his later teachings when he changed his name to David Koresh, were so accessible, so engaging, that, decades later, surviving Branch Davidians express frustration at not being able to recall his exact words. It took an effort to learn from him—you had to listen carefully, you had to think about what you were hearing. But his demeanor was so warm, so relatable, that you gratefully absorbed, rather than painstakingly memorized, the lessons, and applied them afterward in all you did.

Vernon clearly surpassed Lois as a biblical interpreter and teacher. By 1983, two years after beginning private study with her, Vernon felt confident enough to begin correcting what he perceived as Lois's mistakes, in particular the publishing of *Shekinah*. Vernon insisted that the point had been made—the Holy Spirit was feminine. (In fact, he claimed that he'd received a similar message from God years earlier.) It was time to move forward, retaining that important truth, but emphasizing other things. Lois wasn't ready to step aside and recognize Vernon as the new leader. But she was apparently convinced enough of his emerging powers to agree to shut down *Shekinah* after printing a final edition. Clive Doyle was in charge of New Mount Carmel printing and remembers that, in this concluding *Shekinah*, a picture of Lois seemed to indicate that she had two black eyes. It was probably a matter of a photograph taken in poor lighting, but Vernon told Lois these apparent shiners symbolized the beginning of her losing prophetic sight, or wisdom. He was ready to succeed her, and felt fully qualified to do so.

So did George. He sensed his mother's weakening grasp on leadership, and deeply resented Vernon's now obvious status as her intended successor. There were still some at New Mount Carmel who weren't impressed by, or actively disliked, Vernon Howell, who at age twenty-three looked, and still often acted, like a kid. They gathered to listen when George taught that one of Satan's voices was music—didn't Vernon sing and play guitar?—and that Vernon advocated oral sex, which George declared was sinful. George's supporters were still in the minority at New Mount Carmel, but no longer by a wide margin, and they were louder and more aggressive than Lois's and Vernon's adherents. Though George never specifically advocated it, violence seemed imminent. Utilizing the bully's classic tactic of presenting himself as the victim, George sent a telegram to McClennan County district attorney Feazell. It referenced the notorious religious leader of Peoples Temple, who only a few years earlier had led more than nine hundred followers to their deaths in the jungles of Guyana:

Have Jim Jones type character in Waco Texas making death threats to me and family and proclaiming mass murder at New Mount Carmel Center Waco Texas Route 7 Box 471B 76705 at Branch Davidian 7th Day Adventist Association headquarters. Need investigation now. Character's name is Vernon W. Howell and Perry Jones. I live on property at Route 7 address.

Feazell declined to investigate.

Lois could have contacted the sheriff and asked for enforcement of the restraining order on her son, but didn't. Perhaps she was weakened by the onset of breast cancer that would kill her in another two years. Lois may have believed that a clash for control between George and Vernon was inevitable, so they might as well get it over with. If her protégé was the true prophet that she believed him to be, then surely God would tip the scales in Vernon's favor. Lois could have resented Vernon's eagerness to assume leadership before she was ready to give it up. For whatever reason, she didn't intercede. When another fire broke out, burning the administration building to the ground and leaving only a concrete vault standing, George claimed that it was Vernon's fault, and, to a lesser extent, his mother's. They were supposed to be in charge, so any disasters were their responsibility. It was clear, to Vernon most of all, that something besides another building was about to combust.

Vernon did the unexpected. Along with a few followers, he moved to a rented house in Waco. They didn't resign from the Branch

Davidians/Living Waters; they just withdrew from New Mount Carmel. For a while, others sympathetic to Vernon rather than George visited him there, and enough stayed to overcrowd the small place. In search of more room, they temporarily relocated thirty miles east down State Highway 84 to the tiny town of Mexia, where someone gave them permission to park their cars and set up temporary shelters on a church campground. A place was needed to settle, though only for a while—Vernon assured the two dozen or so people with him that they would eventually return to New Mount Carmel. But in the interim, he acquired twenty acres in Palestine—not the Holy Land, but property bristling with pine trees in aptly named Palestine, Texas, another forty miles east. Vernon agreed to pay $40,000 to the previous owner, in monthly installments of $400. The price was relatively low because the land included an electrical easement with thick power lines. Living conditions were primitive there for Vernon and his followers. Most slept in cars, trucks, or old buses that the group acquired. A few enterprising souls set up lean-tos. Eventually everyone pitched in to build a log cabin large enough for a rudimentary kitchen and small meeting hall. There was no power or running water in the camp. Though the spartan conditions seemed appalling to outsiders, they reflected a lifestyle choice sometimes adopted by Christian groups divesting themselves of all potential distractions from their worship of God.

Spirits among everyone there were high. Vernon, whose prophetic voice they trusted, assured them that everything would work out; this was all part of God's plan. Vernon was so confident that, in the middle of the move to Mexia and then Palestine, he and a very special companion took time to travel to Israel. That trip set in motion a drawn-out series of events that culminated in flames.

CHAPTER FIVE

The Lamb

When he joined Lois Roden on her 1983 trip to Israel, Vernon Howell was essentially a tagalong. But in 1985, he returned to the Holy Land for a specific purpose. In the Book of Revelation, Mount Zion is measured to ensure that there is enough room there to accommodate the 144,000 chosen, who would return to the Holy Land rather than translate to some heavenly place. Vernon wanted to personally carry out this holy mission. His additional intention was to ensure that his first child was born in Israel. Months earlier, Vernon Howell had married Rachel Jones, the fourteen-year-old daughter of longtime Branch Davidians Perry and Mary Belle Jones. Though the girl was under sixteen, the age of consent, her parents gave permission, making the union legal under Texas state law. Rachel almost immediately became pregnant, and was early in her second trimester when she accompanied her husband overseas.

In Jerusalem, Vernon and Rachel lived in a small apartment often rented out to foreign visitors. For a time, Vernon spent his days studying with rabbis willing to share knowledge. If he had any notion of dazzling these teachers with all he already knew, he was mistaken, though they were impressed with his eagerness to learn more. Vernon brought along his guitar, and sometimes played songs he'd written himself that celebrated faith. Eventually, he made his way up Mount Zion, southwest of Jerusalem's Old City. A wall had been built along the summit, and this was where Vernon, like most other visitors, undoubtedly sat. He looked, estimated, and satisfied himself that there would be sufficient space for the 144,000. Vernon had done what Revelation required.

But obeying the biblical mandate to measure Mount Zion turned out to be the least of Vernon's accomplishments on this trip. He returned to the camp in Palestine, Texas, a changed young man, suddenly, manifestly self-confident, even cocky. The difference was discernible to everyone there. They were surprised, too, that he and Rachel were back before their child was born. In spring 1985, baby Cyrus was delivered in Texas, not Israel as Vernon had intended. What happened in Israel, and why he had returned earlier than planned, was not something he immediately revealed. Vernon disseminated amazing details by degrees, first to a few confidants, then gradually to those with him in the Palestine camp, and, eventually, back at New Mount Carmel to new followers, but only after he felt certain that they were sufficiently devoted to be trusted. Later, during protracted telephone conversations, he also shared his story with siege negotiators from the FBI.

The facts, as Vernon related them, were these: While in Israel, he was "taken up" to Heaven by seven angels, who didn't have wings. Instead, they roamed aloft in *merkabah*, a Hebrew term for celestial chariots, and described at length in the first chapter of Ezekiel. With Vernon on board, they soared past the constellation Orion, and when they arrived at their exalted destination, Vernon was granted critical information, which he explained as three connected parts.

For his first heavenly insight, Vernon was reminded of Cyrus, king of Persia, mentioned prominently in Isaiah 45. Babylon conquered Israel in 586 BC and took many Jews into captivity. But when Cyrus and his Persian army defeated the Babylonians forty-seven years later, they freed the Jews, returned them to their homeland, and, with the Persian king's own money, rebuilt the Temple there. Cyrus is described in Isaiah as a "messiah" of God, meaning one appointed by the Lord to provide a special service. Several messiahs are mentioned in the Bible, but Cyrus is the only gentile so designated. Vernon Howell was informed that he was this same Cyrus, whose name in

Hebrew is "Koresh." Vernon must take that as his name. ("David" was added by the newly dubbed Koresh in tribute to the Throne of David, which Jesus would occupy after He returned.) Like his biblical namesake, David Koresh would rescue the righteous from Babylon.

Second, as explained by David Koresh, the Book of Revelation was written by a priest named John during the first century AD, but it described events that would occur much later, at history's end. In this apocalyptic chapter of the Bible, someone identified as the Lamb is the only one capable of opening the great book in the hand of Him who sits on a heavenly throne—to do this, the Lamb opens, in order, the Seven Seals on the back of the book. As each seal opens, more truth is revealed and more cataclysmic events occur. After the Fifth Seal, the end is under way, and the openings of the Sixth and Seventh Seals unleash horrors that eradicate the sinful world, making way for the return of Jesus and the establishment of a new, one-thousand-year Kingdom of God on Earth. Most interpreta-tions, of Revelation and other books of the Bible, identify the Lamb as Jesus. But Isaiah 53:10 states that the Lamb "shall see his seed," and, according to the Bible, Jesus was childless. Vernon—now David Koresh—was about to become a father. He, rather than Jesus, was the Lamb in Revelation, and only he could open and interpret the Seven Seals, initiating the End Time. While horrific, this apocalypse was preliminary to final glory, the return of Christ and the establish-ment of a godly, rather than sinful, world.

Third, the duty of the Lamb went beyond the opening of the seals. Revelation describes Babylon waging war on the Lamb and his followers, who must die. But their souls rest under an altar "for a little season," and then, after other righteous "fellow-servants" are also slaughtered, the Lamb returns at the head of the forces of God, "and the Lamb shall overcome them." The Lamb's martyred followers are also exalted: "They that are with him are called, and chosen, and faithful." Adjusted for the modern day, "Babylon" meant any govern-ment oppressing true religious faith.

Simply put, as an integral aspect of the Lamb opening the Seven

Seals, Koresh and his followers were commanded by God to fight, and lose to, modern-day Babylon. Their deaths were a necessary step to bring about the End Time, during which they'd triumphantly re-emerge. Previous iterations of the Davidians/Branch Davidians/Living Waters saw their duty as preparing the way. Koresh and those who believed in him would be essential players in the final confrontation itself.

Vernon Wayne Howell wouldn't legally change his name until 1990—secular details were always afterthoughts. But to his followers in Palestine, Texas, he was immediately David Koresh, the returned messiah Cyrus, and the Lamb of Revelation who would lead a holy war against Babylon and usher in the End Time, just as the Bible prophesied. It was all quite impressive.

But it was also unoriginal. One hundred and sixteen years earlier, another prophet claimed virtually the same things. David wasn't the first self-proclaimed Koresh.

CHAPTER SIX

Cyrus Teed

yrus Teed got his childhood education on the banks of the Erie Canal rather than in classrooms. Born in 1839 to financially challenged parents, Cyrus quit school at age eleven to help support his family by working as a "hoggee," guiding animals pulling boats down portions of the canal. It was exhausting labor, requiring walks of as much as thirty miles per day for a miserly monthly wage of $8. Cyrus was a bright, observant boy, and since his job didn't require much concentration, he focused instead on the passengers aboard the packet boats that his teams towed. In *The Allure of Immortality: An American Cult, a Florida Swamp, and a Renegade Prophet*, Teed biographer Lyn Millner describes these passengers as "wealthy people and intellectuals, the pious and not-so-pious, preachers and prostitutes." The youngster apparently learned from everyone. When he wasn't working, Cyrus, whose maternal grandfather was a Baptist preacher, often read the Bible. Most of the religion-minded in the American northeast at that time were familiar with William Miller and his apocalyptic prophecies. Cyrus undoubtedly was aware of Miller, and observed how his predictions of an imminent End Time attracted flocks of followers.

Cyrus had no intention of being a canal worker all his life. In 1859, at age twenty, he began apprenticing with his uncle, a surgeon in Utica, New York. Cyrus developed an abiding interest in both the human body and the human life force. His immediate goal, despite his scant formal education, was medical school. In the same year, Cyrus married his sixteen-year-old second cousin Fidelia. When she became pregnant with the couple's son, the Teeds moved to Bing-hamton so that Cyrus could attend Eclectic Medical College of the City of New York, one of a few dozen institutions around the country offering an alternative education in medicine. The "eclectic" version relied heavily on homeopathic remedy, and disparaged common practices such as bleeding or purging patients. Eclectic physicians be-lieved that the body's self-healing tendencies should be trusted.

After a break for Union Army service in the Civil War—his enlistment was short-lived; severe sunstroke resulted in early discharge—Teed graduated and joined his uncle's medical practice in Utica. But his real interest soon turned to alchemy; Teed built a laboratory adjacent to his home. Most nights found him hard at work in his lab, attempting through various experiments to turn lead into gold. Teed would claim that around midnight on an unspecified date in October 1869, he succeeded—and that was only preliminary to what happened next.

According to Teed, after making his alchemic breakthrough, he lay down on a couch in the laboratory to rest; his mind convulsed with "momentous possibilities for the future of the world." If lead could be transformed into gold, why couldn't mankind achieve immu-nity from death? That cogitation was interrupted by the appearance of a female angel, "clothed with the sun, and the moon under her feet, and upon her head a crown of twelve stars." This exactly matched the description of the angel in Revelation 12:1. She informed Teed that he was "to redeem the race," though in the process he must die. Over years to come, Teed disclosed additional details, including that after a major event, a violent clash, Teed would "translate" to more godlike form, and his followers would be among the chosen people to enjoy new, immortal life on a sinless earth. As the Lamb of Revelation, he would open the Seven Seals to initiate these climactic events. Teed claimed that he was also a new iteration of Persian king Cyrus, liber-ator of the Jews and God's gentile messiah. He took the name "Ko-resh," the Hebrew pronunciation of Cyrus's name. The new age he ushered in would be known as "Koreshanity." (This was a third age;

the first two were Judaism, led by Abraham, and Christianity, led by Jesus.) It was all foretold in the Bible, if you knew where to look and how to interpret what you read. Now, Teed—Koresh—did.

He did not immediately reveal his holy mission, or his new name, to the public. Instead, as Cyrus Teed he embarked on a series of lectures in which he claimed that, by observing celibacy and making certain dietary adjustments, it would become possible to live forever. He wrote lengthy, turgid commentaries involving economics—governments used unfair taxation to rob citizens. Alchemy was no longer mentioned; instead, he cited incomprehensible pseudoscientific jargon that he claimed proved the earth was hollow, and everyone lived inside it. Such claims attracted entranced followers and scathing coverage in major newspapers. On August 10, 1884, *The New York Times* reported Teed was soliciting money in Syracuse by claiming to be "a new messiah." The local district attorney declared that he was ready to bring charges "at any time" for fraud. In June 1892, the *Times* wrote that the husband of a Teed enthusiast was suing him for $100,000, claiming alienation of affection. Among other things, the suit claimed that Teed convinced Sidney C. Miller's wife, Jeanne, to give the huckster $5,000.

Teed moved his operations from New York to Chicago, where his activities continued attracting press coverage. "His escapades made news," biographer Millner says. "There were sex scandals, accusations that he was starving children, and the science got coverage, especially the hollow Earth stuff." But in the 1890s, Teed completely recreated himself, identifying now by the single name Koresh and, with a few followers, moving to land he acquired in Estero, just outside Fort Myers, Florida. The group called itself the Koreshans, and within a few years numbered in the hundreds. This was due in part to response to Teed's newsletter, *The Flaming Sword*, named for the burning weapon God placed to prevent Garden of Eden entry after Adam and Eve were banished. It was in "The Clock of Ages Strikes the Hour of Revolution" in the March 25, 1898, edition of *The Flaming Sword* that he publicly announced the coming End Time and his role in it:

*One of the supreme factors of the change about to startle the world
as the most marvelous of possibility, is that the change is to be
brought about by the intellectual process of one man, who not only
knows of the coming changes, but who inaugurates the method. . . .
The world is not mobilizing for peace, but for war, though a war
that the Divine peace may succeed. The governments of the world
will be broken to pieces and dissipated as "the chaff of the summer
threshing floor." There is no escape. Prophetic declaration predicts
the end in the midst of catastrophe. . . . God's chosen people will
await the call for the gathering of Armageddon. The Flaming Sword
is the sign of the prophet.*

Koresh continued writing *Flaming Sword* editorials, though they
weren't all about the coming Armageddon and his crucial role in it.
He wrote frequently about economics and science, utilizing dense
arguments that defied comprehension but still seemed persuasive. All
his essays and public lectures on religion were laden with references
to biblical passages that proved his points. The "hollow Earth" theme
remained one of his favorite topics. The Koreshans became prominent
in Estero; photos show them dressed in suits and ties or fashionable
dresses. Their community boasted a sawmill, dormitories, a bakery, an
infirmary, a general store, an art hall (where Teed/Koresh sometimes
preached), and a printing press, where staff produced not only *Flaming
Sword* newsletters, but an endless series of pamphlets and books at-
tributed to "Koresh." One tome, *The Cellular Cosmogony, or, the Earth
a Concave Sphere*, was dedicated by Koresh "to the Firstfruits of the
Resurrection: This little work is part of the skirmish line of the army
of the revolution." The Koreshans also engaged in local politics; since
Fort Myers's population at that time was only a few thousand, Teed's
hundreds of followers had the potential to decide any close election.
This caused considerable consternation among many non-Koreshans,
who previously viewed their neighbors as harmless, often entertaining,
oddballs. (The Koreshans invited outside visitors by signs and buttons
bearing the hollow Earth slogan, "We live inside! Drop in and see us!")

By 1906, Millner says, outside animosity against Koresh and his followers had escalated: "Fort Myers was pissed off—there was an election and the Koreshans were voting as a bloc, getting the candidates they wanted elected and taxes for improvements within their compound. There were accusations locally of Teed philandering, of unhappy people in Estero who couldn't escape." Within the Koreshan community, the leader faced a dilemma. After being promised the End Time and glorious roles during it, some supporters inevitably grew impatient. Prophets who predict an imminent event must eventually deliver, and it had been eight years since Koresh described the final events in his *Flaming Sword* editorial. Something had to give, and on October 13, 1906, it did.

A Koreshan visiting Fort Myers quarreled with a town marshal; voices were raised, a crowd gathered, and punches were thrown. Koresh was nearby, meeting some friends arriving by train. He interceded in the argument, and (witnesses differed) either swung at the marshal first or was assaulted by the officer. Either way, Koresh went down, his glasses were broken, and, his followers later claimed, he suffered head injuries that would kill him two years later. Millner disputes this: "He was in poor health toward the end of his life; he was possibly diabetic. But his followers wanted to believe about the End of Days."

From their perspective, everything fit. Koresh, the Lamb, was attacked by an agent of Babylon. It was straight out of Revelation and proved Koresh's prophecy to be correct. Now the Lamb had to die so he could be transformed and the End Time commence. But Koresh didn't die as quickly as they anticipated. He lingered, gradually becoming a bedridden invalid. Koresh's hair turned white, he lost weight, and he complained of headaches and shooting pains in his left side. He finally expired on December 22, 1908, after asking a bedside nurse to feed him a teaspoon of salt. With almost his final breath, he wheezed that "every sacrifice should be seasoned with salt." Then he was gone, and his faithful at Estero placed their leader's body in a zinc bathtub. They gathered around to watch Koresh translate into higher form, as he had prophesized.

Five days later, Fort Myers health officials insisted that the decomposing corpse be buried. Koresh was placed in a shoreside tomb, which in 1921 was washed out to sea during a hurricane. By then, many Koreshans had long since lost faith and left Estero. Those remaining turned to their fallen leader's writings for clues: perhaps Koresh's "translation" wasn't intended to happen right away. They chose to stay and wait; in the interim, they reprinted pamphlets and other collections of Koresh's teachings. Some in the sinful world might still be saved before the Lamb returned to smite Babylon down. Their patience would be rewarded. It was only a matter of time.

Almost seventy-seven years after the first Koresh's death, Vernon Wayne Howell, utilizing virtually the same story and many similar details, presented himself to followers as chosen by God to be Cyrus-known-as-Koresh, Lamb of Revelation and opener of the Seven Seals. The parallels defy coincidence. Howell adopted Teed's prophecies as his own. How did it happen?

CHAPTER SEVEN

Connection

In 1931, the Koreshans remaining in Estero published many of their leader's key religious teachings in a single volume. As described in its foreword, the purpose of *Koreshanity: The New Age Religion* was "to acquaint the reader with the principal tenets of Koreshanity and to interpret the character and true identity of Dr. Cyrus R. Teed (Koresh)." The hope was that readers would then feel encouraged to seek out more of Teed/Koresh's books, and learn, then embrace, all his prophecies and wisdom. The book was printed (there is no record of how many copies) and put on sale. A privately published title, *Koreshanity* failed to gain much attention.

The Koreshans didn't give up. Like many books written by Koresh himself, *Koreshanity* was published by the group's own Guiding Star Press, and Guiding Star titles were usually available in Estero and Fort Myers bookstores. In 1948, popular author Carl Carmer, who often wrote about colorful characters from his native state of New York, was on vacation in the area, dropped into a bookstore, saw the various "Koresh" titles, and bought two. He did not specify which. But he was intrigued enough to track down some of the Koreshans, who told him all about Cyrus Teed's 1869 encounter with the angel in his laboratory at Utica, New York, and everything that happened afterward. Carmer, intrigued, included the tale in *Dark Trees to the Wind*, a collection of his short nonfiction stories published in 1949. The book remained in print for decades. Its Koreshan chapter was titled "The Great Alchemist at Utica." Books by Carmer, whose work appeared in *The New Yorker*, *The Atlantic Monthly*, and *Town &*

Country, always attracted attention. Koresh, dead for over forty years, did not posthumously become a household name. But now there was a more current record of him.

In 1961, remaining Koreshans deeded three hundred acres of the group's land to the state of Florida. Koreshan State Park was officially dedicated in 1967; visitors toured buildings, read historical markers, and learned about Teed/Koresh. Old copies of *The Flaming Sword* became prized by scattered collectors of materials pertaining to religious and/or American history. While still mostly regional, information about Cyrus Teed–turned–Koresh was readily available to anyone interested.

In 1971, *Koreshanity: The New Age Religion* was reissued by supporters. The new edition was visually unimpressive, with a drab blue cardboard cover, a stiff, formal photograph of "Dr. Cyrus R. Teed (Koresh)," and 171 pages mostly devoted to Koresh's "credentials" as the Lamb of Revelation. Each credential is bolstered with specific biblical passages, many obscure, and often linked together. The thirtieth credential is one of the longest; "The Man of Sin, the Son of Perdition" relates in detail how Koresh, or "the Lord Cyrus," must appear to be "a man of sin," who, through a process including burning, undergoes "radical transformation" while God perfects him as "the resurrected Messiah."

In March 1993, during the extended events at Mount Carmel, very few public library systems in the United States included a copy of *Koreshanity* in their collections. Most copies were in major city libraries, such as those in New York, Los Angeles, or Chicago. There was also a copy in the much smaller Waco-McLennan County Library. A date stamped in the front inside cover of this second edition of *Koreshanity* indicates that the library acquired its copy in November 1972, about a year after publication.

Waco-McLennan County reference librarian Sean Sutcliffe says there is no way to track how and why such an obscure title was acquired; existing library records don't go back that far. Someone may have donated it, or, more likely, a patron made a special request for the library to acquire the book. A discolored patch inside the book's back cover indicates where an old-fashioned library card holder was once pasted. When the library system switched to electronic tracking, library cards were removed from all its books, and those cards have since been discarded. Sutcliffe says that no means exist to discover who may have checked out the book once it became part of the library collection.

It's almost impossible that *Koreshanity* was requested, read, and deliberately plagiarized by Vernon Howell before his trip to Israel in 1985. J. Phillip Arnold notes, "David wasn't a reader. He only read the Bible." But Arnold, an eminent religious scholar, also says, "Most prophets don't claim to be the Lamb. And David and Teed are the only two who also claimed to be Cyrus, to be Koresh. It's too coincidental." Catherine Wessinger, professor of Religious Studies at Loyola University of New Orleans and collaborator with Bonnie Haldeman and Clive Doyle on their memoirs, said, after perusing *Koreshanity* for the first time, "It's too close. The book was in the Waco library, and the parallels, the specifics, are too close."

But someone who lived just outside Waco at Mount Carmel in 1972 and knew about the Koreshans could have asked the local library to acquire *Koreshanity*, then might have passed along critical details to Vernon Wayne Howell by means that allowed the young man to believe Cyrus Teed's 1869 vision and later revelations were actually his own.

Lois Roden was a dedicated religious scholar. She traveled extensively, participating in discussions with representatives of many religious groups, and read a great deal about other sects and their beliefs. Teed biographer Lyn Millner says, "If she somehow heard about Koresh and the Koreshans and wanted to know more, the information was available."

It's possible Lois visited Koreshan State Park in Florida. She may have first learned of Cyrus Teed and his vision by reading *Dark Trees to the Wind*. But it's certain that, in 1977, when she needed a startling new prophecy to establish her own right to lead the Branch

Davidians, Lois announced that she'd been visited by an angel. The celestial visitor's message to Lois was that the Holy Ghost was feminine, proof that God was both male and female. This message brought Lois badly needed validation. It was also taken virtually word for word from Cyrus Teed's account of his 1869 angelic visitation, and also from "God the Lord Is Alternately Male and Female," an article in the January 23, 1892, edition of *The Flaming Sword*. Four years before twenty-one-year-old Vernon Wayne Howell arrived at Mount Carmel, Lois Roden was cribbing from Cyrus Teed to gain control of the Branch Davidians. By 1984, she was ill, in early stages of breast cancer, and faced with the increasing probability that her unstable son George would bully his way into succeeding her. George claimed leadership by right. Lois and, before her, Ben Roden became leaders by convincing other Davidians that they were prophets, true messengers in communication with God. If Lois's protégé Vernon Howell was to become the next leader at Mount Carmel, he would have to do the same.

From his arrival at Mount Carmel in 1981 through the early months of 1984, Vernon was Lois Roden's grateful student, as mentioned earlier. Then he began criticizing her, pointing out what he described as errors in her judgment, something previously unthinkable. Months before his 1985 trip to Israel, Vernon believed himself to be Lois's superior. Instead of correcting him, she accepted the criticism. She would have to, if she had convinced him that he had a biblically mandated mission much greater than her own—greater, in fact, than anyone else's in history.

Religion scholar James Tabor suggests that "what may be happening is that she's giving him possible phrases, seeds of ideas, and with the brain that he had, he could have embellished them. All Lois has to do is give him the kernel idea, and on his own he will decide, 'This is actually about me.'"

Arnold agrees: "Lois in bed with David at night might have whispered that he would be Koresh someday, and reveal the meaning of the Seven Seals. She suggests the story, and David feels he's caught up on a chariot and the rest."

Even as a child, Vernon Howell believed that God communicated with him. He aspired to be anointed a prophet. A suggestion from Lois that he might be the greatest of all prophets, and, even more, the Lamb who finally reveals the Seven Seals, would surely have been intoxicating. When he allegedly received this amazing revelation is illuminating. Lois Roden was not with Vernon and Rachel Howell in Israel; if she was the catalyst for his claim, Lois probably suggested that he must fully experience his vision thousands of miles away from her. Vernon's eagerness to believe would do the rest. Then George Roden couldn't claim that Vernon was just parroting nonsense fed directly to him by Lois. It may be that, in late 1984, Vernon removed himself and his followers from Mount Carmel for a reason other than trepidation of gun-toting George.

However it happened, Vernon Wayne Howell took Cyrus Teed's prophecies and made them his own. He probably did not realize that he did. David Koresh preached not only with fervor, but conviction. That combination eventually made the second Koresh much more famous than the first.

CHAPTER EIGHT

Palestine and Points West and East

Back at the camp in Palestine, David Koresh pondered his next move. He was called on by God to do great things, and had to prepare. An obvious first step was finding more followers; the Lamb needed an army for the coming clash with Babylon. He'd already pried away everyone willing to listen to him from Mount Carmel. A logical fresh recruiting ground was the General Conference of Seventh-day Adventists scheduled that summer in New Orleans at the city's famous Superdome, only a few hundred miles from Palestine. Like Victor Houteff and Ben and Lois Roden before him, Koresh believed that Adventists were the most likely converts. He drove to the convention, walked in uninvited, and was rebuffed when he asked to address the attendees. Koresh was offended by the rejection. He drove back to Palestine, loaded his guitar and sound equipment, then made the return trip to New Orleans. Denied the opportunity to proselytize inside, he resorted to blasting his self-composed evangelistic songs at SDA conventioneers in the massive arena's parking lot. The impromptu concert didn't attract any new followers.

A new plan was needed, not only to recruit additional followers, but to bring in the money necessary to travel and find them, then defray the additional expenses of bringing them back to Texas. All of the men and most of the women in the Palestine camp already worked. Many commuted two hours each way to jobs in Waco. Though they all contributed money toward camp expenses, Koresh never asked them to turn over their entire paychecks. Still, even with only a few dozen people living there, it was already a financial stretch. Someone suggested to Koresh that there were supposed to be lots of jobs in California, and wages in that state were higher than in Texas. There were many Adventists in the Los Angeles area; this was where Victor Houteff brought together the first Davidians. Why not an L.A. satellite base to both recruit and bring in more money? There was no thought of abandoning Texas; it was Koresh's frequently expressed intention to eventually reclaim Mount Carmel ("New" had been dropped) from George Roden. But he was enthusiastic about expanding to Los Angeles. Everything about L.A. worked; there was an SDA college in Loma Linda, and longtime Branch Davidians Don and Jeannine Bunds lived in nearby Pomona. Both disdained George, and remained generous contributors to Mount Carmel and Lois Roden; they'd surely offer at least temporary hospitality to Texas guests.

Koresh didn't talk much about another reason he found Los Angeles so compelling. L.A. was the music capital of America, and he still retained aspirations of show business success. For someone who'd just learned he was the Lamb in Revelation who would reveal the Seven Seals, it wasn't much of a stretch to anticipate rock 'n' roll superstardom. He'd use this celebrity to evangelize, of course. In fall 1985, when Koresh, his wife, baby, and a few others—including Perry Jones and Clive Doyle—headed west, he took his guitar and rock star aspirations with him.

As Koresh had expected, the Bunds welcomed them. The first arrivals stayed in their home. When additional room was needed for more followers from the Palestine camp, Koresh rented a house in the L.A. suburb of La Verne. Everything went as they'd hoped. Almost everyone found work that paid much better than in Texas, and since Koresh and his followers lived dormitory-style, California expenses were minimal. A shuttle system soon evolved. Koresh made regular trips back to Palestine—he was still the leader there, after all—and several others alternated between the two locations. One of these was

Bonnie Haldeman; Koresh's mother later wrote that she separated from his stepfather after Roy Haldeman's heavy drinking became too much for her to bear. Bonnie left her younger son, Roger, with his father; in California, she found cleaning jobs for herself and some of Koresh's female followers. "This was a new adventure for me," Bonnie wrote in her memoir. "I was tickled to go to California."

David spent much of his time on or around the Adventist college campus in Loma Linda, preaching to any students who'd listen on their way between classes. But the first important recruit was discovered by Perry Jones. In January 1986, twenty-two-year-old Marc Breault, a Loma Linda graduate student, was shopping at a supermarket when Perry approached him, complimenting Breault's Dallas Cowboys T-shirt and asking if the tall, thick-bodied young man might be from Texas. Hawaii native Breault said no, and, in response to Perry's next question, explained he was studying at Loma Linda with the plan of becoming a Seventh-day Adventist minister. Marc's eyesight was so poor that there was some question the church would appoint him to such a position. He was very concerned about it. Perry, who'd worked with Lois Roden on *Shekinah*, identified himself as a "religious journalist." For some time, the pair stood in a store aisle enthusiastically discussing various religious topics. Then Perry mentioned "a young man only a couple years older than you. I think he has inspiration from God." Breault was skeptical, especially when Perry added that the inspired young man was his son-in-law. But he agreed to meet Koresh, who showed up at Breault's apartment the next day. After a series of Bible studies with Koresh, Breault was convinced that no one knew more about the Bible than his new acquaintance. He left the Adventists to join him.

The income provided by his California followers opened up new recruitment horizons for Koresh. Thanks to previous outreach by Ben Roden, there were some small groups of Branch Davidians in Australia. Aussies Clive Doyle and his mother, Edna, had come to Mount Carmel at Ben Roden's invitation. In 1986, Koresh flew to Australia, bringing Clive with him to make introductions. They were met at the airport by a young Branch Davidian woman named Elizabeth Baranyai. After a rough start—the Australian Branch Davidians didn't understand some of Koresh's American catchphrases and jargon—he won over quite a few. Within months, some began arriving in Los Angeles to join the group there. Besides Baranyai, they included Graeme Craddock and eighteen-year-old twins Peter and Nicole Gent. All would become familiar names in Branch Davidian lore.

But in terms of recruitment, of introducing the Koresh message to others and engaging them so completely that they felt compelled to know more, Marc Breault initially surpassed Koresh. From the time he joined the group, Breault impressed everyone, Koresh most of all. It helped that he played keyboards, and could join Koresh's band, which was still in a formative stage. More importantly, Breault lived and breathed scripture. He occasionally felt that God was sending messages to him. These messages weren't as clear as those Koresh described experiencing in Israel, but he encouraged Breault to keep himself open to such communication. Surviving Branch Davidians agree that, among all his followers, Koresh loved Breault the most.

Breault was well acquainted with Adventist organizations in his home state of Hawaii. The Diamond Head Seventh-day Adventist Church in particular boasted a membership bristling with bright young men and women who enthusiastically studied the Bible. It was logical for Breault to request permission to speak there, knowing in advance that it was likely most of the church elders would reject his message. It was the insatiable seekers, the Adventists who always wanted more biblical knowledge, that comprised his target audience.

Branch Davidian survivor Paul Fatta remembers that "I was head deacon there, for five years I was part of that church. I was active in Young Adults for Christ, with Scott Sonobe, Mark and Jaydean Wendell, Neil and Margarita Vaega, Steve and Judy Schneider—all really good friends of mine. We were vegetarians and not drinkers. We'd go on hikes, have potlucks, all clean, wholesome fun." Everyone in the group was accomplished in some way. Fatta owned Dial-a-Ride, "a service for people who, for whatever reason, couldn't use mass transit," somewhat similar to modern-day Uber. Jaydean Wendell was a former policewoman. Steve Schneider, who demonstrated impressive knowledge of the Bible and speaking skills, attended graduate school with the intention of becoming an SDA minister.

Everything changed in 1987. "One Friday night, we had a Sabbath sundown service, nothing big, maybe thirty people there," Fatta recalls. "A guy named Marc Breault was visiting and he was leading the study, talking about how God works and the seven feast days. One of the church elders stood up, and he says, 'Marc, I know you're bringing this up, but it's not really the doctrine of this church. It should be taken to the leadership and they can decide if we should research it.' And they stopped his Bible study, actually shut the lights off."

This offended Fatta: "I wasn't even agreeing with what Marc was saying, but I didn't like the idea that the church hierarchy was going to tell me if I could think something was the truth or not." In the church parking lot, he invited Breault to come back to his house and continue the lesson—anyone who wanted should come along. About a dozen did, including members from Young Adults for Christ. Afterward, Fatta allowed Breault to use his place to hold Bible study: "I started listening to Marc and thought, 'This is really interesting. He talked about how the psalms and prophecies in the Bible tie into the Book of Revelation.' For me, it was like a light came on. I couldn't sleep at night, thinking about it."

The other Young Adults for Christ were equally enthused. Fatta and Steve Schneider wondered where Breault had learned it all. Both men believed that God "sends messengers from time to time." After Breault returned to California, they decided to call him and ask if God revealed these truths to him. If he said yes, then he was a prophet, and they must follow him. But Breault said no, he learned from someone at Loma Linda, whom he identified as Vernon Howell. (Koresh still made occasional use of his former name.) The two truth seekers from Hawaii decided that they must go to California and meet "the source."

When they arrived in L.A., Schneider broke away briefly to visit friends in Washington state. Fatta picked up Sherri Jewell, who'd been his girlfriend in Hawaii. A teacher and school administrator, she'd broken up with him and taken a job in Anaheim. They were still on friendly terms, and Fatta wanted company when he met Marc Breault's mentor. It was a Saturday, and when they drove to Loma Linda, congregants were just leaving Sabbath services at an SDA church. A few people stood outside, handing out leaflets with a banner headline reading, "*Your kids are like the daughters of Babylon.*" Fatta was impressed: "Standing right in front of Loma Linda University Church, they're calling them out—pretty bold." He asked one, "I'm looking for Marc Breault, or how about this guy Vernon Howell?"

He was directed to "a guy with long hair, wearing polyester pants and glasses. He had a Bible out, and right there he's giving a Bible lesson to some young people. I stood in back and listened. Everything seemed on the up-and-up, all biblical. Afterward, I introduced myself and said, 'I came from Hawaii because Marc Breault said he got his information from you. I want to hear more.'" Howell—Koresh—was receptive. Immediately afterward, Fatta says, "I got a thirteen-hour Bible study with him, and it wasn't boring. He was nailing the scripture and the truth based on the Word of God. I ended up going back to where they were staying. There were some people there from Australia. When Steve [Schneider] ended up coming, and he knew his Bible inside out, he was amazed at what David was revealing from the scriptures. It meant a lot to me that Steve had the same reaction."

Back in Hawaii, Fatta pondered for a few months: "You need to do that, when you're asking God for more truth. I felt that David was delivering [it]." After having prayed, asking the Lord, "If this is wrong, close the door," Fatta sold his business, home, and most of his possessions, then joined Koresh and Breault in California. Steve and Judy Schneider did the same. Most of the Diamond Head Young Adults for Christ followed. Sherri Jewell gave up her school district job in Anaheim to join Koresh.

Steve Schneider's persuasive gifts helped swell the L.A. ranks even further. Along with Marc Breault, he became Koresh's most effective recruiter. One of his early successes was initially drawn to Koresh less for the message than an aspect of his music. In the summer of 1987, nineteen-year-old David Thibodeau came to Los Angeles from Maine to begin a one-year drumming course at the Musicians Institute of Technology in Hollywood. The teenager considered this a critical step toward rock stardom, but by year's end realized that he, like most of the school's other students, more likely faced a music career eking out a marginal living in cover bands. After graduation, he supported himself working in the gift shop of Mann's Chinese Theatre; though he still dreamed of something better, he was currently part of a band where other members "were into the rock life for its kicks rather than its ambitions."

Thibodeau often dropped into the Guitar Center shop on Sunset Boulevard to purchase drumsticks. While there one spring night, he met two shoppers, one serious-looking and athletic, the other grubby in jeans, a T-shirt, and wearing "aviator-type shades" that hid his eyes. The serious-looking fellow introduced himself as Steve Schneider, who said that his grungy companion was David Koresh. Schneider asked if Thibodeau was a drummer; if so, Koresh's band needed a drummer. Schneider was the band's manager. Thibodeau was put off by the business card Schneider handed him: it read "Messiah Productions"; biblical excerpts were printed on the back. The teen from Maine wasn't particularly religious. He told Schneider that a Christian band didn't interest him.

While Koresh stood by silently, Schneider explained that he and Koresh weren't "traditional Christians." Besides, the band was great, and was "going to be huge." At this point, Koresh finally spoke. A lot of scripture involved music, he explained. He wasn't out to convert Thibodeau. He'd like them to play some music together and "see where we can go from there." Thibodeau visited Koresh in Pomona, jammed with him a few times, and agreed to give the band a try. He wasn't impressed as much by what he considered Koresh's limited musical skills ("Good on guitar, not that good as a singer") as he was with Steve Schneider. So far as Thibodeau was concerned, having a manager was the important professional step. Being in Koresh's band was part of the package.

Rehearsals progressed; another Koresh follower who'd been playing drums was switched to bass. Between practices, Koresh sometimes talked about the Bible. Schneider shared personal recollections of being expelled for drunkenness from an Adventist college in England, moving to Hawaii and living like a heathen. But he'd married a fine woman named Judy, went back to school in pursuit of a graduate degree in comparative religion, joined Diamond Head Seventh-day Adventist Church in Honolulu, met Marc Breault, met Koresh through him, and, after some initial doubts, he and Judy joined Koresh. The music business was one part of something bigger. Thibodeau was intrigued. He also enjoyed quiet conversations with Koresh that were about music rather than religion; they drank beer as they chatted, and Koresh didn't try pressuring him for money like Thibodeau thought a religious phony would have done. He joined some of Koresh's and Schneider's Bible studies, and, he wrote later, "For the first time, the Bible came alive for me." Thibodeau didn't become a full-fledged convert, but he stayed around, willing to hear more.

The Bunds' house in Pomona and the rent house in La Verne filled up. Innovative business ventures helped fill group coffers. Neil and Margarita Vaega had owned a bakery in Honolulu. After they moved to L.A. to join Koresh, he asked them to open a bakery business there. But the new operation turned into something even more profitable than expected. Rather than baking and selling plain bagels and whole wheat bread, the Vaegas and Bonnie Haldeman developed a regular sales route among neighboring office buildings. There, they sold fresh bagels with cream cheese and thick sandwiches to workers eager for tasty lunches without the inconvenience of leaving their desks. And, after initially working as crew members for other bosses, some of Koresh's followers formed their own landscaping and roofing companies; all the profits went to him.

There was enough money for Koresh to extend recruitment efforts across the Atlantic Ocean as well as the Pacific. Besides Australia, he and Schneider traveled to England, where enough Adventist elders were concerned about them to issue blanket warnings to their affiliated SDA churches:

> *Their tactic, if you try to engage them in logical debate, is to become illogical. Then if you switch to illogic, they switch to logic. They are cunning and clever. They cannot be beaten. Their methods are calculated, brain-washing. Their policy is to agitate and confuse, and to bring in new light.*

Barred from Britain's Adventist churches, the American visitors had sufficient funds to rent nearby meeting halls. SDA college graduate student Livingstone Fagan came to hear David. Fagan was about to complete a two-year program and was wondering, *Now what?* Many of his personal questions regarding biblical truth remained unanswered: "You came out [of graduate school] with a piece of paper from an institution." At the meeting, David's words convinced him that "there were still threads to be gathered. David invited me to come to the U.S., and I wanted to." Fagan eventually moved to Texas with his wife, their two young daughters, and his mother.

In England, as always, Koresh's recruiting focused almost exclusively on SDAs. There—and often in Australia, and Hawaii, and California—if he couldn't make his case in person, he'd record cassette tapes and send them along with Schneider or Breault or whoever was representing him. They'd play the tapes, and that way potential new followers still could hear the truth from the Lamb's own lips. On these tapes, geared for SDA audiences, he often identified himself as an Adventist, insisting, "As Adventists, we all believe . . ." or, "As Adventists, we already know . . ."

Koresh frequently made the point that he, like everyone else, was a sinner who needed God's forgiveness. On a tape sent to prospective followers in Australia, he says matter-of-factly, "Let's face it. We are bad. That's why, in the message of Revelation 18, it says, 'Once Babylon is falling, it's falling.' So, we turn back to the prophets of Isaiah;

let's take a look at Isaiah's prophets real quick. We know that in Isaiah chapter 12, with [our] fall, 'And in that day'—this is verse 1— 'thou shalt say, O Lord, I will praise thee: though thou wast angry with me, thine anger is turned away, and thou comfortest me. Behold, God is my salvation; I will trust, and not be afraid; for the Lord Jehovah is my strength and my song; He is also become my salvation.' Ain't that something?"

If an audience didn't appear sufficiently engaged, Koresh knew how to get their attention. Clive Doyle remembers, "At a program in England, where most of those who had come to listen were Black, David suddenly said, 'God hates Black people.' And there was this shock. Then he said, 'And God hates yellow people. And God hates white people. God loves people of light. Are you people of light?'"

Koresh always emphasized that nothing about God and the Bible was simple. Claiming faith was easy; being faithful was hard. An open mind and extended study were required. Anyone following Koresh was committing to a life of sacrifice. He was careful not to tell too much too soon; the entire prophecy of the opening of the Seven Seals and the coming of the End Time would prove overwhelming to neophytes. Those who joined and stuck with him in California and elsewhere were invited to come to Texas and immerse themselves in study led by Koresh. Then, gradually, they would absorb the complex prophecies and be prepared for all the events of Revelation.

Koresh did not intend to educate his growing flock in the woodsy Palestine camp. Mount Carmel was still the appropriate home for the Lamb and his faithful. In November 1987, a challenge from George Roden offered him an opportunity to reclaim it.

CHAPTER NINE

Shootout at Mount Carmel

T hings did not go well for George Roden after Vernon Howell and his supporters left Mount Carmel in 1984. There was an initial, if limited, triumph. George insisted on another election for Branch Davidian president, and with Vernon's adherents gone and only his mother as an opponent, this time he won. But attaining the title he'd sought for so long didn't bring George much satisfaction. Lois, freed from day-to-day responsibilities, alternated between Waco and the Palestine camp, trying to bring about a reconciliation. Her health continued failing, and breast cancer killed her in 1986. Lois's demise eliminated Mount Carmel's stabilizing influence. Many Branch Davidians still living there wearied of George's constant haranguing and left. With only a few die-hard followers remaining on the property, and finances running low as a result, George was reduced to renting empty cabins to outsiders. There weren't many applicants; George had to settle for whoever was willing to live in rudimentary housing on barren land. Inevitably, some new tenants found Mount Carmel appealing because of its relative isolation from town—and the law. Renters in one house stocked and peddled printed pornography. Another Mount Carmel cabin became a drug lab. If George had knowledge of either illegal enterprise, he overlooked it. Everything paled beside George's abiding obsession, which was to permanently eliminate competition for Branch Davidian leadership by Vernon Howell, or David Koresh, as he was now calling himself.

Even after Lois's death, the two were in occasional contact, mostly through letters where each accused the other of apostasy and fraud. George was aware that Koresh wanted Mount Carmel back. David believed the property was crucial to his ministry. The Palestine camp couldn't support more than the few dozen already living there. As his following grew, Koresh needed a place where he could gather everyone together, not only to celebrate festivals like Passover, but to be present for Bible studies that gradually prepared them for the dramatic events to come. There was enough space for that at Mount Carmel. He had to have it. In late October 1987, George provided an opportunity. There was no one left at Mount Carmel to question George's increasing delusions of God-granted powers. Though there's no record of whether he did so by letter, phone call, or in person, George challenged Koresh to a puzzling duel.

A small portion of the Mount Carmel property was used as a cemetery. Longtime residents who wanted to be buried there were obliged. George disinterred the coffin of Branch Davidian Anna Hughes, who had been resting in place for two decades. Jesus raised the dead; now George Roden declared that he and Koresh must compete to see who could do the same. Whichever one resurrected Anna first would prove himself the rightful, God-anointed leader, and master of Mount Carmel. The loser must abandon the claim, and the place, immediately.

Such a competition was in conflict with Koresh's claims about his God-mandated role as the Lamb. Other than the ability to open the Seven Seals and subsequent responsibilities to help bring about the new Kingdom of God on Earth, Koresh boasted of no additional powers. He couldn't turn water into wine, heal the sick—or raise the dead. If George claimed that ability, then George was nuts, which Koresh already knew anyway. He had no intention of facing George in such a farcical confrontation. But Koresh did think that the ludicrous challenge could result in him reclaiming Mount Carmel.

Koresh still maintained friendly relations with McLennan County sheriff Jack Harwell and his deputies. He drove from Palestine to Waco, and informed the lawmen that George Roden had illegally dug

up a corpse; wasn't that desecration of a grave? They should immediately go out to Mount Carmel and arrest him. They told Koresh it
wasn't that simple. No arrest could be made without proof. If he came
back with pictures of the desecration, then the sheriff's office would
investigate.

Koresh still had a few informants living at Mount Carmel. He sent
word for one to take photographs without alerting George. Within
days, Koresh was back to see the sheriff, brandishing pictures of Anna
Hughes's dirt-crusted coffin, which was draped with the flag of Israel
and displayed in the Mount Carmel chapel. To Koresh's dismay, he
was told that this still wasn't enough. How could the lawmen be
certain there was a body in the coffin? They needed to see a photo of
Anna Hughes's corpse. When Koresh promised to get one, the lawmen offered a friendly warning. George Roden was dangerous; lately
he was reputed to walk around lugging an Uzi. If Koresh attempted
to get the necessary photo for evidence, he'd better be careful. Koresh understood that as permission to arm himself and whomever he
brought along.

Paul Fatta was one of seven followers Koresh included on the
mission. In early November, Fatta recalls, "We went to Walmart and
bought hunting [camouflage] suits and guns, the first guns I know of
that we had. Then that night about 3 a.m., we went over to Mount
Carmel for reconnaissance. But George had moved the casket from
the church."

Koresh and his squad spent a nervous day out of sight, probably
in the thick brush behind the property. After dark, Fatta says, "We
moved from house to house. It turned out that the casket had been
moved from the church to a little work shed, though we didn't know
that. At one house, we talked to the people there. David said that
they should leave the property, we were investigating George, and
nobody was getting hurt. They left, but on the way out, they went
to George. George comes running out, wearing a black cowboy hat
and [with] an Uzi on his hip. There were eight of us, we each had a
gun, but nothing like an Uzi. George yells out, 'Is that you, Vernon?'

David goes, 'George, just leave the property. We don't want anyone getting hurt.' And George starts spraying bullets all over the place."

Koresh and his followers took what cover they could and returned fire. The battle went on for an estimated forty-five minutes; no one involved was a marksman. Then someone—Fatta remembers it was Koresh—made a lucky shot that smashed the magazine of George's Uzi, jamming it and preventing him from firing. George's thumb was nicked by a metal splinter. Before the intruders could take advantage, sirens wailed and cars full of McLennan County deputies barreled up the hill. Despite Koresh and his followers insisting that George started the shooting, the eight of them were ordered to put aside their weapons and lie facedown on the ground. That command was particularly unpleasant because Mount Carmel was infested with ants. The men protested that they'd come with guns only because that was what the lawmen had cautioned them to do. "But we all got thrown in the back of the police cars," Fatta says. "When we got to the station, the sheriff says, 'Boys, you can't do this in America. But, hey, I appreciate that you cooperated and didn't give my men any trouble.'"

District Attorney Vic Feazell didn't want to prosecute the case. George Roden was crazy; he'd instigated the quarrel. "But there'd been shooting, and David came to where George was," Feazell says. "I thought they'd all get off. An assistant D.A. wanted the case, and I let him take it."

Bonnie Haldeman wrote that after his arrest, her son called and begged her to bail him out, pleading, "I just can't take much of jail." Even the holding cell scared him. Bonnie raised the necessary $5,000; Paul Fatta's father arrived to provide bail for his son. Though it took longer, the other six were also bonded out.

The trial was set for April 1988. In the interim, Koresh and the other seven defendants returned to the Palestine camp. On January 16, two reporters from the *Waco Tribune-Herald* visited there. David chose not to talk with them, though he posed for photos. Perry Jones took the journalists on a tour, which didn't take long. They wrote, "Reports from Palestine law officials that 'they're living in boxes' are not far off. The 5-by-7-foot plywood [shanties] contain small wood-burning stoves bought on sale from Payless Cashways. . . . Light comes from kerosene lamps. There is no insulation. 'Our heads are warm, but our feet are cold,' Jones said. Each box has its own private bathroom—a plastic bucket." But Jones explained, "This is all temporary. We're hoping to get back home [to Mount Carmel]."

Thanks to George Roden, they did. Weeks before the trial of the eight from Palestine began, George was brought into court. Someone—Perry Jones seems likely—brought to the authorities' attention that George had been at Mount Carmel in violation of the old restraining order that remained in effect. There was also a matter of no one paying taxes on the property for nineteen years; McLennan County had been attempting to collect over $60,000 in overdue payments for several months. George responded to being dunned for back taxes with a number of legal briefs questioning the court's right to harass him. He used such offensive language ("Maybe God will make it up to you in the end and send you herpes and AIDS the last seven plagues and shove them up you goddamn bastards [sic] asses") that, late in March, a judge sentenced George to six months in prison for contempt of court.

Koresh was flush with money earned by his followers in California; he was quick to make the delinquent tax payments, and, since the restraining order was finally in effect and George was barred from the property, received the court's permission for him and his followers to take possession of Mount Carmel. They found the place in terrible disorder. Bonnie Haldeman wrote, "Goats were running in and out of the buildings." Non–Branch Davidian renters were sent on their way. In the lengthy cleanup process that ensued, Koresh and his people found and destroyed mounds of printed pornography. When drug paraphernalia was discovered, they summoned the sheriff to take it away.

There was also a stash of guns. As part of the trial process, Koresh and everyone else involved had to surrender their weapons to the sheriff. Any guns in George's possession at Mount Carmel were also supposed to be confiscated. Feazell recalls that Harwell was astonished to receive a call from Koresh soon after he returned to the Mount Carmel property: "David says, 'Sheriff, I don't want anybody to get in trouble, but you guys missed a room. We've got twelve more rifles.' Jack [Harwell] came to my office and said, 'You won't believe what just happened.' David was that honest."

When the trial convened, the defendants couldn't help feeling nervous despite their belief that God was on their side. Fatta recalls, "We were facing anywhere from five to ninety-nine years in the Texas state prison. That would have been bad." They were represented by Waco attorney Gary Coker, who was paid in part with a Harley-Davidson motorcycle owned by Koresh.

"Coker's whole defense was, 'George Roden is crazy. These guys were just defending themselves,'" recalls *Tribune-Herald* reporter Tommy Witherspoon, who covered the trial. Journalist Carlton Stowers remembers, "The county courthouse had these really steep steps in front, and during the trial they [Branch Davidians] actually tried to bring [Anna Hughes's] casket up those stairs, like pallbearers at a funeral or something. On the way up, they sort of dropped the casket, like an Abbott and Costello routine." The judge wasn't amused, and commanded, "Get that thing out of my court." The guns used in the shootout were wheeled into the courtroom in a shopping cart. That didn't amuse the judge either.

The jury acquitted seven of the defendants, and told the judge they couldn't arrive at a verdict on Koresh. County D.A. Feazell waived a retrial. Koresh had Mount Carmel back, and was free to bring far-flung followers there. He felt some trepidation about George Roden getting out of prison and making his own gun-wielding raid on the property. Clive Doyle remembers Koresh posting armed guards at the entrance.

Instead, George, after being freed, retreated to Odessa, Texas, where he was occasionally visited by his few remaining followers. George never stopped claiming that he was the rightful Branch Davidian leader, and anointed by the Lord as a messiah. In letters written to loyalists, he described Koresh and his followers as "the devil and his imps." In October 1989, Wayman Dale Adair, brother of a Branch Davidian who'd split off from Mount Carmel completely, dropped by to visit George. There was a quarrel, and George killed Adair. He was tried, found not guilty by reason of insanity, and eventually confined to a mental hospital in Big Spring, Texas. Over the next years George escaped twice, but was captured, once in New York City. In December 1998, shortly after escaping for a third time, George's body was discovered on the Big Spring hospital grounds. He'd died of a heart attack.

CHAPTER TEN

New Era at the Anthill

About sixty followers joined David Koresh in reclaiming Mount Carmel. Perhaps half had lived there before. They, at least, knew what they were returning to. But the others had joined Koresh in scenic Southern California, Hawaii, Australia, and England. To many of them, "Mount Carmel" was a Promised Land. Koresh and his veteran followers talked often about how they longed to return there. Some of the newcomers had spent time at the camp in Palestine, with its rickety shacks and lantern-lit nights and bucket baths. Fabled Mount Carmel was surely a step up from that.

So, arrival at Mount Carmel was a shock. Even after cleaning up the messes left by George Roden and his trashy renters, the property remained an eyesore. Central Texas's heat left the ground cracked beneath swatches of sun-blasted yellow grass. Shade was virtually nonexistent because trees were stunted. The only blossoms danced atop stems of weeds. Flies and mosquitoes buzzed through the air, and ants swarmed on the ground, so many that newcomers nicknamed their home "the Anthill." Some houses lined the hilltop, though "hovels" was a better description. There was water and electricity, but no air-conditioning or heating. Walls were thin; wind whistled through. Being inside was no more comfortable than being outside. Meals, always taken together by the group, provided sustenance rather than traditional fare. Bananas and popcorn were staples. Sometimes, these two items comprised entire meals. Decades later, Kathy Schroeder spoke for all the newcomers to the property: "We hated Mount Carmel."

This was exactly the reaction that Koresh wanted.

"What the conditions did, they weeded out the people who were just there for a good experience," Paul Fatta says. "The question for everyone was always, 'Are you here for the truth?' It was a test. A lot of people came, and then left. The doors weren't locked, the gates weren't locked. Among those who really wanted the truth, nobody's going. We shared that goal and the discomfort that came with it."

Those who stayed did not automatically become friends. They were pilgrims sharing the same holy quest, and their rigid schedule left little time for socializing. The "daily" was observed twice, in the morning and late afternoon. These were gatherings for reflection and prayer, though Kathy Schroeder says that prayer mostly consisted of scripture readings. "We had the philosophy that if you were going to pray, the best thing to pray would be God's own words," she says. In between the dailies was whatever work fell to each individual. Some had jobs in town, a few homeschooled their children, and there was always lots of manual labor to be done. One of Koresh's pet projects was the gradual tearing down of the houses, then using the flimsy materials to build a single, sprawling edifice that eventually included offices, a chapel, a kitchen and cafeteria, a bare-bones gymnasium, water towers, a central tower commanding 360-degree views of the entire property and the roads leading to it, small boxlike bedrooms on the first and second floors, and the concrete vault left standing when the old administration building burned down years earlier. The tear-down and building took several years. No one at Mount Carmel had to concern themselves with how to fill idle time.

Koresh wasn't always present; he commuted between Mount Carmel and Los Angeles, with some recruiting trips to Hawaii and overseas. Marc Breault and Steve Schneider also traveled and recruited. In Koresh's absence, Perry Jones took charge at Mount Carmel. Many living there found Perry to be as irritating as the voracious fire ants. He constantly carped at those he felt weren't exhibiting the proper, obedient spirit. But he was considered Koresh's second-in-command, so his irascibility was tolerated.

When Koresh was in residence, on most nights he gave group

Bible studies, and that's what his followers were there for. Schroeder says, "I felt, 'Fine, I've got to do this or that, follow rules and all this weird stuff,' but that was okay as long as there were those Bible studies." An individual Bible study with Koresh was a rare, prized experience. Everyone's attitude toward him was extremely respectful, but Koresh didn't encourage adoration. He frequently cautioned, "I don't want you to worship the person, but the teaching. I'm just a messenger of the truth. I'm like a Dixie cup that God will crumple up and throw away when He's done with it."

Yet Koresh's Bible studies convinced everyone that the truth was being conveyed by someone special to God. To Clive Doyle, Koresh was not reciting: "He was *receiving.*" Sometimes, Koresh said that when he taught, it felt like watching a movie in his head and describing the action. Mostly his presentation was low-key, but there were always moments when he was caught up in his own descriptions, and his voice rose and fell to considerable dramatic effect.

The Bible studies were not one-man shows. Koresh invited debate, not only with himself, but between his students. It was important to explore every word, every biblical nuance. The process seemed endless because there was so much to learn. Koresh's starting point was usually the Book of Revelation, but he invariably linked one important portion of that book with another part of scripture somewhere else in the Bible. Everything, Koresh taught, was inexorably connected, and led to the Bible's final pages with the prophet John's graphic description of the chaos to come. Perhaps the most thrilling aspect of Koresh's teaching was the concept that the prophets of the Bible were writing about modern times as much or more than their own. These were current events, not old news. Prophecies were about to come true. Though Koresh never mentioned a specific date, he sometimes alluded to things happening in 1995. He made the Bible come alive, seem vital, as no one else in his audience's experience had.

If the effect was enthralling, the effort to achieve it was laborious, for Koresh as well as his students. People came from varied educational backgrounds; some learned faster than others, and given the complexity of the subject matter, everybody at times felt they'd fallen hopelessly behind, and begged Koresh to explain something again. "Eighty people might be listening to him for five hours," Kathy Schroeder explains. "Maybe you needed seven repetitions before it finally clicks. But if people asked, David would do it over and over until everybody got it." Clive Doyle adds, "If you said you'd missed something earlier, or, 'I got all of it but this part,' he could go right back to that part and say it exactly the same way again."

Everyone understood that Koresh's teachings about the Seven Seals were crucial. They believed him when he said that only he had the ability to teach the subject, and that the Lamb must open the seals one at a time. Among all of mankind, they were the first to learn these things. Every aspect of each seal must be discussed, and all scriptural passages related to each aspect explored before the next could be taken up. The endless details were intimidating; Koresh promised that if everybody kept listening, they'd eventually understand. The first four seals contained warnings and announced the arrival of various angels and creatures in preparation for what was to come. The Fifth Seal, Koresh taught, explained what was going to happen to him and his followers. For them, he couched Fifth Seal prophecy in both biblical and modern terms.

"He taught that there would be a big battle between the forces of the world and David and his people," teenaged Kiri Jewell testified in 1995 before a congressional committee in Washington, D.C. "The world would win and we would be killed, but we'd come back in a cloud and smite the wicked and retake the world. The details would change as David received more messages from God, but there was never a time when we didn't expect to get killed by the feds, who David said were Babylon. While we waited for this to happen, we [were to build] up an army for David so the battle would be a big one and all the world would know about the power of David and God."

Not all Koresh's faithful would die right away. Revelation 6:9–11 promised that the souls of those slain first would lie beneath an altar while the rest waited "for a little season" to be killed in their turn. When the Sixth Seal was opened, the sun and moon would be darkened, and with the opening of the Seventh Seal, the Lord would return. And when the End Time came, if those listening to Koresh remained faithful and did all that was required, they would have a place among the Elect. Three blessed groups would be gathered. The Bible—and Koresh—explained it as God reaping His harvest. The most fortunate would be the Wave Sheaf, the very best of the harvest. Then would come the first fruits, prime souls. Finally, there would be the great multitude, believers spared in the Final Judgment. Koresh's followers, the army of the Lamb, would be among the Wave Sheaf . . . if they persevered. If they didn't, the opposite of glory awaited. Anyone exposed to the Lamb's message, but who rejected it, was doomed.

Accordingly, Mount Carmel students felt obligated not to discuss what they learned from Koresh with any outsiders who might scoff at his teachings. Even hearing the truth secondhand and disbelieving it would condemn family and friends to being blotted out when Jesus returned to make His judgments. Kathy Schroeder says, "If we shared with people we cared about, and they didn't believe, then their blood was on our hands." Everyone at Mount Carmel was considered "in the message." When God told Koresh that He was ready and the time came, those who weren't in the message would suffer their deserved fate.

Koresh was a night owl who didn't concern himself with anyone else's circadian rhythms. Around 7 p.m., he'd summon everyone to gather in the chapel, and teach for as long as the spirit moved him. He might finish, tell everyone to turn in, and summon them back soon afterward if he suddenly felt inspired to teach some more. Even when he finally wore down, it was common for at least a few followers to beg Koresh not to stop; the exhilaration of learning the truth held their exhaustion at bay. Koresh sympathized; he said he wished that everyone could instantly know all that he knew. But there was only one Lamb. Everyone else had to meet the challenge of learning.

But it became clear that even the Lamb couldn't require his followers to exist without any recreation. In time, Koresh permitted purchase of video equipment and allowed movies. The Mount Carmel kids—who sat through Bible study along with the adults—were sometimes rewarded with ice cream. Perry Jones made the rounds of Waco supermarkets, getting donations of day-old doughnuts and other pastries that were doled out to grown-ups when Koresh felt it was appropriate.

These limited treats were understood to be minor, very occasional pleasures. The real satisfaction came from doing what God and the Lamb required. Failure to listen, to *hear*, was fatal. In Revelation, six angels cry out warnings and unleash torments; a seventh, greater than the others, has the mightiest message, but Prophet John is not permitted to record the words. This seventh angel holds a small book, apparently the same one with the Seven Seals to be opened by the Lamb. Koresh taught that he was not only the Lamb, but also the seventh angel, who could now cry out "as a lion roareth." He wrote a song about it called "Seven Thunders," and sometimes sang it to followers, or in small clubs or cafés around Waco:

> In the days of the voice of the Seventh Angel
> When he shall begin to sound
> The battle has gone before
> Going to come to the ground.
> The mystery is finished as he hath declared
> To his servants the prophets
> Won't you beware? Won't you beware?

CHAPTER ELEVEN

The Privileges of the Lamb

T hough Koresh would have forbidden followers to head into Waco at night for dinner in a restaurant or to catch the latest hit film at a local theater, he sometimes ventured out to his own favorite haunts, and brought his guitar. "We ran into Koresh on and off, mainly because he played his guitar, mostly in the Chelsea Street Pub," remembers *Waco Tribune-Herald* photographer Rod Aydelotte. Even as he claimed biblical destiny as the Lamb, David also pursued a career in music. Koresh explained to his Mount Carmel faithful that "sometimes you have to use a hook to bring people in." Young sinners were more likely to listen to the message when it was expressed in song. In 1991, he ordered some of his followers to build a stage in a Waco bar called the Cue Stick. They purchased and installed a sound system, and, for a time, David Koresh and his group became the house band on Saturday nights.

He didn't confine his efforts to occasional shows in Waco. Some of his time in Los Angeles was spent seeking the attention of record labels rather than recruiting for the Branch Davidians. In L.A., Koresh and his band rolled in a shiny "Messiah Productions" tour bus (which sometimes did double duty shuttling recruits to Texas). Koresh's backup musicians, all selected from among his followers, sometimes took the stage wearing T-shirts emblazoned with "David Koresh/God Rocks." He hired an artist to place biblical images and scriptural passages on the body of his guitars. When no recording contract was forthcoming, he adopted a more commercial style in both his songwriting and performances. Drummer David Thibodeau, who previously enjoyed playing Koresh originals because his music wasn't like anybody else's, wasn't pleased: "The new songs sounded unoriginal, and David wasn't that good a singer, anyway." No one was converted after listening to Koresh play. But he kept trying, in Los Angeles and Waco, and his followers didn't rebel. It was what Koresh wanted, and when he was questioned about it during Bible study, he replied that the Bible promised the Lamb privileges in recognition of the work and great sacrifices required of him. Revelation 19:7 made it plain: "Give honour to him."

They obeyed, though they didn't always like it. Paul Fatta says, "David was never trying to win popularity contests." Kathy Schroeder is blunter: "David was an asshole. He was arrogant. But he was not manipulative."

This, to his followers, was key. They were free to question him at any time about anything. Koresh invariably cited scripture to justify his doing whatever troubled them. Schroeder says, "I didn't like everything he said. I argued with him. We sometimes butted heads. He'd say something, and I'd press him and make him tell me why something meant what he said. And every time I did, he had a response. He never said that he didn't know. He always knew. And, eventually, his responses made sense whether I liked it or not."

Almost everyone at Mount Carmel was originally Seventh-day Adventist. Belief in prophets and their prophecies was ingrained in them even before they left the SDAs to follow Koresh. The earliest Davidians believed Victor Houteff was a prophet equivalent to the Bible's storied Elijah. Branch Davidians were convinced that Ben and Lois Roden, in the holy tradition of true prophets, received and communicated messages from God. Clive Doyle, whose Mount Carmel tenure dated back to Ben Roden, says, "It's the nature of prophets that those who follow each of them feel that this is the one, the final one, and then it often turns out not to be the case." For Doyle, for everyone at Mount Carmel, David Koresh was unquestionably the final one. As the Lamb, he was the ultimate prophet, because it was his role to bring about the End Time and the new, better world to follow. If, in his human guise, Koresh did troubling things, the Bible still said they must honor him. Koresh himself willingly acknowledged personal flaws, citing Psalm 40:12 when admitting that his sins were "more than the hairs of mine head." And, as Dick Reavis writes in *The Ashes of Waco*, Koresh also taught that "God does not have to present Himself in a way that man likes, wants, or understands. The believer's duty is to accept God and His commandments on God's terms, not ours."

So, no one challenged Koresh when he picked the movies to be shown on special nights after exhausting Bible study. Films starring Arnold Schwarzenegger were common, because he liked the actor. Another unquestioned decision was recurring; Koresh sometimes allowed Branch Davidian kids to attend public schools, and other times he insisted that they be homeschooled by their mothers. There was no consideration of whether it was good for the children to seesaw back and forth. What mattered was what Koresh wanted at that particular time. He, through God, knew best.

No one was supposed to smoke, but Koresh began puffing cigarettes. He justified this with Psalm 18:8, where smoke emerges from God's nostrils. Many followers practiced vegetarianism. Koresh mandated that meat be occasionally served (beef and poultry, never the pork abhorred in the Jewish faith), and he insisted that everyone eat what was put before them. As he reminded, the priests in the Bible made animal sacrifices, and afterward the meat was eaten. Those in the message could do no less.

As the last, greatest prophet, Koresh could and did rescind mandates of his Mount Carmel predecessors. In particular, he banned the sale of Bible study audiotapes. Ben and Lois Roden enthusiastically peddled recordings of their teachings—it was a good way to raise money. But prohibiting selling tapes of his teachings allowed Koresh crucial flexibility. He could alter a prophecy without having to concern himself with contradicting what tape purchasers might have heard him saying previously. A good example was Koresh's original 1987 prophecy that, based on his interpretations of Daniel 11,

Matthew 24, and Revelation 7–16, he and his followers would travel to Israel. Once there, they would fight along with the Israeli army against United Nations forces led by the United States. Citing what he called his "Mount Zion" vision, Koresh said that this End Time would come in Jerusalem. That's where the Lamb and his followers would die, the first step toward their glorious return. There was no doubt about any of this—it was right there in the Bible. But four years later, during the Gulf War, Koresh began teaching that Armageddon might occur at Mount Carmel instead. He cited the same biblical passages. One of the privileges of the Lamb was the flexibility to change his prophecies. Within a few years, Koresh would explain to FBI negotiators that prophecy predicted what *would* happen *if* nothing changed.

In spring 1986, Koresh revealed a privilege of the Lamb that was hard for most of the Branch Davidians to accept, especially his wife, Rachel. While he and his followers were still camped in Palestine, he told Rachel that God had instructed him to take an additional wife. This was a violation of secular law. Koresh said that God's law, whatever God wanted done, superseded laws of man. There were passages in Revelation and Isaiah and, especially, Psalm 45:9–16 ("With gladness and rejoicing shall they be brought") supporting what God was telling him, the Lamb, to do. Rachel wasn't immediately persuaded until, she said, God visited her in a dream to tell her the same thing. Her husband must take an additional wife, and, soon, he did. It was Clive Doyle's daughter Karen. Clive didn't argue. This was a command from God. Then Koresh announced an alteration of the Lord's original message: he was to take additional *wives*. They soon included Rachel's sister Michele, Robyn Bunds (daughter of longtime supporters Don and Jeannine), Australian Nicole Gent, and Hawaiian Dana Okimoto. They were told by Koresh that their selection was an honor; not every woman was worthy. When pregnancies began resulting, he said it was in fulfillment of biblical mandate: the Lamb was spreading his seed.

Not all the young women's parents initially approved. Jeannine

Bunds later recalled that she and husband Don "were really upset," but Koresh "just kept talking to us and he convinced us that this was the way it was supposed to be." The elder Bundses were finally persuaded by Koresh's assertion that whenever Robyn became pregnant, "She's going to have a baby for God." Australians Bruce and Lisa Gent capitulated after arguing with daughter Nicole. She insisted that she and Koresh had discussed marriage for four days, and, once she agreed, it wasn't for her parents to say yes or no.

Koresh told followers that he was obeying spiritual law by taking multiple wives, but once he and his followers were back at Mount Carmel, he didn't want secular officials to know about it. David Thibodeau remembers that Koresh enlisted young male followers to join his new wives in "sham marriages" that would provide legal cover. Greg Summers "married" Aisha Gyarfas; Jeff Little posed as Nicole Gent's husband; Cliff Sellors joined Robyn Bunds in fabricated matrimony; and Thibodeau was paired with Michele Jones. The women performed "wifely" duties for their ersatz spouses, mending and washing their clothes and performing other small chores. Sex, however, was solely David Koresh's prerogative. Some wives were in California rather than Texas. The number of women spiritually married to him continued increasing. In 1993, Robyn Bunds told a reporter that Koresh maintained a half dozen wives in La Verne, while male followers lived in Pomona. When he was in California, he stayed with the women in a La Verne rent house. There was one room where the females slept in bunk beds, and a private bedroom for Koresh, where he spent each night with the wife of his choosing. He referred to his wives as "the House of David." When Thibodeau asked Koresh why he required so many women, he replied, "It's like winning in the bedroom. If you don't win in the bedroom, son, you're not going to win on the battlefield."

Some of these multiple unions didn't last. Dana Okimoto left Koresh and returned to Hawaii, taking with her the two children they'd had together. Robyn Bunds repudiated him not long after she gave birth to his son. There were others among the Branch Davidians who were never comfortable with Koresh's spiritually mandated harem.

But Koresh said he was acting on God's instructions, and used biblical passages to support his claim. If he was wrong about this, then perhaps he was wrong about everything else, and this was something most of his followers would not even consider. The quality of his teaching was impressive, and obvious even to outsiders who listened, years later, to recordings that Koresh allowed to be made, but not sold. (David's tapes were sometimes sent to current followers living elsewhere.) Religion scholar James Tabor says he has listened to about fifty hours of Koresh's Bible studies. "I've never met anyone who knows the Bible better than me," Tabor says. "But [Koresh] pointed out dozens and dozens of things I'd never noticed. He was picking out things I'd read, but had never put together." Koresh taught brilliantly, and his followers felt it was not only their honor, but their holy obligation, to believe all he said.

Perhaps most of all, following Koresh required belief that spiritual mandates took precedence over secular customs and laws. Malcolm Gladwell wrote in *The New Yorker* that it ultimately didn't matter to Koresh's faithful that some privileges he claimed were "at odds with virtually every social convention of modern life. [And] no one became a Branch Davidian if he required the comfort of religious orthodoxy."

The Lamb reveled in his privileges; his followers accepted them with the same conviction as they did his prophecy that he was leading them toward death—and a new, better life beyond.

CHAPTER TWELVE

A New Light

Mike Schroeder was not a religious man before he met Steve Schneider in Miami, Florida, and began attending some of Schneider's Bible lessons. Mike believed all he heard there, and enthusiastically told his girlfriend Kathy all about it. She recalls them deciding that "either the whole thing was real, or nothing was real." Schneider urged them to visit David Koresh at Mount Carmel. In 1988, soon after the couple married, they drove from Florida to Texas, bringing with them Kathy's three children from a previous marriage. When they arrived, they were told Koresh was in California. Since they'd already come so far, they decided to keep going and meet Koresh there. After spending the night at Mount Carmel—dinner was bananas and popcorn, and Kathy thought that Perry Jones "was a very strange man"—they set off for Los Angeles, where they met Koresh and attended one of his Bible studies. Though Kathy didn't like his "arrogant" personality, she was enthralled by his scriptural interpretations. The Schroeders returned to Florida, thought about it, sold everything they owned, and in the summer of 1989 returned to Mount Carmel. They intended to join the Branch Davidians and live there. The ride to Texas was uncomfortable for Kathy, who was pregnant. She was still thrilled, because she and her husband were going to spend their lives together "living for God." Then, when they arrived at Mount Carmel, Koresh informed Kathy that if she and Mike wanted to stay, they couldn't be married anymore.

"David had just brought what he called 'a New Light' from

California," Kathy Schroeder remembers. "It was about not just the single women [among the Branch Davidians] being his, but all the wives, all the women." Koresh explained that this latest message to him from God was solidly based on biblical prophecy. Psalm 45 described how women "with gladness and rejoicing" will "enter into the king's palace," and, "instead of thy fathers shall be thy children, whom thou mayest make princes in all the earth." And that scripture connected to Revelation 4:4 and 5:10, which describe "four and twenty elders" who would help rule over God's Kingdom on Earth after the End Time. Koresh was the king of Psalm 45, and the twenty-four elders represented his offspring, who, along with their father, the Lamb, had critical roles to play.

Obviously, quite a few women would have to bear his children to reach that sacred number. It would be an honor for them to give birth to holy babies. And, if they'd been married to someone else under secular law, it was also a blessing for their former husbands, who would make a meaningful sacrifice by obeying God's command. The women who had been their wives were Koresh's wives now. Under the new rule, these men would have an additional opportunity to earn God's favor. Except for Koresh, God wanted every Branch Davidian male to be entirely celibate; even masturbation was forbidden. Relieved of preoccupation with sex, all the men could fully devote their thoughts and energy to study of the Bible and service to the Lord.

"It was a tough sell," David Thibodeau wrote in his memoir. "In David's spiritual logic, he saw himself assuming the burden of sexuality for the entire community." Initially, the only person who felt entirely sympathetic to him and the effect of his edict was his mother, Bonnie, who had reconciled with her husband and lived with him and Koresh's half brother, Roger, at Mount Carmel. Almost immediately, Bonnie wrote in her memoir, many of the Mount Carmel women began competing for the right to bear future leaders of God's Kingdom: "I tell you, it was not easy on David to have a bunch of wives."

Koresh did his best to placate his male followers by explaining that all worldly relationships were temporary, anyway. In their next lives, the ones they were earning by loyally following the Lamb, they would find their perfect, permanent mates. These would be drawn from their own bodies, as Eve was from Adam's rib in the Garden of Eden. This didn't offer any immediate comfort, but it had to do. Everyone at Mount Carmel had already given up significant material and physical comfort to concentrate on learning and following God's Will. In general, Branch Davidian survivor Livingstone Fagan says, "We had to be brought to a place where our love of God was greater than our love for anything else. When there are things you love, God challenges you to see if you love Him more. God set up our Waco experiences to facilitate our progression." For many, this New Light of Koresh's was God's greatest challenge, besides the duty of dying alongside the Lamb at the hands of Babylon before returning in glory. Most of the men reluctantly accepted it.

Upon the Schroeders' arrival, Kathy followed Koresh's new rule. Mike, she says, "put 150 percent of his soul" into following the teachings of his new leader, but giving up his wife was still difficult. So, Koresh told Mike that he could not live at Mount Carmel, where constant contact with Kathy might be too painful. Instead, he would spend most of his nights and many of his days at an auto repair shop that the Branch Davidians recently opened a few miles away. Mike had no mechanical skills, so he would have to learn them—that would help keep his mind off the mandated end of his marriage. Whenever Mike did spend a night at Mount Carmel, to avoid the temptation of reasserting his marital rights he was instructed to sleep outside in his car. Finally, it was strongly suggested to Mike that he burn any photos he had of Kathy; this, he was told, was one of the best ways to move on. He burned them.

The new, L-shaped multistory facility lent itself to the new arrangements. All the men had their rooms on the first floor. Women and children were on the second, and Koresh's bedroom was also upstairs. In the evenings after Bible study, he chose his companion for the night. Kathy Schroeder says the women most eager to be honored "hung around" in hopes of being selected. Others, willing to comply but not eager to do so, went on their way and returned if Koresh summoned them. "He had his favorites," Kathy recalls. "We all knew that they were Rachel [his secular wife], Michele [Jones, Rachel's younger sister], Aisha Gyarfas, and Judy Schneider." But Koresh made sure that all the women were at least occasionally included. Sex was preceded by an individual Bible study, and conception was the ultimate reward. Soon, at any given time he had several wives in various stages of pregnancy.

Kathy Schroeder's pregnancy by her secular husband kept her from being chosen until after her son Bryan was born: "And since I was always one of the ones giving him trouble, arguing, in Bible study, the fact that he finally included me two times says something about him." The first time Koresh selected her, she remembers, "He was feeling sick, feverish. I think I was really just a body next to him. That time I just got a sermon that was very basic. We used the missionary [position]." She noticed that "David was really a big man, he could just stick his arm under my back and move me."

The second time was much better. "He gave me a personal Bible study. The feeling was so comforting, [like] my God speaking directly to me. Sex was just part of it. The sermon made every touch not feel like sex at all, just a culmination of my relationship with God that I'd had all my life."

The special moment ended when Koresh was called away. Schroeder says, "We were in David's room back by the gym. One of the other ones, Aisha, was having her baby [by Koresh], and he had to leave. Afterward, he named that baby 'Startle' because of the interruption."

Men relegated to other parts of the compound often endured excruciating emotional agony when Koresh took their former wives to his bedroom for sex. One night, David Thibodeau encountered Steve Schneider slumped over and holding his head in his hands. Schneider blurted how frustrated he was by Koresh's "new teaching," and that he almost couldn't stand the idea of his wife being with him. But, Schneider concluded, "If your wife had a chance to marry the Lamb, would you want to hold her back?" Wayne Martin was equally torn. He didn't want to give up his wife, Sheila, but decided that "if David is the Lamb, it wouldn't be fair for me to keep her from having this part of the truth."

Koresh couldn't resist occasionally rubbing it in. He taunted the other men, saying, "I got all the women. Aren't you jealous?" Sometimes he added, "We're all God's guinea pigs here. My lot is to procreate, yours is to tolerate. I'd swap with you any day." After a few months, the Branch Davidian men noticed that Koresh's most frequent choices of bed partners were the group's most attractive women. As always, he had a reason: "Shouldn't God's children be beautiful?" He even prophesied that, come the End Time, he'd have outside women, too. In particular, Koresh insisted that pop star Madonna was promised to him by the Lord. He taped a photo of the controversial entertainer on his motorcycle.

Eventually, eleven Branch Davidian women cumulatively gave birth to seventeen of Koresh's children. He claimed that siring these babies reaffirmed prophecy. Everything learned from the Bible and communicated to him by God was true. The infants were proof. There were other children at Mount Carmel, offspring of Branch Davidian couples before their marriages were undone by Koresh. There was an unspoken pecking order among the kids: the Lamb's offspring, part of future holy leadership come the End Time, were special, and treated as such. Even perpetually grumbling Perry Jones crabbed only about unruly youngsters who weren't Koresh's children. Koresh began teaching that his children weren't children at all, but rather old, sacred souls from Heaven who returned to earth in the form of infants. When the time came, they would assume mature forms and wisdom.

It was inevitable that some would not accept Koresh's "New Light." People always came and went, from among the Los Angeles–based followers as well as at Mount Carmel. But almost always in Texas, they were relative newcomers unable to handle primitive living conditions and endless Bible study. Now, in the summer and early fall of 1989, some longtime followers departed rather than dissolve their marriages. Mark and Jaydean Wendell left. This was a blow; as a former policewoman, Jaydean was especially useful in monitoring relationships with local lawmen. It was a great relief to Koresh when, after an absence of several months, the Wendells and their three children returned. They hated what the New Light required, but their belief in Koresh as the Lamb and the accuracy of his prophecies was such that they decided he must be obeyed.

A few women who'd been cohabitating with Koresh prior to his revelation of the New Light departed; they hadn't minded sharing him with a few other women, but had no desire to serve him in an ever-growing harem. Both Dana Okimoto and Robyn Bunds took children of Koresh's with them. Jeannine Bunds, Robyn's mother, left after she failed to become pregnant with the Lamb's holy child. Jeannine's adult son went with her. Her husband, Don, remained loyal to Koresh.

But the biggest blow was the loss of Marc Breault, whose loyalty and own spiritual fervor earned him a place as Koresh's most valued follower. Breault had recently married Elizabeth Baranyai, the young Australian woman who helped introduce Koresh to longtime Branch Davidians in her country. Breault's devotion to Koresh, once so complete, turned to disdain. Once Breault decided that the New Light was intolerable—he had absolutely no intention of handing over his wife—he began recalling a number of other worrisome edicts and acts by Koresh. Breault's anger was such that he determined David Koresh must be brought down.

Koresh talked incessantly about the Book of Revelation's End Time. Because of New Light, his own had begun.

CHAPTER THIRTEEN

Rumblings

Marc Breault couldn't leave the Branch Davidians right away. He was at Mount Carmel, and his wife, Elizabeth, was in Australia, ostensibly rallying the Branch Davidians there to accept and support Koresh's teachings. But when he contacted her to explain why he no longer wanted to follow Koresh, he discovered that she felt the same. In a letter to her husband, Elizabeth wrote, "You are my only love, the love of my life, and I don't believe I will be able to go through with what is being asked." Since she was in Australia and Koresh was in the U.S., she was at least temporarily safe from his New Light. But Koresh sometimes came to Australia to visit current Branch Davidians and recruit new ones, so the distance wasn't permanent. Breault determined that his first course of action must be to go to Elizabeth. This required some deception—Koresh approved every trip into Waco by his followers, let alone going overseas. Breault knew that an open declaration he was leaving would spark an immediate reaction from Koresh, who'd utilize all of his unequaled persuasive skills to keep his most valued follower by his side. So, Breault invented a reason to accompany Koresh to Los Angeles on his next trip (the purchase of new musical equipment) and, once there, used money secretly sent to him by Elizabeth to purchase a ticket to Australia. After joining his wife, he had an immediate plan to move against his former mentor.

David Koresh was unsurpassed at citing scripture to justify his actions; no one knew the Bible better. But Marc Breault came very close. It was known among other Branch Davidians that Koresh believed Breault might possess prophetic powers, less than his own, but still formidable. During their four years together, Koresh encouraged Breault to examine his nightly dreams for possible messages, and used him, along with Steve Schneider, as a designated emissary. Australian Branch Davidians knew Marc Breault and respected him. So, he started there.

Bruce and Lisa Gent, parents of twins Peter and Nicole, had returned to Australia. Peter and Nicole were at Mount Carmel, where twenty-one-year-old Nicole was one of Koresh's wives. She'd returned to Australia for a short time to give birth to his son, then returned to Texas with the baby boy. Breault wrote to the Gents at their home in Melbourne, explaining that God had directed him to speak to "any Branches who would give ear." Breault had "new light" that contradicted things being taught in Texas. He had his own scripture to cite—Psalm 74, which describes someone blaspheming in the name of the Lord. Breault wanted an opportunity to make his case.

Koresh was openly devastated when Breault defected from Los Angeles. He claimed the loss of his follower and friend made him physically ill; for a time, he took to his bed with chills and fever. When he learned Breault was in Australia and openly requesting a chance to refute Koresh in front of the Branch Davidians there, he responded. There were phone calls to Breault from Steve Schneider, pleading Koresh's case. Koresh himself went to Australia and debated Breault in front of a Branch Davidian audience. Breault held his own, and wrote in his memoir that when the exchanges grew heated, the police were called, and Koresh immediately flew back to the U.S. The faith that some Australian followers had in Koresh was shaken. Breault looked for further opportunities in America.

Robyn Bunds was deeply offended by Koresh's introduction of the New Light. She'd accepted her place as one of several Koresh wives, but the idea of being reduced to one "House of David" bedmate among many was too much. She'd had a son by him whom he named

Wisdom. Robyn and the toddler lived with the Branch Davidians in California. She was not the only member of the Bunds family who lost faith in Koresh. Her mother, Jeannine, had been among his most ardent believers. It was Jeannine and Don Bunds's generosity in opening their Pomona home to Koresh when he first arrived that enabled him to begin building a Southern California base. When he announced the New Light, Jeannine slept with David, expecting conception of a holy child. But when no pregnancy resulted, Jeannine had second thoughts. Soon, Robyn was joined by her mother and brother as skeptics of someone they'd once believed implicitly. When Robyn made known her intention of leaving the Branch Davidians, Koresh's response was to whisk toddler Wisdom back to Mount Carmel. To him, Robyn was just one among many women. Wisdom was the Lamb's progeny, intended by God to become one of twenty-four elders after the End Time. Koresh still tried coaxing Robyn back into the fold, but retaining the child was his priority. Surely, Robyn would never challenge the Lamb further.

For a time, Robyn dithered. Then, after communicating with Breault, she turned to the police in La Verne, California, where Koresh maintained the rent house for himself and selected women. Robyn claimed that her son was taken to Texas without her permission; she wanted him back. The La Verne lawmen contacted authorities in McLennan County. Koresh insisted to followers that his children were special to the Lord and belonged to Him, but secular law favored Wisdom's mother. After police visited Koresh at Mount Carmel, he immediately returned the boy to Robyn. She renamed him Shaun, and supported Breault's further efforts to bring David down.

Breault contacted U.S. Immigration officials, alleging that some Branch Davidians in the U.S. had extended their stays beyond visa limits. More sham marriages at Mount Carmel followed, these not to cover multiple marriages by Koresh, but to gain citizen status for some foreign followers. Now Immigration had the Branch Davidians on its radar. The McLennan County sheriff's department was also warned of illegal foreigners in residence at Mount Carmel. Since federal authorities were investigating, the local lawmen didn't get directly involved, but they still took notice. To this point, they'd always felt that the Branch Davidians were odd but not in any legal sense criminal, Koresh's 1987 shootout with George Roden notwithstanding. Koresh was still on friendly terms with the sheriff. But now, they were alert to possible wrongdoing at Mount Carmel, too.

Koresh realized it. Though he still taught that the End Time wasn't quite imminent, these Breault- and Bunds-related rumblings were troubling. Koresh advised his mother and stepfather to move from Mount Carmel to a rent house in Waco. Bonnie later said that "I think he knew down the road what was going to happen." Robyn Bunds had taken Koresh's son, and it was clear Marc Breault had no intention of letting up.

Sex-related scandal was natural media fodder all over the world, and Australia was no exception. Tipped off by Breault to salacious goings-on at the Texas headquarters of a cult leader, in early 1992 producers of the popular Australian TV newsmagazine A Current Affair sent cameras and a crew to Waco. When his Mount Carmel loyalists argued against cooperating, Koresh explained that it was a worthwhile risk. The godly qualities of life there might somehow outshine everything else being alleged. They didn't. Australian audiences were treated to an hour of scenes suggesting lewd sex, mistreatment of children, and impossibly unsanitary living conditions. For the time being, viewership was confined to Australia, but that was bad enough. Breault's efforts in his wife's home country had already reduced opportunities for finding new members. After A Current Affair's broadcast, Koresh could forget recruiting there.

The big event at Mount Carmel every year was the spring celebration of Passover. Branch Davidians the world over were encouraged to travel to Texas and mark the high holy day with the Lamb himself.

For a few days every April, Mount Carmel's population would double or even triple. It was not uncommon for as many as three hundred celebrants to gather there. Every inch of space was jammed with sleeping bags. Koresh's Bible studies were standing room only. Great fellowship was enjoyed by all. Mount Carmel residents enjoyed their hosting duties, and visitors left feeling spiritually refreshed, because Koresh's teaching was never more inspired. Then in 1992, Clive Doyle alleges, Marc Breault spoiled everything.

In early April, reporters at the *Waco Tribune-Herald* were tipped that the Branch Davidians planned a mass suicide at Mount Carmel during their Passover gathering. In his memoir, which describes in detail several of his attempts to discredit Koresh, Breault does not mention this. Doyle says he has no doubt that Breault was the one who provided the information for "the 1992 story that we were about to commit suicide." However the Waco journalists received the tip, they followed up immediately. Reporter Mark England contacted Koresh, who said, "Hey, I'm not ready to die." He explained that, although he taught followers about the End Time, "the end of time is just a process. We've got to know what God requires of us in this generation . . . just be informed what the word of God has stated by the prophet. Hey, all we can do is hope for salvation. That's what we teach."

England quoted Koresh in a *Tribune-Herald* story that appeared on April 18, when the Mount Carmel Passover celebration was already in progress. In his story the next day, "The Davidians Observe Passover," England followed up by noting "about 150 people" gathered peacefully to celebrate at Mount Carmel. Steve Schneider assured the reporter, "People are here for life. You mention a word like 'death,' and I'm out of here myself." This was a deft sidestep; Koresh assured his followers that they would live beyond their initial demise at the hands of Babylon during the End Time. An unidentified spokesman from the sheriff's department supported the Branch Davidians: "They've got a right to believe what they want to believe. I think the unknown is causing them a lot of problems. People don't understand their religion." So far as the *Tribune-Herald* was concerned, that ended any Branch Davidian–related controversy for the time being. Still, England and his editors wondered if there might be something more. Quietly, England continued gleaning information about Koresh and his followers, with the aim of publishing something more substantial should it be merited.

Koresh talked his way past the Passover accusation, and, though he'd lost his young son Wisdom, that incident seemed safely behind him. But Koresh's ongoing beliefs, edicts, and personal actions left him vulnerable to additional legal and media scrutiny. Though he still retained a solid core of followers, Koresh had no doubt that Babylon was beginning to close in.

CHAPTER FOURTEEN

The Guns

The lives of the Branch Davidians were dominated by one overriding fact: they viewed every facet of their lives, every action taken, every word spoken, from a spiritual rather than secular perspective. Koresh and the Bible were their guides. Nothing was done by whim, or with any concern about how the outside world would react. All that mattered was doing whatever was necessary to stay in the message. No aspect of their lives was separate from their religious beliefs.

"We followed what the Bible wanted," Kathy Schroeder says, and, in example, tells what she calls "the grasshopper story." At Mount Carmel, "One of my sons killed a grasshopper, and I made him eat it. In the Bible, [the Book of] Leviticus tells you what foods are edible. Anything that is edible and you kill, then you must eat it, because that is the only reason to kill it." In all things, she says, "We lived for God."

That meant not only tolerating, but welcoming, living conditions more spartan than imposed on monks in monasteries or nuns in convents. Mount Carmel's new, single building was constructed of cheap materials culled from the flimsy shacks that previously served members as their homes. Everyone knew that the place was a firetrap. There was a gymnasium and swimming pool—living for God required exercise to maintain the envelope of flesh their souls occupied on earth—but even these were basic. Individual rooms were tiny and sparsely furnished with a narrow bed (or bunk beds, if there were children), desks if kids were being homeschooled, a "closet" consisting of a shelf and hangers behind a curtain, and, in the women's rooms, a chamber pot. Mount Carmel kids had the daily chore of carrying the overflowing pots outside, digging a hole, dumping in the contents, and covering them up. (Occasional hepatitis B infections resulted.) The men used a primitive outhouse connected to an ancient septic tank.

Sponge baths were the most common ablutions. A rudimentary shower was rigged outside, with a screen to provide minimal privacy. None of the individual rooms had electricity. In cold weather, a little warmth was provided by space heaters plugged into the few outlets in various parts of the building. During the summer, fans replaced the space heaters. Air-conditioning might be considered essential everywhere else in Texas, but not at Mount Carmel—except in Koresh's room, cooled by a window unit. Only the kitchen/cafeteria had running water. Meals were basic, mostly relying on staples that could be purchased cheaply and in bulk by Perry Jones, who did the grocery shopping. Steve Schneider joked that living at Mount Carmel was like camping indoors.

Maintaining such a basic lifestyle was relatively inexpensive. Koresh estimated that it cost about $30 to $35 per month to feed each person. Add in minimal utilities, property repair, and taxes, occasional luxuries like a television and videotape machine, and some costs for medicine (Branch Davidians mostly relied on public clinics), and Mount Carmel's average monthly budget totaled around $15,000, or $125 for each man, woman, and child. Income was derived from donations by wealthy followers, regular contributions from followers living and working in Southern California, and a portion of the income from those Branch Davidians living at Mount Carmel who worked at outside jobs. Wayne Martin had a law practice. Perry and Mary Belle Jones's son David was a mailman. Rachel Koresh, David's first and legal wife, worked as a grocery store checker at H-E-B, a mainstream chain. Others worked for roofing and landscaping companies. Older residents had Social Security and pension checks. Individual bank accounts were allowed.

Almost everyone at Mount Carmel had at least some income,

and Koresh's better-heeled followers made up the difference for those who couldn't contribute much toward group expenses. (It would later emerge that Koresh also kept a substantial amount of cash on hand for emergencies.) But Koresh, eager for additional income, decided that he and his followers needed to establish new moneymaking businesses in Waco, just as they had in Los Angeles. Paul Fatta, who'd operated a very successful start-up business in Hawaii, was his advisor, though Fatta emphasizes that "David was the shot caller." Fatta's role was to help implement Koresh's business schemes whether he agreed with them or not.

Koresh's initial business project was in keeping with his own interest and talents—a car repair service. He'd always been handy at fixing cars. The Branch Davidians opened a repair shop a few miles from Mount Carmel. Koresh and a few other men with sufficient mechanical skills were able to fix most automotive problems, and they also acquired old beaters that could be cleaned up and resold. Reasonable prices were charged, and competent service was provided. A steady income stream resulted, but it still wasn't enough. Koresh's next idea turned out to be another moneymaker—and a step that moved himself and his followers inexorably toward the end.

In September 1990, David Thibodeau met a woman who mentioned that she knew a licensed gun dealer named Henry McMahon. As a youngster, Koresh was an avid hunter of small game. It occurred to him that there might be considerable profit to be made through the purchase and refurbishing of secondhand weapons, which could then be sold at the gun shows that are ubiquitous in Texas. Koresh arranged a meeting with McMahon, who'd had some work done on his cars at the Branch Davidian garage and was a very satisfied customer. At Koresh's request, McMahon got the Davidians started in the firearms business, explaining what customers at gun shows looked for in the way of bargains and hard-to-find weapons. Soon, Branch Davidian display tables began appearing at shows in Waco and Austin and Fort Worth. Early on, the wares offered consisted of old handguns and rifles that had been cleaned up and, if necessary, repaired. But Koresh learned the gun business as quickly and comprehensively as he'd absorbed the Bible. Soon, he no longer bought all his stock from Mc-Mahon; he was just as adept as the veteran dealer at going to shows and buying weapons that, once repaired and polished, could be resold at a significant profit.

Koresh also noticed that guns were not the only popular items at these shows. Hunting apparel, particularly vests with pockets for cartridges and other necessary shooting oddments, was always popular with gun show customers. Mount Carmel women set to work crafting deluxe hunting vests. They purchased the basic garments in local discount stores like Walmart, then gussied up the vests with roomier pockets and other accoutrements, including attachments for holding hand grenades. Grenades were illegal for citizens to own, but acquiring a vest that could accommodate them was especially attractive to militarists anticipating some form of all-out combat. The Branch Davidians also began offering MREs (Meals, Ready-to-Eat), canned fare they purchased in bulk from military surplus stores and resold at the gun shows to hunters and survivalists. Business for the vests and MREs was so brisk that a mail order system became necessary. The Branch Davidians named their operation the Mag Bag, and the mailing address they used for it belonged to the car repair shop.

In late 1991 or early 1992, Henry McMahon had a new suggestion for Koresh. U.S. presidential primary campaigns were under way. Republican incumbent George H. W. Bush seemed likely to be unseated by any one of several Democratic Party challengers, all of whom promised tighter gun laws and ownership restrictions if elected. The National Rifle Association's formidable publicity machine blared warnings that, come January 1993, any Democratic president taking office would almost certainly order sales of fully automatic rifles to cease immediately. (Semiautomatic guns fire single shots or short bursts when the trigger is pulled; fully automatic weapons fire continuously until the trigger is released, or ammunition is emptied from the magazine.) Those who already owned fully automatic weapons would undoubtedly be "grandfathered," or allowed to keep them.

This, McMahon explained, created an instant, rabid market among gun enthusiasts who wanted to acquire fully automatic firearms before a gun-hating Democrat president made purchasing them illegal. Semiautomatic weapons could be converted to fully automatic with some tinkering and the addition of a special type of lower receiver.

McMahon suggested a partnership. The Branch Davidians should buy the semiautomatic rifles and items necessary to convert them, then perform the conversions. Because only licensed gun dealers could sell fully automatic rifles—and the Branch Davidians weren't licensed—McMahon would handle that. Anyone selling, or buying, such weapons was required to register them with the government and pay fees of a few hundred dollars. Otherwise, sales and ownership were illegal and could result in arrest, hefty fines, or even imprisonment. Those converting the guns also had to register the work and pay a tax. But this window of opportunity was limited; either McMahon and the Branch Davidians jumped in right now, or else Bill Clinton, or whoever the new Democratic president was, would shut down sales.

Koresh taught that spiritual rather than secular laws were what mattered, but nothing in the Bible prohibited those in the message from taking advantage of a time-sensitive loophole in Babylon's laws. By spring 1992, the Branch Davidians began buying significant numbers of rifle conversion kits. These purchases were entirely legal; no law prohibited owning semiautomatic guns or the parts needed to convert them to fully automatic. It was only against the law to convert them without filing the required paperwork or paying taxes. The Branch Davidians did neither.

At Mount Carmel, a few followers with mechanical aptitude learned how to perform the conversions. Koresh, always thinking of the future and End Time, saw an opportunity to not only make money, but to begin building a private arsenal for the coming battle with Babylon. Fully automatic weaponry would allow the Lamb and his followers to put up the kind of fight God demanded before succumbing. Besides guns, there were also purchases of grenade "hulls," legal so long as they were not packed with explosives, which the Davidians also acquired.

The Branch Davidians at Mount Carmel were, for the most part, intelligent and perceptive. Many realized that secular laws were being broken. They didn't protest because, since they always looked from a spiritual perspective, it didn't matter. David Koresh spoke with authority from God, and only God's laws should be followed. The guns were converted for godly purposes. Against that, Babylon's conflicting laws must be ignored. This belief was so ingrained that, Kathy Schroeder says, she, like everyone else, didn't "really think about" gun-related secular illegality. It was insignificant. The killing and eating of a single grasshopper mattered. Illegally converting and selling fully automatic weapons didn't. They were doing what God wanted. They didn't care about anything else.

In only one instance did some of his followers wonder if Koresh was following God's Will or his own. The Bible mandated that the Lamb was entitled to his privileges. Was it possible for him to take a privilege too far?

CHAPTER FIFTEEN

The Girls

The adults of Mount Carmel waged a daily struggle to keep themselves worthy in the eyes of God. Simply accepting Koresh as the Lamb wasn't enough, come the End Time, to assure their places in the Wave Sheaf, and glorious life afterward in the new Kingdom of God on Earth. Koresh badgered them not to feel superior because they were, for the moment, "in the message." God would regularly provide challenges that could only be met by the truly faithful. They must accept everything God required of them, at peril of being deemed unworthy. All previous obedience could be negated by a single failure to wholeheartedly honor God's wishes.

Parents among the Branch Davidians had an even greater responsibility. Until their children came of appropriate age, the youngsters would be judged by the acts of their mothers and fathers. Not just the parents' own souls, but their children's, were at constant risk. This additional responsibility continued until sons or daughters reached the approximate age of twelve. Up to that time, Mount Carmel's children listened to Koresh teach just as their parents did. They endured the same spartan living conditions, and were assigned simple work duties. Corporal discipline reinforced the expectation of obedience and good behavior. But the onset of puberty also signified the moment when they must assume what God required of all "believing" adults—absolute acquiescence to whatever the Lamb and the Bible declared that God demanded of them.

For boys, it meant accepting responsibility for their own souls.

For girls, once they were confirmed as postpubescent, it meant that, and more.

Secular law in Texas is specific in terms of the legal age for young women to have sex and/or marry, and regards polygamy as illegal. With parental permission, girls can marry at age fourteen. In 1984, Koresh's marriage to fourteen-year-old Rachel Jones was within the law because her parents approved. Outside of marriage, in Texas the age of consent is seventeen. Even if her parents agree, any adult male having sex with a girl not his wife under age seventeen is guilty of second-degree statutory rape. If the girl is under fourteen, the charge escalates to first-degree felony. This doesn't mean that adult men in Texas never have sex with willing, unmarried, underage girls, but it does mean that they risk prison when they do. Committing polygamy is also criminal, with the potential of a prison sentence.

So, when Koresh announced in 1986 that God required him to take an additional wife or wives, he did so with the understanding that, under secular Texas law, he was committing a crime. (Unless Branch Davidian lawyer Wayne Martin specifically informed him, David may not have known that polygamy constituted a third-degree felony, with a maximum prison sentence of ten years.) Koresh was sufficiently concerned about secular repercussions to ask that several male followers join in legal marriages to the various women. It was just a matter of putting names on a form.

But another aspect of Koresh's polygamy placed him in even greater legal jeopardy. Karen Doyle, daughter of longtime Branch Davidian Clive, was fourteen. Michele Jones, Koresh's sister-in-law, was twelve. Nicole Gent was sixteen. To the law, and to outsiders, even sexual contact with a single legally underage child might seem repulsive, but religion scholar Catherine Wessinger suggests that Koresh was acting as a result of cultural indoctrination: "David's mother got pregnant with him when she was very young [fourteen]. He came from a section of Southern culture where young girls got pregnant or married and no one thought very much of it."

David believed that he had permission from God, and scripture confirmed it for most of his followers. Years later, still offended by secular objections, Livingstone Fagan wrote, "You often hear them talk with great self-righteous indignation about David and his having sex with under-aged girls. But in truth, none of these people know what happened or why. They don't know any of these girls they speak of, nor do they care about them. . . . By reproaching David, they are reproaching God."

When he announced the New Light in 1989 dissolving secular marriages between followers and claiming all the Branch Davidian females as his wives, David's decree offended some enough for them to leave. Those who stayed, obeyed. The Lamb needed to sire twenty-four children to serve as the magistrates described in the Book of Revelation. Some of the additional women he initially bedded were in their thirties or even older: Judy Schneider, Sheila Martin, Jeannine Bunds, Jaydean Wendell, Lorraine Sylvia, and Katherine Andrade. Babies resulted: daughters Mayanah with Judy, Chanel with Katherine, Hollywood with Lorraine, and son Patron with Jaydean. God's Will was being honored, and special, holy children were the reward.

But the Lamb's eye was drawn to younger breeders. In her 1995 testimony to congressional investigators, fifteen-year-old Kiri Jewell indicated that Koresh was choosing future partners even before they reached puberty:

"David took me on a motorcycle trip with some of the guys to Mount Baldy [in California] when I was about seven. On that trip, he took me for a ride down a mountain ski trail on the chairlift. There wasn't any snow, but it seemed like we could see the whole world. That was when David said to me personally that one day, I would be one of his wives."

Kiri was puzzled; when she told her mother, Sherri Jewell was thrilled. Three years later, Koresh moved forward with Kiri, whose testimony about the experience so repulsed the congressional panel that its chairman apologized to her for what she'd had to relate.

"My mom and Lisa [Ferris] and I went to Texas [from California] for Passover in 1991. David took the three of us to a motel. There were two chairs in the room and one bed that we all slept in. We were there for two or three days, just mostly hanging around the room. David preached to us."

At one point, the two adult women went shopping, leaving Kiri alone with Koresh.

"I took a shower and then I was brushing my hair, sitting in the chair, and then David told me to come and sit down by him on the bed," the teenager testified. "I was wearing a long white T-shirt and panties. He kissed me and I just sat there, but then he laid me down. He took his penis and rubbed it on the outside of my vagina while he was still kissing me. I had known this would happen sometime, so I just laid there and stared at the ceiling. I didn't know how to kiss him back. Anyway, I was still kind of freaked out. When he was finished, he told me to go take a shower . . . in the bathroom, I realized I was all wet and gooey on my legs. That freaked me out more. I just stayed in the shower for about an hour. When I came out, David was in his jeans and the bed was made. He told me to come here again. This time, he read to me from [the Bible's] Song of Solomon. I was ten years old when this happened."

Only "sometime later," Kiri said, did her mother ask what had happened in the motel. "She said, 'What? Did he take you?' I just said, 'Yeah.' She wasn't mad or anything. I asked my mom what would we do if we ever left there [Mount Carmel]. She said, 'We'll never leave, so why ask?' I never liked it there, but I wouldn't leave my mother, so I figured I'd be there with her to the end."

Koresh didn't penetrate ten-year-old Kiri, but the sexual act he did perform met the legal standard of an unlawful act with a minor, whether her mother consented or not. Under Branch Davidian understanding of spiritual law, the Lamb was exercising his prerogative. Kiri knew what was coming next. She told the committee, "Aisha [Gyarfas] was older than I was. She was probably thirteen when I was six or seven. She became one of David's wives when she was fourteen and had a baby for him." Though Koresh said he was acting on God's instructions, he was still concerned about potential repercussions from those not entirely in the message. Kiri said, "Once she [Aisha] was pregnant, I never saw her. She was kept hidden because she wasn't an adult. It was Passover, and there were a lot of people coming from all over and she didn't, she wasn't supposed to be seen pregnant because she was so young."

Some surviving Branch Davidians say they were then, and still remain, skeptical that Koresh was following God's command rather than satisfying his own very human urges. David Thibodeau wrote in his memoir, "There's nothing in the [Seven] Seals that specifically commanded David to have sex with underage girls. It was his personal vision that impelled him, not a clear Biblical example . . . there he was, deep in the heart of Texas, locked solid into the Bible Belt, where his sexual practices were bound to cause trouble. If he didn't understand that, he was an idiot." Besides, Thibodeau wrote, "I had a hard time believing that a girl of 12 or 13 could really know what she was doing in agreeing to have sex with a man twice her age, particularly in a closed community where sleeping with the leader was considered a supreme honor."

Kathy Schroeder disagrees. She remembers that to her, and many others at Mount Carmel, "David with underaged girls, I don't think it was a concern. At the time, everybody was more concerned about themselves, and where they stood with God. I think that the girls had to be twelve. If that's the age where you become accountable for your soul, then why can't you have sex?"

Sherri Jewell was divorced from Kiri's father, David Jewell, who lived in Michigan. He had never been a Branch Davidian. He was already divorced from Sherri when she met Koresh in California and joined the group. Kiri sometimes spent time with her father in Michigan; the adult Jewells were sufficiently cordial to agree on the girl visiting her dad.

In October 1991, David Jewell was contacted by Marc Breault, who said, "I've got something to tell you, and you're not going to like it. It's about your daughter Kiri, and I have reason to believe she's in extreme danger." Over several months, Jewell became convinced that David Koresh was about to take Kiri as a wife. The child was scheduled to come stay in Michigan with her father over Christmas, a holiday that the Branch Davidians did not recognize or celebrate. Just before Kiri was supposed to return to Texas, her father told her that he had a court order allowing him to keep her in Michigan. She felt "shocked and scared."

David Jewell initiated court proceedings to give him sole custody of his daughter. Sherri Jewell and the Branch Davidians took legal steps to thwart him. A Michigan court date was set for February 1992. In the interim, Sherri and Steve Schneider urged Kiri in phone calls to "remain true to David [Koresh]." Sherri warned her daughter that Koresh "had given beer to Rachel Sylvia, who was then eleven or twelve, to soften her up. My mom said I needed to hurry up and get back, or I'd lose my place to Rachel. She told me, 'It's time to fight. Are you ready?'"

Steve Schneider flew to Michigan to advise Sherri Jewell at Kiri's custody hearing. Marc Breault appeared to testify on behalf of David Jewell. Perhaps perplexed by the complicated religious ramifications, the court ruled that the Jewells would have joint custody of the child. Sherri Jewell agreed to let Kiri stay in Michigan for the time being. She would only have done so if instructed by Koresh, who apparently wanted to avoid any additional court hearings in Waco. Between illegal guns, multiple wives, and sex with underage girls, Koresh and the Branch Davidians remained in great peril from secular law enforcement. He didn't feel that he and his followers were prepared for assault by Babylon's forces yet.

But when the first legal investigation came, it had nothing to do with those three secular crimes.

Lois Roden is pictured on the front page of her newsletter, *Shekinah*. The Lord revealed to her that the Holy Spirit is both masculine and feminine.

(The Texas Collection, Baylor University)

The son of Branch Davidian leaders Ben and Lois Roden, George Roden claimed group leadership should be his by right of succession, and fought David Koresh for the role. Commanding the Branch Davidians was not his only ambition.

(The Texas Collection, Baylor University)

David Koresh poses with his legal wife, Heather, and their infant son, Cyrus.
(Getty Images)

A century before Vernon Howell renamed himself David Koresh and announced himself as the Lamb in the Bible's Book of Revelation, Cyrus Teed proclaimed himself to be Koresh and the Lamb. (Ralph Lauer)

This copy of *Koreshanity: The New Age Religion* was acquired by the Waco-McClennan County Public Library in November 1972, almost nine years before Vernon Wayne Howell arrived at Mount Carmel and joined the Branch Davidians.
(Ralph Lauer)

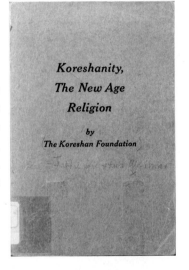

Koreshanity,
The New Age
Religion
by
The Koreshan Foundation

Kiri Jewell with her father, David Jewell. Following the Mount Carmel conflagration in April 1993, fifteen-year-old Kiri testified to a Congressional investigative committee that David Koresh first made sexual contact with her when she was ten.
(Getty Images)

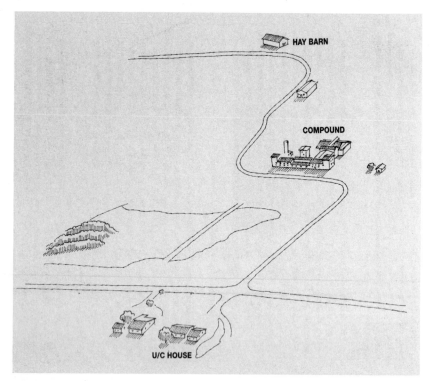

This map shows how ATF agents set up their undercover or "U. C. House" directly across from Mount Carmel. There was scant cover from the road to Mount Carmel. (September 1993 Treasury Department Report)

ATF agents in the Bellmead Civic Center staging area scramble to grab their combat gear immediately after being informed that the Branch Davidians "know we're coming." Four agents died, and sixteen more were wounded in the subsequent raid. (Bill Buford Collection)

After exiting two cattle trailers amid a hail of virtually point-blank gunfire, ATF agents took what cover was available—mostly behind cars—and began returning fire. (Bureau of Alcohol, Tobacco & Firearms website)

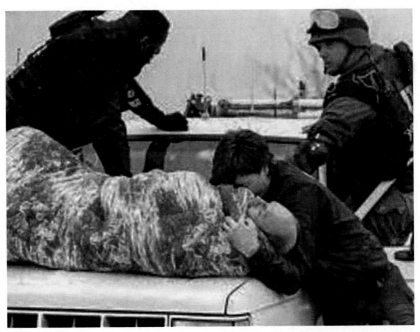

After a cease-fire was finally in place, ATF dead and wounded were taken away from Mount Carmel on whatever vehicles were available. One critically injured agent was held in place on the hood of a truck inching down the curving Mount Carmel driveway. (Bureau of Alcohol, Tobacco & Firearms website)

Global news media descended on Waco during the fifty-one–day siege of Mount Carmel by the FBI. Many media groups set up elaborate camps. (The Texas Collection, Baylor University)

When the FBI denied them direct contact with the media, besieged Branch Davidians wrote messages on sheets and hung them out Mount Carmel windows.
(The Texas Collection, Baylor University)

Prominent defense attorney Dick DeGuerin was hired by Bonnie Haldeman to represent her son, David Koresh. DeGuerin's consultations inside Mount Carmel with his client resulted in Koresh's offer to surrender peacefully with his followers if he was first allowed to write explanations of the Book of Revelation's Seven Seals. (Getty Images)

An Army tank driven by an FBI agent deliberately crashes into the rickety wall of Mount Carmel on the morning of April 19, 1993. Fifty-three Branch Davidian adults and twenty-three children died in the ensuing fire and collapse of the building. (Associated Press)

Following the conflagration, federal agents and Texas Rangers searched the smoking wreckage for bodies and evidence. The concrete vault, where ammunition was stored and women and children sheltered and died when the roof collapsed, was left partially intact. (Getty Images)

During the siege, numerous protestors joined the crowds surrounding the Mount Carmel siege site, including Timothy McVeigh, perched here on the hood of his car. On April 19, 1995, McVeigh blew up a federal building in Oklahoma City, a lethal indication that events in Waco spawned a lasting legacy of rage. (FBI Website)

CHAPTER SIXTEEN

Child Protective Services

Marc Breault was thorough in his efforts to bring down David Koresh. He contacted U.S. senators and congressmen as well as state and local authorities, alleging the types of criminality best suited to get their attention. Potential rape of twelve-year-old Kiri Jewell worked in a Michigan court; claiming toddler Wisdom had been snatched from his mother, Robyn Bunds, was successful in California.

Breault was less successful on Koresh's home turf, in part because McLennan County lawmen were already familiar with the Branch Davidians, and considered them strange but essentially harmless. When the *Waco Tribune-Herald* was convinced enough by Breault's claims of mass suicide at Mount Carmel during Passover 1992 to publish articles about the possibility, no one from the sheriff's department went out to check. Koresh's assurances to reporter Mark England that he contemplated nothing of the kind was sufficient for Sheriff Harwell and his deputies. But, based on his claims of child abuse on the Branch Davidian property, Breault had better luck with another arm of local government.

In February 1992, Child Protective Services in McLennan County opened an investigation into these child abuse accusations. Specifically, they were concerned that corporal punishment at Mount Carmel crossed the line into physical abuse; for even minor misbehavior, children there were allegedly being beaten to a point where their physical wellbeing or even their lives were in danger. Koresh was notified by CPS official Joyce Sparks that she and her staff would visit

Mount Carmel to interview him, other parents, and children. Full cooperation was requested. If abuses were confirmed, CPS would take appropriate action. Sparks would be in touch to arrange the first visit.

Koresh's reaction was twofold. First, he believed that this inquiry, and the threat of their children being taken from them, violated the Branch Davidians' right to religious freedom. Everything they did was Bible-based, including physical punishment of children (Proverbs 23:13–14: "Withhold not correction from the child: for if thou beatest him with the rod, he shall not die. Thou shalt beat him with the rod, and shalt deliver his soul from hell"). God told them how to punish their kids, not some Babylon child protective agency. Second, even on a secular basis, he didn't think he and his adult followers were doing anything wrong. To Koresh, spanking kids hard was perfectly normal. He often spoke of how he'd been frequently beaten during his own childhood. In her memoir, Bonnie Haldeman said she divorced one husband after he repeatedly spanked her infant son for crying. Though Bonnie admitted that occasionally "I might have whopped him," she denied Koresh's claims that she and her second husband, Roy Haldeman, sometimes beat him black-and-blue, even when he was a teenager.

At least in Koresh's mind, he'd suffered regular beatings, and in spite of them, or, perhaps, because of them, he turned out to be the Lamb. No coincidence was involved in God's plans. James Tabor speculates, "David was raised in a culture that included corporal punishment. I think he convinced himself that it was holy." Joyce Sparks, in her 1995 congressional testimony, was somewhat less generous: "[David] thought he was the law, so he didn't have to answer to anyone. . . . I mean, he was the Lamb of God, so his interpretation was beyond question to him."

Because of that conclusion, and based in large part on his own childhood experience, Koresh mandated corporal punishment at Mount Carmel—but within certain guidelines. First, no child could be spanked immediately after any transgression, because at that moment his or her parents were probably too angry. The spanking must be administered twenty-four hours later, when parents were calm. Before the spanking, the parents would explain to the child why whatever he or she had done was wrong. An adult's hand to child's flesh was forbidden: a wooden kitchen spoon, known as "the helper," was utilized instead. (Kathy Schroeder's son, Scott Mabb, remembers that every family used its own individual spoon as a paddle.) Children could only be struck on the buttocks. After the spanking, the child would be hugged by the parent. Every spanking followed the same format. Kathy Schroeder describes it as "a ritual. You'd swat, then you'd hug the kid, [and] rub the bottom. The paddle did the pain, and the parent did the love." Paul Fatta, who lived in Mount Carmel with his son Kalani, says, "It was the farthest thing from child abuse." Bonnie Haldeman wrote that "they didn't leave bruises," but that wasn't always true.

Scott Mabb remembers, "I had a long rap sheet. I was known for lying as a kid. My friend was Kevin Jones, the second-oldest of David Jones' kids. I'd gotten there [to Mount Carmel] at [age] eight."

When Scott and Kevin kept getting in trouble, they were forbidden to spend any time together. One day, Scott was outside doing a noxious daily chore: "It was 'dumping the [slop] bucket,' taking the bucket out and then you dug a hole and buried the stuff in it. I was doing that when Kevin came over, even though I told him I wasn't allowed to be with him. We were spotted, and it got back to Mom and Perry [Jones, Kevin's crotchety grandfather]." Kathy Schroeder says, "I got called in. Perry was there, we were in the dining room with Scott. Kevin had told Perry that Scott came up to him. Scott said it was the other way around, and Perry called him a liar."

Thus began, Scott recalls, "the worst spanking of my life." Urged on by Perry Jones, Kathy gave her son "five licks" with the wooden spoon. Then Scott was told to admit he'd lied. He denied it, and got five licks more. The pattern repeated until Scott's buttocks were badly bruised. The boy never admitted lying.

More than thirty years later, Scott Mabb remembers the incident as a positive moment in his life: "Maybe today, this would have been looked on as a bad thing. I, as an adult forty years old now, can argue that this was the turning point in making me what I am now, someone almost allergic to lying. What hurt me more than the spanking was my mom not believing me. I learned that it's not the lie that does the damage, it's how lying convinces people that you're always lying, even when you're not." In fact, Scott says, "I can't remember a time when I got more love than in Waco."

Spanking-as-love extended to infants. Kiri Jewell shocked congressional investigators in 1995 when she claimed she'd seen eight-month-old babies paddled with "the helper." Kathy Schroeder says spanking started even earlier than that: "We disciplined kids from six months. They could get a swat to stop an action." This way, "they would get trained."

Joyce Sparks made her first visit to Mount Carmel accompanied by two other CPS staffers and a pair of McLennan County deputies. She spoke with Koresh, some parents, and several children. Sparks was permitted to meet with whomever she liked, and see whatever she wanted. But she left following her first and all subsequent visits feeling frustrated. Everyone, even the children, seemed to have their answers prepared in advance. No adult had seen children being excessively disciplined, none of the children said they had been hurt.

Sparks decided to try a different tack. She testified to Congress that "we ended up interviewing [a] little boy on the back of a flatbed trailer outside [Mount Carmel]. His eyes were darting around, and he was clearly frightened. He was being very careful what he said. . . . When I met with David Koresh after that, he knew every question I had asked the child. He must have sat the child down and interrogated him to get every single bit of information, because then he [Koresh] was explaining everything to me."

After learning some of Breault's allegations, the district attorney's office became involved. Vic Feazell remembers, "There was even a surprise inspection, just showing up at the [Mount Carmel] gate and asking to come in. They let us in, let us talk to whoever we wanted to, and then asked us to stay for an ice cream social, because that's what they were doing when we got there, giving the kids ice cream." So far as Feazell was concerned, no further investigation was required: "They seemed like healthy, happy kids. The sheriff was invited any time to show up. My investigator, J. L. Crawford, was told that any time he was in the [Mount Carmel] neighborhood, to swing by. There was never anything."

Joyce Sparks was unconvinced. In particular, she found her one-on-one conversations with Koresh to be frustrating. He responded to every question, but his detailed answers weren't helpful. She later testified to Congress, "He just used the scriptures to tell you what was right, and what he thought the law was."

After seeing the *Waco Tribune-Herald* articles about the possibility of mass suicide at Mount Carmel during 1992's celebration of Passover, Sparks's supervisors forbid her from making a scheduled Mount Carmel visit. When she called Koresh to explain, he insisted that "this is not in our plans," and offered to bring any children she requested to her office to be interviewed. Then he launched into a complex explanation of the scriptural passages that dictated the Branch Davidian rules for raising children. Sparks interrupted: "David, we have to keep the religion separate." Koresh replied, "I can't do that." It was the truth, but by the secular law being followed by Sparks, religion wasn't relevant if children were being abused.

On April 30, 1992, Sparks reluctantly closed her investigation after nine weeks of interviews: "We knew that babies were being spanked, but we never saw a bruise, so it was difficult for us to do anything with that." But several months later, she thought there was a second chance to prove Mount Carmel children were being abused.

David Jewell allowed twelve-year-old Kiri to come to Waco and be informally interviewed by Sparks about Koresh's alleged sexual acts toward her. Kiri told the same story she later shared with Congress. Sparks testified that "she [Kiri] was scared to death that she was telling me and he [Koresh] might find out. . . . When I interviewed her, I asked, 'How did you feel when this was going on?' She said, 'Well, I felt scared, but I also felt privileged.'"

Sparks testified that Koresh would not admit to her that he had sex with underaged girls: "He was very cautious. But I did my homework. I studied what he asked me to [in the Bible], and Psalm 45 was a real important psalm to him, and it is the wedding psalm. So, he was much too smart to tell me that he was doing that, but all of his teaching said it was okay. . . . There are a lot of references in the Old Testament that would lead one to believe that it was okay."

Texas law said it wasn't okay. But any hope Sparks had of successfully bringing a case against Koresh was dashed when Kiri refused to formally testify. Sparks said it was because Kiri knew Koresh would be present in court when she did: "She [Kiri] said that she sometimes wondered what it would be like if David was right, if his teachings were right, and she thought that she would die and burn in hell for telling."

At the conclusion to her own 1995 congressional testimony, Sparks was asked, "Do you feel that Koresh's followers can accurately say that he was fully investigated and found innocent [of child abuse]?" Sparks replied, "Not at all."

Even though Child Protective Services closed its case, Koresh believed that the CPS investigation, coupled with newspaper coverage of potential Mount Carmel suicide, indicated that more, and much worse, was imminent. The forces of Babylon were on the move against the Lamb and his followers, and time was running out. When the End Time came, he and the Branch Davidians were going to still be at Mount Carmel.

Koresh announced, "We may not get to Israel. The devil doesn't want us to go, so he is going to block it. It looks like persecution is coming."

CHAPTER SEVENTEEN

The Message Evolves

P art of Marc Breault's strategy was to contact relatives of Branch Davidians living at Mount Carmel. As he did with elected officials, reporters, CPS staff, and lawmen, Breault would warn that their family members were in terrible danger because of David Koresh. In February 1992, he contacted Steve Schneider's sister Sue, who told him that she'd recently received a troubling call from her brother. Steve said he was calling to say goodbye, because he was probably going to do something that caused him to die. But there was good news, too. He'd be resurrected soon afterward. His death and subsequent resurrection would be part of something Sue thought he described as "the end." Steve said he wouldn't be the only one to die and come back. It would be true of everyone at Mount Carmel.

Schneider's message to his sister coincided with the beginning of Child Protective Service's investigation. Like Koresh, Schneider believed it was a probing persecution by Babylon, a means of testing the Branch Davidians' resolve. Koresh had let them know exactly how resolute he and his followers were. Joyce Sparks testified to Congress that "[Koresh] repeatedly told me, 'You can't understand me unless you understand what I believe.' And I came to understand that, so I started watching how his beliefs manifested his actions. It was real clear. I mean, he said, 'The enemy will surround the camp, and the saints will die. . . . There will be blood and fire, an explosion at the end.' And he believed that, and the people that followed him believed that as well."

Surviving Branch Davidians agree that, in the wake of the CPS investigations, the tone of Koresh's teaching changed. It was as though everything he'd previously taught was preliminary. Now it was time for his followers to fully understand what had begun to happen, and how they must take specific steps to prepare for fulfillment of his most crucial prophecies.

It began prior to Passover in April. Branch Davidians everywhere understood that they were welcome to come to Mount Carmel for celebration and teachings by Koresh, then return to their homes. This time, Koresh made it clear that everyone who'd received the message was required to come, and the truly faithful should stay. This was probably their last Passover. Special dispensation was extended to those who had joined for a while, then left. They would be forgiven for this transgression if they returned now and fully recommitted to the message. Foreign followers received extra coaxing. Australian Graeme Craddock had visited Mount Carmel several times without making it his permanent home. Steve Schneider convinced him to return for Passover 1992 and stay. This way, Craddock could actively participate in what was soon to come. Articles in the Waco paper about potential Mount Carmel mass suicide during Passover were brandished as proof: See how Babylon spreads lies about us? This propaganda is part of an excuse to attack us.

After Passover, Koresh made certain that his followers at Mount Carmel, now expanded to about 130, understood what was required next. Some of it was harrowing, even for long-term Branch Davidians.

"There was a new sense of the end in his teaching," Kathy Schroeder recalls. "It was now all about the Seven Seals, it was about breaking the seals wide open. We knew that we were the Wave Sheaf, the ones to return with Christ on Judgment Day, and that meant we had to die before Judgment Day." Everyone's acceptance of this pleased Koresh, and has puzzled outsiders since. Why would rational adults follow someone who encouraged them to die as part of bringing about the end of the world?

That question ignores two key factors. First, almost all of Koresh's followers had at one time been part of the Seventh-day Adventist Church, which bases its teachings on following biblical law in order to be judged positively during the End Time. The dead as well as the living are at peril, so it doesn't matter whether this judgment occurs within days or centuries of the present time. You do as the Bible instructs, or else you have no hope. SDA canon also includes the belief that there are occasionally prophets who communicate spiritual messages, Ellen G. White being the most recent among them. This belief in prophets and prophecy remained imbued in the former Adventists, who found in Koresh confirmation of all they already believed, and, additionally, fulfillment of personal yearning for even more Bible-based knowledge than SDA clergy provided. Koresh was everything that the Adventist Church promised, and more. Based on the God-inspired interpretation of scripture that most of his followers already believed in, Koresh had proven himself to be the Lamb of Revelation.

Second, Koresh was prophesizing the End Time, but not the end of the world. Rather, God was only bringing its current, sinful iteration to an end. Koresh foretold a glorious new era, with the Lamb and the Wave Sheaf standing first among the blessed elect who'd enjoy perfect existence in the resulting Kingdom of God on Earth. Just as his followers were sure that they had to die, they were equally certain that their deaths would only be temporary if they remained faithful to God and the Lamb. It was all in the Bible, and anything contradicting what the Bible and Koresh taught was the work of Satan and Babylon.

Koresh began graphically describing the battle that loomed. Kathy Schroeder says that post-Passover 1992 was "when he started teaching, 'If you can't kill for God, you can't die for God.' It was just a deeper progression of the message that we'd known all along." In his memoir, David Thibodeau wrote, "David did say that we should never allow ourselves to be attacked without fighting back. Jesus may have gone meekly to the cross, but we should follow His command, according to the apostle Luke, to defend ourselves against anyone who threatened to destroy us. . . . We should not start any kind of violence, but we must respond fiercely to any armed assault."

For that, they needed guns, lots of them. When Babylon came for them at Mount Carmel, it would be in force. Henry McMahon was not their only source of arms. Gun dealers around the country received orders from the Branch Davidians, who used credit cards for the purchases. Kathy Schroeder says that she and her husband, Mike, whom Koresh allowed to work together for once, "applied for as many credit cards as we could around March, April 1992, something like that. We didn't put our real income [on the applications]. They [the credit cards] were mostly used for gun purchases. I had to make the monthly payments, but we figured we were going to be gone and we wouldn't have to worry about it anyway." Each card was used until it was maxed out.

Once the Branch Davidians accumulated enough guns, Koresh mandated practice. Some of his followers already had been firing at targets around the Mount Carmel property, but now it was organized for everyone to participate. Koresh began by occasionally alternating teaching the Bible and gun skills. Now, Kathy Schroeder says, "A Bible study didn't necessarily just denote a period of time sitting down with the Bible open. Anytime we gathered with David, it was a Bible study, but sometimes it would entail David looking at guns. It could entail David teaching us how to load magazines. That was all a part of gatherings, practicing cleaning [guns], loading, different tests for your eyesight. David would take a whole evening and just take a whole bunch of guys and ask them what their vision was, give them [eye] tests, different things to see who he was going to give which weapons to."

There was separate target practice for men and women. Both fired at targets. The women were limited to fewer shots. The men also had to take apart and rebuild their weapons and load and change clips, while Koresh looked on and used a stopwatch to ensure that no one was too slow. Except for seasoned shooters, everyone started with small-caliber guns, then moved up to more powerful weapons as they demonstrated sufficient aptitude. Kathy Schroeder had been in the military; Koresh mostly supervised the men's shooting, and relied on her for reports on how individual women were faring. "He'd ask me in a Bible study, 'How did so-and-so do?'" she says. "He'd ask, 'Who do you think would be responsible [enough] to have a fully automatic?' Things like that."

Koresh leavened the new responsibilities of becoming battle-ready with more recreation than usual. Branch Davidian David Jones already owned a boat, and Koresh bought another. There were outings where everyone swam or water-skied. After some dirt tracks were cut around the Mount Carmel property, the group acquired dirt bikes, more motorcycles (Koresh already had one), and go-karts for the kids. Kathy Schroeder says, "Everything was very serious, things were imminent, but another aspect was that David said, 'We're going to enjoy this last summer that we have.'"

Koresh's belief that the CPS investigation was only the first attempted persecution by Babylon was soon reinforced. An FBI investigation of the Branch Davidians was launched at about the same time that the CPS inquiry was closed. On April 20, 1992, the office of U.S. senator Donald Riegle of Michigan received a fax. The name of the sender was later redacted, but it probably came from David Jewell, who lived in Michigan. The cover page noted that the contents concerned "Allegation against religious cult."

The next day, Riegle sent a letter to the FBI, stating that a constituent had contacted his office regarding concerns about "a religious cult in Texas known as the Branch Davidian Seventh Day Adventists." Accompanying materials, supplied to the senator's office by the constituent, alleged that Vernon Howell, aka David Koresh, "may have been planning a mass suicide for the members of his religious sect." This was a touchy allegation for the FBI, which had come under widespread criticism in 1978 for ignoring warnings about the

Peoples Temple outpost in the jungles of Guyana. More than nine hundred members of that group either committed suicide by ingesting poison or were forcibly injected at the order of their leader, Jim Jones. A congressman who had come to the community known as Jonestown to investigate was murdered at a nearby airstrip, along with members of the media and some Jones followers who had chosen to leave the settlement. The last thing the FBI wanted was to find itself blamed for another Jonestown. The material originally received by Riegle also alleged "holding people against their will, which may constitute violations of the Federal laws pertaining to involuntary servitude and slavery."

FBI agent Byron Sage, who oversaw a number of the agency's offices in Texas, including Waco, recalls that he was instructed to look into "potential for Jonestown-type cult activity and mass suicide. We went out, contacted local authorities, and the main allegations that we heard about were abuses of children, which was not our jurisdiction."

But any request from a U.S. senator's office received full agency cooperation, so Sage dispatched an agent in Waco, who he remembers "interviewed Vernon [Howell] and found the complaint [about suicide] to be unfounded. I wrote that up, sent it [the report] in, and closed the case."

The fact that he'd been interviewed by the FBI on the heels of the CPS investigation reinforced David Koresh's belief that the final persecution by agents of Babylon was under way. He would have been more alarmed had he read a July 1992 report from the FBI field office in Waco. It was apparently intended for eventual transmission to Senator Riegle, and listed the various ways the Waco office investigated the allegations without finding anything falling under their agency purview. The final paragraph of the report concluded, "All logical investigation having been conducted, San Antonio [the main office of the FBI's regional Texas district] is considering this matter closed."

But the immediately preceding paragraph foreshadowed future tragedy: "It was brought to the attention of the Federal Bureau of

Investigation (FBI) office in Waco that ATF may possibly have a firearms violation regarding captioned subject"—meaning Vernon Howell, aka David Koresh. "[Redacted name] advised he received information that subject may possibly be converting AR-15 rifles from semi-automatic to automatic weapons. . . . Alcohol, Tobacco, and Firearms (ATF) SA was provided information about them [the Branch Davidians] to include a diagram of the house the captioned subject is living in, as well as photographs of the interior of the house."

ATF was also investigating the Branch Davidians.

CHAPTER EIGHTEEN

The ATF

I n 2015, an article published by the Center for American Progress declared that "the Bureau of Alcohol, Tobacco, Firearms and Explosives, or ATF, is an accident of history." This is an exaggeration—but not by much.

The lineage of the ATF essentially reflects the history of American government's efforts to restrict and tax goods that many citizens didn't want restricted or taxed. Its origins date back to 1862, when Congress created a Treasury subdepartment called the Office of Internal Revenue to collect taxes, including tariffs on imported distilled spirits and tobacco. A year later, so much evasion had been uncovered in one tariff category that three full-time "detectives" were hired to specifically pursue alcohol-related tax evaders. It was a limited area of inquiry; most Americans were happy to quaff liquor from American distillers.

In 1919, ratification of the Eighteenth Amendment expanded the agents' responsibilities. All manufacture, sale, and transport of alcoholic beverages was prohibited (hence the term "Prohibition"). Powerful leaders of organized crime stepped up to provide thirsty citizens with what they wanted, new law notwithstanding, and the government responded in 1920 by establishing the Bureau of Prohibition Investigation Division. Eliot Ness gained renown for pursuing Al Capone. Popular mythology depicts Ness as an agent for the Federal Bureau of Investigation, which was created in 1908. But Ness was not employed by the FBI.

By 1927, with many Americans continuing to swill bootleg liquor in defiance of the law, the Prohibition unit reorganized into the larger Bureau of Prohibition. The ATF's modern-day website notes that during this era, "vast criminal fortunes corrupt[ed] enforcement officers, prosecutors, judges, juries and politicians." Agents charged with tracking and arresting such an array of miscreants faced daunting odds. Lawbreakers were everywhere. Because its personnel were now engaged in enforcing law rather than tax compliance, control of the Bureau of Prohibition transferred from the Department of the Treasury to the Department of Justice. That lasted until 1933, when adoption of the Twenty-first Amendment ended Prohibition and the bureau, renamed the Alcohol Tax Unit (ATU), switched back to Treasury.

A year later, with gun violence on the rise and organized crime wielding especially fearsome arsenals, Congress established the National Firearms Act. Registration of specific weapons, in particular machine guns and "short-barreled" shotguns, was required, and taxes were imposed on sales of firearms. Four years after that, the Federal Firearms Act regulated "interstate shipment of firearms and ammunition, and prohibited their receipt by felons; required dealer and manufacturer licensing; and imposed firearms marking and record-keeping requirements." In 1941, the duties of the ATU were expanded to enforcing the nation's gun laws.

Following the 1968 assassinations of Martin Luther King and Robert F. Kennedy, Congress passed the Gun Control Act, stepping up firearms licensing and regulation and adding tight restrictions on "destructive devices" like bombs. The ATU was reorganized as the Alcohol and Tobacco Tax Division (ATTD) and additionally assigned enforcement of the Gun Control Act. Responsibility for enforcing explosives regulations followed in 1972, when "functions, powers and duties relating to alcohol, tobacco, firearms and explosives were transferred from the Internal Revenue Service to the Bureau of Alcohol, Tobacco and Firearms." The ATF formally became an independent bureau on July 1, 1972. Congress kept piling on additional responsibilities: gun tracing (sales and ownership); interstate cigarette smuggling; arson for profit.

Even as the FBI attained celebrity-like status (thanks in part to a popular television series starring Efrem Zimbalist Jr.), the ATF became a public punching bag. In his novel *The Famous and the Dead*, author T. Jefferson Parker deftly described the cause of ATF's inevitable unpopularity: "ATF had it rough because most Americans liked alcohol, tobacco and firearms—and disliked regulation." Of ATF's designated areas of enforcement, guns by far dominated agents' activities and public attention. The powerful National Rifle Association inundated NRA members, and, even more critically, members of Congress, with accusations of ATF assaults on Second Amendment rights.

As a result, while other federal agencies, the FBI especially, enjoyed widespread congressional support, ATF leadership struggled during every budgetary cycle. Republican presidents in particular recognized political opportunity. In 1981, newly inaugurated Ronald Reagan announced plans to abolish the ATF as a stand-alone agency and fold it into the Secret Service. But the NRA convinced the president otherwise: a former NRA lobbyist told *The New York Times* that his clients "always loved to have an agency on the edge that is a whipping boy." ATF remained independent—and also chronically underbudgeted, understaffed, underequipped, and generally unappreciated. About the time it began investigating the Branch Davidians, ATF, the agency responsible for enforcing gun laws across the nation, had just over 4,000 employees and an annual budget of $366 million. This contrasted dismally with the FBI's 22,000 employees and $2.03 billion annual budget. Money was so tight that some ATF agents in charge of divisional offices instituted agent fines for minor infractions like showing up late to meetings. They used the proceeds to purchase essential but non-agency-funded equipment.

ATF's punching-bag status was also reflected in the way the agency went about its vital business. Agent Jerry Petrilli remembers, "We constantly were told to be very careful with what we did and how it could be interpreted. In particular, there was concern about the NRA with its influence with Congress. ATF struggled with that. Whatever we did was likely to be misrepresented, misinterpreted."

NRA-fueled public paranoia about ATF's alleged intention of eventually confiscating even legally owned firearms frustrated the agents, who were themselves proud gun owners. "Our reputation was, 'We're coming to take everyone's guns away from them,' and that wasn't true," says Bill Buford. "In all my career, I didn't know a single [ATF] agent who didn't own firearms, who wasn't a hunter. What we were doing, we were enforcing gun laws, not taking guns away. But the pressure was always on [us]."

Prospective agents almost universally applied to ATF after experience in the military, public police forces, or the Border Patrol. They saw working for the agency as a means of continuing careers in law enforcement, experiencing the challenges of investigation without the tedium of too much desk duty. Military veterans and their families were especially enticed by what agent Blake Boteler describes as "the difference between military and law enforcement." In the military, combat requires the near inevitability of injury or death for some participants on both sides of battles. Federal law enforcement seeks minimal risk to all involved. That doesn't always happen, but it's far less likely if agents are experienced and consider use of guns to be a last resort. ATF's record for bloodless enforcement was sterling—and so far as its agents were concerned, nobody outside ATF seemed to care, or even notice.

ATF's dubious reputation didn't prevent other agencies from requesting its assistance in highly volatile situations. Only a few months before ATF began its Branch Davidian investigation in Waco, many of the same agents who subsequently participated in the Mount Carmel raid were ordered to Los Angeles. There, they assisted in quelling the late April 1992 riots immediately following a jury's exoneration of four police officers charged with using excessive force in the arrest of suspect Rodney King. South Central Los Angeles erupted in violence and flames. Los Angeles police were unable to end the chaos, and were reinforced by the California National Guard, the U.S. military—and the ATF, whose agents in L.A. were mostly tasked with executing search warrants for guns stolen from pawn shops and providing escorts for fire inspectors. No accolades for ATF resulted, but none were expected. Its agents felt satisfied that they'd done their duty, and had responded promptly when requested to support other law enforcement organizations.

That was the case again almost two months later. In early June, a UPS driver contacted the McLennan County sheriff's department to report that he'd delivered a suspicious package to a car repair shop just outside Waco. After hearing his story, the local lawmen called the ATF and asked for assistance. As always, the much maligned agency complied.

CHAPTER NINETEEN

Investigation

In 1992, Davy Aguilera had been an ATF special agent for five years. In a court affidavit describing his duties, Aguilera wrote that he investigated suspects "who have unlawfully possessed, transferred or shipped in interstate or foreign commerce firearms and/or explosive devices which were not registered," and that he had "successfully participated in the prosecution of several of these individuals." When Aguilera met in Waco with Lieutenant Gene Barber of the McLennan County sheriff's department on June 4, it seemed like the beginning of another potential case.

UPS driver Larry Gilbreath had told Barber that, while making the latest in a series of deliveries to a car repair business on FM 2491, one of the boxes he dropped off had broken open. The contents were about fifty "pineapple" hand grenade husks, which could potentially be filled with explosives. Owning empty grenade shells was not illegal, but filling them with powder and arming them for use was. The sight of so many shells alarmed Gilbreath, and he informed the local lawmen that over the previous months he'd delivered many packages to the repair shop, most addressed to David Koresh or Mike Schroeder. One delivery, Gilbreath recounted, was listed as a "quantity of black powder." The combination of grenade shells and powder was troubling. The lawmen recognized Koresh's name; most remembered his 1987 shootout with George Roden. That caused them sufficient concern to contact ATF and request a meeting, where they told the visiting agent about Koresh and his odd followers at Mount Carmel. Aguilera felt that there were possible grounds for an ATF investigation, and asked to be informed of any additional information regarding deliveries to the garage.

On June 9, Barber contacted Aguilera again. Gilbreath, now watchful for suspicious shipments, reported that UPS delivered several additional parcels to the repair shop; as always, a description of their contents was required for UPS services. Gilbreath checked, and one of the packages contained sixty ammunition magazines for M16 and AR-15 rifles. Aguilera knew that semiautomatic AR-15s were often converted to fully automatic M16s, either legally with appropriate registration and tax payments, or else illegally. The size of the ammunition magazine shipment indicated that, if there was such an illegal operation involving David Koresh, it might be substantial.

So, Aguilera began the painstaking process of tracking down Koresh's gun and munitions purchases. It required considerable time and effort because the law did not allow computerized collection of gun-related sales and transaction information from dealers and individual brokers. Aguilera had to ascertain the companies that sent such shipments to Koresh at the garage, then contact each shipper individually to request copies of the written transaction records they were required to make available to him.

In addition to his records search, which involved numerous dealers from around the country, Aguilera also interviewed Robert Cervenka, who owned property adjacent to Mount Carmel. Cervenka told the ATF agent that, beginning about January 1992, he heard machine gun fire from somewhere on his neighbors' land. Cervenka said that he knew machine gun fire when he heard it, because he was a military veteran. Lieutenant Barber told Aguilera that Cervenka made a similar complaint to the sheriff's department in November 1991. At another Barber-Aguilera meeting, the lieutenant provided the ATF agent with aerial photographs of Mount Carmel that had recently been taken by the sheriff's department. The photos showed a school bus buried in the ground next to the long, L-shaped main building. It was presumably connected to the building by an underground tunnel. There was also a large, nearby excavation in progress; its purpose was unknown.

Soon, Aguilera's records search led him to Hewitt Handguns in a town near Waco. The small business was operated by Henry McMahon and his girlfriend, Karen Kilpatrick. McMahon held the appropriate licenses to sell guns and munitions, and kept all required transaction records. When Aguilera visited him at his shop on July 30, McMahon produced records of Koresh purchases that partially included 104 AR-15/M16 upper receiver groups with barrels, 260 AR-15/M16 magazines, 91 AR-15 lower receiver units, 26 assorted hand and "long" guns (rifles), two cases (approximately 50) of "inert practice" hand grenades, 40 to 50 pounds of black powder, over 8,000 rounds of AR-15/M16 ammunition, and an M76 grenade launcher. None of the items, by themselves, were illegal to own.

McMahon explained to Aguilera and another ATF agent that he and Koresh were in business together. It was possible to assemble AR-15 rifles from parts, then sell the newly built firearms at gun shows for lower prices than most dealers charged. Koresh couldn't buy some of the parts or sell the assembled weapons because he wasn't a licensed dealer, but he did have money that McMahon lacked for their purchase. McMahon had the necessary sales license. Koresh and other Branch Davidians assembled the guns, McMahon sold them, and they split the profits. So far, a half dozen Mount Carmel–assembled weapons had been sold. McMahon anticipated selling many more. The agents had bad news for McMahon: anyone manufacturing and selling more than fifty weapons was liable for an 11 percent federal tax on the proceeds, and for keeping appropriate records of the transactions. McMahon immediately terminated the AR-15 deal with Koresh; the taxes and the additional paperwork weren't worth the potential profits.

But, during the same July 30 meeting with the ATF agents, McMahon caught the federal lawmen by surprise. While they were still at Hewitt Handguns, McMahon called Koresh and told him that ATF agents were there asking questions about the arsenal he'd apparently accumulated at the garage and/or Mount Carmel. Koresh's response, according to McMahon's later congressional testimony, was,

"Well, if there's a problem, tell them to come out here." McMahon gestured toward Aguilera, inviting him to take the phone and talk to Koresh, but Aguilera waved him off. At this stage of his investigation, before he'd obtained a warrant authorizing him to look wherever he liked at Mount Carmel or the garage, the last thing Aguilera wanted was to confront Koresh, even at Koresh's invitation. If he went to see him while warrantless, he could only look where Koresh allowed—and the Branch Davidian leader surely wouldn't let him anywhere near cached, illegally converted weapons. Meanwhile, McMahon's call alerted Koresh to ATF's investigation, giving him an opportunity to hide or discard anything incriminating. In the aftermath of the McMahon meeting, Aguilera checked to see if Koresh had the required manufacturer and dealer licenses. He didn't.

Based on his experience in previous investigations, Aguilera felt certain that David Koresh was involved in firearm illegalities substantial enough to justify a search warrant. He wrote and submitted a report on what he'd discovered so far to ATF headquarters in Washington, D.C., requesting approval to move forward to federal court with a search warrant request. In the interim, which Aguilera realized might last several months—there was nothing so apparently urgent as to jump the Koresh investigation to the front of ATF's lengthy investigative line—he continued conducting interviews and tracking records of David's arms and munitions purchases.

In August, while Aguilera awaited word from ATF leaders in Washington, an incident occurred at Ruby Ridge, Idaho, that further tarnished ATF's reputation, even though they were only one of several federal agencies involved.

Randy Weaver, a former Army Green Beret, moved, with his wife, Vicki, and their children, to rural northwest Idaho in the 1980s to escape what they considered an increasingly out-of-control world. The Weavers purchased property along a creek and lived there in a rustic cabin. Weaver came under federal notice in 1985 for alleged threats against President Ronald Reagan, the pope, and additional officials, and was interviewed by the FBI and local lawmen. Though Weaver was reputed to be a member of the white supremacist Aryan Nations and supposedly maintained a substantial arsenal, he wasn't charged with breaking any laws; it couldn't be proven that he had threatened the president and others.

But soon after the fruitless FBI interview, Weaver became friendly with an ATF informant working undercover as a gun dealer. In October 1989, ATF charged Weaver with illegally selling the undercover informant two shotguns, whose sawed-off barrels violated minimum lawful length. A grand jury indicted him for possession of illegal weapons in late 1990, and Weaver was arrested in early 1991. After making bail, he did not appear for trial. U.S. marshals, trying to avoid potential violence, spent months negotiating with Weaver, who refused to surrender peacefully. Finally, in August 1992, a half dozen marshals scouted Weaver's property in advance of a planned raid to arrest him. They encountered Weaver's fourteen-year-old son Sammy and adult family friend Kevin Harris. Shots were fired; Sammy was killed, and so was one of the U.S. marshals. The Weavers retrieved their son's body and, along with Harris, barricaded themselves in their cabin.

Idaho state lawmen surrounded the cabin. They were reinforced by an FBI Hostage Rescue Team (HRT), FBI snipers, and ATF agents. Within a day, FBI snipers wounded Randy Weaver and Harris and killed Vicki Weaver. The leader of the HRT team was Dick Rogers, soon to serve in a similar assignment in Waco. It was days before everyone else in the Weaver cabin finally surrendered.

It turned out that, during the entire siege, Randy Weaver never fired a shot. Most of the post-siege media coverage was sympathetic toward him; so was a jury that acquitted Weaver and Harris in 1993 for the murder of the U.S. marshal. Weaver was sentenced to eighteen months in prison for missing his original court date and violating bail conditions. Upon his release, he sued the government, filing wrongful death claims for his son and wife. In 1995, the government agreed to pay Weaver and his daughters a total of $3.1 million.

In the late fall of 1992, the wave of bad publicity following Ruby Ridge was such that all of the agencies involved badly wanted to avoid another illegal arms confrontation that could potentially turn deadly, especially if it involved women and children. Excessive caution before moving forward on any case seemed appropriate. Though no direct link to the Idaho debacle has ever been established, on November 2, 1992, Davy Aguilera was notified by ATF headquarters that he had not accumulated enough evidence regarding David Koresh and illegal guns to justify a search warrant request. He needed something more.

Events at Ruby Ridge affected Mount Carmel, too. David Thibodeau later wrote, "Randy Weaver was not a man we admired." The Branch Davidians believed that the white supremacist groups Weaver allegedly aligned with were "tainted by anti-Semitic rhetoric . . . his ideas were repellant [sic]." But Koresh and his followers also believed that the killing of Weaver's son and wife "was an ominous portent . . . our community also lived by beliefs that the mainstream society might not tolerate forever."

Koresh, already aware, thanks to Henry McMahon, that ATF was in the process of investigating him, took Ruby Ridge concern further. Appealing to his followers' beliefs that no group anywhere matched their own importance, and to their impression that the FBI, U.S. Marshals, and ATF represented the elite forces of Babylon, Koresh suggested that Ruby Ridge might be Babylon's rehearsal for an attack on Mount Carmel.

CHAPTER TWENTY

The Investigation Continues

The turndown of Agent Aguilera's warrant request didn't mean that ATF officials wanted his Branch Davidian investigation closed. Within the agency, rumors were already spreading about a big operation pending in Waco. Just about everyone hoped to be involved, especially members of ATF's Special Response Teams (SRTs), select agents trained for volatile operations involving armed suspects and, possibly, hostages. This was a relatively new program in ATF, one reflecting an increasingly agitated, gun-centric society where such situations were becoming too common. Whatever was going on in Waco—the ATF grapevine indicated it involved some bizarre religious cult and illegal guns—was so substantial that, for the first time in agency history, there might be some form of interdivisional cooperation, agents from several different regions mounting a joint operation. Some ATF agents from the Dallas office first heard the rumors while participating in the Weaver siege at Ruby Ridge. Another, working out of New Orleans, was tipped by his friend Davy Aguilera that something big was going to go down, and he would probably want to be part of it. Agents joined ATF to be in on the action—it was natural that most of them hoped for a chance to participate in what promised to be the agency's biggest operation yet.

But that would only be possible after Aguilera came up with enough evidence for the big shots in Washington to overcome post–Ruby Ridge qualms. The pressure was almost entirely on him; there was no possibility of more agents being assigned full-time to assist as he went about his Koresh investigation. He had only occasional help. Thinly stretched ATF usually had everyone assigned to their own significant tasks, though it sometimes happened that an agent would be temporarily transferred from one case to another. Special Agent Blake Boteler had been pulled from undercover infiltration of a gun-toting biker gang to help out at Ruby Ridge; when he was subsequently selected to participate in the Mount Carmel raid, he was yanked from undercover again, and reinserted in the gang after the raid was over.

Additionally, Aguilera's virtually sole responsibility to come up with all the information about Koresh and his Davidians reflected an acknowledged agency deficiency. "We [ATF] had no one whose [full-time] job it was to just gather and supply intelligence," SRT team leader Jerry Petrilli says. "Whoever was investigating something had to do most of that himself." In 1992, there was not yet widespread internet access for use as a research tool. Everything Aguilera did required either personally locating paper records, or else tracking down potential sources and interviewing them.

By the time Aguilera received his November 1992 turndown, he'd already been on the Koresh case for over four months. The suspect knew about Aguilera and the investigation. He'd had time to destroy evidence or ramp up his illegal operation. After November, Aguilera continued doggedly tracing and interviewing gun dealers who'd sold items to Koresh, but that tack alone apparently would not turn up evidence his bosses considered sufficient. Koresh had enough guns, gun parts, and conversion materials to make it likely he was engaged in crooked arms possession and sales. But nothing that Aguilera had learned so far proved beyond doubt that Koresh did anything illegal. Appearance alone, no matter how well substantiated by circumstantial evidence, wasn't going to be enough. Aguilera needed eyewitnesses who could testify more specifically to Koresh's criminality.

So, in December 1992, Davy Aguilera turned most of his investigative attention from paperwork to people. The first, and most obvious, was Joyce Sparks of Child Protective Services. An ATF agent temporarily assigned to help out Aguilera spoke with Sparks on December 4. She related the frustrations of her own Branch Davidian investigation, including one interview with a seven- or eight-year-old boy who told her that "all the adults had guns and they were always practicing with them." When she pressed Koresh to show her any guns at Mount Carmel, he made her wait for thirty minutes, supposedly so he could move all his followers out of the main building; Koresh insisted that he kept the gun storage area a secret from them. Then Koresh took Sparks on a short tour. When Sparks saw "a buried school bus from which all the seats had been removed," a bullet-riddled old refrigerator at one end of the bus, and three rifles lying on the bus floor, Koresh told her that the bus was where he practiced his target shooting. That kept the noise muffled; he didn't want to disturb his neighbors. Sparks added that Koresh also told her he was "the Messenger" from God, the world was about to end, and when Koresh "reveals" himself, the recent riots in Los Angeles would be nothing compared to what would happen in Waco. According to Sparks, Koresh promised that this would be a "military-type" thing, and "nonbelievers would suffer."

Based on information from the McLennan County sheriff's department—they'd been involved in the Robyn Bunds custody issue—in December 1992 Aguilera traveled to La Verne, California, where he met and interviewed several members of the Bunds family, all former Branch Davidians. Robyn Bunds told Aguilera that, in the La Verne rent house, Koresh made followers watch violent movies about the Vietnam War, and referred to these as "training films." Followers armed with loaded guns stood guard duty around the house. Koresh himself slept with a gun under his pillow. While cleaning the house, Robyn found some gun parts that her brother later explained were from a "machine gun conversion kit."

Robyn's mother, Jeannine, said that before leaving Koresh and the Branch Davidians at Mount Carmel, she participated in shooting drills with AK-47 rifles. In July 1991, she witnessed Koresh blasting at targets with a machine gun. Based on this testimony from Robyn and Jeannine Bunds, plus Sparks's description of Koresh's end-of-the-world claim, Aguilera now had information from multiple sources that indicated Koresh not only had illegal weapons, but might even use them in some fashion against nonbelievers in Waco.

Then Jeannine Bunds added more. Koresh, she claimed, "had fathered at least 15 children from various women and young girls at the compound." Jeannine said that she had personally delivered several of these children. Aguilera noted in his affidavit that "according to Ms. Bunds, Howell annuls all marriages of couples who join his cult. He then has exclusive sexual access to the women." Some of them, Jeannine alleged, were as young as eleven. Enforcing the law against statutory rape was not within ATF purview, but linking Koresh to the sexual assault of little girls would add urgency to ATF's warrant request. Aguilera was equally encouraged by his discovery that multiple foreign Koresh followers living at Mount Carmel—who came from "Jamaica, [the] United Kingdom, Israel, Australia and New Zealand"—were likely overstaying time limits on their entry permits. That, too, had nothing directly to do with ATF's responsibilities, but Aguilera noted that "it is a violation of Title 18, United States Code, Section 922 for an illegal alien to receive a firearm."

Aguilera interviewed Jeannine Bunds again in early January 1993. He showed her photographs of various guns and munitions; she identified pictures of an AR-15 rifle and "pineapple-type" hand grenades "as being items which she had seen at the Mount Carmel Center while she was there." On this same California trip, Aguilera also spoke with Deborah Sue Bunds, Jeannine's daughter-in-law. She told of witnessing Koresh firing a machine gun, and hearing him talk about how he wanted to acquire more of them.

On January 6, Aguilera received results from an inquiry he'd directed to ATF explosives enforcement officer Jerry Taylor. Based on his receiving regular, substantial deliveries of items including potassium nitrate, aluminum, magnesium, and black powder, Taylor concluded that it was likely Vernon Howell aka David Koresh was assembling "improvised explosive weapons such as grenades and pipe bombs," violating Title 26, United States Code, Section 5845. This officially confirmed what was obvious anyway.

ATF's Firearms Technology Branch in Washington, D.C., advised that "the firearms parts which Howell has received, and the method by which he has received them, is consistent with activities in other ATF investigations in various parts of the United States which have resulted in the discovery and seizure of machine guns. . . . The firearms parts received by Howell could be used to assemble both semiautomatic firearms and machine guns." This was another official affirmation of the obvious that should impress any judge considering the issue of a Mount Carmel/car repair service search warrant.

Aguilera met with former Branch Davidian David Block, who related seeing plans and equipment for assembling illegal arms at Mount Carmel. SRT team leader Bill Buford conducted a phone interview with Poia Vaega, a New Zealander who graphically described suffering sexual abuse by Vernon Wayne Howell and one of his male followers before she and her husband broke free from the Branch Davidians. She also told of Howell passing around "his personal AK-47 machine gun for the group to handle and look over."

At this point, Aguilera's affidavit to support a search warrant request was practically writing itself. The proverbial cherry on top was supplied on January 3, 1993, by Marc Breault, whose testimony to Aguilera was both succinct and damning. According to Aguilera's affidavit, while living at Mount Carmel from early 1988 until September 1989, Breault

> . . . participated in physical and firearm shooting exercises conducted by Howell. He [Breault] stood guard duty with a loaded gun . . . those who stood guard duty were instructed by Howell to "shoot to kill" anyone who attempted to come through the entrance gate of the Mount Carmel property. On one occasion, Howell told him that he wanted to obtain and/or manufacture machine guns, grenades and explosive devices. Howell stated that he thought that the gun control laws were ludicrous, because an individual could

easily acquire a firearm and the necessary parts to convert it to a machine gun, but if a person had the gun and the parts together, they would be in violation of the law.

Here was a witness who had heard "Howell" admitting that he knew he was breaking the law.

ATF had all of the information from former Branch Davidians and firearms/explosives experts that agents could have hoped for, but a balky judge might point out that, confronted with these statements, Koresh and his loyal Branch Davidians could simply deny everything their former members had claimed. It would be one side's word against the other's. Experts specified how all the guns and munitions delivered to Koresh could be used to assemble illegal weapons and explosives, but, even so, ownership of the necessary firearms and parts still wasn't illegal. The whole point of the warrant request was to receive permission to raid Mount Carmel. Then ATF agents could seize and confiscate illegally converted weapons. That would prove Koresh's guilt, as well as that of any cult followers who were also involved. ATF wanted substantive supporting evidence beyond testimony from former Branch Davidians.

Photos of the Branch Davidians' target practices seemed to be one of the best options. On October 2, 1992, along the road adjacent to Mount Carmel, ATF erected a "pole camera" focused on the compound area. Agents installing the camera thought they heard gunfire from somewhere on the Branch Davidian property near the compound. This was promising—useful photos might be obtained almost immediately. But the picture quality was so poor that the first camera was switched out for a second. That camera recorded two small planes seeming to land just behind the compound, but again the picture quality was so poor that specific details like tail numbers weren't discernible.

There was another problem with the information Aguilera and

ATF had gathered from former Branch Davidians. None of Koresh's former followers were speaking from recent experience. All of them had already left Mount Carmel by spring 1992, when Joyce Sparks and the CPS investigation convinced Koresh that the long-anticipated persecution by Babylon was beginning, followed in short order by the visit from the FBI. Breault, the Bundses, and the others were unaware that, during the summer of 1992, Koresh's teachings focused on the now imminent opening of the Seven Seals by the Lamb, and specific preparations for the subsequent battle against Babylon. Most critically, all the ATF informants had left Mount Carmel while Koresh still kept the group's guns under lock and key in a single room. They didn't know that Koresh subsequently tested all his followers' eyesight and marksmanship, then handed out personal firearms to adults who'd displayed any degree of competence. Many adults at Mount Carmel, though not all, now had guns and ammunition magazines in their rooms, which were along narrow corridors on the first and second floors of the compound. If instructed by Koresh, they could be ready to fire in all directions within minutes. But ATF's agents relied on what it had heard from the former members, and felt certain that if Koresh chose to resist a raid, it would take significant time—likely half an hour or even more—just to arm his followers and position them to fight. It was a crucial misjudgment.

So, too, was the federal agents' inherent belief that almost no one, Branch Davidians included, ever really meant it when they claimed they would die fighting. Based on their individual experiences, which spanned hundreds of raids where suspects pledged to resist to the last man, the agents felt confident that Koresh and his followers would reconsider the minute they saw armed, armored agents surrounding them. During ATF's information-gathering process, Aguilera and other agents heard lurid tales of illegal and immoral goings-on at Mount Carmel. What they didn't hear was any objective information about what Koresh taught and his followers believed, not just about the End Time, but their prominent roles in the Kingdom of God on Earth to come. Death, for them, wouldn't be the end, but rather a required preliminary to a glorious new beginning. The Lamb and the Bible told them so. J. Phillip Arnold, whose professional career has been dedicated to studying religious history and faiths, says that anyone doubting David Koresh and his followers' sincerity about dying in a mandated fight should have considered it from the Branch Davidians' perspective: "If you believe in God, and if you believe that God has told you to do something, wouldn't you do it?"

But the ATF didn't have the relevant information or the insight necessary. What they did have was belief in their own abilities, and a sense that here, at last, was an opportunity to demonstrate to doubters that ATF was law enforcement at its finest. The Branch Davidians were a group of misfits motivated by twisted religious beliefs, which was the general public's definition of a cult. ATF would prove that a cult could be stopped before wreaking havoc on innocent people or themselves. This would be ATF's moment—and ATF's alone.

The FBI's Byron Sage recalls, "My office got a second complaint [about Howell and the Branch Davidians] in November 1992 or December. I called our Waco office and told the senior agent there, 'We've gotten two complaints now about them [the Branch Davidians], and I don't want a third. Please make sure that this [your investigation] is done as thoroughly as needed,' and he said, 'Okay, we'll make sure.' But our office was the same place in Waco as the U.S. District Attorney's office, same building, and an assistant U.S. attorney hears our agent mention Howell, and says, 'What about Howell?' Our agent tells him, and the assistant [U.S. attorney] levitates off the floor. He says, 'You guys can't do that. This is close to the chest, but the ATF has an undercover operation targeting the Branch Davidians and Vernon Wayne Howell. You all cannot go out there and possibly tip off David [Koresh] to the ATF interest in him, or raise their suspicions.' My agent told him, 'Maybe they [the ATF] need our assistance.' He said, 'I'll get back to you.' I told my agent,

'Ride hard on this. If we close the case again, it's got to be that there's no foundation. . . .'

"Within an hour, the assistant U.S. attorney is back, all sheepish, he gets me on the phone with [my agent] and says, 'ATF is planning a raid on the facility at the end of this month or early March [1993].' I said, 'Fine, but I need you to ask them if they need FBI assistance, because we want to interview Vernon Wayne Howell. And we can do that while he's in custody, presumably.' And the ATF sent word through him to me: 'We don't need FBI assistance.' After he told me this, I had [sent] a letterhead memorandum back to headquarters, and then to the congressman [who'd raised the second complaint]. On the bureau copy I made a note in the margin, 'At the direction of U.S. assistant district attorney, advised hold in abeyance or stand down.'"

In early December 1992, ATF decided it would never get the additional evidence against Koresh that it wanted with the misfunctioning pole cameras. Since mechanisms had failed, reliable human eyes would be substituted. Agents began scouting the area around the Mount Carmel property, searching for an ideal spot to place undercover operatives. It was another step toward tragedy.

The Undercover House
and the Helicopters

D ouble Ee Ranch Road was a narrow track bisecting scraggly properties and fronted at varying intervals by small residences. Some of the road was comprised of hardpacked dirt and pebbles rather than asphalt. Because there weren't a lot of houses, everyone living in them knew their few neighbors at least by sight and usually by name. The only exception to the drab ordinariness of the houses was the Branch Davidians' hulking facility set some two hundred yards back from the road, and reached by a long, curving driveway. Directly across the road from that building was a rent house; its occupants moved out in late 1992, informing neighbors, including the Branch Davidians, that the owner intended to do some repairs and rent it out again. Some of Koresh's followers hired on to assist with roofing and other modifications. At year's end, the house still stood empty, though it was rumored along Double Ee that a single mother and her fourteen-year-old son would move in soon.

It came as a surprise on January 11, 1993, when eight men, who appeared to be in their late twenties or early thirties, took possession instead. They looked clean-cut; their cars, parked in a cleared area in front and beside the house, were relatively new models. Some of their neighbors dropped by over the next few weeks, just to introduce themselves. The newcomers weren't especially friendly. They said that they were enrolled at Texas State Technical College, a popular blue-collar institution that trained students in various trades related to manufacturing, aviation, and medicine, among other fields. Tuition, compared to nearby Baylor University, was relatively low. The modest Double Ee Ranch Road rental property was typical of group living spaces rented by TSTC students struggling on limited budgets.

The eight men were ATF special agents working undercover. Their nickname for their new lair was "the undercover house," or "the U.C. house" for short. As soon as they took possession of the property, they began unloading boxes containing surveillance equipment, mostly cameras to be trained on the Branch Davidian property across the road. They had a fine view of the front of the massive building, but could see very little to the side. The slope of the Mount Carmel hill was vexing; it obstructed some views. A dirt track was cut on the Branch Davidian property—people sometimes jogged along it. An array of cars and trucks was parked along the front of the building. There wasn't a lot of traffic in and out, but every day some of the Branch Davidians living there drove away, apparently to day jobs or on errands. Ranch equipment dotted the property, including a circular "horse walker," where steeds could be tethered, then walked around and around as part of their training process, but the agents didn't see any horses. A short walk down the road offered a view of one side and the back of the building. There was thick brush in the back, and some sort of garage consisting mostly of cinder blocks. The top of the buried school bus was visible, as was the gaping crater where, every day but the Branch Davidians' Saturday Sabbath, men worked on continuing excavation.

The agents set up their cameras, connecting what seemed to be thousands of wires, and making sure that the lenses didn't poke so close to the windows that they might be visible outside. They believed that the Branch Davidians probably had night vision equipment, which discouraged them from using their own. Almost instantly, there was a problem; they couldn't get the cameras to work. Special Agent Dave DiBetta, expert with such equipment, was summoned to see what was wrong. He discovered that the problem was with the agents, not the cameras. They'd been set up properly, but the wrong controls were being pushed, or used out of order. Di-Betta patiently demonstrated what he'd thought the undercover men knew all along: "You push *this*, then you set *this*." He left shaking his head; how mechanically inept could these guys be? In another few weeks, he soon found out: they still couldn't get the cameras to work. DiBetta returned; this time he put numbered stickers on the various controls. They should push 1, then 2, then 3, and so on. And still, the cameras only sporadically were operated as intended. The undercover agents were selected for their youthful appearance rather than technical skills.

For eight days, the agents worked alternating four-man, twelve-hour shifts, observing Mount Carmel at all times, attempting to record all the comings and goings as well as any outdoor activity that could be observed from the U.C. house. But it was difficult to discern what, if anything, was happening after dark. The agents were particularly challenged to keep a constant eye on David Koresh. The only photo of him that they had for reference was a grainy copy of his driver's license. It was hard to tell if they were seeing him or some-one else. After a week, they reported to the ATF divisional office in Houston that it was impossible to observe and record everything happening at Mount Carmel at night. They were told to keep careful watch during the day, and do their best after dark; but 24/7 observation was mostly reduced to daylight-to-dusk.

The important thing, the agents and their Houston supervisors believed, was that the Branch Davidians didn't realize that their new neighbors were undercover ATF agents rather than TSTC students. They were confident that the suspects had no idea.

Their Mount Carmel neighbors figured out the eight arrivals' real identities within the first few days that the agents were in place. Branch Davidian Jaime Castillo was out jogging around the Mount Carmel track on January 11 when he saw new people moving in across the road—eight men, not a woman and her teenage son.

Castillo reported what he'd seen to Koresh, who ordered Neil Vaega to reconnoiter. Vaega grabbed a six-pack of beer—Koresh allowed a limited supply of this alcoholic beverage kept on hand, to be infrequently doled out as a special treat—and walked across Double Ee to introduce himself. When he knocked, the door opened just a crack. (The agents were busy setting up their surveillance equipment.) Someone glared out at Vaega, grunted hello, grabbed the beer, and slammed the door shut.

Vaega hustled back to Mount Carmel, where he informed Koresh about this odd behavior. "David thought right away that they were INS," Immigration and Naturalization Service of the Department of Justice, Kathy Schroeder remembers. "Some of the British people with us had overstayed their visas. So, David said everybody from outside [the U.S.] had to stay inside indefinitely." Koresh knew that he was already in the crosshairs of Child Protective Services and the FBI. Getting hassled by Immigration, though not as threatening as investigations by other agencies of Babylon, was a nuisance he and his followers didn't need as they prepared for the End Time.

The Branch Davidians surreptitiously recorded the license plates of cars parked across the road. Wayne Martin ran a records check at the McLennan County Courthouse—all of the cars were leased from the same Houston dealer. Perry Jones began wandering over to the rental property, engaging any of the young men living there in conversation if one was standing outside. He reported that to him, they seemed old for college students. A few of the Branch Davidians had attended TSTC themselves. They asked their new neighbors which classes they were attending; who were the instructors? Which buildings were their classes in? Their vague responses indicated to David, who never went over to meet with them personally, that he was right: these were fed spies. Whatever agency they represented was immaterial—Babylon was closing in.

The agents were concerned about Perry Jones's regular visits. They also noticed the sixty-four-year-old observing them from the Mount Carmel tower. Clearly, the Branch Davidians were watching them closely. To deflect suspicion, the agents decided to throw a party and invite their across-the-road neighbors. Partying was, after all, what college students did. They contacted some other ATF agents to come to Waco for the occasion—a few more men, but mostly female agents. No college party would seem typical without girls. Carla Bell recalls that she was working out of the ATF office in Lubbock when she was asked if she'd like to do some undercover work. It was a chance to spend time with her boyfriend and soon-to-be husband, ATF agent Kris Mayfield, who'd also been asked to attend. Along with another "eight or ten" female agents, she agreed to go to Waco for the U.C. house wingding. Some of the Branch Davidians showed up, mingled, and reported back to Koresh that these were federal agents for sure. All the short haircuts, hallway doors shut tight to keep visitors from seeing whatever was stashed inside . . . but the Branch Davidian guests enjoyed the beer being served.

After the party, ATF believed any Branch Davidian suspicion had been deflected. At this point agency officials' main concern, dating back to December 1992, was securing helicopters as part of the raid they now anticipated would occur sometime in late February 1993 or early March. ATF's aerial fleet consisted of five small planes. Helicopters were needed to overfly Mount Carmel in advance of any action, photographing the property from above to provide useful information about where and how agents might make their approach. There was some thought, too, that helicopters might be used to distract the Branch Davidians as agents on the ground approached the compound. ATF contacted the U.S. Army and the Texas National Guard, requesting several helicopters and pilots to fly them—but both organizations turned the ATF request down.

Because serving warrants and raids had never required agents taking control of such a large, sprawling property and building, ATF officials were not familiar with some specific conditions for agency use of Army or National Guard helicopters and flight personnel. ATF was basing its operation on alleged conversion and possession of illegal firearms. Regulations were clear: military and National Guard helicopters could be part of a joint federal agency operation only if a "drug nexus" was involved. ATF had to offer proof that the Branch Davidians were drug dealers, too. This, though ATF didn't realize it, was impossible.

"There were no illegal drugs at Mount Carmel," Paul Fatta emphatically declares. "Remember that a lot of the people had come from the Seventh-day Adventists, and they believed in living a healthy lifestyle." David Thibodeau adds, "David was absolutely against drugs, any drugs. When he took Mount Carmel back over [from George Roden] and found some kind of drug lab, he even called the sheriff and had them come and take everything away."

ATF made a lengthy criminal records check, and compiled a list of eleven Branch Davidians at Mount Carmel who might be drug traffickers. This conclusion was based on relatively trifling past offenses, mostly minor pot busts decades earlier, before any of the individuals listed had begun following Koresh and living at Mount Carmel. ATF also dredged up part of the story about the old drug lab discovered by Koresh in the wake of George Roden's Mount Carmel reign. ATF's revised helicopter requests to the Army and National Guard noted the presence of a meth lab at Mount Carmel years earlier. ATF officials would report later that they contacted the sheriff's office, and were told that there was no record of their deputies removing drug lab equipment from Mount Carmel at Koresh's request. Sheriff Jack Harwell is long deceased, so he can't confirm or deny the story, but former county D.A. Vic Feazell is adamant: "They [the sheriff's department] went and got it."

But National Guard officials were convinced that ATF had sufficient evidence to indicate the possible presence of drug-making facilities on Mount Carmel. On January 6, 1993, the first of several National Guard helicopter flyovers swooped across the property. The Branch Davidian kids were delighted; they pointed fingers and toy guns at the helicopters, pretending to shoot them down. Their parents and the other adults took the overflights as yet more confirmation: just as Koresh prophesied, Babylon was surely coming. Most were pleased rather than alarmed.

"Things were being prepared for the end," Kathy Schroeder recalls. "It was awesome. Exactly how it would come about, we didn't know. We were playing it by ear." Koresh, during Bible study, began discussing "quickening," which he described as "bringing the soul into harmony with the Divine." Wayne Martin warned everyone that they all risked personal destruction for "letting David down," and not perfectly following his rules at all times. "We're the weak links in the chain that leads to God," Martin warned. Everyone needed to shape up.

But the January 6 overflight had another result besides bolstering the Branch Davidians' belief that Koresh's prophecies were being fulfilled. A National Guard airman aboard the helicopter scanned the compound using forward-looking infrared radar (FLIR), which indicated a possible "hot spot" such as a methamphetamine lab. From that moment, agency officials assumed they had direct evidence of illegal drug manufacturing.

ATF also wanted at least some idea of the interior layout of the compound. In mid-January, Texas-based agent Nathaniel Medrano, who was perpetually enthusiastic, volunteered to pose as a UPS driver making a delivery at Mount Carmel. He was to ask to use the bathroom; that simple, nonthreatening request would certainly result in an invitation to come inside. Medrano had been engaged in other undercover work, and had grown his hair long as part of a disguise. He asked his supervisor if he should visit a barber before making the Mount Carmel visit, because UPS drivers all had short haircuts. Medrano was told not to bother.

On January 27, Medrano rode along with an actual UPS driver who was making a Mount Carmel delivery. When they arrived and knocked on the front door, Medrano asked the man who answered if he could use the bathroom. He was handed a roll of toilet paper and directed to the outhouse behind the building. The ATF agent only caught a brief glimpse of whatever lay behind the front door. His long hair gave him away to the Branch Davidians, who instantly guessed he was another federal agent working undercover. Koresh was offended by this blunder. He called Sheriff Jack Harwell to complain about being harassed, though he limited the complaint to the fake UPS employee.

In September 1993, when the Treasury Department issued its findings in a departmental investigation of the Mount Carmel operation, it cited the botched January 27 UPS delivery as the intelligence effort "carried out with the least regard for secrecy" among all of ATF's undercover bumblings involving the Branch Davidians. Medrano, a proud man, took the finding personally. Even though supervisors and fellow agents assured him that it was no reflection at all on him, only his supervisors, Medrano felt that it was a stain on his professional character. He badgered officials to change the wording, but to no avail. In 1996, in ATF's Los Angeles office, Medrano put his gun to his head, pulled the trigger, and fell down dead. Agent Guillermo Gallegos, Medrano's close friend, says, "He was the last person you would have thought would commit suicide, but that report was too much for him."

On January 28, the day after the unsuccessful UPS reconnaissance, two of the agents posted at the U.C. house strolled across the street to call on the Branch Davidians. They found a few men near the horse walker, and mentioned that they might be interested in buying it. One of the agents, Robert Rodriguez, introduced himself as Robert Gonzalez. Gesturing toward the gaping pit and the men laboring there, he asked what they were working on. Later he would testify that the group's only reply was hard stares: "That was one thing they loved to do, they loved just to stare you down." "Gonzalez" asked Koresh if the Mount Carmel building was a church; he replied that it wasn't.

Rodriguez was ordered to go back again, work his way into the Branch Davidians' confidence, and scout Mount Carmel's interior, looking especially for where guns were kept. But where he went inside was limited. "We didn't let outsiders look all around," Kathy Schroeder says. "They were only allowed to see a little bit at a time." On his subsequent visits, Koresh talked with the undercover agent, always with the same few male followers gathered around. The other Branch Davidians made themselves scarce, or simply looked away.

On February 5, "Gonzalez" was permitted to attend a Bible study. Koresh stuck to interpreting scripture: "He knew the Bible very well, that was obvious." The undercover agent wasn't familiar with the Bible himself, but he was impressed with how all Koresh's followers hung on every word: "Obviously, the people there believed what he was teaching."

Koresh took time to talk with "Gonzalez" one-on-one. He explained that his followers were hated by law enforcement, and warned that if "Gonzalez" continued visiting Mount Carmel, he'd be watched by police. He invited the undercover agent to come back. Rodriguez's supervisors were pleased—he'd infiltrated the cult. But after "Gonzalez" left, Koresh told everyone that he was clearly a federal agent. When some followers protested that Babylon's spy shouldn't be allowed among them, Koresh reminded them how, in the Bible, Jesus befriended a Roman centurion.

"Gonzalez" visited Mount Carmel several more times. Once, he participated in target practice with Koresh. The undercover agent brought along a handgun and AR-15. He said he'd only acquired the firearms recently and didn't know much about them. Koresh noticed that the weapons featured some sophisticated add-ons that no rookie shooter would even know about. But he continued inviting "Gonzalez" over. On February 21, he extended an invitation for "Gonzalez" to participate in a two-week Bible course beginning on March 1. If he made it through the course, Koresh said, he would be welcome to move into the compound as a step toward joining the Branch Davidians. Koresh explained, "Maybe I can show you something you don't know, but might really want to know." The temptation to turn a federal agent into a follower was irresistible. By this time, "Gonzalez" had heard Koresh disavow U.S. laws, refer to America as "the Dragon," and predict it would be destroyed. He'd especially emphasized his disdain for gun regulations that criminalized some conversions of semiautomatic rifles to fully automatic.

Rodriguez had reported everything his superiors asked for, with the exception of a full description of Mount Carmel's interior. He could supply that if he attended the two-week Bible course and then joined the Branch Davidians, but ATF officials weren't willing to wait that long. They had most of the necessary information and, besides, there was now added incentive to conduct a highly successful, well-publicized operation.

In November 1992, producers of the popular CBS network news program 60 Minutes notified ATF that their reporters were investigating charges of sexual harassment within the agency. On January 11, 1993, 60 Minutes aired a segment titled "Alcohol, Tobacco, Firearms and Harassment." Several female agents described incidents where they were intimidated or verbally accosted by male colleagues. That was bad enough; worse were the women's claims that when they complained to male supervisors, they were disciplined while the perpetrators weren't penalized. ATF officials' on-camera responses were rote rather than convincing—they wouldn't tolerate such things, they would certainly ensure that nothing like what was alleged could ever happen again, not that they admitted anything had happened. ATF was accustomed to mistrust by conservative members of Congress, who constantly questioned the agency's real motives regarding gun control. Liberal members were traditionally ATF's defenders. But allegations of sexual harassment were especially hot buttons for liberal politicians. If they turned on ATF, the agency would have little remaining congressional support. Adding to the new pressure from the political left were rumors that President-elect Bill Clinton, a Democrat, was considering merging ATF with the FBI. The timing of the 60 Minutes broadcast and the Clinton rumors could not have been worse—an ATF congressional budget hearing was scheduled on March 10. Something positive was needed to balance out the negativity, and there was little doubt what that something should be.

Since July 1992, ATF agents had painstakingly laid the groundwork for the biggest operation in agency history. An inarguable success prior to the March 10 hearing was required so agency officials would have something to brag about. Some risk was involved, but that was true of any operation. The key to success was a well-thought-out plan. For months, ATF had been thinking, and considering options of how best to proceed. Now, it was time to finalize a Mount Carmel plan—and then carry it out.

The Plan

During the summer of 1992, several ATF tactical leaders were summoned to the agency's Houston division office for a meeting.

Jerry Petrilli recalls, "I was in Albuquerque as resident agent in charge there, and New Mexico was part of our Dallas division. I was also unit leader for Dallas's SRT [Special Response Team]. I went to a meeting in Houston. We were told that these guys—I'd never heard of the Branch Davidians—this group was obtaining a large quantity of weapons. There were illegal guns in their compound."

According to Petrilli, Houston agent in charge Phil Chojnacki and Chuck Sarabyn, Chojnacki's number two, called the meeting. Because Waco was included in ATF's Houston territory, they would command any ATF operation there. The purpose of the meeting, Petrilli says, "was to decide, 'Are we going to do something, and, if so, what should we do?' or should we ignore the violation or refer it to another agency? We had the county sheriff saying, 'We want some help.' We decided there was no other agency to refer it to, and we'd work with the [McLennan County] sheriff. This group represented a danger to the community, and the longer we waited, the more the potential [for danger] would increase. The feeling was, 'Shit, we've got to do something.' So, people like me, like [New Orleans SRT unit leader] Bill Buford, started thinking, 'What is the right thing to do?'"

During the next seven months, while Aguilera investigated, then was informed by his Washington, D.C., superiors that he hadn't gotten enough evidence and investigated some more, additional tactical meetings were held. Participants correctly assumed that, at some point, they'd get the go-ahead for a Waco operation, and wanted a plan in place when they did. Early get-togethers involved informally suggesting and critiquing various options. Coming up with an effective, relatively safe approach to the Mount Carmel compound was the most challenging aspect. The compound was built atop a sloping hill, with no ground cover anywhere around it. The suspects allegedly had fully automatic weapons, and could fire on anyone approaching from inside their building's walls. If they saw agents swarming toward the compound and got to their guns in time, the ATF force risked slaughter.

"We felt very comfortable throwing out ideas," Petrilli says. "One of mine was, 'Could we have a diversion? How about a helicopter hovering overhead [above the building] and dropping sandbags on the roof, so it sounds like we're coming down on ropes?' And somebody else said, 'What if the sandbag goes through the roof and kills a child?' We'd suggest things and talk about why something wouldn't work."

The presence of women and children inside Mount Carmel was constantly factored in, as was the arsenal allegedly available to Koresh and his followers. Aguilera shared information as he gathered it: the Branch Davidians practiced with their guns, and some of them were probably decent shots, if not quite marksmen. But Koresh kept the firearms locked away when they weren't in use. Every morning except Saturday Sabbath, most of the Branch Davidian men worked on the pit outside the compound. That suggested "dynamic entry": if agents could get inside the compound before the Branch Davidians had time to react, they should be able to prevent anyone in the group from getting to their guns. But former Branch Davidian-turned-informer Marc Breault later said that, because David's followers would defend their leader to the death, "I strongly advised the ATF that if they were going to arrest Vernon, they do so with no force, that they somehow lure Vernon away from [Mount] Carmel."

That sounded sensible, until planners heard conflicting reports from agents in the undercover house. While the agents there no longer kept 24/7 watch on the compound—which the planners didn't know; they assumed surveillance was still continuous—they believed that Koresh had stopped leaving Mount Carmel at all. If this was the case, then he couldn't be nabbed while eating lunch in a Waco restaurant, or stopping to fill up his personal car, a gleaming Camaro, at a local service station. The planners learned, when it was much too late, that the undercover agents were wrong. During their weeks of observing Mount Carmel, Koresh continued occasionally leaving the compound to go into town. They just didn't see him doing it. But, based on the erroneous information that was received, attempting to arrest Koresh somewhere away from his followers was ruled out by operation planners.

Two years after the Mount Carmel raid, Chuck Sarabyn testified to Congress that one enthusiastically explored option was utilizing Child Protective Services to lure Koresh away from the compound. This was considered a possibility even after undercover agents reported that Koresh never left Mount Carmel. Sarabyn told a congressional panel that ATF asked if a CPS staffer could call Koresh "and say, you know, 'We want to talk to you,' or whatever." Then, somewhere near CPS's Waco office, ATF would arrest him. Joyce Sparks was the CPS staff member ATF contacted, and she said that she was willing to try. Sparks testified to Congress that Koresh was always "very open to meeting with me." But her supervisors were concerned about the risk involved, and ordered her to decline.

There was another obvious option besides CPS's Sparks. McLennan County sheriff Jack Harwell had a friendly relationship with Koresh. On a few occasions when local lawmen had some business with him, Harwell simply drove to Mount Carmel, knocked on the front door, and asked Koresh to come downtown for a meeting. He always complied. It was a request from the sheriff's department that initiated ATF's investigation of Koresh; they communicated frequently with Harwell and his deputies. But Harwell said later that ATF officials never discussed specifics about the raid with him. The sheriff told a few reporters he'd known for years that he would gladly have gone to Mount Carmel and told David that he needed to come downtown to talk to ATF investigators. Harwell was certain Koresh would have agreed. But the sheriff claimed that he was never asked for his assistance.

Another aspect never discussed in any detail by planners or agents was the Branch Davidians' religious beliefs, and how these might cause them to react to any ATF approach on their property.

"We called them a cult, but their religion had nothing to do with it," remembers agent Mike Russell. "It [the planning and subsequent operation] was all based on their illegal firearms. We didn't consider anything about religion." Three decades later, Petrilli agrees: "During these [planning] meetings, we did not discuss what they [the Branch Davidians] believed. We didn't have that information. One of our [ATF's] admitted weaknesses was intelligence. We did not have dedicated intelligence officers to gather that kind of information."

Like much of the general public, ATF agents had little respect for anyone involved in a "cult," a term popularly defined as a group of potentially dangerous people weak-minded enough to follow and obey a religious charlatan. Agent Dave DiBetta says that the planners "underestimated the people in there with him [Koresh]. I told them, 'They have a Harvard-educated lawyer, a nurse, a post office guy—these are decent jobs, and you need some ability to do them.' But I guess they [the planners] felt that if you follow a guy with crazy beliefs, you're a sheep, and they never realized that it doesn't take much ability to pull a trigger. They thought they [the Branch Davidians] were so sheepish, and didn't realize how much fervor they had."

By mid-December 1992, the tactical planners were not only certain that a Mount Carmel operation was inevitable, but felt that it was time to get specific about how the action would unfold. Initially, they decided on "surround and call out," or what civilians would describe as a siege. Eight years earlier, a joint ATF/FBI operation in Arkansas successfully utilized surround and call out to subdue the Covenant, the Sword, and the Arm of the Lord, a religion-based group violating gun laws. The siege lasted three days, and then the suspects surrendered. No one on either side was wounded or killed. Covenant leaders were convicted, and the group broke up. This was exactly the result that ATF wanted at Mount Carmel.

Agent Kris Mayfield says that "in late fall [of 1992] or early 1993," his supervisor instructed him "to go gather up equipment" for a "possible surround and call out." Mayfield was temporarily serving in San Antonio. When operations of any significance were planned, ATF was required to sign for temporary use of equipment that was considered outmoded or surplus by the U.S. military. These materials, Mayfield says, "were kept in huge warehouses on military bases. Think of the warehouse in that Indiana Jones movie; they were warehouses like that." San Antonio had several military bases, and Mayfield was given approval by his supervisor to pick out and sign for use of appropriate equipment. "I found light towers for lighting up an area while it was surrounded, and personal equipment like sleeping bags," he says. "There was cold weather equipment—it was still winter months— and rain gear. In all, I signed for the use of about $1 million worth of equipment. The figuring was, if we did surround and call out, we'd have to wait until they came out, then look for evidence. We figured maybe ten days, possibly two weeks. I signed for all this stuff, and once you signed, you had thirty days to pick everything up or else you lost your hold on it. It was now into January [1993]. . . . So, as the end of January approached, I remember emailing our team leaders and saying we were right at the end of the thirty days. And I get the word back, 'Plans have changed. We won't need that equipment.'"

Sarabyn later explained to congressional investigators that "basically, we weighed the options of assault versus siege. But if we did a siege . . . there was a big fear of everybody committing suicide. Second, you know, if we tried to do a siege, we knew that there were machine guns in there. We knew that there were hand grenades."

Besides being well armed, Sarabyn said, the suspects had large quantities "of food and water that could last for a long time . . . I think they had MREs for three months and, you know, their own water well . . . [and] we were concerned about the destruction of evidence, you know, that if they made those machine guns, if they made those hand grenades and we said, 'Hey, we're here to do a search warrant, come out,' and they don't come out, they could take them apart as quickly as they put them in." When dynamic entry was decided, some of the planners didn't feel they had sufficient information to move forward. Even the smallest details, they believed, could make the difference between operation success and failure. Petrilli says, "We, the tactical people, wanted to know specific things. We wanted to know, when Robert Rodriguez went out to shoot with them [the Branch Davidians], whether their guns were already loaded when they brought them out, or whether they had to load them where they were shooting [target practice]. If they didn't have the guns already loaded, then that was a few extra seconds we'd have for our operation. Inside the compound, we wanted to know about the separation of the men and women, where they lived." Rodriguez could supply some of the information, but nothing about the layout of most of the compound because he wasn't allowed to see most of the Mount Carmel interior. Planners had to rely on descriptions provided by former Branch Davidian members who hadn't been inside for at least a year.

The plan that came together required ATF agents from three divisions—Houston, Dallas, and New Orleans—to make their way to the front and side of the compound without arousing the suspicion of male Branch Davidians who would supposedly be outside excavating the pit that ATF suspected was to eventually serve as a bunker. It was decided that the agents would arrive at Mount Carmel in cattle trailers pulled by pickup trucks, which were a common sight along Double Ee Ranch Road—the Branch Davidian men would surely think the trailers had turned up their sloping driveway by accident. Snipers placed across the road in the undercover house, and perhaps in one or two positions blocked from U.C. house view by the Mount Carmel slope, would be ready, if needed, to provide covering fire. And, just to make certain that the Branch Davidians didn't immediately suspect a trap, three Texas National Guard helicopters would swoop down just behind the compound—the attention of the men working in the pit would be focused on the helicopters. Meanwhile, agents would rush out of the trailers. The New Orleans contingent would run to one side of the compound with ladders, climb to the roof, and secure the supposed gun room and Koresh's bedroom (with luck, he might be in there).

Houston and Dallas would, as legally obligated, announce themselves at the front door with shouts, then immediately use a ram to batter the door open. Houston agents would secure the first floor; Dallas agents would rush up the stairs and take control of the second floor, then clear the compound's central tower. The Branch Davidian men wouldn't be able to get to their guns. The group's women and children would be separated from the men by female ATF agents, then calmed in another part of the compound. Evidence necessary to bring Koresh to justice would presumably be easy to find—illegally altered guns, drugs, and a drug lab somewhere in the compound. Koresh would be arrested, along perhaps with an obvious co-conspirator or two. So long as they didn't resist, once the incriminating guns and drugs were confiscated and their leader led away, the remaining Davidians would be left at Mount Carmel, under the watch of ATF agents tasked with continuing to search the premises and making certain no evidence was destroyed by Koresh's followers.

ATF was a division of the Treasury Department, and administered by agency director Stephen Higgins, a thirty-two-year ATF veteran who had been in charge for the past eleven years. The agents in the field liked Higgins; thirty years later, many still describe him as "a nice man." Traditionally in the ATF, operations were planned at division level, and only those of particular consequence had to be okayed by high-level officials in Washington before being carried out. There were thousands of warrant services and raids in the course of any year, most of them involving minimal personnel and risk—too many for agency higher-ups to be involved in each one. Rarer still was ATF officials turning to their Treasury Department supervisors for permission to go ahead. But the proposed Mount Carmel operation was the biggest in agency history, so on February 12, 1993, the plan was presented to Director Higgins for his approval.

Higgins later testified that "the first question I asked when presented [with the] plan was, 'Why don't we just arrest him [Koresh] somewhere away from the premises?'" This, the director remembered, "led to a long discussion about the things [planners] had looked into doing and the reasons they had concluded that [they] weren't going to work, couldn't be successful, so now we were down to the remaining options." There was no discussion about the Branch Davidians' religious beliefs: "I am not sure anybody truly knew what went on in his [Koresh's] mind." Director Higgins approved the dynamic entry plan. It would be appropriate, once a date was selected for the operation but before it commenced, to request additional approval from the Treasury Department. No one was concerned about that; one of the things ATF agents and officials appreciated most was that they were almost always allowed to rely on their own best judgment.

Back in Texas, Blake Boteler was asked to leave his undercover biker gang assignment to look at Mount Carmel and share any observations. He was driven out along Double Ee Ranch Road by Robert White, second-in-command for the Dallas SRT. Boteler remembers that he was concerned by what he saw: "I said to Bob White, 'That place is as big as a Holiday Inn, and there's no ground cover around it.'" But the use of cattle trailers to transport agents to the compound was believed to be sufficient deception, especially with swooping helicopters to divert the Branch Davidians' attention.

A final decision was made. The operation would be conducted on Monday, March 1. For three days prior, most of the ATF agents involved would receive additional training at Fort Hood, the military base about sixty-five miles southwest of Waco. Members of SRT teams in all three divisions involved, plus additional agents whose skills were considered useful to such a massive effort, had previously been instructed not to request vacation days during late February or early March. Now, they learned they'd be going to Mount Carmel by way of Fort Hood. After so many months, ATF was finally ready to roll.

The Branch Davidians at Mount Carmel were ready, too. Though they didn't know when Babylon was coming, they were sure it would be soon. David Thibodeau wrote that "the prophecies" were about to be fulfilled, and it was a relief to everyone there, "confirmation that we had been true to David's teachings, and hadn't put up with all the hardships of life on the Anthill for nothing." They were ready to fight as instructed by the Book of Revelation. Later, Kathy Schroeder would say simply, "We had automatic weapons. We had good reason." They didn't fear an assault; they welcomed it.

Davy Aguilera finally received permission to write a "probable cause affidavit" and submit it to the federal court in Waco, along with a request for a Mount Carmel search warrant, a warrant to arrest "Vernon Wayne Howell AKA David Koresh," and a request for the warrants to be sealed from the public in order to retain the advantage of surprise. The affidavit, submitted on February 25, 1993, described at length the guns, parts, and munitions delivered to Koresh, and the implications of what he and his followers could do with them— things within ATF's jurisdiction. But it also included allegations of child abuse, polygamy, and statutory rape, offenses that were not ATF's legal concern.

The warrants were granted. The operation could go forward, and did, but not on Monday, March 1, as planners intended. There was a last-minute switch to Sunday, February 28. Participating agents were told that the *Waco Tribune-Herald* was to blame, and that the newspaper's irresponsibility might ruin everything.

"The Sinful Messiah"

Like any journalists employed by a daily newspaper in a medium-sized town, reporters at the *Waco Tribune-Herald* were constantly on the alert for any unusual activities or intriguing gossip that might provide the basis for a good story. This was especially true in Waco, where, longtime *Tribune-Herald* photographer Rod Aydelotte says, "The big news was mostly car wrecks and tornadoes," supplemented by coverage of Baylor University and local high school athletics. Opportunities to write about something different were rare, and much desired by most of the newspaper's reporters.

In April 1992, when reporter Mark England wrote several stories about rumors that Branch Davidians at Mount Carmel would commit mass suicide during Passover, no one killed themselves. But England mentioned to his editors that there might be more to write about the group. Everyone knew they were odd, and a few years earlier there'd been a shootout between their current leader and a rival. Additional research might result in at least a few more stories that would intrigue readers, maybe even offer the basis for a full-scale investigative series. During the months that followed, England was still responsible for writing non–Branch Davidian stories, but he and Darlene McCormick, another *Tribune-Herald* reporter, also followed up on anything they heard about the community at Mount Carmel. Their intention was to compile sufficient information to warrant writing a series.

Six months after the suicide-at-Passover coverage, McCormick heard rumors that a government investigation was in progress involving the Branch Davidians possibly possessing illegal guns. She soon tracked down basic information: it wasn't just that the group reportedly owned illegal firearms; they supposedly were making them, doing something involving conversion from semi- to fully automatic. This comprised a perfect combination for front-page coverage in Waco, where religion and guns were integral to city culture. In October, McCormick contacted Assistant U.S. Attorney Bill Johnston at his downtown office to ask whether he had any knowledge of David Koresh and his followers breaking gun laws. McCormick also asked Johnston if a federal investigation of that allegation was in progress. He refused to confirm anything, then immediately warned the ATF that Waco's daily newspaper was working on a story that might compromise their investigation.

Journalists interpret "no comment" as confirmation that something is afoot. McCormick kept digging. A source—Branch Davidians and ATF officials all felt certain it was Marc Breault—alleged Koresh maintained a harem who bore him multiple offspring. McCormick called Koresh, and remembered later, "I didn't get anything solid" about his supposed polygamy. But Koresh was eager to allude to the possibility: "I did get quite a long talk or sermon about how, 'You, too, could become one of the queens of Heaven.' He told me all about his Heaven, that he was the next Messiah, that he wanted everyone to go to Heaven with him, that he would rule up there."

Tribune-Herald editors were now certain that an investigative series was warranted. Added to religion and guns, sex was the perfect third component for a potential blockbuster. Mark England began a series of interviews with Koresh. This alerted Koresh that probing *Tribune-Herald* stories were coming at some point, and, from McCormick's questions as well as England's, he could anticipate the subject matter. After a few conversations with England, where Koresh deftly avoided providing any specifics about guns or polygamy, he told his followers that the reporter's calls were additional proof. Babylon, whose loathsome forces included journalists as well as federal agents, was continuing to close in.

If so, they were taking their time. ATF's investigation continued through the rest of the year and into January 1993. The *Tribune-Herald* didn't publish any scandalous Koresh/Branch Davidian stories; just as the agency knew what the newspaper was up to, the reporters and their editors were aware that ATF was pursuing a Mount Carmel case. In both law enforcement and journalism, timing is crucial. ATF was working toward a late February/early March operation and didn't want the *Tribune-Herald* to run any stories beforehand that might either put Koresh on high alert, or else panic him into destroying evidence. Raid planners were also concerned that an alarmed Koresh and his followers might launch some form of public assault. Editors at the newspaper, besides a determination to serve the public's "right to know" that a group in their community was violating federal law and moral standards, also wanted their eventual series to have maximum effect. Running the stories too soon, especially if they caused ATF to postpone or even call off a Mount Carmel raid, might dissipate potential impact, particularly if nothing happened as a result of the stories and the Branch Davidians went on about their questionable business. But waiting too long, and publishing after an ATF action against Koresh, would make the paper appear to be reporting after the fact, rather than breaking the potentially most important story in Waco history.

In early January 1993, the *Tribune-Herald* series was ready for publication. After being reviewed and approved by publisher Randall Preddy, the stories were forwarded to Cox Enterprises in Atlanta, which owned the media chain that included the Waco paper. Cox officials were concerned enough about potential Branch Davidian retaliation that they dispatched Charles Rochner, Cox vice president for security, to Waco. He would determine proper precautions to take. The series was titled "The Sinful Messiah," catchy phrasing reflecting its main theme: an obviously flawed, self-proclaimed prophet and his flock were committing legal and venal sins in the name of God.

In mid-January, just as ATF agents took up residence across from Mount Carmel in their self-styled undercover house, *Tribune-Herald* managing editor Barbara Elmore called Assistant U.S. Attorney Bill

Johnston to ask whether he thought the Branch Davidians would make some type of violent retaliation against her newspaper after the "Sinful Messiah" series was published. For the first time, Johnston openly acknowledged the ongoing ATF investigation, and told Elmore that agency leaders feared publishing the stories prior to their raid would ruin the operation. He suggested that ATF and newspaper officials meet to discuss the situation.

On February 1, Chuck Sarabyn and Special Agent Earl Dunagan met with Elmore in Johnston's office, where he made introductions and left them to talk. According to Sarabyn, he asked that publication of the series be delayed until after ATF executed a Mount Carmel search warrant; they hoped to do so in three weeks, on February 22. If the newspaper cooperated, ATF guaranteed *Tribune-Herald* reporters "front row seats" at the raid itself. They could come along on the operation. No other paper or media outlet would have anything approaching that access. Elmore said that she would have to consult Preddy, her publisher. She later insisted that no specific raid date had been discussed, only that ATF expected to act within two to four weeks.

Two weeks later, Dunagan informed Elmore that the raid was now set for March 1. She replied that the newspaper had not yet made a decision whether to hold the series; she'd pass on this new information to her bosses. Dunagan assumed that the *Tribune-Herald* was cooperating. Elmore felt that ATF understood no agreement had been reached. Mark England was instructed to interview Koresh by phone, this time to get a reaction to the news that the investigative series was coming. The reporter called Mount Carmel on February 22. Koresh asked England to come out to Mount Carmel, but he refused. On February 24, Mark England drove north to Dallas, where he had been instructed by his supervisors to stay until after the "Sinful Messiah" series was published, out of Koresh's and the Branch Davidians' reach.

On February 24, Phil Chojnacki, ATF's Houston special agent in charge and the leader of the Mount Carmel operation, met with Charles Rochner, *Tribune-Herald* publisher Preddy, editor Robert

Lott, Elmore, and two other newspaper officials. Chojnacki thanked everyone for the newspaper's cooperation. They informed him that publication had only been delayed so that a security plan could be put in place at the paper's editorial offices and printing plant. ATF's ever-evolving raid schedule had nothing to do with it. Chojnacki agreed that there should be concern for newspaper employees' safety, but asked again that the series be postponed. Koresh was acting relaxed; publication might agitate him and disrupt ATF's plans. But Chojnacki wouldn't confirm a March 1 raid date; he said only that it would take place "fairly soon." Asked if that meant seven to fourteen days, he refused to confirm or deny. Instead, Chojnacki said that he hadn't yet obtained warrants for his operation. He wanted to know if he'd receive advance warning of publication, and whether he was really being told that the newspaper was proceeding despite his request to delay the series. Lott said that the newspaper's most important consideration was the public's right to know. They couldn't be concerned with the timing of ATF's operation. Chojnacki was angry when he left; Preddy thought the ATF leader understood that they'd consider his request again, and get back to him.

But after the meeting, the newspaper executives decided they hadn't heard anything persuasive from Chojnacki. He wouldn't give a definite date for the Mount Carmel raid. They'd been waiting to print their stories since late January. They decided to publish the first articles in the series on Saturday, February 27. Activity at the newspaper's editorial office and printing plant was minimal on weekends. They'd have a chance to gauge the Branch Davidians' reaction while there was less immediate danger to employees.

Chojnacki was sure the series was about to be published, and assumed the first stories would appear on Sunday, February 28. Sunday was the day newspapers traditionally reserved for printing their very biggest stories—readers had more time to read carefully, instead of taking quick glances before rushing off for weekday work or Saturday morning errands. Chojnacki called Sarabyn: they'd scheduled the raid for Monday, March 1. Could it be pushed forward two days, to Saturday, February 27? Sarabyn didn't think so; most of the ATF agents involved in the raid were scheduled to arrive at Fort Hood on Wednesday and Thursday. There was too much training to be done, too many last-minute details that must be handled, to try to pull off the operation on Saturday. But the raid could be bumped up one day, to Sunday rather than Monday. Chojnacki checked with his bosses in Washington. They were fine with that. The operation was rescheduled for Sunday. Maybe ATF would catch Koresh and the Branch Davidians absorbed in reading about themselves.

On Friday, February 26, *Tribune-Herald* publisher Preddy gave final permission to begin publishing the "Sinful Messiah" series the next day. That afternoon, he called Chojnacki to notify him. The publisher told Chojnacki that he was welcome to come by the newspaper's printing plant about 12:15 a.m. on Saturday, where he could peruse the first copies off the press. At the ATF agent's request, *Tribune-Herald* editors read each article running in the series one more time, to make certain there were no mentions of ATF or any planned agency operations. After they did so, Cox vice president Rochner called Chojnacki to assure him that there were none.

About 8 a.m. on Saturday, February 27, ATF undercover agent Robert Rodriguez went to Mount Carmel and, maintaining his role as across-the-road neighbor "Gonzalez," brought along that day's *Tribune-Herald*. The first "Sinful Messiah" installments, blazoned across the front page and continued at length on inside pages, focused mostly on Koresh's alleged polygamy, which included underaged girls, and CPS investigations of child abuse at Mount Carmel. David, after reading the stories, was predictably agitated; he talked about how "they" were going to be coming.

"Gonzalez" stayed for a short time, and returned in the afternoon. Saturday was observed by the Branch Davidians as their Sabbath, and Koresh talked to his followers in Mount Carmel's chapel. The ATF agent reported afterward that, as usual, all women sat on the right side of the aisle, and men on the left side. He estimated there were about seventy-five adults. Koresh "was concerned . . . after he made the statement that, 'Now, for sure, they'll be coming,' [he said] 'Remember what I taught, how we have rehearsed,' and, 'Don't be hysterical when the time comes, just do as you have been taught.'" He did not elaborate on what he'd taught his followers to do. But the agent didn't see any guns, or signs that the group was preparing for imminent assault. After returning to the undercover house, Rodriguez called Sarabyn at Fort Hood, and reported this. Rodriguez was unhappy when ordered to go back to Mount Carmel on Sunday morning, to see if the Branch Davidians were going about their usual morning schedule or else preparing to fight. Rodriguez suggested that being there just prior to the raid was too risky; what if he was stuck inside when the cattle trailers arrived? He was told that if he was out of the compound by 9:15 a.m., he ought to be all right.

On Saturday morning, Branch Davidian Steve Schneider called the *Tribune-Herald* newsroom, and complained to city editor Brian Blansett about the stories that appeared in the paper that day. He told Blansett that Koresh wanted an opportunity to tell the *Tribune-Herald* the "real story" of the Seven Seals and not "seven days of lies." Blansett said he'd call Schneider back. Then the city editor called Mark England, who was still in Dallas, telling him that Koresh wanted another interview. Rochner, the Cox Enterprises security official, suggested that England could interview Koresh face-to-face in a restaurant; Rochner and a cop would observe nearby. England drove back to Waco, but, after arriving, he informed Blansett that he didn't want to interview Koresh again. *Tribune-Herald* reporter Tommy Witherspoon had been tipped by an informant that ATF would raid Mount Carmel on Sunday morning. If that was the case, there wasn't really time to interview Koresh. *Tribune-Herald* editors and reporters had to prepare instead to cover the raid.

Blansett didn't call Schneider back.

• • •

On Saturday evening, Bonnie Haldeman, now living in Chandler, Texas, seventy-five miles northeast of Mount Carmel, received a call from a friend who'd read that day's first installment of "The Sinful Messiah" series. She asked Bonnie, "What's going on in Waco?" and described horrible stories that were "all about your son." Bonnie called Koresh and asked about the articles. Though he told her, "It's nothing," she asked if he wanted to send his wife, Rachel, and their kids to stay with her, just in case something happened. (Bonnie was aware of Koresh's other wives and children, but chose never to discuss them with her son.) David repeated that there was no problem, and, besides, "God will take care of us." He ended the call by asking Bonnie to come see everybody at Mount Carmel soon. His mother replied that she couldn't come right then—she was going to be working that day and the next—but she might be able to come the following weekend.

Saturday night at Mount Carmel found a cluster of Branch Davidian men speculating on what form Babylon's looming attack on them might take. This assault, they felt certain, was coming soon. Koresh told them as much after reading the accusatory stories in that day's *Tribune-Herald*, which did not even consider the spiritual obligation of obeying God's commands rather than secular law. What would Babylon unleash on Mount Carmel? Maybe a combination of flamethrowers and napalm, the modern equivalent of a biblical "lake of fire." Their community of 130—almost twice as many as the ATF's estimated 75—included 45 women, and 43 children aged fifteen or under. Perhaps, when the time came, the women and children should be moved to the concrete bunker by the cafeteria, where some guns and a lot of ammunition were stored. They'd be safer behind the thick walls there. Most of the men had automatic weapons, but few were expert in their use. Could they offer sufficient resistance to satisfy God's expectations as written in the Book of Revelation? Steve Schneider, passing the group and sensing their shaky nerves, told them, "Don't worry. The prophecies are being fulfilled." He reminded them of what Koresh taught: in the final moments, the Lamb and his faithful would experience "translation." In one form, translation required the physical act of death, of actually experiencing dying before your soul was freed. But translation could also consist of a spiritual rather than physical act, with souls simply taken up to Heaven without literal death. This was a way God rewarded true believers.

On Saturday night, the Branch Davidians were ready. Seventy-five miles away at Fort Hood, the ATF agents were, too.

Fort Hood

From early to mid-February 1993, ATF agents participating in the Mount Carmel operation began receiving word that before the raid, they'd deploy to the Fort Hood Army base in Killeen for special training. Like the operation itself, this was unprecedented in agency history. They were proud and excited to be part of it.

Some of the eighty agents designated for this special training still weren't entirely certain of what they'd be doing when the operation took place, or even where in Texas they'd be doing it. "I didn't know it was Waco," agent Guillermo Gallegos recalls. "I did not know the magnitude. I had only been told I was going to work with Houston on this. I didn't know other divisions were involved."

Most of the operation planners arrived at Fort Hood on Wednesday, February 24. Everyone else reported on Thursday, when they were briefed on the operation, and informed they'd engage in three days of special training. They'd sleep in barracks on the base, and move out to Waco before dawn on Monday, March 1. The operation, initially named "Prairie Fire," had been renamed "Trojan Horse." The traditional go-word "Execute" was changed to "Showtime." The latter was tacit acknowledgment that, as always, ATF critics would be on the lookout for anything, no matter how minor, to offer as proof the agency aggressively preyed on decent, gun-owning American citizens.

The briefings at Fort Hood included a visit from undercover agent Robert Rodriguez. He talked about what he'd observed at Mount Carmel and inside the Branch Davidian facility. David Koresh controlled everything there, Rodriguez emphasized. His followers were devoted to him. The agents comprising his audience were left, agent Blake Boteler says, with the impression that "they were capable of fighting us. But we never thought they would put up the kind of opposition that they did. We thought, 'Maybe somebody will stick a gun out and shoot at us down a hall' once we were inside." SRT leaders explained the specific assignments of their squads—Houston and Dallas to enter through the front door, with Houston to secure the first floor and Dallas to proceed upstairs and secure the second. New Orleans had the trickiest task, rushing to the side of the compound, climbing ladders to the roof, smashing windows, and entering through the openings to take control of the gun room and Koresh's bedroom. None of the agents felt overwhelmed. They were seasoned pros, and they were up against sheeplike religious nuts.

Friday and Saturday were hectic. Agents trained at Fort Hood's Military Operations in Urban Terrain (MOUT) site, where multistory buildings provided an opportunity to rehearse raid responsibilities. Some of the training almost exactly approximated what they'd encounter at Mount Carmel, especially placing ladders on the sides of buildings and scaling up. There was little difficulty getting inside through doors or windows, but the mock Mount Carmel interior layout at Fort Hood was pure guesswork. No one knew how many rooms were on each floor, or vital information about the distance between rooms, the width of staircases, the exact number of people living on each floor. Tape and ropes marked approximated distances.

Agents on the New Orleans team had an especially critical task to rehearse, using special tools to "break and rake" on the roof. First, a three-man team must break the window glass of the gun room, then "rake" remaining sharp glass shards from the window frames so the agents could wriggle inside without getting cut. Roof entry into Koresh's room posed a different challenge; a window air conditioner unit blocked the way. Agents would have to shove the unit into the room, then clamber in after it.

Much of the training focused on the cattle trailers, the process of loading into them, then exiting on the double. Here, many of the agents felt uncomfortable. "These were 'metal pole' trailers," agent Sam Cohen remembers. "They had all these metal poles [as basic framework] inside, and plywood all along the sides and a tarp on top. It was hard to see out. I thought it was claustrophobic." But the agents were assured that they wouldn't be in the trailers for long; it was just a short drive from the staging area to Mount Carmel. Exiting the trailers was practiced for several hours. By the end of that exercise, agent Mike Russell says, "We got so we could get thirty agents out in twenty-five seconds." There was also practice riding in the trailers; agents were taken out on fifteen-minute trips, which approximated the trailer drive time from the Bellmead Civic Center staging area to Mount Carmel. This theoretically allowed those who would make that trip to acclimate themselves to the trailers' tight quarters and jouncing ride.

On Friday, February 26, agents learned two pieces of unwelcome news. One had nothing to do with their Waco mission. A building at the World Trade Center in New York City was bombed that day by terrorists. The device exploded in a parking garage. Six people were killed, and almost one thousand were injured, the majority of these while participating in panicky emergency exits. Officials and teams from many federal agencies, including ATF, rushed to the scene. Throughout government law enforcement bureaucracy, attention was riveted on New York.

Chuck Sarabyn had an additional announcement for the agents. He told them that operation leader Phil Chojnacki respectfully asked management of the Waco daily newspaper to hold off publishing an investigative series about Koresh and the Branch Davidians until after the Mount Carmel raid took place. Chojnacki's modest request was accompanied by a promise that, if the paper cooperated, its reporters would be given special access to interviews, but the editors refused. The series was going to run on Saturday, even though it might alert Koresh to the pending ATF operation. So, the decision had been made that the raid would now take place on Sunday, rather than Monday, morning. Agent Kris Mayfield says, "The impression was left with us that there had only been one meeting with the paper." The agents weren't surprised by the *Tribune-Herald*'s refusal to cooperate. They believed that the media was always antagonistic.

That didn't prevent ATF higher-ups from wanting reporters primed to write laudatory stories after the Mount Carmel raid was successfully completed. Agent Sharon Wheeler of the Dallas office was told to alert a presumably supportive TV reporter that, on Sunday, there would be some potentially good story material resulting from the execution of a search warrant in Waco. Wheeler told her bosses that she couldn't alert just one station; she then received permission to contact all of the major TV affiliates in Dallas, asking for weekend contact numbers for reporters. Wheeler later testified that she did so. "I was asked by Channel 5 if it involved the World Trade Center bombing, and I said, 'No.' We were planning on having a press conference when the raid was over."

SRT team leaders weren't upset when they learned that the operation was being moved up a day. Jerry Petrilli says, "The original idea was, we'd train [through Saturday] and then have a day of rest on Sunday before going out on Monday. I was pleased with no day of rest. We were refining skills, our teams had got really sharp, so why rest for a day and lose that momentum?"

In between training exercises, team leaders and their squads made plans beyond the basic dynamic entry itself. There were dogs on the Branch Davidian property, a pack of them, and, according to undercover agent Rodriguez, some were aggressive. A number of these dogs were kept behind a fence in a pen area near Mount Carmel's front door. ATF had no more desire to shoot dogs than it did suspects. It was decided that an agent carrying a fire extinguisher would be among the first to emerge from the trailers. If any dogs appeared threatening, the agent would spray them, hopefully discouraging any attack. Agent Robert Champion was assigned this role. If that didn't work, the dogs, regrettably, would be shot.

Panic-stricken children were a particular concern; nobody wanted to frighten little kids. Female agents from several ATF offices learned they'd been brought to Fort Hood to form a fourth entry team, and go inside Mount Carmel immediately after Dallas, Houston, and New Orleans SRTs gained control of the premises. Then the female agents would move Branch Davidian women and children away from the men, and give candy to the kids. The possibility that the Branch Davidian women might be as potentially violent as the men was not considered.

Always, the vital element of surprise was emphasized. Without catching the Branch Davidians entirely off guard, any opportunity for a smooth, nonviolent confrontation would surely be lost. Usually, ATF raids took place at or just before dawn, a time when most suspects still lolled in bed or were slowly gathering their wits after waking. But, according to agents at the undercover house, and from Mount Carmel infiltrator Rodriguez especially, it was only after breakfast and a morning "daily" religious gathering that Mount Carmel men grabbed tools and went outside to work on the ever-deepening pit. So, it would be around 9:30 a.m., perhaps a bit closer to 10 a.m., when the adult male Branch Davidians were separated from immediate access to the guns locked up on the third floor inside. This was when the two cattle trailers loaded with a total of seventy-six agents would swoop up the driveway, and dynamic entry implemented. If the Branch Davidian men outside tried to get to the guns, they'd have to go through battle-tested ATF agents to do it. "We knew," Sam Cohen says, "that they had towers for observation, superior firepower, and the [advantage of] high ground. The only advantages we had were superior training, and surprise."

Even when caught completely by surprise, the agents believed, Branch Davidian men might not meekly surrender. "We expected that we might have to fight them hand-to-hand," agent Rory Heisch recalls. Guillermo Gallegos says that his role was to follow the Houston SRT inside, and "secure" any presumably unarmed Branch Davidian men who resisted: "I had lots of flex handcuffs to detain individuals as we went."

Always, briefings emphasized that, when the raid took place, the

Branch Davidians' guns would be inside, and the men would be outside. No one doubted that the suspects would be taken by surprise. As the Treasury Department report published seven months later bluntly stated, "It does not appear that anyone in ATF's leadership asked the obvious questions, beginning with, 'What happens if . . . '"

At Fort Hood, some of the agents did ask their team leaders what would happen if the Branch Davidians somehow learned about the imminent raid, and armed themselves accordingly. "At Fort Hood, someone [from the New Orleans team] specifically asked SRT team leader Bill Buford about a contingency plan," agent Keith Constantino says. "Bill told us, 'If this goes belly-up, run like hell.' Ninety-nine percent of the time when we did these [raids], we knew there were bad guys with guns behind the door. You have to have some contingency plan if things go wrong. So, this flustered some of us. All the experts were doing the planning, and this no contingency thing was a big hiccup to us." Agent Mike Duncan says that, upon realizing there was no "what if" plan in place, he reminded himself that geography often had a lot to do with suspects' responses: "Taking up arms and shooting law enforcement officers? Maybe in Los Angeles, but in Central Texas, it's never going to happen. Not here."

On Thursday and Friday nights, the agents at Fort Hood ate their dinners in a base mess hall, or else got in their cars and drove to fast-food joints nearby; Pizza Hut was a favorite. Mike Russell recalls that on these two nights, "there was some carrying on, some drinking." Establishing camaraderie was important; some agents from different divisions were meeting for the first time, and on Sunday they'd be entrusting each other with their lives. The married agents made sure to call home before climbing into the barracks' bunks. For a few agents, such close confinement didn't lend itself to blissful sleep. "I had driven to Fort Hood with another agent, Milton Bonaventura," Keith Constantino says. "We were sleeping in the barracks, with people snoring and farting and playing cards all night. Getting a good night's sleep was out of the question. So, me and Milton left, checked into a motel, and got a good night's sleep."

But Saturday night, February 27, was different. There was no drinking or card playing. Instead, agents practiced administering IVs to "wounded" comrades. No one stayed up late; everyone would have to be up at 3:30 or 4 a.m. on Sunday to prepare for the mile-long car caravan drive to the raid staging area in Bellmead. The agents were always self-disciplined and purposeful on the night before an operation, but this time there was additional incentive to be ready. On Saturday, copies of the *Waco Tribune-Herald*'s "Sinful Messiah" series were delivered to Fort Hood, and many of the agents read and discussed the disturbing articles. They'd already known they were raiding Bible-beating weirdos who had illegal, fully automatic guns. Now many of them learned for the first time that the weirdos' leader allegedly had lots of wives and was raping little girls, and all the children living in the Mount Carmel compound were in daily peril of excessive beatings. "All of us started reading it and going, 'Wow,'" Guillermo Gallegos recalls. Most went to bed on Saturday night determined not only to confiscate illegal guns and arrest David Koresh, but to save those kids. It added an edge.

Agent Carla Bell said she and others had an additional concern: "We were thinking, 'God, I hope they [the Branch Davidians] have at least one [illegally converted gun],' to make our warrant look good."

The agents acquired a lot of new information during their days of training at Fort Hood, and some of it—the lack of a contingency plan, what they'd read in the first installment of the "Sinful Messiah" series—upset them. But they would have been even more concerned if they'd been aware of one final, unexpected obstacle. Unbeknownst to the agents, only last-minute pleas and a specific assurance from ATF director Stephen Higgins prevented Treasury Department officials in Washington from calling off Operation Trojan Horse.

Surprise Promised

On Friday, February 26, ATF director Stephen Higgins remembered that Lloyd Bentsen, recently sworn in as Treasury secretary in the Clinton administration, hailed from Texas. Bentsen had previously represented his state in the U.S. Senate. Now, he was Higgins's boss, since ATF was a Treasury bureau. When the Mount Carmel operation succeeded on Sunday, as Higgins expected, there would hopefully be mention of ATF's triumph in media throughout the country, but especially in Texas, Bentsen's home state. That surely meant, despite any other pressing duties occupying Bentsen, someone would bring raid-related stories to his attention. As Higgins later explained to congressional investigators, he decided it would be appropriate to give Bentsen a heads-up before the Sunday raid took place and the secretary saw subsequent coverage.

Higgins was under no obligation to request permission from Bentsen or any other Treasury Department officials in Washington to carry out the Mount Carmel raid. Ron Noble, in February 1993 a Treasury advisor, and soon to be appointed the department's assistant for law enforcement, later testified before a congressional investigative committee that ATF was not, and had never been, required to notify "main Treasury" prior to operations of any size. In 1992 alone, the agency executed 10,134 federal warrants, and assisted various state and local agencies with another 12,884 search warrants. Requesting permission from Washington would have hampered the agency's ability to act quickly, and would have required countless Treasury officials from doing anything all day other than reviewing ATF proposals. By submitting advance notice of the pending raid, Higgins was taking an extra step out of consideration toward his new boss.

But beyond representing additional courtesy, the notification itself was perfunctory, a single typewritten page describing in minimal detail the Mount Carmel plan without requesting permission to carry it out. The memorandum was composed by Special Agent Christopher Cuyler, ATF's liaison to the Treasury Department. Cuyler later testified that he based what he wrote on details he'd overheard in a February 11 meeting, "and then from talking to various division chiefs in our headquarters." Apparently, Cuyler didn't listen closely, or else what he heard was based on inaccurate information. His terse description contained several errors. Among them, Cuyler claimed that Koresh had been acquitted of attempted murder, that he "has been involved in a shootout with a rival religious cult," and that "in general the [Branch Davidian] women are not allowed outside the main compound." He concluded the memo with the assurance that "a well-reasoned, comprehensive plan has been approved which allows for all contingencies." That was completely wrong.

On Friday afternoon, February 26, Cuyler transmitted the memo to Michael D. Langan in Washington, the Treasury Department's acting deputy assistant director for law enforcement. Langan was one of many Treasury Department staffers acting in a more senior role until Congress confirmed nominations for new Clinton administration appointees. Secretary Bentsen himself had just attained congressional approval. If Cuyler hoped Langan would immediately bring his Mount Carmel memo to Bentsen's attention, he was mistaken. The newly sworn-in secretary was in London, attending an international economics conference.

Even if Bentsen had been in his Washington office, on February 26 he would have had no time to peruse the Cuyler memo. Nine minutes before the Mount Carmel message reached the Treasury Department at 2:27 p.m., the terrorist bomb blasted the World Trade Center, in what a department official described as "the biggest terrorist attack in this country's history." Swarms of ATF officials, special agents, and explosives experts were ordered to the bombing scene. Acting Treasury officials and advisors in Washington were focused on New York City, not Waco. Ron Noble later admitted to congressional investigators that "I didn't even know [the city of] Waco existed. I am sorry to say that to those of you from Texas."

But on Noble's recommendation, later that afternoon Cuyler met with Langan and John P. Simpson, Treasury's acting assistant secretary for law enforcement. Cuyler didn't have much more to share that hadn't been in his memo. He noted that the raid had been moved from Monday to Sunday because the "Sinful Messiah" series had been published, and there was concern it might put Koresh on high alert. Simpson was troubled by what he heard; after his meeting with Cuyler, he contacted ATF director Higgins to ask about possible alternatives to the pending Mount Carmel raid. Was the use of so much force really required? Higgins pointed out that ATF was simply informing the Treasury's Office of Enforcement, not asking permission.

Simpson remained concerned. He convened a late Friday afternoon meeting with Noble, Langan, and Stanley Morris, a former director of the U.S. Marshals Service who, like Noble, was currently a Treasury Department advisor. Morris took considerable issue with what little ATF had chosen to share about its February 28 raid plans: Why was so much force necessary to execute this warrant? How could ATF be certain that there wouldn't be a shootout, if the Branch Davidians were well armed? What precautions were being taken to assure not only the safety of participating ATF agents, but also the Branch Davidians inside the Mount Carmel compound? Noble agreed, and told Simpson that, based on the information provided, he didn't believe the raid should be permitted to go forward. That led to further discussion: Did Simpson, for the moment the senior Treasury Department enforcement official on hand in Washington, actually have the authority to call the raid off? Simpson decided that he did. He called ATF director Higgins and ordered the Mount Carmel operation to be shut down.

Half an hour later, Higgins called Simpson back; first on this call, then in a later conference call including Simpson and Ron Noble, the ATF director asked that Simpson reconsider his stand-down order. Force was needed, Higgins emphasized, because Koresh was un-likely to surrender peacefully, and because ATF feared the Branch Davidians would destroy evidence, or even commit mass suicide if more restrained warrant execution efforts were attempted. ATF knew that, at the time they scheduled the raid, Branch Davidian men would be separated from the cult's women and children, would be outside while the females and kids were inside, and, besides, all their guns were closed away in a room whose access only Koresh controlled. The raid, precisely as planned, had to be made on Sunday, February 28, because of the Waco newspaper. Waiting any longer gave Koresh opportunity to alter the Branch Davidians' daily routine.

Above all, Higgins stressed, the agents in charge of the raid had instructions to cancel the operation, call it off immediately, if the element of surprise was compromised, or even if, on February 28, the Branch Davidians appeared to change their daily routine in any way. Surprise was the key. If that critical element was lost, the raid would be called off.

Simpson and Noble took Higgins at his word. Simpson informed the ATF director that his original decision was revoked. With the un-derstanding that the agents in charge would shut the Mount Carmel operation off if the element of surprise was lost, Simpson gave permis-sion for the raid to go forward on Sunday.

According to the Treasury Department investigative report issued seven months later, on Wednesday, February 24, reporter Tommy Witherspoon had informed his editors that he'd received a tip from a source he did not identify. This source told Witherspoon that ATF intended to raid Mount Carmel on Monday morning, March 1. Witherspoon was a veteran reporter whose beat included the court-house and sheriff's department. He did solid work, much of it based on developing a wide array of sources who were proven providers of accurate "inside" information. If Witherspoon trusted this source, so did his editors. Reporters and photographers were assigned to the story, and told to be in the newsroom early on Monday morning.

The Treasury Department report also stated that on Thursday, February 25, Witherspoon tipped a friend, KWTX-TV cameraman Dan Mulloney, about ATF's planned Mount Carmel raid on Monday, March 1. Mulloney also heard about it from another source: his girlfriend worked at American Medical Transport, a Waco ambulance service. ATF had contacted the company to arrange for several ambulances to be on hand near Mount Carmel on the morning of March 1, in case any injuries were incurred during the raid. Mulloney's girlfriend told him all about it.

When ATF raid leaders decided to move the operation from March 1 to February 28, Witherspoon's source immediately contacted him about the change, and the reporter informed his editors. On Saturday, February 27, Witherspoon and Mulloney played racquetball; they talked about the new date. Also on Saturday, *Tribune-Herald* reporters and photographers were instructed to report to the newsroom on Sunday morning at 8 a.m. for their special Mount Carmel assignments.

So on Friday, as ATF director Stephen Higgins promised John Simpson and Ron Noble that surprise would not be lost, to some extent it already was. Had Higgins known that local Waco media already knew about the imminent Mount Carmel raid scheduled for midmorning on Sunday, would he have called off the operation? What really mattered was that David Koresh and the Branch Davidians were taken by surprise. On Friday, then all day on Saturday, they would have been.

Early Sunday morning, that changed.

Surprise Lost

A lot of moving parts intersected in the hours leading up to the ATF's Sunday morning raid on Mount Carmel. The first of these came on Saturday afternoon. After spending some of Saturday morning at the compound with the Branch Davidians, undercover agent Robert Rodriguez met with ATF operation commander Phil Chojnacki. Chojnacki had one predominant inquiry—when Rodriguez was inside Mount Carmel, had he seen any guns? Rodriguez said that he hadn't. This was what raid planners hoped to hear. Besides the Branch Davidians being upset by the articles published in the *Tribune-Herald* that day, life at the compound seemed to follow its regular schedule.

At 5 p.m. on Saturday, Rodriguez returned to Mount Carmel and stayed until almost midnight. When he returned to the undercover house across Double Ee Ranch Road, he spoke with Jim Cavanaugh, the Dallas office's assistant special agent in charge, who was supervising the agents there. Cavanaugh listened as Rodriguez phoned Sarabyn to report that there still was no indication the Branch Davidians anticipated an assault on Sunday morning. The undercover agent was upset when Sarabyn ordered him to go back to Mount Carmel on Sunday morning, just before the operation was scheduled to begin. Rodriguez believed that Koresh might not let him leave by 9:15 a.m., his Mount Carmel departure time mandated by Sarabyn. If he was still there when the raid commenced and shooting resulted, Rodriguez believed, he might very well be cut down in a crossfire. But Sarabyn told him to make the Sunday morning compound visit anyway. Then ATF would know for certain whether the Branch Davidians suspected something was about to happen. Rodriguez grudgingly agreed. Cavanaugh, listening to the conversation, wondered whether the undercover agent was cracking from the strain.

There were lots of small, last-minute details to attend to. Phil Lewis, third in seniority to Chojnacki and Sarabyn in ATF's Houston division, served as the operation's support commander and had been in Waco for almost a week. His job was to "get everything in place that was needed, ranging from medical and communications support to port-a-potty rentals and tents, all that." The last-minute switch of raid date from Monday to Sunday meant that Lewis spent many frantic hours at ATF's Waco command post rearranging things—these ranged from when medevac helicopters would be on hand to transport anyone potentially wounded to changing the date on the McDonald's Happy Meal vouchers intended for the Branch Davidian kids.

The date change wasn't the only news that caught Lewis by surprise. Until Chuck Sarabyn informed him around midweek, Lewis still believed that Child Protective Services was cooperating in luring David Koresh away from Mount Carmel just before the raid. "With him not present at Mount Carmel to give commands, there was a reasonable chance of our operation working," Lewis says. "I had been in the planning meetings, and I believed that this [Koresh being away from Mount Carmel] was part of the plan. But right before, in Waco, Chuck told me, 'We're not arresting Koresh [away from the property].' He said CPS management had decided not to do it. I asked, 'So, how are we getting Koresh away from the compound?' He said, 'Oh, we're not going to worry about that.'"

The element of surprise was still considered essential. But ATF was a noticeable presence in Waco on Saturday. The agency booked 153 hotel and motel rooms in town for Sunday night, and reserved some of them for Saturday night as well. Several dozen agents slated for supporting roles during and after the raid arrived in Waco on Saturday. Chojnacki and Sarabyn met with some of them around 8 p.m. at a

Best Western motel. The group included arrest and support teams, explosive specialists, dog handlers, and laboratory technicians. National Guard members attended the meeting, too. One ATF staffer ordered fresh doughnuts from a local grocery store; these would be picked up in the morning and taken to the staging area in nearby Bellmead. The McLennan County sheriff's department had agreed to supply coffee there. Final arrangements were made for ambulance services and portable toilets. Charlie Smith, assigned to fly one of ATF's small planes over Mount Carmel the next morning, remembers that during and after the Best Western motel meeting, everyone was confident: "Everybody expected we'd just be in and out [at Mount Carmel], like all our other deals. I worked out of Houston, and liked to play golf. I set up a tee time back home for Sunday afternoon. I figured I'd fly the [Mount Carmel] mission on Sunday morning and still have plenty of time to fly back to Houston for golf."

Some of the ATF personnel went about their errands wearing jackets emblazoned with the agency name. They wore the jackets because it was chilly, with intermittent rain. Two years later, newly appointed ATF director John Magaw told congressional investigators, "It's not that they didn't want to do it, [it's that] they didn't think about operational security." In his 2007 article, "What Really Happened at Waco" for The Huffington Post, James Moore wrote that ATF "booked a room at the [town's] convention center for a 4 p.m. Sunday news conference," and a "front page newspaper series, commandeered local hotel rooms, media tips from government officials and law enforcement warnings meant that, if the Branch Davidians did not know that [ATF] was coming, they were the only souls in a five-county region who did not."

On Saturday night, the Branch Davidians still didn't know. ATF and local lawmen meant to keep it that way. Even though there would be ATF agents moving on the back country roads around Mount Carmel early on Sunday morning, the decision was made not to place roadblocks sealing off the area until just before the raid commenced. Even a fleeting glimpse of roadblocks might tip off the suspects; better to wait until the last possible minute.

Branch Davidian Kathy Schroeder was out of bed early on Sunday, February 28. One of Schroeder's assigned tasks was to prepare breakfast for everyone, a daunting daily task with 130 to feed. By David's order, this morning meal was served at 6 a.m. Everyone ate together in the rudimentary cafeteria; permission was rarely granted for anyone to take a meal in his or her room. On this day, as usual, Schroeder remembers fixing a communal breakfast of oatmeal, millet, and eggs, ordinary but filling fare for people following a rigorous daily routine.

An exception to routine on this morning was Paul Fatta, who had to drive ninety miles south to Austin; the Branch Davidians had a table at a gun show there that weekend. Fatta was supposed to be accompanied by Steve Schneider—business was usually brisk at these gun shows, necessitating at least a pair of Branch Davidians on hand—but Koresh was concerned about the next installment of "Sinful Messiah" stories being published that day. Steve was acting as David's conduit to *Tribune-Herald* editors and reporters; Koresh instructed him to stay at Mount Carmel instead of going to Austin. Fatta wasn't upset. Since he now had extra room in his car, he brought along his fourteen-year-old son, Kalani. Even at gun shows, there were usually a few tables selling sports collectibles, and Kalani loved baseball cards. The teen was glad to ride down to Austin with Dad. They drove away before 7 a.m. No roadblocks were yet in place to prevent their passage.

Not long after Kathy Schroeder began fixing the Branch Davidians' breakfasts, six ATF agents assigned to block attempted escape from the rear of the Mount Carmel compound checked into the staging area at Bellmead Civic Center. Then they were driven past Mount Carmel and dropped off behind the Branch Davidian property. They stealthily picked their way through thick brush, and set up well back of the main building; there was no cover for about seventy-five yards from the edge of the brush to the sprawling facility. The agents settled in for what they anticipated would be up to a three-hour wait.

Just after daybreak, Charlie Short and copilot Eddie Pali flew ATF's small Partenavia twin-engine aircraft on a reconnaissance mission over Mount Carmel. Short remembers that "there was a little rain, it was overcast, and the [cloud] ceiling was coming down." Besides Short's holstered handgun, there were no firearms on the plane, but there was an 8mm handheld movie camera. "Somebody handed it to Eddie just before we took off," Short remembers. "They said to take a film of the operation, but Eddie didn't know how to use it."

Short and Pali cruised over Mount Carmel and didn't see anyone outside. Short radioed back to the ATF command center that everything was quiet: "Then I throttled [the plane] down and kept flying around, staying out of the way of the place [Mount Carmel]. We were going to be up in the air until everything started, flying back in then at about 1,500 feet with the three [National Guard] helicopters below us. The idea was, the helicopters would fly by the place and distract the people in there."

At 7 a.m., there was a meeting at Waco's KWTX-TV station. News director Rick Bradfield gave maps of the Mount Carmel area to cameramen Dan Mulloney, John McLemore, and Jim Peeler. Mulloney and McLemore were instructed to position themselves near the intersection of FM 2491 and Double Ee Ranch Road. This was the way that ATF agents were most likely to come. Peeler was ordered to the more remote intersection of Double Ee and Old Mexia Road. Even with a map, he wasn't confident he could find his way there. Mulloney and McLemore were expected to return with footage of ATF entering the Mount Carmel property and confronting the Branch

Davidians. Peeler would film prisoners being taken away. About 7:30 a.m., Mulloney and McLemore took up their assigned positions not far from the FM 2491/Double Ee Ranch Road intersection. Peeler became hopelessly lost, and had no idea if he was anywhere near where he was supposed to be.

Chuck Sarabyn briefly stopped at the Bellmead staging area, then drove on to the TSTC campus, where Phil Chojnacki was preparing to ride in one of the three National Guard helicopters that would do a Mount Carmel flyover and provide a distraction just before the ground raid commenced. After that, Chojnacki expected to observe the operation as the helicopters hovered near the compound. Phil Lewis was at the command post to handle radio communications, and there were five additional agents who would join National Guard pilots in the helicopters; Davy Aguilera, whose long, painstaking investigation provided the bulk of evidence on which the operation was based, was among them. These ATF agents carried only holstered handguns. None of the three National Guard helicopters had mounted weapons or carried long-range firearms. Their interiors were crammed with their agent passengers.

In the undercover house across Double Ee Ranch Road from Mount Carmel, two sniper teams prepared to take up positions by front windows. Jim Cavanaugh manned the phone, keeping in touch with Chojnacki and Sarabyn, who had returned to the TSTC base from the Bellmead staging area. An additional two-man sniper team was part of the six-agent contingent already in place behind the compound. Everything was going as planned.

Undercover agent Robert Rodriguez reluctantly drove onto the Branch Davidian property about 8 a.m. on Sunday. He'd told Koresh the night before that he'd return in the morning, and Koresh mentioned it to his followers; they weren't surprised when "Gonzalez" knocked on the front door. The previous morning, he'd brought along copies of the day's *Tribune-Herald*. He did the same on Sunday. A few Branch Davidians who were permitted to interact with "Gonzalez" greeted him. Koresh had assured everyone at Mount Carmel that "Gonzalez" was a government spy, but he should be allowed inside the compound anyway. He'd hear the truth being preached, and who knows? He might listen and believe; even Babylon's spies had souls, too.

The Branch Davidians, Sherri Jewell foremost among them, took the Sunday newspapers "Gonzalez" brought, glanced at the articles, and pointedly began laughing and mocking them. Such lies! Then Koresh walked over. When he made no immediate effort to take the paper and read the latest allegations against him, the undercover agent took the initiative: "I asked him to explain to me why Marc Breault [quoted extensively in Sunday's articles] was saying these things, and what was the difference between his teachings and Marc Breault's." It was a canny request; Koresh was glad to explain the differences at length. This gave "Gonzalez" an opportunity to surreptitiously glance around the front area inside the compound. He didn't see any guns. The men weren't outside working in the pit yet, but it was still relatively early, and cold and nasty out besides. Koresh didn't seem any different than usual. The Branch Davidian leader yammered on; the agent resisted taking too many glances at his watch. He was determined to be out of Mount Carmel by 9:15. Already, he'd been there almost thirty minutes.

Reporters, photographers, and editors gathered in the *Tribune-Herald* newsroom at approximately the same time Rodriguez arrived at Mount Carmel. A few learned for the first time that they'd be covering an ATF raid on the Branch Davidians. They were broken into groups to ride to the Mount Carmel area. Tommy Witherspoon and fellow reporter Marc Masferrer were teamed with photographer Rod Aydelotte. Masferrer was relatively new to the newspaper's staff; Witherspoon and Aydelotte were old hands. The editors made location assignments, and the Witherspoon-Masferrer-Aydelotte team got a prime one, directly across Double Ee Ranch Road from the compound.

Aydelotte's photography assignment was specific: editors expected the ATF operation to be conducted jointly with the McLennan County sheriff's office. "I thought the sheriff [Jack Harwell] was just going to knock on the door and tell David to come out," Aydelotte recalls. "That was the assumption we had; I was going to shoot pictures of that." He and the two reporters left for Mount Carmel in Aydelotte's 1986 Honda Accord.

At the TSTC command center, Chuck Sarabyn awaited word from Rodriguez. He knew (Jim Cavanaugh in the undercover house must have notified him) that the agent entered Mount Carmel around 8 a.m. He ought to be coming out soon to describe what was going on in there.

About 8:30 a.m., Koresh decided the Branch Davidians needed a few more copies of Sunday's *Tribune-Herald*. He told David Jones, whose day job was mail delivery for the U.S. Postal Service, to get in his car and go buy additional copies. Jones, like his children and his father, Perry, lived at Mount Carmel. Soon after Koresh made his request, Jones drove out of the compound. He took his car, which was the same one he used for work. There were still no roadblocks in place. Because of his postal route, Jones knew all the narrow byways around the Mount Carmel property. Daily copies of the *Tribune-Herald* were usually available at service stations accessible by Double Ee Ranch Road and Old Mexia Road. Jones drove in that direction.

• • •

At 8:30, Jim Peeler used his cell phone to call fellow KWTX camera-man Dan Mulloney, who was in his assigned place near the intersec-tion of FM 2491 and Double Ee Ranch Road. Peeler said that he was lost. Mulloney did his best to offer directions, but after they talked Peeler remained confused. He was still dithering on the side of Old Mexia Road when he saw a yellow Buick rumbling toward him. The car had "U.S. Mail" painted on the door. At that moment, no chance encounter could have been more welcomed by the TV cameraman, who was wearing a KWTX windbreaker. A mailman would surely know his way around the area.

David Jones pulled up behind Peeler's car and asked if there was a problem. Peeler poured out his frantic tale of being a TV cameraman and having to film this important raid at "Rodenville" that was about to happen and he'd tried and tried to find the place and could the mailman please help him figure out how to get there? Jones pointed toward Mount Carmel; portions of its roof were clearly visible. He and Peeler chatted a moment more. Peeler mentioned that there might be some gunfire involved. Then Jones got in his Buick, turned around, and rushed back to Mount Carmel.

Peeler retreated to his own car, and drove toward the intersection of Double Ee and Old Mexia Road. He'd been so close, and hadn't realized it. When Peeler arrived a few minutes later, he found that a roadblock had been set up by ATF agents and officers of the Texas Department of Public Safety. The TV cameraman parked nearby and got his equipment ready.

At approximately 8:45 a.m., David Jones parked beside the Branch Davidian building and rushed inside. In the front area of the massive facility, he saw David Koresh engaged in conversation with Robert "Gonzalez." Koresh, as usual, was doing most of the talking. A few Branch Davidians were also there. David Jones's father, Perry, was among them, and the son pulled his father away to whisper the ur-gent news: ATF was coming *now*. Perry Jones was alarmed. Koresh had to be informed immediately. But he was talking to "Gonzalez," who everyone knew was Babylon's spy. Both Joneses realized that "Gonzalez" shouldn't know that *they* knew.

So, Perry Jones went over to Koresh and said, "David, you've got a telephone call." The Mount Carmel phone was in a front room away from where Koresh and "Gonzalez" sat. David Jones could relay the news to his leader there without "Gonzalez" overhearing. But Koresh, deep into lecturing the ATF undercover agent about all the reasons that his biblical interpretations were superior to Marc Breault's, ignored Perry. The elder Jones tried again: "David, it's London, England, on the phone." That caught Koresh's attention; several of his British followers remained in America well past the exit date designated on their visas. Someone in England might be calling to warn about a problem with U.S. Immigration. Koresh excused himself to "Gonzalez" and went to the phone room. David Jones was waiting there, and filled him in.

The ATF undercover agent waited for several minutes. None of the other Branch Davidians engaged him in conversation while Koresh was away. Then Koresh came back, and Robert Rodriguez knew instantly that something had gone wrong. He testified later, "When he left [to take the supposed phone call], I mean, everything was as we always were, normal, talking, discussing the Bible. When he [Koresh] came back, he was just completely, I mean, he was nervous, he was shaking real bad." Koresh blurted to "Gonzalez" that "they got me once"—an apparent reference to his arrest in the 1987 Mount Carmel shootout with George Roden—"and they'll never get me again." The undercover agent saw "people in front of the door, people behind me, there was no place for me to go. . . . I quickly broke eye contact with him, I looked down toward the book [the Bible], and I said to myself, 'He knows. I need to get out.'"

Koresh went to one front window, then another, scanning the long driveway. He turned, still appearing shaken, and said, "They're coming, Robert. The time has come." Rodriguez remembers that "I needed to get out and advise my superiors of what was going on. . . . I was really trying to act as normal as I could. And there was [sic] people coming in toward the side where the door, the exit, was." The agent said to Koresh, "Well, David, I need to go. I need to meet somebody." Koresh repeated, "They're coming, Robert. They're coming." Rodriguez said, "I have to meet some people for breakfast." Branch Davidians kept arriving in the front compound area, gathering around, listening intently. The agent fleetingly wondered about the sniper team back at the undercover house, who were surely observing the building. Did they have any idea what was happening? Then Koresh abruptly turned to the agent, extended his hand to shake, and said, "Okay, Robert. Good luck." Rodriguez was so nervous that, afterward, he couldn't remember whether he opened the front door himself, or if a Branch Davidian stepped up and opened it for him.

Even outside, Rodriguez didn't feel safe. The Branch Davidians knew an attack was coming; if some of them already had their guns, they might shoot him as he walked to his car. He said later that the thirty feet between Mount Carmel's front door and his vehicle comprised the longest walk of his life. As he walked, he looked across Double Ee Ranch Road to the undercover house. To Rodriguez's horror, "all the windows [there] were open, you could see the cameras in there, and there was [sic] two snipers." If he could see all this, if any of the Davidians came outside and looked across the road, they could, too. But no one followed him outside. Rodriguez got into his car and drove a few hundred yards to the undercover house, where Jim Cavanaugh was waiting for him.

After hearing Rodriguez's blurted report, Cavanaugh advised him to call Chuck Sarabyn at the TSTC command post. Rodriguez made the call: "I told him. I said, 'Chuck, they know. They know.'" The undercover agent was stunned when Sarabyn responded by asking him if he had seen any guns, and what Koresh had been doing as Rodriguez left Mount Carmel.

Phil Lewis was standing near Sarabyn when he took Rodriguez's call. He remembers, "Robert was talking so loud that I heard his half of the conversation as well as Chuck's. The bottom line, the gist of it, it was very clear. Robert says, 'They know we are coming.' And Chuck is asking questions about that. Chuck hangs up, and he was just hyped. He put the phone down, he turned, he looked like he was going to run out the door. I grabbed him, saying, 'Chuck, what are you going to do?' I was hoping he'd say 'We'll have to think about this.' But he said, 'I think it'll be okay if we go quickly.' He ran out the door toward the helicopters."

Rodriguez wanted to reemphasize to Sarabyn that Koresh knew ATF was on its way; they'd be waiting when the cattle trailers full of agents arrived. The operation had to be called off. He got into his car and raced toward the TSTC command post: "I wanted to have a more lengthy conversation with him [Sarabyn] about the events."

Out on the TSTC runway, Sarabyn consulted with operation commander Phil Chojnacki, who was preparing to fly out to Mount Carmel and observe the raid from above in one of the three National Guard helicopters. The 'copters were warming up for the flights, and the roar of their rotors made conversation difficult. The ATF leaders moved about fifty feet away. Sarabyn told Chojnacki that Rodriguez reported that Koresh knew raiders were coming, but the undercover agent added that Koresh was shaking and reading the Bible. Based on what Rodriguez told him, Sarabyn said, Koresh wasn't ordering anyone in Mount Carmel to do anything to prepare for an assault. Chojnacki wanted to know if Rodriguez had seen any guns. Sarabyn said that he hadn't. Chojnacki asked Sarabyn's opinion of what should be done, and Sarabyn said that he believed the operation could still be executed successfully, if they hurried. Chojnacki replied, "Let's go." Sarabyn left for the Bellmead staging area. His discussion with Chojnacki lasted about three minutes.

Seven months later, the Treasury Department's report on the ATF's now notorious raid on Mount Carmel included speculation on why Chojnacki and Sarabyn allowed the operation to continue after they learned that the element of surprise was lost. Investigators concluded,

> A raid of the scope, expense, and logistical complexity contemplated by the planners of the Waco operation can generate a momentum that, if unchecked, can be inexorable. By the time Rodriguez left the Compound on Sunday morning and reported to Sarabyn, all was poised to go forward. . . . The [ATF] agents had been drawn from seven different ATF field divisions and 18 different cities, and could not be kept in the Waco area indefinitely. . . . No one associated with the venture could have doubted the fantastic cost and effort it would take if the operation were aborted or put off for another time.
>
> It is difficult to measure what effect the operation's built-in momentum may have had on the raid-day decision to go forward. . . . Decisions that now appear flawed may well not have been decisions at all, but simply steps taken along what seemed at the time to be a preordained road.
>
> . . . Neither Chojnacki or Sarabyn had any experience remotely comparable to the raid attempted on February 28. The bulk of their experience was with typical street enforcement actions. Nor had they had any meaningful training in operations of this magnitude, or any relevant military tactical experience that might have compensated for that lack of training. As a result, they were ill-prepared for the command of a large-scale, high-risk assault on a large, heavily-armed structure.

· · ·

At Mount Carmel, Kathy Schroeder, still in the kitchen, was instructed by someone to go to a meeting in the chapel. Koresh had said to. She remembers, "When I got there, I realized that there were only women present. We waited fifteen, maybe twenty minutes. Almost all the women were there. Some were reading the newspaper [with Sunday's "Sinful Messiah" stories]." Throughout the chaotic day, there would be repeated incidents of miscommunication among Branch Davidians, who were scattered throughout the sprawling compound. This was the first. Schroeder recalls, "David came in the room, and he stopped about halfway and said, 'What are y'all doing here?'"

Though Koresh had been shaken when he first learned that an attack was coming, he'd recovered control of himself. Schroeder says, "He [David] had a gun over his shoulder and a black vest on, a vest that was made to put [ammunition] magazines in. I believe it [the gun] was an AK-47. And then he said, 'Go back to your rooms, and watch.'" Many Branch Davidian adults had guns and ammunition in their rooms. Koresh was giving the women an order to take up their posts and prepare to fight.

Schroeder stopped back at the kitchen on her way to the first-floor room she shared with her four children. They were the only mother and kids living on the first floor; women and children on the second floor had complained that Schroeder and her brood were too sloppy with their slop buckets. On this morning, Schroeder had decided to let her kids sleep in while she made breakfast for everyone else. Now, she poured some bowls of oatmeal and took them back to her room. Schroeder woke the children and gave them their food. Though she was proud to have been assigned an AR-15 by Koresh, the weapon wasn't in her room because it had been "taken to be worked on," presumably converted from semi- to fully automatic.

The first-floor room assigned to Schroeder and her children faced out to the front of the compound, with a view of the driveway. The dog pen was just below and to the side. While her children ate, Schroeder took up a position by her window and watched, as David had instructed.

Sarabyn reached the Bellmead staging area at approximately 9:10 and informed the agents that the Branch Davidians knew they were coming, but that the raid could still be successful if they hurried. The cattle trailers left for Mount Carmel about fifteen minutes later.

• • •

Robert Rodriguez arrived at the TSTC command center. He jumped from his car and asked those he saw there, " 'Where's Chuck? Where's Chuck?' They advised me that he had left [for the raid staging area at Bellmead Civic Center]. At that time, I started yelling. . . . I was upset, because they were continuing with the raid, because I knew what was going to happen." Rodriguez apparently reached the TSTC command post just after Sarabyn arrived at the Bellmead Civic Center staging area and ordered the agents waiting there into the cattle trailers. Rodriguez testified later that he shouted, "'Why, why, why? They know we're coming.' If I remember right, everybody was really concerned." But their concern didn't help: "I went outside and I sat down, and I remember starting to cry."

Tribune-Herald photographer Rod Aydelotte and reporters Tommy Witherspoon and Marc Masferrer turned onto Double Ee Ranch Road around 9:30 a.m. They were surprised not to have encountered any roadblocks. Aydelotte guided his car past Mount Carmel—no one seemed to be outside. It was eerily quiet. The three journalists needed a place where they could set up to observe and photograph the arrest they presumed was coming anytime. Two convenient houses were just across Double Ee from the compound. Witherspoon suggested that Aydelotte pull into one of the driveways; they'd ask the people inside if they'd seen anything going on at the compound, and whether the *Tribune-Herald* staffers could park in their driveway and cover the Mount Carmel raid from there. Aydelotte picked one and turned in. Only later would the journalists realize that they had just parked in the driveway of ATF's undercover house.

KWTX cameraman Dan Mulloney was parked about a mile from the intersection of FM 2941 and Double Ee Ranch Road, the best route from Bellmead Civic Center to Mount Carmel. At about 9:35 a.m. he saw two cattle trailers pulled by pickup trucks approaching. The interiors of the trailers were concealed on top by tarps and along the sides by plywood, but the views through their back gates weren't entirely blocked. Mulloney jumped into his car and followed the trailers. He could see, through the cover gap in the back gate of the second trailer, someone wearing a vest and combat helmet. Mulloney waved, and the geared-up individual waved back. Mulloney followed the trailers by "about twelve to fifteen car lengths" as they made the left turn onto Double Ee Ranch Road.

At 9:40 a.m., Witherspoon climbed out of Aydelotte's car, walked up to the door of the house across the road from Mount Carmel, and knocked. He recalls, "A guy opened it, and I say, 'We understand that a possible news event might be occurring,' and before I can say anything more, he yells, 'Just get the fuck out of here!' So, I go back to the car, and we back out of the driveway, and Rod, the photographer, starts to drive [down Double Ee]. The front passenger side of his car, where I was sitting, was the side of the car toward the [Branch Davidian] compound. I looked back over my shoulder and saw the cattle trailers coming, and I yelled, 'Here they come, Rod!' Then the helicopters came up from our left, and the cattle trailers went up the driveway.

"And then it all exploded at once."

The Raid—Early Moments

I t's impossible for participants in gun battles to be objective about them afterward. Their memories are skewed. They attempted to shoot people who tried to shoot them. Those who lived may have friends or loved ones or, at least, comrades-in-arms who died. When survivors in such events offer their personal recollections—during subsequent trials, through interviews with the media, on the pages of memoirs written after the fact—even the most honest are telling the truth only as they remember it. When there are survivors on both sides, discrepancies inevitably center on specific moments. In the case of the ATF raid on Mount Carmel on the morning of Sunday, February 28, 1993, there's absolute disagreement from surviving participants on two key points. One version must be completely wrong. Three decades later, remaining ATF agents and Branch Davidians still disagree about critical elements at the beginning of their bloody struggle that morning. Their conflicting memories reflect immutable enmity. Neither side in any way forgives the other.

The controversy begins, as it almost inevitably must, with who fired first.

Kathy Schroeder remembers that, about 9:45 that morning, she was still watching out the window of her first-floor room at Mount Carmel. Trusting David, certain that Babylon's attack was imminent because he said so, she told her four children to put on their shoes in case they had to run. The words were hardly out of her mouth when she saw two "cattle cars" pulling up outside the front of the compound: "My room was behind where the dogs were in the pen. The first shots that day were when they [ATF agents] shot the dogs. I'm sure of it. Just a few shots and yips from the dogs. Then, after that, there was a lot of shooting. My gun was being worked on, so I didn't shoot. I told my kids to hide under their bunk beds. I ducked down."

ATF agents agree that the dogs were shot, but not until the Branch Davidians fired first. In their memories, no shots were yet fired when the first few agents from Cattle Trailer #2 called out to announce themselves at the compound's front double doors. These doors opened, and David Koresh appeared. "What's going on?" he asked, grinned "weirdly," and slammed the doors shut. A fusillade of gunfire erupted through the doors, spraying out at the men in front of them. One of the agents was hit on the thumb. Most of the other agents, still descending from the trailers, were also engulfed in fire from the compound. These shots were coming all along the first and second floors, from windows facing the front of the building. Sam Cohen, stuck in the pack struggling to exit Trailer #2, recalls "[bullet] holes start[ed] appearing in the canvas on top of the trailer. You could hear the rounds hitting the metal poles along the sides. I was, like, trying to move down a fatal funnel, thirty of us trying to get out in one small area. Mike Russell right in front of me stepped out and took a bullet through the trap[ezius] muscle." The agents who'd briefly glimpsed Koresh vividly recall that when the Branch Davidians' bullets plowed through the front doors, which were metal with Styrofoam insulation, "Styrofoam streamers" and "white, flakey paint" pattered down around them "like a snowstorm."

Some surviving Branch Davidians insist that ATF agents were the first to fire, and their initial target was David Koresh. "I remember, the last thing before they [ATF] started shooting, David telling us, 'Everybody stay calm,'" David Thibodeau says. "He wanted to get it resolved." Thibodeau and Clive Doyle both insist in their memoirs that the agents fired first, at Koresh. Thibodeau wrote later that Koresh opened the door and essentially pleaded with the agents not to shoot, yelling, "There are women and children in here!" Only after their leader was fired upon, Thibodeau wrote, "the general feeling among other survivors . . . is that several people simply returned the ATF's barrage of bullets in the shock of the moment, in a natural impulse of self-defense provoked by the unexpected brutality of ATF's assault."

Mike Russell says there's obvious proof that the Branch Davidians opened fire when Koresh appeared at the front double doors and momentarily faced ATF agents: "If we had fired first at the front door while he was standing there, we had marksmen. He [Koresh] would have been killed right there."

Several members of the media, eyewitnesses that morning who were not aligned with either ATF or the Branch Davidians, are unequivocal: the Branch Davidians fired first. Tommy Witherspoon, huddling with his *Tribune-Herald* colleagues in a Double Ee roadside ditch across from the compound, says, "The firing started from the compound at the ATF." Fellow reporter Marc Masferrer testified later, "I believe the firing started inside the building, from the building." KWTX cameraman Dan Mulloney, who trailed the two cattle trailers in his car all the way up the Mount Carmel driveway, testified that "In my opinion, the gunfire originated from the compound."

What all agree on is that the front compound doors slammed shut, and a gun battle lasting almost two hours commenced.

The next point of irreconcilable contention involves the helicopters.

At 9:29 a.m., three National Guard helicopters lifted off from the ATF command center runway. The helicopter fleet consisted of a Black Hawk UH-60, carrying five ATF agents, including Davy Aguilera and Dallas special agent in charge Ted Royster. It was accompanied by two smaller UH-58 models. ATF operation commander Phil Chojnacki, the ATF agent in command of the operation, was a passenger in one of the UH-58s. They were supposed to arrive at Mount Carmel just before the two cattle trailers, and divert the Branch Davidians' attention from their property's driveway by making a few passes above and behind the compound. But their timing was off;

Tribune-Herald reporter Witherspoon saw the helicopters and cattle trailers arrive simultaneously. There is no disagreement that as the helicopters approached Mount Carmel, they took fire from Branch Davidians shooting from upper floors of the compound, and from a platform high up its water tower. When they were still several hundred yards away, the big Black Hawk and both UH-58s were hit, one more severely than the other.

The National Guard pilots at their controls testified later that none of the helicopters were armed with mounted guns, or had on board any guns capable of accurate fire at the compound from that distance. They were certain that there was no return fire from their aircrafts. The six ATF agents—five in the Black Hawk, Chojnacki in one of the damaged UH-58s—had no weapons other than sidearms, which lacked the power to inflict even minimal damage at that great range. Blake Boteler observes, "The six ATF agents on the helicopters, they were what we called 'empty holsters,' not part of tactical teams, just there as observers. Not one was SRT [a specially trained member of an ATF Special Response Team]. If we were going to fly and rake the compound [with gunfire] from above, we would have had SRTs up there." Rather than machine gun barrels, all that protruded from any of the helicopters was one cameraman dangling from a banana sling, unsuccessfully attempting to film the raid.

By National Guard and ATF accounts, two of the damaged helicopters turned immediately and made emergency landings in a field behind the Branch Davidian property. The third helicopter, Treasury Department investigators reported, "circled overhead to watch for additional attackers." Then it, too, landed in the field, where Chojnacki prevailed on its pilot to fly him back to command headquarters.

Surviving Branch Davidians vehemently disagree. Thibodeau says, "The roof of our tower was just riddled, and you could tell from the holes that the bullets came from above, little bits of stuff dangled inside." Weeks later, when Koresh hired prominent Texas attorney Dick DeGuerin, the Houston lawyer, after being allowed to enter the compound, viewed the damaged roof. Almost thirty years later,

DeGuerin declares, "There is no doubt. They [the Branch Davidi-ans] were fired upon from the air. There were many [bullet] holes." Immediately following the raid, some Davidians told others inside the compound that they'd seen a helicopter hovering directly over-head and firing. Survivors still allege that one of the five Branch Davidians who died that morning, possibly two, were killed by fire from a helicopter. Just over seven weeks later, when Texas Rangers scoured the Mount Carmel property for physical evidence of all that had occurred, its preserved roof would have been handy proof one way or the other whether one of the three-helicopter fleet barraged defenders from above. But the roof, as well as most of the rest of the compound, had by then been obliterated by fire and bulldozers. No evidence remained to prove what the helicopters did or didn't do— only conflicting memories.

Who fired first, and what did the helicopters do? These disputed el-ements of the gun battle happened in the very first few minutes. But both sides generally agree on all that occurred after that, except for a moral as well as legal question: During the next two hours, who com-mitted murder, and who killed in justified self-defense?

The Price of Prophecy

Gunfire from Mount Carmel didn't slacken after the front doors slammed shut. Most of the ATF agents who'd exited the cattle trailers took what cover they could find, and there wasn't much—the pickup trucks used to pull the trailers, the Branch Davidians' cars and vans parked in front of the compound, the hulk of an old air-conditioning unit abandoned near the building. Some of the agents were only a few yards from the windows where defenders fired at close range. A few of these agents crawled up against the base of the building itself; when they glanced up, they could see gun barrels belching bullets from directly overhead.

Initially the Branch Davidians felt thrilled, even empowered. Kathy Schroeder, crouched down in her first-floor room, says that "when the agents were outside our door, the Seventh Seal finally came alive for me. The prophecies were being fulfilled. This was just another phase of it." After years of teaching and preparation, the forces of the Lamb were clashing with Babylon. David Koresh was right all along. Their fierce joy was demonstrated by their shooting positions, flush against window frames, guns protruding out as they fired waves of bullets. At last, the great moment had come. Then another portion of Koresh's prophecy became evident. The Branch Davidians were fighting as he'd foretold, but there was also the matter of them having to die.

Above the compound, Charlie Short and Eddie Pali circled in their small, two-engine plane. They'd remained after the helicopters retreated. It was frustrating. They had no guns to provide covering fire for their embattled comrades below. Short recalls, "It was still cold and rainy. There were clouds. When I looked down right at the beginning, it looked like Christmas lights on the front of the compound, [from] the explosions of the guns sticking out. But then that stopped; whoever was shooting from inside backed away from the windows. They kept shooting, but I couldn't see the flashes anymore." Agent Mike Russell says, "They made one mistake, a thing that surprises me they did not realize in their training. It looked like they set up by saying, 'You take this window, and you take this window.' But if you stand right at the front of a window, you make yourself a target. So, they learned quick to back away from the windows while they were shooting."

Once they were behind even minimal cover, the ATF agents began shooting back. Six had powerful AR-15 rifles; these weapons had been requested for all of the SRTs, but agency leadership allowed only a half dozen. Many of the agents wielded lower-power MP5s; a few had shotguns, others just their handguns. But they were well-trained marksmen, the SRTs especially, and they returned fire at the windows. It was hard to see individual targets—afterward, several agents would say that they never, in the course of the long fight, saw the entire body of a single Branch Davidian. Instead, there were brief glimpses of arms or hands or faces, nothing more. The agents guessed from muzzle flashes where shooters stood and fired through the windows there. That backed the defenders up, but they kept firing.

The Branch Davidians' stock of ammunition was virtually inexhaustible. Within minutes, many of the ATF agents had expended most of the limited magazines they brought on the raid. Some veterans began shouting for everyone to save some ammunition; the Branch Davidians might pour from the building in an attempt to overrun them. It was hard for the agents to hear each other above the roar of defender gunfire, the crackling of their own radios, and the penetrating hum of Charlie Short repeatedly flying low over the compound. He was making a desperate effort to draw the fire of at least some Branch Davidians who were shooting at the agents on the ground. A few SRT team leaders, still in touch by radio with Jim Cavanaugh in the undercover house, pleaded with him to call Short off—his well-meaning effort was only adding to the confusion. For the moment, Phil Chojnacki and Chuck Sarabyn weren't in any position to offer leadership. Chojnacki was still in an adjacent field with the downed helicopters, and Sarabyn, who'd ridden in Trailer #1, was pinned down like everyone else.

Agents close to the building were not only ducking bullets, they were being sprayed by shrapnel from exploding hand grenades dropped or tossed out of windows. Jerry Petrilli and Sam Cohen suffered numerous wounds from the grenades, though none were debilitating. Eric Evers was hit by gunfire five times, in the arm, side, chest, and back, and somehow survived. Carla Bell, sheltering with several other agents behind a battered white van, recalls that the ground "seemed like it was jumping, from all the bullets hitting it." Even in the midst of battle, some agents retained a sense of humor. Claire Rayburn leaned from cover to fire at a window, and was shot through a finger. She later said that she inspected her mangled digit and thought, *I won't be getting that one manicured anymore.* There was no humor to be found in the fate of agent Steve Willis. He was shot through the head and fell dead beside a car. Looking down from his plane, Charlie Short saw Willis, his friend and occasional copilot, looking "like a dead deer, with his head blown away."

But the defenders were taking casualties, too. The first was especially unsettling. Koresh had escaped injury from ATF bullets through the front doors, but Perry Jones wasn't so lucky. Clive Doyle, running down a compound front hall, saw Jones "crawling on his hands and knees, screaming that he had been shot." It was an abdominal wound; when Doyle and another Branch Davidian dragged Jones to a back room, the old man screeched in agony. He begged Doyle, or anyone, to shoot him and end his suffering. Jones's loud cries added to the din. There was nothing immediately to be done for him; Doyle left him, only to be told by someone else that Winston Blake was shot.

Doyle hurried to Blake's room and saw his slumped body: "The carpet was wringing wet, and there was blood everywhere. I knelt down and tried to find a pulse on his neck, but I could not find one."

Branch Davidian women and children lived on the facility's second floor. Often, to prevent individual room overcrowding, some children slept in rooms with women who were not their mothers. Nine-year-old Heather Jones shared a room with Judy Schneider and infant Mayanah, Judy's daughter by David Koresh. When the gun battle erupted, Heather and Mayanah, as the group had practiced, rolled themselves up in a mattress. As Heather peeked out from this rudimentary shelter, she saw Judy take a rifle and begin firing out the window. But Judy leaned too far, and an ATF bullet plowed into her hand. She shrieked and dropped her gun.

Dying for God was excruciating. If the Branch Davidians had hoped to put up a good fight, then somehow be painlessly "translated" to await the return of the Lamb and Jesus, they were disabused of that fanciful notion. But most kept fighting and, much to the ATF agents' dismay, unlimbered a weapon even more fearsome than the illegally converted, fully automatic firearms.

Pride of place among the Branch Davidians' extensive arsenal was held by a Barrett .50 caliber rifle. Kathy Schroeder remembers David "bringing it out in a Bible study and showing it to everybody. He called it 'the Bear,' and said it had armor-piercing bullets." The Barrett was only semiautomatic, but that was plenty. It had the power to fire its chunky bullets through almost anything.

Many of the ATF agents sheltered behind cars; whenever possible, they crawled behind the front areas containing engines, because they'd been taught that the engine blocks inside could stop almost any bullet. But not one from the Barrett. The first time that mighty weapon boomed, loud and distinct above the rest of the battle noise, the agents realized that every one of them was now vulnerable. Even the sound of the Barrett being fired was demoralizing. Sam Cohen recalls, "The only thing I can compare it to is a big bass drum in a Fourth of July parade, how, when it's pounded, you feel the reverberations in your chest." Blake Boteler remembers a near miss: "It felt like somebody slapped me in the face, just the pressure as a bullet [from the Barrett] rushed by and hit the ground. That ground was hardpacked caliche. That bullet from the Barrett blew a hole the size of a cantaloupe. The Barrett shots came in five-round bursts, KLUNG-KLUNG-KLUNG-KLUNG-KLUNG. They hit the cars, and chunks of engines flew off and tore into agents' legs." Mike Duncan says succinctly, "Talk about a morale-sucker." But inside Mount Carmel, the morale of at least one Branch Davidian was sagging to the brink of hysteria. As tapes reveal, he panicked as soon as bullets began flying.

At 9:48 a.m., within minutes of the first shots, Branch Davidian Wayne Martin used the phone in his first-floor office in the building to call 911. He shrieked to the operator, "There are seventy-five men around our building shooting at us!" Gunfire was clearly audible in the background. The number on the operator's screen indicated the message originated from Mount Carmel. The operator transferred the call to McLennan County sheriff's office deputy Larry Lynch, who was on duty. Lynch muttered, "God almighty, that fuckin' newspaper," immediately assuming the *Tribune-Herald* articles were responsible for whatever was happening. Lynch instructed the operator to inform his department leaders that he had Mount Carmel on the line. Martin put down his phone for several minutes, then picked it up and screamed, "Tell them to fall back, we got women and children in danger! Call them off! We're under fire," hardly the tone or words of someone gladly dying at the hands of the forces of Babylon as foretold by David Koresh and the Book of Revelation.

Lynch had no formal training as a negotiator, but he proved himself instinctively adept. In a soothing voice, he advised, "Do you have weapons in there? Cease fire, do not fire anymore." Martin, somewhat calmer but still shouting, replied, "I have a right to defend myself! They fired first! They're still attacking! There's a chopper with more guns going off!" Lynch could hear many guns. He asked, "Who's firing now?" and Martin replied, "They are." Lynch said, "Don't return fire," and Martin said, "We haven't been." A moment later the Branch Davidian attorney yelled again, "Tell them to back off!" Lynch muttered to himself, "I can't believe this." He attempted to keep Martin on the line while operators tried to link up a call with ATF, at both the agency's TSTC command center and the undercover house. It might still be possible to get everybody calmed down, and stop this thing before it got worse.

But on the east side of the compound, it was already worse.

Teams of agents from ATF's New Orleans division were tasked with scaling ladders to the roof, entering and controlling Koresh's bedroom and the gunroom from there. The presumption that all of Mount Carmel's guns were kept in the gunroom was based on information from former Branch Davidians who left Carmel before Koresh passed out many of the guns for followers to keep in their rooms. Four agents were assigned to breach the bedroom, and three the gunroom. While other agents on the ground had all they could do to find cover as the Branch Davidians opened fire, these agents had to lug ladders and special break-and-rake equipment as they dodged bullets and hustled as quickly as possible around the east side of the building. Co-team leaders Kenny King and Bill Buford led these ladder contingents; King had agents Conway LeBleu, David Millen, and Todd McKeehan. Buford's team included Keith Constantino and Glen Jordan. Both teams managed to reach the east side of the building and put their ladders in place.

LeBleu was the first of the King team up its ladder; as soon as he reached the roof, he raised his shotgun to provide cover for the three behind him. Millen approached Koresh's bedroom window and performed break and rake, but as he did, rifle fire exploded from inside the room and King was hit four times and badly wounded. McKeehan was hit once in the chest and died instantly. His body lay motionless on the roof. Millen rolled away to join LeBleu; they began firing at a Branch Davidian gunman up in the Mount Carmel water tower. King, terribly wounded, tried to reach McKeehan, but before he could he was hit twice more and rolled off the roof, bouncing hard into a courtyard toward the rear of the compound. He was so close to the building that defenders there could not see him. Using his one hand that still functioned, King flicked on his radio and hissed that he was bleeding badly and needed medical help to have any chance of survival. But the Branch Davidians' fire prevented any of the ATF medics from coming to his aid. King lay there bleeding for almost two more hours.

Millen and LeBleu remained on the roof, trying to provide cover for Buford's team, who had been able to break the gunroom window and crawl inside. There they saw lengthy wooden gun racks with a few rifles stored on them. Though they didn't know it, much earlier that morning Paul Fatta had gathered most of the guns in those racks and taken them to sell at the gun show in Austin. A Branch Davidian was in the doorway as they entered; they fired and he disappeared. But shots began raining in on them through the gunroom walls, which were so thin that they were easy for bullets to penetrate. The agents shot back; both sides were firing blind, but there were more Davidians and fully automatic guns bombarding the agents than there were agents firing back. Jordan and Buford were both hit several times. Constantino stayed in the room, providing cover fire as the other two agents crawled out the window and tumbled down below.

Constantino had a chance to shoot at a Branch Davidian he could see in the doorway; the agent hesitated momentarily before firing because he thought the figure lurching toward him might be a member of King's team, who had perhaps secured Koresh's bedroom and now was coming to help the Buford team. But it was Branch Davidian Scott Sonobe; both men fired. Sonobe was hit and staggered out of the gunroom. Bullets still smashed in through the walls. With Jordan and Buford out and, hopefully, down safely, Constantino tried to dive through the window to the roof, but cracked his head on the window frame. Stunned, he slipped on the rain-slicked roof and slid over the edge, falling hard, breaking his hip, and causing severe damage to his pelvis and legs. Millen was able to safely descend by ladder. LeBleu, choosing to go last, continued providing covering fire. Branch Davidian bullets cut him down, and he fell dead near McKeehan's corpse on the roof.

Kris Mayfield remembers the fourth ATF death: "I saw Robert Williams killed. He had his MP5 up, I distinctly remember there had been no shooting for maybe two seconds and then there was a *ka-boom*, not the .50 caliber, but a high-caliber, and Robert just falls back." When Mayfield tried to reach Williams, he recalls that when he stepped on grass beside the body, "there was a squish that came from all the blood."

Martin remained on the phone with Lynch. At one point, David Koresh got on the line. His voice was steady as he informed the lieutenant, "We've known about this. I've been teaching about it for four years. We knew you were coming and everything." To Koresh, the ATF and the McLennan County sheriff's department were all part of the same Babylon force. He added, "You see, we knew before you knew." When Koresh began citing biblical references, Lynch asked him to stop talking theology and focus on practical matters. Koresh responded, "Theology really is life and death." Lynch countered, "Let's remain as calm as we can." He repeatedly suggested a cease-fire. Koresh was willing to think about it. And, while he did, there were more deaths.

Peter Gent was the sniper in the water tower. Besides whoever was firing the Barrett .50 caliber, Gent was the pinned-down ATF agents' main nemesis. Those agents closest to the compound were actually safest from first-floor fire; the fence in front was high enough to provide extra protection, and the angle of fire toward them from the first floor was tricky. But Gent had superb firing angles. Several agents tried to pick him off, but they had to rise up, fire, and immediately duck before they could be hit by return fire from Gent or from inside the compound. Finally, Gent was hit, and toppled inside the water tower out of sight. Several agents initially claimed credit, but consensus was later reached that Gent was killed by agent Lowell Sprague. It would be several days before the rest of the Branch Davidians knew for certain that Gent was dead. They didn't risk climbing up the water tower, and thought for a time that he might have somehow escaped during the firefight.

ATF snipers in the undercover house across Double Ee Ranch Road also took aim at the Branch Davidians. Unlike the agents pinned near the front of the massive building, who had to shoot up a slope, the ATF snipers could fire almost on a line from their windows into the windows of Mount Carmel. That helped drive the Branch Davidians back from the windows. One who kept leaning out was Jaydean Wendell. Formerly a policewoman in Hawaii, she wrapped her children in mattresses in her second-floor room and then sent out volleys of shots from her window at the ATF agents on the ground below. Like Judy Schneider, she leaned out too far, but unlike Judy, she was killed rather than wounded. Her body sprawled near the window. Her children stayed huddled in their mattresses.

Peter Hipsman, somewhere on an upper floor, was hit in the side by a bullet that did extensive internal damage. Like Perry Jones, Hipsman writhed in agony. He begged someone to put him out of his misery. That couldn't be done without David Koresh's permission— and Koresh was badly wounded, too.

Over the years, it's been widely accepted that David Koresh was shot when he briefly opened the front doors of Mount Carmel and confronted ATF agents. That wasn't the case. Perry Jones, standing as usual near David, was hit by ATF fire, but his leader wasn't struck. During the ensuing fight, the next conclusive sighting of Koresh came when he spoke with Larry Lynch, using a cell phone rather than the phone in Wayne Martin's first-floor office. But Koresh still had his rifle, still wore his protective vest, and, apparently, he roamed the halls and floors of the compound. If few of his followers saw him, that was because many were preoccupied firing at the ATF agents from their windows.

About forty-five minutes after the first shots were fired, two ATF agents, Charles Smith and Charles Giarrusso, managed to enter the back portion of Mount Carmel on the first floor. Branch Davidians, nearby but out of sight, were firing out at the ATF, but at least for the moment they hadn't seen Smith and Giarrusso, who were supposed to link up with King's and Buford's squads after they'd secured the gun-room and Koresh's bedroom. Instead, they saw the two ladder squads violently repulsed, and McKeehan and LeBleu killed. Both bodies lay on the roof.

Suddenly, there was movement on the catwalk above the floor where Smith and Giarrusso stood. The first shouts of "Cease fire!" began to echo around the Mount Carmel halls as, the two agents later reported, whoever was on the catwalk fired down at them. They returned fire, and their assailant, whom they did not see clearly, dropped. Koresh was shot through his left side by a bullet that chipped his hip bone. That shot or a second one also hit his right thumb and wrist. Koresh said later that he never fired at the agents. No matter who fired when, the Branch Davidian leader was severely wounded. He crawled away as both his followers and attackers received word that they should stand down.

ATF agents, and later agents of the FBI, mistakenly believed that, at any time inside Mount Carmel, David Koresh could issue a command and all his followers would instantly obey. That was rarely possible; the Mount Carmel facility was simply too sprawling. Even on ordinary days, it took time for instructions about anything to reach every Branch Davidian, many of whom would be hard at tasks in the far reaches of the building. It was impossible to achieve full, instant compliance on the morning of the ATF raid. Defenders were scattered everywhere, including the underground passages to the buried school bus and massive pit. When Wayne Martin, Steve Schneider, and Lieutenant Larry Lynch reached agreement that everyone should put down their guns, ATF agents immediately were informed on their radios. Most heaved sighs of relief, and moved to tend to their wounded and dead. But inside Mount Carmel, shouting messengers running down halls had to spread the word, and many of the Branch Davidians, half deafened from the concussive gunfire and reeling emotionally, either didn't hear or were too distracted to comprehend what they were being told.

When ATF agents stood up, shots were fired at them. The agents immediately assumed that the cease-fire was a Branch Davidian trick to make the agents show themselves, then mow them down. They took cover again, some fired back, and Branch Davidians inside and ATF agents outside began shouting imprecations and obscenity-laced commands: "Leave us the fuck alone!" "Get the fuck outside without your guns!" There was very little distance between assailants. Both sides mistrusted the other.

Full-scale firing resumed. ATF medics gallantly risked their lives ministering to fallen agents, even when the wounded lay out in the open. Medics Tim Gabourie and Ken Chisholm rigged IVs and plugged wounds with whatever materials they had on hand. They also directed other ATF agents to offer emergency care, calling out instructions even as they performed their own ministrations. Gabourie, especially, put his life on the line, dashing some forty yards without cover to reach a badly wounded agent. As he ran, he was targeted with the .50 caliber Barrett, and one of that gun's heavy bullets smashed the medical bag out of his hand. He grabbed what he could and kept going. While administering first aid to one agent, Gabourie also tossed gauze bandages, an IV bottle, and a thermal blanket to Guillermo Gallegos, who was tending to fallen Larry Shiver, wounded in the left thigh. Gallegos covered Shiver's body with his own, and whispered, "Larry, you'll be the first one on the ambulance when it comes, but you gotta hang with me."

The scene was just as grim inside Mount Carmel. Both Perry Jones and Peter Hipsman were gravely wounded, and pleading to be put out of their misery. Medical supplies inside the compound were scant. During the first cease-fire, David Thibodeau came upon Koresh propped against a wall in an upper-floor hallway. Koresh said, "This fed jumped up out of the blue, firing from the hip. A bullet spun me all the way around, like a 250-pound man kicking you in the side. I was getting numb, but I managed to crawl away." Koresh thought he was dying, and the followers gathering around him thought so, too. But while Koresh lived, he was still in charge.

The cease-fire hadn't held, and something needed to be done about that. Kathy Schroeder says, "I remember being in front of David when Neil Vaega came and asked permission to finish Perry off, and David didn't answer and Neil left. I was still there when he [Neil] came back a second time and asked again, and I don't remember whether David answered him or not. All I know is, he [Neil] came back a third time, and said it had been done. Neil told me that Peter [Hipsman] had been shot on the third floor, fourth floor, the top floor of the tower, somewhere, and he had an abdomen wound, and he was also shot in the head, but he was still alive, and he [Neil] finished him off, and I think he said it took two shots to finish him off."

A second cease-fire was negotiated. That one fell apart, too, for the same reason. Kathy Schroeder remembers "people yelling up and down the halls," trying to spread the word. A few Branch Davidians inside Mount Carmel either still didn't hear, or were too caught up in the struggle to stop shooting. ATF agents were all perilously close to running out of ammunition. Weeks later, Texas Rangers assigned to Waco as outside observers and investigators estimated that, on February 28, the Branch Davidians fired anywhere from 12,000 to 15,000 rounds, to ATF's 1,500. After the second failed cease-fire, Carla Bell remembers thinking she and other agents would escape with their lives only if the government sent tanks to rescue them. There was a pond nearby on the property. She watched rounds skipping off the water and wondered if she could reach the pond without being cut down. To make room for other agents behind the white van they used for cover from Mount Carmel gunfire, Bell and another female agent got inside the vehicle. Someone had been living in it: "There were school-like lockers, and jugs of urine. Afterward somebody also found a machine gun, though we didn't see it. They had the .50 caliber that they were using [inside Mount Carmel], and they fired it at us, but they kept aiming too high." There was a tree behind the van; by morning's end, it was reduced to splinters.

At 11:39 a.m., a third cease-fire was arranged, and this one held. ATF agents who were unhurt began helping their wounded to move away from the building. Some had to be carried. County ambulance drivers refused to bring their ambulances onto the property; agent Davy Aguilera took the wheel of one and steered it along the Mount Carmel driveway. KWTX cameraman Dan Mulloney contributed the pickup he'd driven in behind the cattle trailers. Those trailers, and the trucks that pulled them, were too perforated with bullet holes to be of further use.

The ATF casualty count was four dead and sixteen wounded, totaling more than a quarter of the seventy-six agents who'd ridden the trailers in. Those still able to walk had to make their way a few hundred yards to Double Ee Ranch Road while wondering if any trigger-happy Branch Davidians would shoot them in the back. Agent Dave DiBetta wrote later, "There was no leadership at all. . . . We got to the main road looking like a defeated army." Department of Public Safety officers who'd been manning the FM 2491–Double Ee intersection covered the bodies of the four dead agents with their raincoats. But as a helicopter swooped down to convey the most badly wounded to a local hospital, the wind from its rotors blew the raincoats off. Blake Boteler recalls, "There was blood all over where we walked back down Double Ee Road. It was a surreal deal."

Witherspoon, still on the job as a journalist, "fell in with some of the ATF agents. . . . One was a woman wearing riot gear. I said to her, 'Tell me about it,' and another agent, a guy, bumps me with his shoulder and says, 'Come on, man, can't you see we've been through it?'" That relatively gentle brush-off was better than the agents' reaction to TV cameraman Dan Mulloney. McLennan County sheriff Jack Harwell shouted, "You never should have been here in the first place; get out of here," at him, and Mulloney recalled being "physically and verbally abused," then knocked to the ground by some retreating ATF agents.

Most of the agents thought they'd go back to the staging area, rest and rearm, then return to Mount Carmel. The Branch Davidians thought so, too, especially after agent Wade Brown turned to face the building, raised his arms, and shouted, "We're coming back." They were just as shell-shocked as the ATF agents, and with added reason. The Branch Davidians had long anticipated that their battle with Babylon would end with them all being translated from life to death, ready to await the triumphant return of the Lamb to lead them again. Instead, they were still inside Mount Carmel, with Babylon's army apparently determined to come back for more. The survivors inside considered their five dead to be lucky. Kathy Schroeder says, "Coming out of my room after the cease-fire—I don't know that there was any 'You can come out now' general announcement—I saw Jaydean's body because I was supposed to get her gun, and then I had to clean her blood off the gun. She had three kids and a baby, and now those kids had no mom. I was sad for her children, but happy for her, because she'd done as God commanded."

Four Davidians—David Koresh, David Jones, Judy Schneider, and Scott Sonobe—were wounded. Larry Lynch had spent much of the third cease-fire on the telephone, asking Wayne Martin to tell everyone inside Mount Carmel to relax, to take deep breaths. Now, with the shooting over and ATF safely across Double Ee Ranch Road, he asked the lawyer, "Let us know what we can start doing for your wounded, okay? Do you need any medical supplies that we could send in?" There were murmurs on the other end of the line; then Martin said, "We don't want anything from your country. That's what our wounded are telling us. They don't want your help."

All the blood and death of the morning were, apparently, preliminary. The Branch Davidians and ATF agents were ready for more.

The Raid—Aftermath

A s the ATF agents retreated down Double Ee Ranch Road, the Branch Davidians inside Mount Carmel did their best to regroup. There was a brief sense of triumph—they'd beaten Babylon back!—but that was quickly tempered by certainty that their foe would return. Clive Doyle wrote, "Our feeling after the ATF agents left the immediate proximity of the building was that we were in for it; they were going to come back in force, probably that night. . . . So, word was passed around that we needed to be vigilant."

Kathy Schroeder was asked to go to the kitchen and bring back some Cokes for the weary defenders. While fetching the drinks, she saw ammunition boxes scattered around the cafeteria, and a crate of grenades on the serving counter. Sharing the general consensus that ATF was coming back, she also visited the adjacent, concrete-walled storage room where some guns and most grenades and ammunition were kept and took an AR-15 for herself. She didn't want to be unarmed when ATF attacked a second time.

By the time the soft drinks were consumed, any elation was entirely replaced by two critical concerns. First was Koresh's condition. It was assumed he was dying, the Lamb fulfilling his spiritual destiny by succumbing at the hands of Babylon's forces before returning at the head of a holy army to defeat them forever. David Thibodeau wrote, "He [Koresh] lay on blankets in the hallway upstairs. . . . He was now shaking and semi-conscious, moving in and out of pain, his eyes rolling up into his head. He was deathly pale, and his glasses were misty with fevered sweat." Koresh certainly expected to expire.

He was helped to the telephone and left a message on his mother's answering machine: "Hello, Momma. It's your boy. They shot me and I'm dying, all right? But I'll be back real soon, okay? I'm sorry you didn't learn the Seals, but I'll be merciful, okay? I'll see y'all in the skies."

Then a few hours passed, and he didn't die. There had to be a reason, and when some of his followers asked why only a few of the Mount Carmel defenders had died so far, Koresh said it was the Lord's Will: "Nobody else has to die. God said this is enough." This explanation fit neatly with Revelation 6:9–11, which foretold that, in the initial battle with Babylon, the souls of those first slain would rest beneath an altar "for a little season, until their fellow servants also and their brethren, that should be killed as they were, should be fulfilled." The rest of the Branch Davidians at Mount Carmel were still going to die at Babylon's hands, just not yet. And until God revealed it to him, Koresh couldn't tell when "yet" might be.

Mount Carmel had several phone lines, none especially reliable. Compound pets had a habit of chewing on the wires, and even when the wires were relatively intact, phone service there was spotty. During the early afternoon of February 28, though, the phones operated efficiently. Steve Schneider spoke with ATF agents at the TSTC command post, and notes on the call kept by the agents reported, "All calm, positive negotiations." That wasn't the case as Wayne Martin continued his diatribes to Larry Lynch, claiming at one point that the ATF raid on Mount Carmel was similar to the botched, murderous federal actions at Ruby Ridge, where a mother and her son were killed by federal officers. There was also a moment of afternoon panic at the compound, when helicopters began circling overhead. The Branch Davidians assumed it was another fleet of ATF gunners. In fact, they were helicopters from TV stations maneuvering for close-ups. It took some time for Lynch to reassure Martin that it was the media, rather than a fresh assault by ATF. The FAA promptly declared the skies over and around Mount Carmel to be a no-fly zone.

ATF's retreat had not been entirely complete. Agent Robert

White assigned a few volunteers to set up perimeters, mostly around the southwest corner of the Mount Carmel property. It was intended as a first line of defense should the Branch Davidians launch an armed attack somewhere in the direction of Waco's city limits. It was hard to guess what Koresh and his followers would do next.

ATF agents weren't certain what they were doing next, either. At first, it appeared that they would be returning to Mount Carmel, perhaps to set up a siege rather than attempt another dynamic entry. Blake Boteler recalls, "A bus picked us up, and took us to an Elks Lodge or Moose Lodge or something. We were told, 'Everybody get more ammunition and dry socks. It looks like we'll have to go back.' I'd lost the chin strap to my helmet. I'd seen a helmet on the right front seat of the bus, a bloodied helmet, but it had a chin strap. I went back on the bus, took the chin strap off, and I remember squeezing bloody water off it. Later I learned that it was [dead ATF agent] Robert Williams's helmet."

Sam Cohen took the dry socks and ammunition, "but what I wanted was a high-powered rifle. We stayed at that hall for a while, and then they told us to go to some hotels."

When the exhausted agents got to their rooms, they immediately called spouses or parents or close friends to say that they were all right. Since they'd been told to stand down, the agents assumed that fighting at Mount Carmel was over, at least for that day. They were wrong. About the same time ATF got most of its agents settled in to bathe and rest, one more man was dying a few hundred yards behind the Branch Davidian building.

As the Mount Carmel battle raged, two Branch Davidians, Mike Schroeder and Bob Kendrick, were at the group's car repair shop several miles away. Both men lived as well as worked there. For the past few weeks, they'd allowed Englishman Norman Allison to stay there, too. Allison had briefly been a full-fledged Branch Davidian before abandoning David and Mount Carmel to seek his fortune as a rapper in Hollywood. A month before the ATF raid, he straggled back. David spurned Allison's request to rejoin the Mount Carmel faithful. Kendrick and Schroeder, out of pity, said Allison could sleep at the garage until he figured out what to do next.

Just before 10 a.m. on Sunday, Kendrick spotted helicopters hovering near the location of Mount Carmel. He alerted Schroeder, who began frantically calling the compound. The line was busy, and stayed that way because of Wayne Martin's ongoing negotiations with Larry Lynch. Schroeder kept trying, and finally, as the battle was winding down, managed to reach Steve Schneider. When Schroeder asked what he should do, Schneider replied, "I guess you get in your car and try to get here." Schroeder grabbed a 9mm handgun, Kendrick had two more, and, with Allison as an unarmed passenger, they hopped into a pickup truck and drove toward Mount Carmel. Roadblocks kept them from reaching there. Schroeder remembered that Mary Belle Jones, Perry Jones's wife, lived in a trailer about two miles off and behind the Mount Carmel property, with a few elderly Branch Davidian women whose constitutions couldn't withstand the bare-bones compound. The three men drove in that direction, then left the car to attempt approaching Mount Carmel on foot, through the thick brush behind the property. Kendrick, older and ill with heart disease, lagged behind and eventually dropped out. Schroeder and Allison plodded on, Schroeder in the lead.

The six-man ATF team put in place to prevent escape from the rear of Mount Carmel had endured a long, frustrating day. When the cattle trailers came under fire in front of the compound, the agents in the back of the property moved forward and tried to support them. But there was considerable open ground between the end of the brush and the back of the building, and gunfire kept them at bay throughout the lengthy battle. When the final cease-fire took hold, Jack Grabowski remembers, his team was instructed by radio to leave the Branch Davidian property: "We got to the outside of [a] fence and waited there. We'd been dropped off early in the morning by a car. We didn't have transportation. Then, some [other] agents came. That made about sixteen of us. They filled us in on what happened . . . we set up a skirmish line. We didn't get more than thirty or fifty feet when we spotted somebody in the brush."

Mike Schroeder thrashed his way through the brush far ahead of Norman Allison. He was determined to get into Mount Carmel and fight alongside his leader. But with the roof of the building finally within sight, he heard voices identifying themselves as ATF, ordering, "Let us see your hands!" Grabowski says, "He started shooting at us. Rounds were returned. One suspect was killed. The other [Norman Allison] said, 'I give up, I give up.'"

The agents took their prisoner and continued walking carefully toward an extraction point identified to them over their radios. For the time being, Mike Schroeder's body was left where it fell.

At 6:20 p.m., this final group of ATF agents returned to the TSTC command post, where they informed someone there that they'd just "killed a guy," and needed to report. After their names were taken down, they waited for further instructions. When none seemed forthcoming, they asked if they should turn over their weapons. They were told, "No, you might still need them."

That, ATF's Operation Trojan Horse chronology concludes in its final sentence, "was a bizarre ending to a long and extraordinary day." But the day was still not over.

Kathy Schroeder spent much of the late afternoon and evening in what was now the gun vault, the concrete-walled room that previously served the Branch Davidians as a food pantry. She says, "It was one of the safest parts in the building. I'd helped rebuild it [Mount Carmel], and I knew most of it was a firetrap. I wanted to have my kids someplace safe if they [the ATF] came again, so I offered to go into that room with them and reload the [gun] magazines."

While she did, Kathy learned that Mike Schroeder had called

Mount Carmel, and was instructed by Steve Schneider to try getting in: "I knew that Mike had given himself completely to David and the message, and so he'd do everything he could." Like many other Americans, the Branch Davidians had their radios tuned to news programs, anxious to hear how commentators described what had happened. "We heard an announcement on the radio that men had come out of Mount Carmel with guns blazing," she recalls. "One was killed, one was captured, and one got away." The trio were trying to get in rather than escape the compound, but Schroeder says she instantly knew their identities and fates. "I knew Mike would not have allowed himself to be captured; he was killed. Bob [Kendrick] was an old man who'd survived about seven heart attacks, and Norm Allison had no backbone, he'd surrender. When I heard that on the radio, when I knew Mike was gone, my first reaction was, 'I knew he was going to beat me to Heaven.' I knew he was better than me. I was proud of him, happy for him, jealous of him."

As night fell, Texas Rangers and Texas state highway patrolmen joined a handful of ATF agents maintaining scattered perimeters around the Branch Davidian property. Ranger George Turner remembers, "It was scary. At one place it was just me, three or four other Rangers, and a couple of highway patrolmen. We were scared to death that they were going to come out. They had all those guns. I had just quit smoking, but I said to one of the others, 'Give me a cigarette,' and the next day I bought a pack of cigarettes. We couldn't have stopped them, if they [the Branch Davidians] had all come out."

But the Branch Davidians spent the same early evening hours preparing to stop reinforced agents of Babylon from coming in. Kathy Schroeder helped hand out guns and ammunition to those who'd previously turned down weapons; at this point, everyone was expected to fight. "It was biblical," she says. "We were going to die. Protecting ourselves [with guns] was only a portion of that." While Schroeder passed out guns and ammo, other Branch Davidians "put things up in front of the windows—cans, potato boxes, bales of hay, wooden objects like the podium from the chapel."

The ATF agents that the Branch Davidians expected might attack Mount Carmel again any minute were busy themselves. In hotel and motel rooms around Waco, they gathered in small groups to try to make sense of the debacle that morning. Agent Robert White remembers that he and other members of the Dallas SRT "were trying to figure out what went wrong, what we needed to do to get everybody's feet back on the ground. In such a traumatic situation, you've got to talk it out. Most of the anger at that point was at the special agent in charge and the assistant special agent in charge, [Phil] Chojnacki and [Chuck] Sarabyn." The agents couldn't understand why the raid went forward after the element of surprise was lost. They felt that a promise to them had been broken, and four good men died because of it. Rory Heisch says, "We were pissed."

The agents who'd participated in the long, bloody fight that morning turned out their room lights still not knowing what they would do in the morning: Go in at Mount Carmel again? Set up a siege?

At Mount Carmel, David Koresh gathered his remaining strength and reached out to tell his side of the story. He made calls to the media, to KRLD-AM, a popular news station in the Dallas–Fort Worth area, and then to CNN. In both instances, he portrayed himself and his followers as an innocent religious group wantonly attacked by federal agents who'd come to slaughter them. He insisted to the radio station, "I begged these men to go away," and was even more descriptive on CNN: "They started firing at me. I fell back in the door and the bullets started coming through the door. Some of the young men, they started firing [back]. I was hollering, 'Go away, there's women and children here. Let's talk,' They fired on us first." He added, "I never planned to use the weapons. The problem is that people outside don't understand what we believe."

Audiences heard Koresh graphically describe the havoc wreaked on his followers by the ATF, including the killing of a two-year-old child, which was not true. But most missed Koresh's comment that, because of the morning's events, everyone was now "in the Fifth Seal." The Book of Revelation promised:

> *And when he [the Lamb] had opened the Fifth Seal, I saw under the altar the souls of them that were slain for the Word of God, and for the testimony which they held, and they cried out with a loud voice, saying, "How long, O Lord, holy and true, dost thou not judge and avenge our blood on them that dwell on the earth?"*

But the significance wasn't lost on two CNN viewers who would soon involve themselves in the matter. J. Phillip Arnold of Houston and James Tabor of Charlotte, North Carolina, were prominent religious scholars whose careers focused on biblical and religious history. Arnold recalls, "The possibilities of the Fifth Seal bothered me, because if David thought the events of the Fifth Seal were dawning on February 28, then he would expect the rest of the End Time to immediately follow." Tabor says, "You don't deliver an apocalypse to an apocalyptic group. The [ATF] raid in a sad way confirmed David's prophecies to his followers more than ever before."

Young Kiri Jewell saw Koresh on CNN, too. She predicted to her father, who watched with her, that the Branch Davidians with Koresh "would die, because he [David] taught it. He told us from the beginning [that] sometime we were all going to die, and I didn't know when and I didn't know how. But I told my dad, the day the raid happened, that none of them were going to get out."

For much of the rest of the night at Mount Carmel, Koresh and Steve Schneider were on the phone, talking to ATF agents who lacked training in negotiation technique. They had, at this time, one specific request of Koresh: There were children inside, a lot of them. Surely Koresh and their parents didn't want them risking injury or even death. At least send the children out—they'd be well cared for, and relatives or friends chosen by their parents would be summoned to take temporary custody of them, until this whole thing got sorted out.

To his followers' surprise, Koresh partially accepted. Two nervous little girls emerged in front of the compound about 9 p.m. on Sunday, and another two children around midnight. Notes were pinned to their clothes, giving contact information for who should be summoned to take custody of them.

While Koresh and Schneider were on the phone with Babylon, the rest of the adult Branch Davidians pondered what would happen next. Six of their number were gloriously gathered up to God. Everyone else had to wait for their turn. Wondering how and when that might happen conjured disturbing possibilities. Even with their deep faith in Koresh and God, and after a long, nerve-racking day, many felt they needed some further comfort beyond scripture and prophecy. Access to anything other than essentials was restricted at Mount Carmel; indulgences of any kind required Koresh's consent. Followers faced the leader's wrath for sneaking a smoke, sipping alcohol, or eating a candy bar or other junk food without permission. According to Koresh, such self-indulgent slipups threatened the guilty one's chances of positive judgment in the End Time and gaining a place in the sinless Kingdom of God on Earth to come.

That, almost always, was threat enough. But on this night, dozens of the otherwise faithful lacked the will to resist temptation. Some had packs of cigarettes hidden in the compound, and curled up in various corners to smoke. Others sneaked nips of stashed liquor. Always, there were a few boxes of doughnuts cadged from local bakeries by Perry Jones. Some raid survivors gorged on the pastries, a final gift from their crotchety comrade. All this was done, they hoped, without Koresh's knowledge. He was badly hurt, and preoccupied with the media, and negotiating on the phone, and everybody in Mount Carmel might die anyway, at any minute. What harm could it really do? God would surely understand.

CHAPTER THIRTY

The FBI Takes Over

On Monday morning, March 1, most of the ATF agents who'd participated in the previous day's raid woke up and turned on the TV news. They were disgusted to hear agency spokesmen assuring interviewers that the crucial element of surprise on Sunday hadn't been lost; other factors outside ATF's control, such as incendiary stories in the media, were to blame for what was a regrettable failure. Mike Russell snarled, "You lying son of a bitch" at his TV screen. Sam Cohen assumed an agency cover-up must be in progress: "When he [an ATF spokesman] said that they [Branch Davidians] didn't know we were coming, I thought, 'They're trying to keep a secret, but at least a hundred people already know the secret, and four of them are dead.'"

The agents who participated in the raid were ordered to attend meetings on Monday. One was a peer counseling session with therapists, who urged them to say whatever was on their minds. Mike Duncan recalls, "Some of us sat there, some cried, some talked about different things. When it got to me, I said, 'I'm so fuckin' mad, I can hardly stand it.' They asked, 'At the Davidians?' I said, 'I'm mad at ATF management. We were not prepared, not trained, we didn't get the equipment we needed. Management lied about the element of surprise.'"

At a different meeting, Dan Hartnett, the ATF deputy director for enforcement, met with the agents. After noting how valiantly they had conducted themselves the day before, he introduced Jeff Jamar, the FBI's agent in charge of its San Antonio division. The FBI,

Hartnett said, would immediately assume command of the Mount Carmel operation. Jamar spoke briefly; Hartnett asked if any ATF agents had questions. They did. Kris Mayfield, normally soft-spoken, snapped that he took offense at the FBI replacing ATF: "We got our asses shot off the day before, but we're still professional enough to do our jobs." Hartnett had a reputation for not tolerating insolence from underlings. Carla Bell, sitting next to her fiancé, whispered to Mayfield, "You just got us transferred to Detroit," which ATF agents considered the worst possible posting. But Robert White stood up and agreed with Mayfield. Then, Mike Duncan chimed in: "My question to you is, when are we going to become a big-time agency like we're supposed to be? . . . You've been leading this organization for years. It's your fault." A barrage of additional questions, all of them hostile, followed. Nothing changed. ATF was out, and the FBI was in.

Soon afterward, Hartnett sent out an undated memorandum to "All Special Agents, All Division Chiefs" titled "Subject: Questions Regarding Waco Incident." Hartnett wrote that the February 28 raid plan "was solid, the tactical approach was well thought out. . . . The plan relied on the element of surprise, and it carefully considered agent safety. But, through no fault of ATF, the plan was compromised, and our teams lost the element of surprise. . . . The tragic consequences were not because of a lack of planning, equipment failure, or unpreparedness of our special agents." The memo concluded, "We prefer that this information not be released outside the ATF."

What the ATF agents didn't know was that the FBI had been part of the February 28 operation since minutes after the first shots were fired on Sunday. Not long after 10 a.m., Byron Sage, supervising agent for twenty-two Central Texas counties including McLennan, received a call at his home in an Austin suburb from his boss, Jeff Jamar. Jamar had heard the first reports of what was happening at Mount Carmel; he instructed Sage, a military veteran and trained negotiator, to get up there and help whoever might be attempting communication with the Branch Davidian defenders. On his ninety-mile drive north to Waco, Sage mused that "the average length of any law enforcement gun battle was about two seconds; I thought it might be over before I got there."

But as Sage approached Mount Carmel, he was turned away at a roadblock because the fight was still in progress. He made his way to "the basement of the police department," where he found Larry Lynch trying frantically to keep negotiations for a cease-fire going. Sage worked with Lynch until the third and final cease-fire held.

As soon as the shooting was over, the FBI received a formal request from ATF requesting assistance. The killing of federal agents brought at least that portion of the operation under the FBI's jurisdiction, but for the moment it was simply one federal law enforcement agency asking another to help out. Jeff Jamar arrived in Waco around 5:30 on Sunday afternoon. After consulting with ATF leaders there, it was determined, according to the Treasury Department's subsequent report, "that if the FBI decides the situation at Mount Carmel will be for the long term, then the FBI should have operational command. The ATF has absorbed heavy losses, and if there's more shooting, they may be perceived as seeking revenge."

Jamar ordered in the FBI's Hostage Rescue Team, agents who were crack shots and mission-tested. They were led by agent Dick Rogers, who also commanded the HRT at Ruby Ridge the previous October. FBI negotiators were summoned to work with Sage. Rogers and his HRT team arrived by jet on Sunday evening. The negotiators, relegated to a prop plane that required a fuel stop en route, didn't get to Waco until 10 p.m.

The FBI contingent assumed control with the attitude that they'd come to Waco to clean up somebody else's mess. "It was always that way," Sage says. "The ATF or other lesser law enforcement agencies, they always looked at us [the FBI] as Big Brother. We were the federal fire department. They called us to Ruby Ridge to clean that up after the U.S. Marshal Service screwed up and got in a gun battle. Then Waco came along."

According to testimony two years later during the congressional investigation of the Mount Carmel operation, the FBI's immediate goal was "to stabilize the crisis situation, establish a dialogue with David Koresh and his followers, and to begin to gather intelligence data regarding Koresh." ATF had almost eight months to prepare. The FBI was coming in cold.

Jamar's first order was to sever Koresh's telephone connection to the outside world. Two lines into Mount Carmel remained functional, but calls in and out of the compound could be made only with the FBI negotiators. Gary Noesner, whom Sage describes as one of the FBI's best, called into Mount Carmel to introduce himself to Koresh just before midnight on Sunday. Noesner sounded friendly and easygoing, but the Branch Davidians weren't charmed. "FBI negotiators, whom I consider to be professional liars, have the job to be Mr. Nice Guy to talk you out of any given situation," Clive Doyle wrote later. "This is what they were doing with us."

Noesner quickly established a relatively cordial phone relationship with Koresh and Steve Schneider, who did much of the talking for the Branch Davidian side. This caused the FBI to erroneously conclude that Schneider was independent of Koresh's control to a certain degree; maybe if Koresh proved too obstinate, Schneider might be persuaded to end the standoff instead. That, Kathy Schroeder is certain, would never have happened: "Steve only said on the phone whatever it was that David told him to."

Other FBI agents frantically sought insights into Koresh's personality and the Branch Davidians' religious beliefs. One of their first sources was the Australian TV documentary presenting Koresh as an obvious charlatan. Agents also perused the *Waco Tribune-Herald's* "Sinful Messiah" series; the local paper published all the rest of the stories in the series on Monday rather than spreading them out over several more days as originally planned. As a result of what they initially saw and read, most of the FBI agents in Waco—668 would be deployed there before the Mount Carmel siege finally ended—had little respect for Koresh and his followers.

• • •

Food rationing was imposed inside Mount Carmel on Monday. David Thibodeau recalls that breakfast was nuts and applesauce. Adults were allowed two MREs each day, and the choices were spaghetti and meatballs or tuna casserole. Thibodeau wrote later that the MREs "tasted like mud." Kathy Schroeder remembers, "There were some good ones, I think the spaghetti and meatballs." So long as they ate sparingly, the Branch Davidians weren't in any immediate danger of starvation. "We had tons and tons of canned foods, and dried foods," Schroeder says. They also collected water in every available vessel—their main outside water tank had been punctured by Sunday morning's gunfire, and much of the water in it had leaked away.

Though they had plenty of food for the long haul, by early Monday evening most of the Mount Carmel defenders still believed their current plight would not last much longer. The first evidence that the FBI was ready to fight as well as talk arrived at 6 p.m., in the form of several Bradley fighting vehicles, combat engineer vehicles, and tanks. These were stationed around the perimeter set by the agents comprising the HRT. Koresh came on the phone to warn, "If you keep getting closer, we'll retaliate." The arrival of these daunting, massive vehicles made clear that, unlike the underarmed ATF, the FBI was capable of forcibly ending things anytime they chose. Koresh, stating the obvious, told a negotiator that "you're the Goliath, and we're David." (Noesner was one among a number of negotiators.)

The wound on Koresh's side was seeping; a medical gauge in the compound registered his blood pressure at 85/40. Koresh once again appeared to be on the verge of expiring. He asked that everyone line up, first the men, then the women, and file past where he lay on blankets to bid him goodbye. Koresh had a few loving words for each follower. They were certain that their own deaths were imminent; surely, they would die after Koresh did, as he'd prophesized. The Branch Davidians considered options after their leader was gone. They might, of course, be slaughtered at the hands of Babylon's reinforcements. Another option was suicide, perhaps in some way taking many FBI agents with them. There was never any full group discussion, beyond how to prepare for being attacked again. Kathy Schroeder says, "I was going to have a hand grenade and some of the other women would gather around me, and I was going to pull the pin if that was the only option. At least then we wouldn't be raped or pillaged. It was a last scenario." ·

Schroeder no longer had to consider what would happen to her children in a new attack. Koresh ordered her to send them out earlier in the day. "It wasn't like David was asking if I wanted them to go. Steve [Schneider] just came up to me and asked if they were ready. I pinned notes on them. I knew my ex-husband would take the three I'd had with him, and I hoped he'd take my little three-year-old [fathered by Mike Schroeder], too."

All during the day and early evening of March 1, the Branch Davidians sent out a total of ten children. Negotiators took this as a sign that David might soon be open to everyone peaceably leaving the compound. Joyce Sparks, the CPS staffer who'd led her agency's investigation of alleged child mistreatment at Mount Carmel, saw the children departing on TV and immediately suspected a different motive. "It was not his biological children he was sending out," she told Congress two years later. Koresh, she believed, was gradually sending out everyone else's children as a delaying tactic.

If it was, Koresh abruptly decided not to delay any longer. By 9:30 p.m., he'd recovered enough strength to warn negotiators, "Look at Revelation 5; What's going to happen has already been foretold." (Revelation 5:12–13 reads, "Saying with a loud voice, 'Worthy is the Lamb that was slain to receive power. . . . Blessing, and honour, and glory, and power be unto Him that sitteth upon the throne, and unto the Lamb for ever and ever.'")

Then, unexpectedly, he made an offer: "Let me show a couple of the Seals on the radio. Based on that, we will work something out that [gets] everyone out." For the next few minutes, details were discussed and agreed on. Koresh would record a tape on which he explained the beliefs held by himself and his followers. If the FBI arranged for it to be played on a national radio network—the agency could review the tape ahead of time—then Koresh, having been given the opportunity to bring his message to the world, would lead everyone out of Mount Carmel to surrender peacefully. If a national station wouldn't play the tape for free, Koresh pledged, the FBI should tell him how much airtime would cost: "I'll pay for it." There would be no mass suicide attempt, because "I'm not having anybody kill themselves." Koresh swore to the FBI negotiators that peaceful surrender was "not an assumption, it's a fact."

FBI leaders were cautiously optimistic. If Koresh meant it, if he followed through, then their work in Waco was almost done, on practically the same day they'd replaced ATF. It seemed too good to be true.

Lost in Translation

Since he'd been wounded, Koresh's energy waxed and waned. At 1:12 a.m. on Tuesday morning, he was upbeat as he continued talking on the phone to FBI negotiators. "I'm gonna eat some chicken soup," he told them, adding that he hadn't eaten for two days. "You put out this broadcast, and we'll all come out. . . . I feel much better since you're doing this for me."

While Koresh ate his soup, FBI agents woke up radio network officials with requests to play the tape that Koresh promised he would record shortly. By 1:50 a.m., they had two commitments, from the Christian Broadcasting Network (CBN) and KRLD in Dallas–Fort Worth. When Koresh was informed around 3:30 a.m., he acknowledged that "I know I'm in trouble when I give myself up to you," and promised that he'd "get busy on the tape." An hour later he called negotiators again, urging, "Make sure it's [played] in prime time." At 5:20 a.m., Koresh had another comment: "If I wanted to commit suicide, I'd have already done it."

FBI agents accepted that comment at secular face value. They did not realize that, for Koresh and his followers, "suicide" did not mean the end. Voluntarily dying, in a manner that they believed God wanted, was entirely different. It would be "translating" from humble human life to an exalted, higher form of existence—to the Branch Davidians, this was the furthest possible thing from suicide. As Kathy Schroeder recalls, "On March 2nd, there was never any plan to come out and surrender. If you have a lion at your door, a lion roaring for you to come out, would you come out?"

Instead, the Branch Davidians had a plan that, while not fully articulated among themselves, would result in their longed-for translation. Schroeder explains, " 'Translation' is going to Heaven, whether it be without seeing death, just having it happen, or [for us] it could have been through a battle and then death and being translated by dying." As usual, Koresh made the decision, then entrusted a few others to spread the word to everyone else. Schroeder said she was informed by Neil Vaega, "who told me that David was making a tape, that after it was aired, we were all going to come out . . . and draw fire from the [FBI] agents. If David wasn't already dead, we would shoot him. [Then] we would all be killed. [There were] a couple of alternatives. These were all just methods that we could go; we didn't have any idea of exactly how it would happen."

But they would come out with guns and hand grenades, the remaining children there among the adults, and die as the Book of Revelation and Koresh foretold. Killing federal agents in the process was optional rather than intended. "The object of the plan was to be translated," Schroeder later testified. "Yes, we had to draw enemy fire at the same time, but killing the agents was not something that I thought about." She admitted that she would have tried to kill them, "If I was told to, yes."

Early on Tuesday morning, Koresh sent out two children and two elderly women, seventy-one-year-old Catherine Matteson, who was legally blind, and seventy-five-year-old Margaret Lawson. The youngsters were taken into protective custody; the women were arrested and charged with murder and attempted murder of federal agents. It was an impulsive act; their jail incarceration lasted less than two days before authorities transferred them to a Waco hotel, where they remained in "protective custody" as the first Branch Davidian adults to exit Mount Carmel since the February 28 raid by the ATF. A few journalists were allowed to interview them. Carlton Stowers spoke with Matteson, and found her to be "a sweet little lady" who was bewildered by all that had occurred. Stowers recalls, "She kept asking what they [the Branch Davidians] had done, she kept saying, 'Why is this happening?'" Matteson and all the Branch Davidians believed that, in following the Will of God as they interpreted it, they had done nothing wrong. Secular law was immaterial.

During the morning, Koresh recorded his tape. It was just under an hour long. He sent the tape out, and FBI agents listened carefully to it. Hearing nothing objectionable, they passed the recording along to the radio stations. Shortly past noon, CBN executives informed the FBI that their network would broadcast the tape at 1:30 p.m. Negotiators told Koresh, and at the appointed time, his words went out on national airwaves. This was an opportunity, he and his followers believed, for the world to hear God's message and renounce sin.

In the words of biblical scholar James Tabor, "That March 2nd thing was a fiasco."

Koresh introduced himself, then launched into a lengthy explanation of "the reasons for the revelation of Jesus Christ." Making only fleeting references to his own current plight ("I'm involved in a very serious thing right now. . . . I am really concerned about the lives of my brethren here and, also, would be concerned even greater about the lives of all those in this world"), Koresh offered a Bible study tailored for an audience similar to his followers, who were already devoted to the study of biblical admonitions and intricacies. The same informal, even folksy, delivery that worked so well when delivered by Koresh in person was less effective as the ramblings of a reedy voice on the radio: "That means the book is not to be pranked with by anyone who would dare think that they can, by speculation or private opinions, unlock the mysteries of the Seals and what they contain." Koresh offered a dire warning—"The importance of the Seals is that if you do not listen, you are going to end up making the worst mistake you've ever made in all your lives."

He explained what he and his followers would do next. As promised to the FBI in return for his message being broadcast, they would "give ourselves over to the world, give ourselves out to you. And this is what I've promised. And this is what we're going to keep." Koresh concluded, "Let's get into unity with one God, one truth, one Lamb, one spirit, and let's receive the reward of righteousness. Thank you very much. God bless you."

Inside Mount Carmel, Koresh's followers listened to the broadcast. After the broadcast, Kathy Schroeder testified later, "We gathered in the cafeteria. We started praying. We were joyful. Everybody was ready to get translated. [We] got kind of loud . . . this prayer was very open and very [about] wanting to die, waiting to get out of here, and we got very loud. Steve [Schneider] came down the stairs and told us to be quiet . . . told us to go back to our rooms and pray and study, because David was talking to God."

So far as the FBI was concerned, they'd kept their part of the bargain and it was now Koresh's turn. Negotiation transcripts show that almost as soon as the broadcast concluded, calls went into Mount Carmel asking if the Branch Davidians were ready to come out. A stretcher was sent in, since it was believed that Koresh might be too weak to walk.

At 3:07 on Tuesday afternoon, an unidentified Branch Davidian woman came on the line to report that everyone was "lining up to say goodbye." About forty minutes later, Koresh informed the negotiators that he was ready, and, a few minutes after that, another Branch Davidian said that they were "on their way, but not out yet." The FBI sent school buses to the front of the compound. Agents would arrest the exiting adults, search them for weapons, place them on the buses, and transport them to the FBI command center at the TSTC facility for further processing. Koresh had advised them that his group currently consisted of forty-three men, forty-seven women, and twenty children.

It was almost 5 p.m. when negotiators were informed that Koresh was now leading his followers in prayer. In fact, he was informing them that he was calling off their longed-for "translation." One reason was that, in Koresh's opinion, the FBI had reneged on the agreement for arranging the national radio broadcast at 1:30 rather than in evening prime time. The other was because of his followers' improper behavior on the night of February 28, when they were reeling emotionally after the failed ATF raid.

According to Kathy Schroeder, "The message [from Koresh] was that we had messed up, and [so] God told David to wait—that if we had all died then, we would have gone to hell for our sins, people drinking liquor, smoking cigarettes, eating all kinds of junk food immediately following the raid." The Branch Davidians were more frustrated than angry by what they believed that God had mandated, Schroeder recalls: "We didn't want to 'Jonestown' it, but we wanted to be translated, to become the Wave Sheaf. We wanted it to be done."

At 5:52, an impatient FBI negotiator called into Mount Carmel and said to Schneider, "Let's do it." Seven minutes later, Schneider called back and reported, "The Lord spoke to David. The Lord told David to wait, not to come out." The negotiator protested that an agreement was being broken. Schneider replied, "I understand, but God has the final word." Koresh, he said, couldn't come to the phone himself "because he's praying, he doesn't want to talk right now."

The Branch Davidians believed that David had the privilege of communicating directly with God. They didn't question David's declaration that the Lord had told him they must not leave the compound as planned, or the reasons that they could not. Whether David believed that God had sent this message to him, or whether he simply decided that he didn't want to die that day and found an excuse not to, can't be known.

But they weren't coming out, and the FBI leaders outside Mount Carmel were furious. Negotiator Gary Noesner wrote later that HRT leader Dick Rogers told siege commander Jeff Jamar, "It's time to teach him [Koresh] a lesson. My people can get in and secure that place in 15 minutes." Noesner argued that although Koresh had reneged, he was still allowing children and, so far, two adults to leave the Branch Davidian facility. If negotiations continued, there could be more. Jamar decided that it was too soon for an assault, but agreed with Rogers that Koresh had to be taught a lesson. He ordered that some of the Bradley armored vehicles be moved closer to the building. That would remind everyone inside that they remained there at the FBI's discretion. As soon as the bulky vehicles lurched forward, Schneider furiously called and demanded that they back away. He was told that the negotiators' bosses "were angry and frustrated." Schneider replied, "Honestly, we were going to come out, but what could we do? God told David to wait." He added that the Branch Davidians' plan remained the same: they were "ready to move when David is," and God would tell Koresh when.

These events—the original agreement, David's tape played on national radio, the FBI's belief that the Branch Davidians were coming out and then their announcement that God told David they must not—convinced the FBI's tactical commanders on the Mount Carmel scene that David Koresh could not be trusted. No matter what he promised, it would likely be a lie. This conclusion affected every decision they made for the duration of what would become a historically long siege.

And these FBI lead agents felt personally embarrassed. They'd told bureau officials in Washington that everything was, apparently, coming to a quick, bloodless conclusion, the kind of result that burnished the FBI's prized reputation as the nation's foremost law enforcement organization. Now, they had to report to their Washington bosses that things hadn't gone as anticipated, and that, for the moment, the leaders on-site weren't sure what to do next.

"There was egg on our face," says former FBI analyst Farris Rookstool III, assigned to the Branch Davidian operation as a "scribe," recording and sharing within the FBI contingent there everything being done. "'God said to wait'—the attitude back in the [command] center was angst. 'What's our backup plan?' But Jamar and Dick Rogers, they had no backup plan."

Byron Sage was determined to keep on communicating in

nonthreatening ways with David and his followers. "As negotiators, you don't have the luxury of being offended," he says. "We had to continue to try to do anything to convince him [Koresh] to come out peacefully."

The FBI waited on Koresh. Koresh waited on God.

Settling into the Siege

Any hope the FBI had that Koresh would quickly be permitted by God to lead his followers out of Mount Carmel was dashed the following morning. In a phone conversation with negotiators, he admitted, "I did let you down yesterday. I have full intentions to keep my word . . . [but] I'm dealing with my Father now, not your systematic, bureaucratic system of government. God has called me to be a warrior, but first, mercy and truth."

This unsubtle message that there would be no swift resolution to the Mount Carmel standoff was bad enough. But for the FBI, Koresh and the Branch Davidians were only part of the problem. The media had descended on Waco, and its voracious appetite for information brought additional pressure. Every day until the siege was over, members of the press demanded something newsworthy. All of them had daily deadlines, and editors or producers expecting better, juicier stories than those printed or broadcast by competitors. The media wanted scoops; the FBI wanted stories that presented the American public with a one-sided perspective: the FBI agents were the good guys, Koresh and the Branch Davidians were the villains.

The FBI began staging daily press briefings. A specific format was rigidly followed. An agency spokesman, sometimes joined by an official from ATF, read a general statement about what was happening that day. Usually, there wasn't much progress to report. The siege settled in to near monotony. Negotiators asked the Branch Davidians to come out, and were repeatedly informed that Koresh was waiting for permission from God. During the press conferences, after reading prepared remarks, agency spokesmen took questions, with their responses often describing those inside Mount Carmel as militant religious zealots who presented a clear and present danger to the public. The word "cult" was constantly used; after the notorious Manson murders in 1969 and the mass Jonestown deaths in 1978, Americans were painfully familiar with the term. The press, hoping for something new and important to report, usually responded with insulting questions: Why was it so hard for the mighty FBI to subdue such a relatively small group? Why did ATF attack Mount Carmel in the first place? If the Branch Davidians were so dangerous, why had they lived so long just outside Waco without launching the kind of attacks on civilians that the FBI now claimed might occur at any time? Above all, when was this going to be over?

"The scripted portion of the press conferences generally went well and served our objectives," negotiator Gary Noesner wrote. "We were less successful later when, during question-and-answer sessions, one or more of the FBI or ATF leaders would shoot from the hip." The press conference audience included everyone in Mount Carmel. ATF gunfire had damaged their satellite dish, but they still had snowy TV reception and their radios. They listened intently to the press conferences. "More than once," Noesner wrote, "during questioning by reporters, officials made offhand remarks casting doubt on the sincerity of Koresh's beliefs, with sarcastic references to his conversation with God. It then fell on our team [the negotiators] to backtrack with the Davidians and explain what they meant. This did not help our cause."

Reporters quickly dismissed the value of the FBI's morning press conferences. "All they wanted to do was demonize the Davidians to us," Carlton Stowers says. Tommy Witherspoon adds, "We had a junior reporter that we'd send to those conferences. Afterward, he'd tell us what the FBI guys said, and we'd debunk everything."

But the media had few options other than parroting what they were told. Besides designated agency spokesmen, all federal officials and agents were prohibited from speaking to the press. Reporters wandered around Waco, hoping to waylay longtime residents who'd have colorful tales to tell about the Branch Davidians. No one did. "I spent a lot of time going around, trying to find people who'd had some contact with the Davidians," Stowers says. "I never found anyone who thought they were dangerous. They were looked at as strange, not scary."

Many in Waco seemed sympathetic to both sides. The Branch Davidians were their oddball neighbors, but the FBI was just trying to do its job. During the first weeks of the siege, a local barbecue donated 1,050 plate lunches to the agents ringing Mount Carmel. A high school home economics class baked and distributed 325 dozen cookies to them. Local gyms offered free access, and a Waco dry cleaners laundered and pressed their clothes. Some reporters built daily stories around that. Their other options were limited. Nobody had access to Koresh or his followers; the FBI controlled the only phone lines in and out of Mount Carmel, and guards at the roadblocks forbade getting any closer to the building. How many stories could be written about Waco citizens not being scared of the Branch Davidians? Some reporters simply repeated FBI press conference propaganda: a story in Australia's WHO magazine (media coverage was worldwide) began, "For someone who claimed to be Jesus, David Koresh was a twisted representative of Christian ideals." Koresh's "religious cult of several hundred members . . . believed that to get to heaven, they had to go through whatever hell Koresh prescribed." The article concluded that, to Koresh's detractors, far from being "a charismatic Messiah," he was "closer to being another Charles Manson or Jim Jones."

The FBI further irked the media by herding them to an assigned press area two miles from Mount Carmel. "We could barely see the compound," recalls Carlton Stowers, using the FBI's press conference term for the Branch Davidian building. "The press area was really just by a roadblock in the middle of a farm-to-market road. It was referred to by everybody as 'Tent City' or 'Media City.' There were rows and rows of TV trucks parked on both sides of the road. Reporters set up tents, awnings, and barbecue grills, because there was nothing to do but wait. All around Mount Carmel, there were so many agents and Army guys and negotiators, and equipment and tanks and everything, that it looked like our government was going to war with another country."

Soon, Stowers says, the press was joined by "people selling T-shirts and other trinkets. Entrepreneurs came out of the woodwork. The same [road] blockade is usually where other people came up wanting a closer look, or even trying to get up into the compound to talk to the Davidians."

Items on sale ranged from T-shirts and bumper stickers supporting the Branch Davidians to similar wares describing the group's sinister intentions. Some shirts and bumper stickers touted militia groups, many of which seized on the events at Mount Carmel to claim the government illegally attacked gun owners acting well within their Second Amendment rights to bear arms. One of these peddlers was Timothy McVeigh, who would soon become infamous in his own right. FBI analyst Farris Rookstool remembers, "I drove out [to Mount Carmel], and saw this guy sitting on the hood of his car. He was selling bumper stickers, T-shirts, items that were very antigovernment. We know it was Timothy McVeigh, because someone from the SMU [Southern Methodist University] school paper took his picture and got his information. Two years later, McVeigh did what he did in Oklahoma City."

One thing the FBI could count on, besides Koresh's continuing intransigence, was the periodic appearance of a few Branch Davidian children, always sent out of Mount Carmel with notes pinned on their clothes by their parents. These notes gave instructions about relatives or friends to whom the children should be sent. By the end of the siege's fifth day, twenty-one youngsters had emerged. They were immediately whisked to the FBI's command center, where their parents back inside Mount Carmel were called and assured, by both the negotiators and the children, that everybody was okay.

From there, they were taken to a Child Protective Services facility in Waco, where they were tended by a special trauma assessment team including CPS staff and volunteers from various hospitals and church-affiliated child care programs. Rachel Koresh, David Koresh's first wife, explained to negotiators the food that they hoped would be provided for their kids: fresh fruit, vegetables, juices, and perhaps kosher hot dogs, but never pork, which was forbidden by the group's dietary principles. Koresh sent out $1,000 in cash to help defray the costs involved.

As proof that the children were being well cared for, the FBI sent in videotapes of the kids at the CPS facility. Most seemed happy and, to their parents, disturbingly energetic. They blamed that on the sugary treats some of the kids gobbled down as the tape was being recorded. Kathy Schroeder says, "Our kids were all juiced up on friggin' candy and soda and shit."

Soon, a greater concern replaced worries about sugar intake. The Branch Davidians believed that their children would immediately be placed with the relatives or friends that their parents requested. Instead, the children remained at the CPS facility for observation. Joyce Sparks recalled that the kids, ranging in age from five months to twelve years old, did not appear in any way to have been abused or neglected. They were, in fact, "in remarkably good psychological condition, considering what they've gone through." The older kids helped care for the younger ones, reading and playing with them. All the children joined hands and prayed before meals. Sparks concluded, "They appear very healthy, are well behaved, and well educated."

Dr. Bruce Perry, an associate professor of psychology and behavioral sciences at Baylor Medical College in Houston, had reservations. He testified to Congress in 1995 that the children believed "they would all be attacked, and that the outsiders would kill everyone in the compound and that Koresh would come back and kill the bad guys, uniting everyone in Heaven . . . all of the young girls were being prepared to be David's wives. . . . One of the older girls expressed distress, now that she had been released from the compound, that she would not be able to be picked by David as one of his brides." Children no older than six, Perry added, "would pick up a toy wooden gun, weigh it as though getting the balance, look down the barrel, and say, 'This isn't a real gun.'"

On March 9, the Texas Department of Protective and Regulatory Services stripped the Branch Davidian parents of their children's custody. No parents were yet charged with any crime, but now, even if they were cleared of legal wrongdoing, they would still have to pass state tests before regaining their kids.

After listening to spokesmen at the FBI press conferences describing mistreatment of Branch Davidian children, Koresh decided to counter with a tape of himself and his kids inside Mount Carmel. He played and talked with them, introduced each one to whoever might see the recording, and also asked followers to explain why they had joined the group, and why they were staying now. Koresh sent the tape out to the FBI; after watching it, the lead agents decided not to release it to the press because it might elicit too much sympathy for him.

Day-to-day negotiations were hit-and-miss. Sometimes Koresh or Steve Schneider would sound almost conciliatory. On March 6, Koresh told a negotiator, "You have to understand that I follow a higher authority and it's not up to me. Bear with this fool for a minute," and three days later Schneider promised, "David is willing to work together."

But inside Mount Carmel, tempers were fraying. Most of Koresh's followers wondered how long their "little season" of waiting was going to last. They weren't privy to most of their leader's conversations with the FBI. "When Schneider is on the phone to negotiators, he's on the first floor, so many of them can at least hear his side of the conversations," Clive Doyle wrote. "But Koresh is always upstairs, so very few can hear him when he's talking. It wasn't like it was on a speakerphone where everyone could hear it."

The only certain thing for the Branch Davidians was that the delay in "translation" was their fault—Koresh said so. Their indulgences on the night after the ATF raid had offended God. Now, they must adhere even more closely to His wishes as communicated through Koresh. Otherwise, their anticipated places in the Wave Sheaf would be lost. It was impossible not to feel fretful while trying to work their way back into the Lord's favor, and the tanks outside didn't help.

Koresh himself was subject to mood swings; discomfort from his wounds was a factor. He described to negotiators how he believed he'd lost three pints of blood, and asked that the FBI send in sutures so the wounds could be closed. The FBI complied, but planted a listening device in the box with the sutures. They did the same with containers of milk for the remaining children, also sent in at Koresh's request. When the milk didn't arrive as soon as he expected, Koresh told negotiators that he'd sent out money to pay for it, so, in his opinion, the FBI was obligated to immediately oblige.

Negotiators were frustrated when David attempted explaining at length what he believed and why, essentially trying to give them the same lengthy Bible studies that he offered to his followers. Some negotiators began referring to these hours-long lectures as "Bible babble," and kept interrupting, asking Koresh to stick to practical matters at hand. Byron Sage says, "If you perceive an individual as being delusional, you do not jump into his delusion. So, the whole issue of religion was kept at bay. Due respect was conveyed to David and Steve, primarily, but we were very careful how we addressed and pursued it."

Koresh assumed that the negotiators shared at least some of his vast knowledge of the Bible and its terminology. They didn't, and inevitable misunderstandings led to egregious errors on the part of FBI spokesmen. Koresh taught his followers, and assumed negotiators would know, that "Christ" is a biblical term meaning "the anointed." According to him, there were three Christs: the relatively obscure biblical figure Melchizedek, then Jesus, and finally

Koresh himself. When a baffled negotiator asked, "Do you want to be addressed as Lamb, Christ, or Lord?" he responded, "My name is David Koresh." He claimed to be *a*, rather than *the*, Christ. But after Koresh made several references about his Christ status to negotiators, they noted in their transcripts that David said he *was* Christ. That was repeated to the media during press conferences, which resulted in viewers and readers believing that Koresh was claiming to be Jesus.

Koresh was frustrated, too: Why couldn't these people grasp what should be obvious? He was waiting for God to tell him what to do, and the Lord would not adhere to the FBI's secular schedule. Sometimes his frustration boiled over into direct threats to negotiators. Once, Koresh snarled, "You do not know you are going to pay. . . . Your talk is becoming vain. You people are so arrogant, so foul, why don't you learn Revelation?" He also instructed Schneider to tell negotiators, "The heavens will open and the ground will shake if you mess with us. Just come on in, and see what will happen."

FBI tacticians were increasingly ready to find out. They were losing patience not only with David, but with their own negotiators. Against the negotiators' advice, just after 9 a.m. on Tuesday, March 9, Agent in Charge Jeff Jamar cut electric power into Mount Carmel. He allowed it to be turned back on so the Branch Davidians could watch that day's press conference, then cut it off again the next day. It was a reminder that the FBI was in control.

Cutting off Mount Carmel's electricity was only a first step. On March 10, the HRT team in Waco transmitted a proposed action plan to FBI headquarters in Washington:

> *Concept of operation: HRT snipers will support a phased operation intended to approach the compound with armored vehicles, demand the surrender of occupants and, if necessary, employ chemical*

agents inside. From existing and reinforced sniper positions, HRT snipers will provide real time intelligence, long range precision and covering fire to tactical elements making the approach and delivering chemical agents.

The HRT tactical team didn't intend to wait much longer.

Negotiators Versus Tactical

The FBI was hampered during the Mount Carmel siege by several factors, some outside the agents' control. First was the agency's traditional approach to chain of command, which was exactly opposite ATF's. At ATF, almost all decisions were made at local field office levels. Operations were planned and carried out with minimal input from, or contact with, supervisors in Washington, D.C. This was Treasury Department tradition. Officials there learned of plans for the February 28 raid on Mount Carmel only as a last-minute courtesy.

But the FBI was a division of the Department of Justice, and their tradition required upper-echelon approval for virtually every aspect of every operation. On especially significant cases, FBI lead agents in the field acted only with clearance from the highest departmental officials, occasionally including the United States attorney general. If ever an FBI operation qualified for hands-on supervision by the attorney general, the Mount Carmel siege did, but for the first dozen days of the siege, America had no attorney general. Clinton appointee Janet Reno was not yet confirmed by the Senate. In her place were several deputy attorneys general acting in her stead, most of them new in the Department of Justice themselves and adjusting to an overwhelming flood of demands and responsibilities. The Mount Carmel siege was just one among many. Jeff Jamar, trying to resolve the impasse in Waco, not only had to make crucial decisions under the watch of the mistrustful media, but to do so knowing that anything he did might elicit Reno's disapproval when she finally assumed office.

Jamar arrived in Waco on the evening of February 28 with the understanding that he had to clean up another agency's mess without any time to plan or prepare, and with the world watching. David Koresh, the leader of what Jamar considered the criminal element in Mount Carmel, almost immediately proved himself to be a liar. He'd promised to come out, and bring all his followers along, if the FBI arranged to have his taped sermon broadcast on national radio. The FBI complied, and Koresh reneged. Jamar would not trust him again. Whenever another moment seemed right to bring the siege to a conclusion, any cooperation pledged by Koresh would not be a determining factor. It would be on the FBI's terms.

The most immediate daily problem for Jamar, though, didn't involve concern about his bosses in Washington or his festering disdain for David Koresh. Every day in Waco, Jamar had to adjudicate between two factions of the FBI agents there under his command. Only a few days into the siege, Gary Noesner described "a growing disconnect between the strategy we were pursuing as negotiators, and the thoughts of the tactical folks on the perimeter." An irreconcilable dispute was inevitable. FBI negotiators accepted a certain amount of give and take with suspects under siege. Theirs was a gradual process of establishing communication, building trust, and eventually persuading suspects that the best option was peaceful surrender. This was, always, a delicate dance. The slightest misstep, even a single word or act perceived by the suspects as threatening, could negate days or even weeks of progress. The negotiators expected the tactical FBI teams in Waco to behave with absolute restraint, refraining from anything other than calmly maintaining an impenetrable perimeter around Mount Carmel. Patience, not intimidation, would carry the day.

But the negotiators did their work on telephones from the FBI command post, miles away from Mount Carmel. Tactical, under the aggressive leadership of Dick Rogers, stood guard around the massive Branch Davidian building day and night, catching glimpses of the assholes who'd already killed four federal agents, shot up many more, and had the potential to rush out anytime with guns blazing. While negotiators offered their compromises, tactical had to run the dangerous errands involved with these agreements, delivering milk and medical supplies to Mount Carmel's front door, bringing themselves well within range of fully automatic guns, let alone the .50 caliber monster that earlier laid waste to the ATF.

Byron Sage, who tried to keep a foot in both negotiator and tactical camps, says, "Every time we [negotiators] got authority to take in things [to Mount Carmel], after we got on-scene authority, young guys from the tactical team had to take them in. We were sending them in to harm's way multiple times, so they had to be asking, 'Why?'"

Sage said that he and Noesner ("A very impressive negotiator, very gifted, very talented") engaged in daily briefings of "department heads," not only of tactical, but also with "intelligence and legal, two times a day at the beginning, one time daily after a month. The problem was, the biggest lesson we learned [from the siege] operationally was the lack of communication between negotiators, top to bottom, and tactical, top to bottom. . . . Our briefing to Dick Rogers was very specific about where we [the negotiators] were headed. But it never got from Dick down to [the] HRT teams. We'd talk to Jeff Jamar about something we wanted to do, and Jeff Jamar might say he agreed, but that it [also] was up to Dick Rogers. We should talk to him. He [Jamar] had more than enough on his plate."

Day by day, phone conversation by conversation, negotiators made incremental progress. When the Branch Davidians felt that all the outside world heard about them was negatives, negotiators sent in copies of newspaper and magazine articles that were at least somewhat sympathetic. When Rachel Koresh took the phone and asked, "What will be the charges against David?" the negotiator responded, "I'd have to check, but the difference between a charge and a conviction is a million miles apart." Koresh demanded the FBI acknowledge that ATF helicopters fired on Mount Carmel. The negotiator admitted that ATF agents on board carried sidearms, but pointed out that the helicopters themselves had no mounted guns. Conciliation rather than argument was the goal.

On March 8, Koresh asked if the FBI could "cut back a bit, and give these people time to think." He said that he had not personally seen some of his followers inside Mount Carmel for days. When a negotiator (FBI transcripts do not identify individual negotiators) replied, "I'm not pushy, but can we get something going?" Koresh said, "We are." His pace was much slower than negotiators preferred, but they accepted it. Koresh was sometimes talking with, rather than at, them.

That changed around mid-afternoon the next day, when Jamar abruptly cut off Mount Carmel's electricity. Steve Schneider immediately called negotiators, demanding to know how the Branch Davidians were supposed to keep recently delivered milk cold for the children if their power was off. Noesner went to Jamar, telling him that much of Mount Carmel didn't even have electrical power, so what, really, was the point? Cutting the power only negated progress that had been made by the negotiators. Jamar, who'd been under pressure by tactical to do something, told Noesner that he saw no inconsistency. If all the FBI did was give, all Koresh would do was take.

Mount Carmel's power was turned back on, but only temporarily. For a time, power was briefly restored each day so that the Branch Davidians could listen to the daily press conferences. These grew increasingly accusatory: Carlton Stowers remembers, "They [the Branch Davidians] were supposed to be dealing drugs from the compound. They were participating in some network of illegal arms dealers. They were laundering money." Infuriated by their inability to make their own case to the media, the Branch Davidians began writing messages on bedsheets, then hanging the sheets out their windows. One message declared: "FBI broke negotiations, we want press." Schneider suggested to negotiators that a "mediator-negotiator" from the media be appointed. He suggested that it could be conservative commentator Rush Limbaugh.

Then Jamar cut Mount Carmel's electricity for good. Schneider told negotiators, "We're through with you people . . . these tactics are causing us to want to stay in even more." Heavy military vehicles began removing obstructions around the building, sometimes damaging Branch Davidian vehicles in the process. Schneider demanded, "How does that action relate to negotiations?" A negotiator claimed he was unaware of "any actions like those," and it might have been true: he was speaking to Schneider from several miles away.

Negotiators tried other tacks. One, attempting to turn Schneider against Koresh, didn't work. Reminded that David had taken and impregnated his wife, Judy ("Don't you miss the way it was?"), Schneider replied, "It's better than it was." But an approach to Kathy Schroeder, who occasionally got on the line, was more effective. On Koresh's orders, she'd sent out her four children, sure that her ex-husband would take his three kids and hoping he would also take three-year-old Bryan, her son with Mike Schroeder. But the ex-husband didn't, taking only his own children, and CPS tapes sent into Mount Carmel showed little Bryan sitting forlornly by himself. "I felt a lot of turmoil," Schroeder said later. "I began thinking, 'I can't let my children go through this Babylonian life without my support.'" On March 11, a negotiator assured Schroeder that, if she came out, Bryan would be waiting to greet her: "You know, Kathy, I think what Bryan really needs right now is a hug from his mommy."

Koresh was upset with her, Schroeder recalls, for smoking after the February 28 ATF raid. When she went to talk with him, "He bitched at me for smoking, and we had a conversation. He used my smoking for an excuse for kicking me out. He also told me I'd be a beacon of the message to inform the world."

On March 12, Schroeder walked out of the compound: "I had to walk to a tank with my hands up. They put zip ties on my wrists, my hands were behind my back. Then they put me in the back of a tank and we started off." She was debriefed at the FBI command center, and then, as promised, "They brought Bryan to me. I got to hold him for a half hour or so." Then agents told Schroeder that Bryan needed to be taken to dinner. Instead, he was given to Mike Schroeder's parents, who had just arrived to take custody. When Schroeder asked to see her son again, she says she was told, "Later. Later. After a while, I realized they'd screwed me."

On the same day Kathy Schroeder left Mount Carmel, Janet Reno was finally sworn in as attorney general. Three days later, on March 15, she was briefed on the proposed HRT plan to end the standoff by inserting gas into Mount Carmel. Reno asked if the military had been consulted; she wanted more input before making a decision.

FBI negotiators in Waco tried to regain lost ground. They had some hope that other Branch Davidians would follow Kathy Schroeder's example and come out. Schneider assured negotiators that everyone who wanted to go was free to do so: "Every day, we check." Schroeder, who decided cooperation was the best way to persuade the FBI to reunite her with her children, called into Mount Carmel. She reported that "they've been super," and that, so far, agents had only asked her "general questions." Everybody still inside should remember that "we're all one body, whether we're in there or out here, you know?" Afterward, one of the FBI's hidden microphones picked up someone remarking, "Kathy sounds like she's becoming one of them."

In a significant negotiating step on March 15, Sage and McLennan County sheriff Jack Harwell met with Schneider and Wayne Martin just outside the bullet-riddled front doors of Mount Carmel. Sage says that he found Martin to be "very shallow. He kept saying things like, 'You've usurped our constitutional rights.'" But Harwell interceded, keeping Martin engaged while Sage concentrated on Schneider: "I felt he [Schneider] and I had a genuine conversation. He ended up giving me seven or eight key elements that were problematic for them, and said answering them would go a long way toward resolving the situation." These included "whether, afterward, would they have access to any seized property, would they have a place to return to, meaning the compound, would they have access to the media, could David continue his ministry in jail? . . . I said, 'I don't have the horsepower to tell you yes or no, but I'll find out.'"

But nothing came of the promising meeting—in great part, Farris Rookstool says, because of specific conversations picked up inside Mount Carmel by the FBI bugs: "Hearing them [the Branch Davidians] discussing the overt act of killing federal agents played into the demonization of these people as unhinged zombies, willing to kill any agent trying to do good."

The same evening, Jamar ordered more combat engineer vehicles (CEVs) in to clear everything within fifty yards of Mount Carmel away from the building. Then they could not provide cover to any Branch Davidians rushing out to fire on FBI agents holding the perimeter. Everyone inside was upset; Koresh and Schneider both told Sage on the telephone that there would be no more meetings in person. Sage warned, "We're running out of patience. I need to impart to you that we need to get this resolved." Koresh and Sage argued. At one point, Sage responded to a lengthy Koresh diatribe with, "That's garbage." Koresh snapped, "You are in ignorance," and warned Sage, "If I'm right, you're in bigger trouble than me."

Noesner realized that tactical was ready to go further. Later, he wrote that a senior agent arriving on March 16 from El Paso to help oversee the HRT said, "No use trying to talk to these bastards. We've just got to go in there and cut their balls off." Koresh sensed that there could be imminent change. On the phone with Sage, he asked, "Are you going to kill me?" Sage said, "No," but Koresh abruptly cut off the conversation. Steve Schneider explained later, "He [Koresh] started bleeding badly. He really had to go." Schneider said that the Branch

Davidians understood the FBI's impatience, "but we're waiting for God." Koresh believed "that what he said [to negotiators] fell on deaf ears." Sage replied, "We've got to show progress."

On March 18, CEVs knocked down Mount Carmel's outdoor diesel fuel tanks. Jamar told Noesner it was necessary; otherwise, the Branch Davidians might use the highly combustible fuel to blow up the tanks and other military vehicles. As an alternative to communicating by phone, the FBI began using an elaborate outdoor PA system, so their pleas for those inside to come out did not have to be filtered through Koresh and Schneider.

Schneider tried placating his adversaries, telling a negotiator, "David is saying that the message is coming to him. Just give us a little time." The Branch Davidians had no illusions that after the siege ended, they would be free to carry on at Mount Carmel. Clive Doyle wrote, "By this time, we knew that everyone who went out was going to jail. That was very obvious." Koresh told a negotiator that more people would come out soon: "It could be some time as early as tomorrow evening, some people will come out. That's a promise. That's a guarantee." Two days later, on March 21, seven more adults did surrender to the FBI. That wasn't enough for tactical; the PA system began blasting a high-decibel outpouring that included sirens, bagpipes, squawking seagulls, crying babies, dentists' drills, crowing roosters, dying rabbits, Buddhist chants, Muslim prayer calls, Christmas carols, and pop tunes, including Nancy Sinatra's "These Boots Are Made for Walking" and Billy Ray Cyrus's "Achy Breaky Heart." The sound was cranked so high that the media, blockaded almost two miles away, complained. But the cacophony continued intermittently.

At night, high-powered beams were directed at Mount Carmel's windows. Everyone inside was soon sleep-deprived. Sage disputes, but Farris Rookstool confirms, that occasionally HRT agents standing guard around Mount Carmel would make obscene gestures toward those inside, or even drop their pants and moon the Branch

Davidians. Koresh instructed his followers to turn to their Bibles, and read Nahum 2 and Micah 2–4. These passages described the Lord taking revenge on His enemies.

On March 23, Livingstone Fagan left Mount Carmel. Schroeder says Koresh sent Fagan, one of his most devoted and articulate followers, out to offer counterpoint to the FBI's increasingly lurid claims about the Branch Davidians. If so, the plan failed. Fagan was taken into custody and confined to a local jail. He was not given an opportunity to address the media, and refused FBI offers to call in to Mount Carmel and assure everyone there that he was all right.

Sage phoned to inform Schneider that his bosses demanded "significant numbers" of Branch Davidians to exit Mount Carmel at once. Schneider refused to let him speak to Koresh, who was "taking some private time" and feeling insulted that the FBI didn't appreciate that so many people had just come out. Schneider said that he and everyone else inside couldn't understand the FBI's attitude: the Branch Davidians were "being slapped for doing something good."

Farris Rookstool says that Jeff Jamar did not understand that dealing with Branch Davidians was different: "Negotiators and behavioral science experts clearly said, 'This is not a hostage negotiation, it's not a robber in a bank, not anything for the classic methods we had been trained in.' There were heated conversations and lines drawn." But failure to bring about a resolution left Jamar frustrated. Two incidents, when outside sympathizers managed to circumvent FBI perimeters and actually enter and stay inside Mount Carmel for several days, embarrassed him.

Something had to give, and on March 24 it did. Noesner was informed that he was being relieved as negotiation coordinator. Typically, someone only served in that capacity for three weeks, and Noesner had entered his fourth. But he later learned that he was replaced after HRT boss Dick Rogers complained that Noesner was impeding tactical's more aggressive reproach; Noesner acknowledged that this was true.

"The real story," Noesner wrote, "was that, with the FBI seemingly helpless to compel the Davidians to surrender, he [Jamar] was feeling the heat. The entire nation was watching. . . . I told him [Jamar] that I didn't think we would get anyone else out after these recent actions. He appeared unconcerned.

"I realized then that he had already determined what he was going to do."

Another Way

By mid-March the Branch Davidians inside Mount Carmel were at a low ebb. They could have come out and been translated up to Heaven on March 2, but many of them had sinned, so God was displeased, and instructed Koresh to keep everyone inside. Now, Koresh waited for God to tell him what to do next, and, so far, God had nothing further to communicate. Meanwhile, the FBI still surrounded them, and showed no sign of leaving. Electricity had been cut off; they warmed their gummy MREs over lanterns. Water was becoming a concern. Outdoor receptacles were shot up during the ATF gunfight, and many water containers stored indoors had also been shattered. Phone negotiations with FBI negotiators hadn't yielded much beyond a few gallons of milk for the remaining kids, and some medical supplies. Tanks were aimed at them, and could begin blasting anytime. Based on what they heard during the FBI's daily press conferences, the world was being told all manner of terrible lies about them; it seemed that outside dark, chilly Mount Carmel, they had no friends at all, no one even trying to understand.

Then three appeared.

Drs. J. Phillip Arnold and James Tabor of Houston knew each other well. Both were esteemed biblical scholars, Arnold at Reunion Institute in Houston and Tabor at the University of North Carolina in Charlotte. On February 28, both listened intently to David's rambling interview on CNN. "David really believed he was there to fulfill a mission," Arnold says nearly three decades later. "These [religious] figures like David are not con artists. They actually believe it [what they are saying], and this is what gives them their power."

Since Arnold was in Houston, about three hours' drive from Waco, he decided to head there on March 7 and offer his insights about the Branch Davidians to the FBI. But when he arrived and tried to speak with their spokesmen at a daily press conference, he was rebuffed. Arnold was particularly appalled by a briefing sign posted by the FBI in the press area: "Koresh wounded in [the] hand, Koresh wounded in [the] side." Arnold says, "Those were the same wounds suffered by Jesus. So, I said to one of the agents there, 'Do you realize what that may seem like, the impression it might give?' But there was no interest."

Arnold wasn't the only potentially useful resource to be turned away. Joyce Sparks of CPS, who'd gotten to know Koresh well and tried to consult with the FBI after the siege was in place, testified later to Congress that the agents there "didn't think they needed to listen. . . . You couldn't get them to even stop and listen to information that could have been vital."

Arnold didn't give up after being spurned at the press conference. He found one agent at the FBI command center who confirmed for him that Koresh said they were currently in the Fifth Seal, and took Arnold's contact information. Then, waiting hopefully for the FBI to call, the Houston scholar coincidentally discovered new, potentially vital information while reading a book about the early 1900s House of David barnstorming baseball team. It mentioned a player identified as a "Koreshan." Arnold remembers, "I did a real double-take." He headed to a library and traced the "Koreshans" to Fort Myers, Florida. From there, Arnold discovered how the prophecies of David Koresh repeated those of Cyrus Teed, who proclaimed himself as "Koresh" and "the Lamb" over a century before David did the same. Arnold says, "In all my studies, I had found no other prophet claiming to be 'Koresh,' and all of a sudden, there were two within about one hundred years of each other." Further investigation revealed that a number of books written by this earlier Koresh remained in print, and one collection of some of his teachings was contained in the collection of the Waco-McLennan County Library.

In mid-March, Arnold was interviewed about the Branch Davidians on KRLD Radio in Dallas. Though he didn't bring up the Cyrus Teed connection, he did explain how Koresh's teaching "was a logical way of interpreting the Bible," although he didn't agree with Koresh's conclusions. Arnold also made another trip to Waco. During a stop in the press area a few miles from Mount Carmel, he met a reporter from CNN that he knew, and did a short interview with her. This time, he mentioned Teed. Arnold also spoke with a reporter from *The Washington Post*. CNN subsequently aired a short feature, and the *Post* published a story, each speculating whether David based his prophecies on ones by an earlier Koresh in Florida. There were no additional media mentions of the subject.

Soon afterward, someone from the FBI finally contacted Arnold: "They said, 'The Branch Davidians heard you on the radio. We're not letting you talk to them, but if you send a copy of your [KRLD] radio program to us, we'll get it to them and let them listen to it again." Arnold remembers, "I also told them about the Koresh-Teed thing. I got the impression that they had already heard something about that, but had no idea of how to use it to get David and his people out."

The FBI shared the KRLD recording with the Branch Davidians. On March 15, Steve Schneider began mentioning Arnold to negotiators. He said that the Branch Davidians wanted to hear more from him.

On April 1, they did. Arnold and James Tabor joined in a lengthy call-in interview with Ron Engelman of KGBS-AM radio in Dallas. Engelman had been actively discussing the Waco siege on his program, which was geared to "constitutionalists," listeners who frequently suspected widespread government overreach. Engelman had even gone to Waco himself in a failed attempt to see Koresh. Arnold and Tabor knew that Engelman would allow them to suggest scriptural interpretations that offered alternatives to any immediate, potentially deadly, actions on the part of Koresh and his followers.

On the air that day, they discussed the same intricate scriptural passages that Koresh used in his own prophecies and teachings. They agreed that events at Mount Carmel had caused the public to think more about the Book of Revelation. Tabor bemoaned media coverage that depicted Koresh "as just kind of a crazy man who rambles." He praised "the systematic skills of the exegesis . . . he [Koresh] knows more than he's been given credit for." Arnold observed that the Branch Davidians "are a community of faith. They should be entitled to all the protection under the Constitution."

They worked their way to the heart of their presentation: the Fifth Seal's instruction to "wait for a little season" allowed flexibility. The Lamb and his followers didn't have to die right now, or even in a few months or years. Revelation 10:11 instructed its narrator to "prophesy again before many peoples, and nations, and tongues, and kings." If Koresh surrendered peacefully to the FBI, even if he went to prison as a consequence, he should remember that Paul, greatest of all apostles, continued his ministry while imprisoned. Religious scholars would surely discuss Koresh's teachings, undoubtedly organize a public forum about them, and, Arnold said, "I think an expositor of the Book of Revelation [who] should be included in such a forum would be David Koresh."

There was the opening, both scholars stressed, if Koresh chose to take it. He would teach all the outsiders. Then the Lamb might not have to open the Sixth and Seventh Seals to bring about the End Time. Koresh told FBI negotiators that prophecy was about what would happen if nothing changed. He now had an opportunity to convince and change the world, but he had to live to do it.

Arnold and Tabor concluded the interview feeling certain they'd offered a persuasive narrative. But, with their attention focused on tanks and FBI agents ringing their home, it was unlikely that, even if their radios were tuned to KGBS, David and his followers had heard much of the Engelman show. The two scholars had to get a tape of the Engelman program to Koresh inside Mount Carmel, and, Arnold says, they didn't trust the FBI: "We had to circumvent them."

Time was of the essence. Every day that passed, the two scholars believed, made it more likely that the siege would conclude tragically. Their tape could make a difference. Arnold and Tabor had someone in mind to carry the tape into Mount Carmel, if only they could get his attention.

During much of March, Houston lawyer Dick DeGuerin was equally stymied by FBI intransigence. On March 9, he was contacted by Bonnie Haldeman, who asked him to represent her son Vernon, now David Koresh. It was a reach for nearly impoverished Bonnie; DeGuerin was a renowned defense attorney whose clients included at various times U.S. senator Kay Bailey Hutchison, U.S. congressman Tom DeLay, and several ballplayers for the New York Mets who'd engaged in a brawl at a Houston sports bar. But DeGuerin always relished the opportunity to participate in high-profile cases, and the Mount Carmel siege qualified. He'd also had several courtroom tangles in trials involving the ATF, which he considered "a rogue organization." DeGuerin agreed to represent Koresh.

On March 10, DeGuerin and Bonnie Haldeman drove to Waco, where, with TV cameras recording the scene, they attempted to enter Mount Carmel so the lawyer could confer with his new client, only to be blocked at one of the checkpoints. The next day, DeGuerin filed a writ of habeas corpus in the Waco court, claiming that, because of the siege, Koresh was literally in federal custody and therefore entitled to meet with his attorney. Judge Walter Smith rejected the argument. The FBI's Jeff Jamar was equally dismissive. For the present, he wouldn't allow DeGuerin inside Mount Carmel. He told the lawyer that he'd be in touch if anything changed.

It was March 28 before DeGuerin heard more. Then Jamar called him in Houston. DeGuerin recalls, "He [Jamar] said, 'We realize we have a common interest, seeing this end without violence. We'll put you in touch with him [Koresh] by telephone, and your conversation with him will be private.' That night, I talked to David Koresh."

This initial conversation began with DeGuerin insisting that he "was not a shill for the FBI. I told him [Koresh] that if the ATF had been like I knew them to be, they probably used excessive force. There were probably going to be murder charges. I wanted to come see him. He said, 'If they come sticking guns in my face, sticking guns at my family, then I'm going to defend myself,' or something of that nature. He said that he was eager to meet with me. He was very lucid, factual. And he said, 'They shot at me first.'" Afterward, DeGuerin again requested that Jamar allow him to meet in person with his client. Jamar told him to come back up to Waco, and "we'll see what we can do."

On March 29, DeGuerin was allowed to meet with Koresh, but told he could only do so just outside the Mount Carmel building. "They [the FBI] said I couldn't go in because they were concerned that the Davidians might try to kidnap me. I told them, 'They may be nuts, but they know that the FBI isn't going to ransom a lawyer.'"

That afternoon, DeGuerin rode up to Mount Carmel inside an armored Bradley vehicle; he remembers that the driver, an FBI agent, said, "'Let's not forget, there are four dead agents.' We rode in the Bradley to about a hundred yards from the front of the compound. Then I was told, 'You're on your own.'"

As DeGuerin walked toward the front door, his shoes "started crunching" over shell cases and flex ties left there during the failed February 28 raid. "The building had bullet holes everywhere," DeGuerin remembers. He knocked; the door opened. "I saw Steve Schneider and Wayne Martin. Behind them was an upright piano that was being used as a barricade. Beyond that, the interior was dark."

After some preliminary conversation, DeGuerin said that he needed to speak directly with his client. Koresh emerged from where he'd been concealed behind the piano: "He had a bandage on his wrist, and he was moving slowly." Koresh stood in the doorway and DeGuerin remained just outside as they talked. Koresh offered his version of the February 28 events, how he got word that ATF was coming, and told his followers to go to their rooms. According to

Koresh, "As they [the ATF] got there, deploying, he [Koresh] stepped out in front, held up his hands, and said, 'Go back, there are women and children here,' The answer was a fusillade of bullets."

DeGuerin counseled that if the ATF used excessive force without being provoked, and if the Branch Davidians fought back, "that's self-defense. Texas law is really clear on that, and this case is going to be prosecuted under state law." It was a case, DeGuerin said, that he and Koresh could win.

DeGuerin told Koresh that he needed to talk with other Branch Davidians, and to examine the scene inside Mount Carmel. As his conversation with Koresh progressed, the lawyer noticed "a pretty strong smell of sewage, and also of garlic. Some of them were treating their wounds with garlic." Koresh asked DeGuerin to describe what conditions would be like in jail. After two hours of conversation, the lawyer said goodbye and was returned to the FBI command center. There, he told Jamar that he would not discuss any details of his meeting with Koresh, and when he next returned to Mount Carmel, he'd need to go inside. DeGuerin was told that he could "enter the compound, but I had to come outside every hour to indicate that I was safe."

DeGuerin returned several times, occasionally accompanied by attorney Jack Zimmerman, who agreed to represent Steve Schneider. The two lawyers were taken upstairs in Mount Carmel and shown the bullet holes in the roof. Zimmerman, a military veteran who'd served in Vietnam, and DeGuerin, an experienced hunter, agreed that the trajectory and nature of the holes indicated gunfire from above, undoubtedly from at least one of the helicopters participating in the ATF raid. They interviewed numerous Branch Davidians, who all echoed Koresh's version of the February 28 attack.

When the subject of DeGuerin's fee came up, Koresh volunteered that he had $30,000 to $40,000 in cash on hand. DeGuerin said that amount wasn't nearly enough; Koresh's legal defense would undoubtedly be lengthy and complex. It was decided that Koresh would engage a literary agent and get a book deal. At least a $2.5 million advance seemed likely from that, even more than DeGuerin would charge. Koresh was concerned that it would look bad to personally profit from the raid and siege, so whatever sum was left over would form a trust fund for Koresh's many children. (No mention was made of Koresh's legal issues beyond the certainty of a trial for murder. DeGuerin says that other potential charges, sex offenses especially, "would have had to have him defended by someone else.")

DeGuerin's involvement in the case gave the media something new to write about. Arnold and Tabor took note. Arnold began prowling the Waco hotel where DeGuerin sometimes stayed, hoping to waylay the attorney and request that he bring the KGBS-AM tape into Mount Carmel for Koresh to hear. Arnold had no luck; at one point he called Tabor in North Carolina to declare that they'd failed. Then he happened to meet DeGuerin's wife as they both used the hotel's bank of pay phones. She brought Arnold upstairs to meet her husband, who listened to the tape and agreed to take it to the Branch Davidians.

On April 4 in Mount Carmel, David Thibodeau later told Tabor, "DeGuerin had a tape player and said to David [Koresh], 'I want you to hear this tape.' They sat in the dining hall, everybody gathered around. Everybody was quiet, listening." Koresh and his followers were impressed. They didn't think Arnold and Tabor were truly capable of explaining the Seven Seals—only Koresh, the Lamb, could do that—but they were still prominent biblical scholars. Tabor says, "They were sure David was going to convince us that he was right." Then, the Branch Davidians felt certain, Arnold and Tabor would share the message with other scholars, who would also spread the truth, and so the world might finally hear and obey. At least for a while, the End Time could be averted.

This was hope they hadn't had before, and a means by which God might be obeyed without requiring anyone else in Mount Carmel to die. Koresh seized on it; perhaps this was the message from God he'd awaited.

Though the FBI had allowed attorneys DeGuerin and Zimmerman to come into Mount Carmel, it was unlikely they'd permit Arnold and Tabor to enter. But the two scholars might still be reached, still be taught. A plan formed in Koresh's mind, and though he had to work through certain details, he felt inspired enough to share his optimism with his attorney—and also shared a new time frame.

After leaving Mount Carmel on April 4, DeGuerin told the FBI that Koresh and the Branch Davidians planned to surrender right after Passover. More information and a specific date would be forthcoming. But approximately six weeks after the initial ATF raid on February 28, the Mount Carmel siege should end peacefully.

A Passover Promise

W hat sounded simple, wasn't. Nothing about the Branch Davidians' faith was simple, including when Passover officially commenced and concluded. The holiday, celebrating the exodus of Israelites from slavery in Egypt, traditionally begins on the fifteenth day of the Hebrew month of Nisan, which marks the onset of spring. Passover lasts seven days in Israel, eight days in many other parts of the world. The Branch Davidians, whose beliefs included rigid adherence to Hebrew laws, had a complicated formula for determining their dates of Passover celebration. It was Perry Jones's responsibility to apply the formula, but now he was dead and they weren't certain which dates in April 1993 were appropriate. The FBI was not tolerant of indecision or nuance. They wanted to know immediately when Passover at Mount Carmel would end and the Branch Davidians would surrender.

On April 6, two days after DeGuerin made his announcement, and after considerable discussion inside Mount Carmel, Steve Schneider told a negotiator that, for the Branch Davidians, Passover would begin at sundown that day and be followed by seven days of religious observance. The FBI believed that meant the suspects would surrender in eight days. Schneider said no, that there wasn't a definite date when they pledged to leave Mount Carmel. Koresh was still waiting to hear from God. The promise was that they'd come out after Passover. That didn't mean the moment that Passover ended. In the meantime, the Branch Davidians wanted the FBI to shut down the noise on the PA system outside their building; it interfered with their Passover worship.

Jamar and the FBI tactical team were furious. Once again, Koresh and his followers were playing bait-and-switch, making a definite promise to come out, making demands because of it, and then reneging. The PA system stayed on. On April 7, a negotiator asked Schneider what the Branch Davidians intended to do when their Passover ended on April 14. FBI transcripts of this phone conversation note, "We got a long, long statement, part of which alluded to the tanks being 'chariots of the gods,' but not [a] clear answer."

The FBI was frustrated, but the mood inside Mount Carmel was hopeful, almost merry. David Thibodeau wrote that he and the other Branch Davidians felt "a wave of fresh hope." Koresh himself seemed optimistic. He convened an impromptu Bible study and quoted the fortieth Psalm: "I waited patiently for the Lord, and He inclined unto me, and heard my cry. He brought me up also out of an horrible pit, out of the miry clay, and set my feet upon a rock."

Over the next few days, negotiators continued pressing Schneider for a definite Branch Davidian exit date. He brushed the queries aside: "David studies, contemplates, and waits for an answer." Then, on April 10, the FBI heard from someone else. A typed letter was sent out from the compound, and it ostensibly was dictated by God.

> Friends: I offer to you My Wisdom. I offer to you My sealed secrets. How dare you turn away from My invitations of mercy. I know your sins and inequities. None are hid from Me. When will you ever fear and be wise? Your only Saviour is My Truth. My Truth is the "Seven Seals."

A number of accusatory paragraphs followed. The one-page letter concluded:

> Learn from David My seals or, as you have said, bear the consequences. I forewarn you, the Lake Waco area of Old Mount Carmel

will be terribly shaken. The waters of the lake will be emptied through
the broken dam. The heavens are calling you to judgment.

Please consider these tokens of grave concern.

Yahweh Koresh.

To the FBI, this was nothing less than Koresh threatening to blow up a Lake Waco dam. Koresh responded to a negotiator's frantic call by explaining the letter "put down" the Lord's words exactly as they were "given" to him. But such prophecies were warnings rather than threats. The Lake Waco prediction was only what would happen if the FBI—if the world—didn't listen. And in that regrettable circumstance, it would be an earthquake, not a bomb, that decimated a dam.

Not long afterward, Schneider called negotiators to tell them that another letter was being sent out. Again signed "Yahweh Koresh," it quoted many scriptural passages and cautioned, "I begin to do my strange work, a work you will not believe though it be told you. Isaiah 28." The body of the letter concluded, "Please listen, and show mercy and learn of the Marriage of the Lamb. Why will you be lost?" Attached were full replications of Psalm 45, describing the Lamb and his many willing brides, and Revelation 19, depicting the terrible fates of "the kings of the Earth, and their armies."

Even as these two letters were being composed and sent out of Mount Carmel, negotiators attempted a new tack to shake the Branch Davidians' belief in Koresh. Arnold thought that the FBI had disdained information he attempted to share, but during the evening of April 10, there was an indication that they'd listened at least once. A negotiator asked Steve Schneider if he'd ever heard of a man named Cyrus Teed, who'd led a religious group similar to the Branch Davidians. Schneider said that he hadn't. The negotiator said that there was a book about Teed, who also called himself "Koresh." Maybe Steve would like to see it.

At 7:29 p.m. on April 11, Schneider told a negotiator that even though Passover was still in progress, three Branch Davidians were thinking about coming out. Also, Koresh didn't know anything about this book that had been mentioned. Could it be sent in?

No Branch Davidians came out, and the book wasn't provided to them. Just after midnight, Schneider talked about the potential destruction of the Lake Waco dam, mentioned that a few people might be coming out in the morning, and asked again about "the Koreshian book." Koresh was interested in seeing it; he wasn't afraid of things like that. If the FBI sent the book in, everyone inside could read it.

Ten hours later, Schneider brought up "the Koreshian book" again: "I wanted to ask about the book by Cyrus Teed. We'd be interested in seeing it." A negotiator replied, "Well, what do we get for it?" Schneider was annoyed. He snapped, "Well, okay then. These people in here are very open-minded. They'd like to know what the book says."

At 12:30 a.m. on April 13, Koresh asked a negotiator how the FBI really felt "about us crazy people," and then launched into a remarkable near monologue lasting five hours and twenty minutes. Koresh talked about subjects ranging from his special status as the Lamb to the number of stars in the universe. He denounced the ATF, reminisced about his impoverished childhood, bragged that "some people say I'm one of the hottest musicians," and, after four hours, agreed with the negotiator that "there should be a peaceful resolution to this matter." Then came eighty more minutes of verbal rambling: Koresh swore he got mentor Lois Roden pregnant. There was no baby because she miscarried. On February 28, the helicopters fired into Mount Carmel. That's how one of his people died. He concluded by requesting the FBI to send in "theologians and scholars," and asked again for "the Koreshian book." That was the last mention of *Koreshanity* on the FBI's negotiation transcripts. The book was never provided to the Branch Davidians inside Mount Carmel.

Almost thirty years later, Arnold says, "That was a real opportunity lost. A book that shows a hundred years before David, there's someone else claiming all the same things. Someone like Steve

Schneider, a scholar who believed in information in books—if it [*Koreshanity*] had been sent in, maybe Steve and some others would have started wondering. There might have been at least a few lives saved."

At 8:30 that night, Dick DeGuerin called in to Mount Carmel and asked to speak to Koresh. The Passover period recognized by the Branch Davidians was ending the next day; he wanted to consult with his client. Steve Schneider told the attorney that Koresh couldn't come to the phone because he was writing another letter. On Wednesday, April 14, it was sent out. The letter was addressed to Dick DeGuerin.

> *Hello, Dick:*
>
> *As far as our progress is concerned, here is where we stand: I have related two messages, from God, to the F.B.I.; one of which concerns present danger to people here in Waco.*
>
> *I was shown a fault line running throughout the Lake Waco area. An angel is standing in charge of this event. Many people, here in Waco, know that we are a good people, and yet, they have shown the same resentful spirit of indifference to our "warnings of love."*
>
> *I am presently being permitted to document, in structured form, the decoded messages of the Seven Seals. Upon the completion of this task, I will be freed from my "waiting period." I hope to finish this as soon as possible and to stand before man to answer any and all questions regarding my actions.*
>
> *The written Revelation of the Seven Seals will not be sold, but is to be available to all who wish to know the Truth. The Four Angels of Revelation 7 are here, now ready to punish foolish mankind; but, the writing of these Seals will cause the winds of God's wrath to be held back a little longer.*
>
> *I have been praying so long for this opportunity; to put the Seals in written form. Speaking the Truth seems to have very little effect on men.*
>
> *I was shown that as soon as I am given over into the hands of*

man, I will be made a spectacle of, and people will not be concerned about the truth of God, but just the bizarrity of me—the flesh (person).

I want the people of this generation to be saved. I am working night and day to complete my final work of the writing out of "these Seals."

I thank my Father, He has finally granted me the chance to do this. It will bring New Light and hope for many and they will not have to deal with me the person.

The earthquake in Waco is not something to be taken lightly. It will probably be "the thing" needed to shake some sense into the people. Remember, Dick, the warning came first and I fear that the F.B.I. is going to suppress this information. It may be left up to you.

I will demand that the first manuscript of the Seals be given to you. Many scholars and religious leaders will wish to have copies for examination. I will keep a copy with me. As soon as I can see that people, like Jim Tabor and Phil Arnold have a copy I will come out and then you can do your thing with this Beast.

I hope to keep in touch with you by letter, so please give your address.

We are standing on the threshold of Great events! The Seven Seals, in written form are the most sacred information ever!

David Koresh

The letter was sent out early on Wednesday morning. At 11:45 a.m., DeGuerin was allowed to call in again to Mount Carmel and talk with David. Afterward, the lawyer reiterated to the FBI that Koresh pledged to come out, accompanied by all his followers, as soon as he completed writing about the Seven Seals and was certain his instructions about copies being distributed had been followed. Koresh estimated it would take him one or two days to write about each seal—so, probably ten days to two weeks in all. Then, he'd come out, and the siege would end. This was Koresh's promise.

Inside Mount Carmel, the Branch Davidians were thrilled. Clive Doyle wrote, "When the word went around that David had made the negotiation to write the Seals and we would all go out together, there was real rejoicing that this was finally over, it has all been resolved. There were just a few days left, and we would be out of there." They hung new signs written on sheets out of their windows, among them "Read Proverbs 1, 2, 3, 4, We Come to Love, Not War" and "Let's Have a Beer When This Is Over."

There was no more discussion of "translating" immediately upon their exit. Rather, Doyle wrote, "We knew we were going to jail. But at least this severe lifestyle we were forced to live—rationing and no water and not being able to take a bath and go to the bathroom properly—would be over. If we did go to jail, we would deal with that when it came."

Koresh apparently accepted that jail was in his future. Once he was imprisoned, he predicted to a negotiator, he'd be asked, "'Do you molest young ladies? Have you beaten babies? Do you sacrifice people? Do you make automatic weapons?' That's what they're going to be interested in—sensationalism." Arnold says, "He [Koresh] was going to be like Jesus in the Garden of Gethsemane or Jesus on the cross. He was facing his fate, accepting it, and God was going to be with him." (Joyce Sparks testified to Congress that she believed Koresh expected to avoid prison: "Remember, he thought he was the Lamb. He always assumed he could talk his way out of anything.")

On Thursday and Friday, both Koresh and Steve Schneider reported to negotiators that progress writing the Seals was on schedule. Koresh was dictating to Branch Davidian Ruth Riddle, who typed his words on an IBM Selectric. Then she and Clive Doyle retyped the material onto a disk in a word processor. On Friday, Koresh informed a negotiator that he'd completed the First Seal and was beginning to write about the Second. On Saturday night, Koresh told a negotiator that he missed Thrifty Maid Hot Sauce, and chatted about the pleasures of eating crayfish doused with the condiment. On Sunday night,

April 18, Schneider said Koresh was hard at work writing about the Second Seal, and that the Branch Davidians were waiting for him to finish all seven. Sixty-two adults and twenty-one children believed that their fifty-day ordeal was about to end.

They were right.

The Limits of Patience

On March 2, David Koresh proved to the leaders and members of the FBI Hostage Rescue Team in Waco that he could not be trusted. He reneged after pledging to lead his followers out of Mount Carmel if his tape about Branch Davidian beliefs was aired on radio for a national audience. Koresh's excuse for not keeping his promise—God told him to wait—was, so far as the tactical team was concerned, an obvious ploy. Koresh's "Bible babble" was bunk. Negotiating with Koresh only gave the con man more opportunities to drag things out indefinitely. Further negotiations were a waste of time.

"The people on the site, the HRT, were very testosterone-driven agents," says Farris Rookstool III, the analyst assigned by the FBI to record agency activities during the siege. "Their job always is to wrap things up in a couple of days."

If daily tension was almost unbearable for everyone inside Mount Carmel, all the FBI personnel outside were under constant strain, too. "It was hard," Rookstool says. "You worked twelve-hour shifts, you were away from home and family, living in motels. Domino's Pizza should have been the official food sponsor." It was toughest for the HRT members guarding the property perimeter, and frequently tasked with delivering milk, medical supplies, and other items to Mount Carmel's front door, knowing they were constantly in range of dozens of gun-wielding suspects who'd already killed four ATF agents. HRT agents fumed while negotiators spent days on the phone with Koresh and Steve Schneider. They preferred a more expeditious means of ending the stalemate. On March 10, when HRT leaders in Waco sent a proposed action plan to agency headquarters in Washington, their proposal was "a phased operation" with tanks approaching Mount Carmel, and "if necessary, employ[ing] chemical agents inside."

By late March, even with negotiators' relatively low-key approach, Koresh was sometimes refusing to speak with them. Lead negotiator Gary Noesner was removed, though hope of talking the Branch Davidians out of Mount Carmel wasn't immediately abandoned. During a March 25 conference call, a Department of Justice official in Washington asked Byron Sage, "Do you think negotiations are over?" Sage replied, "No, sir, even if he's [Koresh] not talking to us, at least we think he's listening to what we've got to say." But negotiators adopted a tougher tone, particularly when disputing Branch Davidian arguments that their religious beliefs were being violated by the government. On March 25, when a negotiator asked, "What will move this along?" Wayne Martin said, "If the government respected our religious freedom." The negotiator replied, "No, not the esoteric stuff."

At 9 a.m. on March 26, another negotiator told Steve Schneider, "We need to get some people out by noon. Per our commanders, ten or more." When Schneider demurred, citing Koresh's decision to wait for instructions from God, he was told, "The God I know wouldn't molest kids, [or] take others' wives. Everyone has their own interpretation of the Bible. When did Jesus, God, ever molest ten- or twelve-year-old girls?" Schneider said, "That's a ridiculous question." When the negotiator reiterated that ten Branch Davidians had to come out of Mount Carmel by noon, Schneider replied, "You can burn us out, kill us, whatever. These people fear God, not you." The negotiator said, "Vernon Howell is a coward and a con man." He concluded the conversation by reminding Schneider, "Get some people out by noon. We've got to see it." When nothing further happened, at ten minutes past noon heavy armored vehicles began clearing the area immediately around the building. The process continued for over twenty-four hours, with remaining cars, fences, and even trees removed. The message was obvious: the tanks could crash through Mount Carmel's walls anytime. The Branch Davidians didn't waver. The siege continued.

In 1995, Joyce Sparks from Child Protective Services in Waco testified before Congress that "about the end of March [1993]," she was contacted by an agent "from the [FBI] command post." The agent, whom Sparks did not identify, told her there was a plan to force the Branch Davidians out of Mount Carmel by using a nonlethal form of gas. The agent wanted to know if CPS personnel could be on hand to assist with the Branch Davidian children. "I asked him what kind of protective clothing my staff would wear, what kind of an effect it was going to have on the children and my staff. We discussed it at some length. There was going to be medical personnel and on-site showers. My concern was that I knew when I was there [inside Mount Carmel], there were propane tanks in the hallway. I wondered if that was going to present a problem."

But about 5:30 that afternoon, Sparks testified, the FBI agent called again "and said, you know, 'Forget it.' What we [CPS staff] assumed was that they had decided it was too dangerous."

The FBI hadn't abandoned the idea of using gas. But another option had emerged, one that Attorney General Reno wanted explored first.

The Branch Davidians had been without sufficient water since the failed ATF raid on February 28. Combatants shot holes in the water tank directly outside the building. That caused a steady leak in the Branch Davidians' main source of water, and indoor water containers were also shattered during the attack. The Branch Davidians set out buckets to catch rainwater, but by the end of March and early April it wasn't raining much in Waco anymore. Inside Mount Carmel, everyone was thirsty. There was still some water in the outside tank, but even though the Branch Davidians were limiting themselves to one or two eight-ounce drinks per day, it was still being depleted. Clyde Doyle wrote that "we didn't have water for washing."

During the first week in April, the FBI explored the possibility that running out of water might force the Branch Davidians to give up. When Koresh sent out tapes of himself and his children, agents saw that the kids' hair was unwashed. If drawn-out thirst didn't do the trick, maybe personal hygiene would. Surely no one inside could stand going for weeks without a bath. Rookstool thought differently: "If you analyze their [the Branch Davidians'] lifestyle, limited water wasn't an impediment to their quality of life. They were at home, in their home, with mostly what had been their everyday life to begin with. They were suffering for God, waiting for God, happy to meditate and pray. This was not something the Bureau [FBI] could understand. In that sense, the HRT became the hostages in the Branch Davidian standoff."

The FBI's decision to wait and see what might happen due to the Mount Carmel water shortage didn't last long. On April 7, two Department of Justice officials met in Waco with representatives of the FBI, ATF, Texas Rangers, and the Texas Department of Public Safety. Afterward, they returned to Washington and reported to Attorney General Reno that the FBI once again requested "utilizing tear gas to resolve the standoff at the compound."

The type of gas proposed was 2-chlorobenzalmalononitrile, a white powder commonly identified as CS gas. Those coming in contact with it suffer eye, skin, and respiratory irritation. The FBI proposed inserting CS gradually into Mount Carmel, utilizing noncombustible "ferret rounds" lobbed or dropped in by tanks. Over forty-eight hours, the Branch Davidians' discomfort would become so unbearable that they would emerge with their hands up, and then be scrubbed down, taken into custody, and the siege would end.

There were potential complications, including the rickety Mount Carmel building itself. In its March 10 action plan submitted to FBI headquarters, the HRT team in Waco added two addendums typed in all capital letters. The first noted, "THERE IS SOME QUESTION WHETHER THE FERRET WILL PENETRATE THE TAR PAPER COVERED PORTION OF THE UNFINISHED AREA [the outside pit]. (DUE TO THE ANGLE) SOME OR ALL OF THE FERRETS MAY NOT PENETRATE." The second cautioned, "HRT HAS TALKED TO MILITARY ENGINEERS AND HAVE DEVELOPED INFORMATION REGARDING THE CONTRUCTION OF THE COMPOUND. IT IS NOT OF GOOD QUALITY." Using tanks to batter holes before lobbing ferret rounds of CS gas into the Mount Carmel gymnasium area might "RESULT IN THE COLLAPSE OF THE ROOF. HRT ADVISED THAT THEY HAVE ON OCCA-SION 'BUMPED' THE COMPOUND USING CEVS [combat engi-neer vehicles] AND IT IS NOT VERY STABLE."

Some studies indicated that large amounts of CS gas could be combustible, and that exposure to significant quantities indoors could result in serious illness or death. But the FBI didn't expect to soak Mount Carmel in CS, just gradually ratchet up the gas levels until the Branch Davidians came out. That plan would be in effect so long as those inside Mount Carmel didn't resist with gunfire. Byron Sage remembers, "Plan A was to give them another chance to come out, continue negotiations while the HRT introduced tear gas into the compound and gradually took away their comfort zone. If they opened up [fired] at us, we'd mobilize Plan B, saturate the place and force them out. Plan B, to put in everything we had, was only if [our] agents and vehicles started taking fire."

On February 28, the Branch Davidians fought back against an assault on Mount Carmel. But that was the outgunned ATF. The FBI had tanks. Surely, even religious fanatics would be too intimidated to shoot at those.

The Branch Davidians guessed that a gas attack might be com-ing. They'd anticipated such an assault long before the ATF and FBI arrived, and stocked up on gas masks purchased at gun shows and survival equipment outlets. They had plenty, but none were sized to fit children. In March, they attempted "test fittings," trying, mostly unsuccessfully, to adjust straps so the masks would snugly cover the kids' faces. Many of the adults also had trouble securing the masks; their faces were much thinner because they'd lost considerable weight during the siege. If a gas attack came, it would be hard to hold out long.

Dick DeGuerin's announcement on April 4 that the Branch Davidians intended to leave Mount Carmel after observing Passover didn't convince the FBI on-site leaders, who believed it was probably just another effort by Koresh to prolong the siege, and extend the media attention he so obviously enjoyed. Their skepticism increased on April 10 and 11, when letters from God or "Yahweh Koresh" prophesized disasters including the destruction of a Lake Waco dam. Koresh kept getting wackier. Just to be on the safe side, on April 13, the date most calendars indicated was the end of Passover in 1993, Farris Rookstool says that the FBI "had buses there outside Mount Carmel" in case the Branch Davidians actually emerged: "The Hostage Rescue Team had the mindset, after those buses weren't filled up, that 'We've got to do something.'"

Koresh's April 14 letter to Dick DeGuerin, promising to surrender after he wrote about the Seven Seals, was considered an additional delaying tactic. For a couple of weeks Koresh could report that he was busy writing, then claim he'd gotten another message from God telling him to wait. The FBI wasn't going to fall for it twice. Time was up.

On April 12, Attorney General Reno received a seventy-eight-page briefing book describing in detail the proposed gas attack on Mount Carmel. It included details on gas insertion, and the assurance that "experience with the effects on CS gas on children including infants has been extensively investigated. Available reports indicate that, even in high concentrations or enclosed areas, long term complications from CS exposure is [sic] extremely rare." FBI analysts warned of potential Branch Davidian mayhem outside Mount Carmel: "The threat posed by Koresh and his followers include both a possible mass break-out or a massive explosion. . . . Koresh will not come out under any conditions other than his own." There was a reminder that the daily siege cost was $129,429, and as of April 15, the total cost was $5,898,247. "In summary, [analysts] are of the opinion that the threat level posed by Koresh is clear but his ultimate timetable is not. Further, they are firm in their belief that we have no clear ability to influence the exit of him and his followers from their compound short of tactical intervention." Gary Noesner, removed from the negotiating process three weeks earlier, wrote later that this briefing was "more a sales pitch for one course of action than a complete presentation of all the information."

Reno still wasn't convinced, and asked for another check on Mount Carmel's water supply. She was told that the Davidians had enough to hold out much longer. On April 14, Army officials explained to the attorney general that they could only offer a general opinion. In similar circumstances, they believed the military would consider "inclusive application" of tear gas "rather than employing an incremental approach." Two days later, Reno requested more information from the FBI, particularly concerning the need for tactical assault. For the moment, she disapproved the gassing plan. FBI director William Sessions called Reno and asked that she reconsider. On April 17, she did: the HRT in Waco could proceed with its plan. According to the subsequent report by congressional investigators, "Attorney General Reno has never fully explained what led her to reverse her decision." The FBI would begin a step-by-step CS gas insertion process on Monday, April 19, and extend it over forty-eight hours if needed.

All the while, Koresh closed himself off from the others inside Mount Carmel and worked, dictating his explanation or "opening" of each of the Seven Seals. Shortly after midnight on April 16, Koresh told a negotiator that his writing about the First Seal was finished. Asked when all seven sections would be completed, he replied, "Not long." Koresh pledged again that once he was finished, and confirmed that copies were in the hands of DeGuerin, Arnold, and Tabor, he would come out of Mount Carmel. When asked, "Are you telling me here and now that as soon as you reduce the Seven Seals to a written form, that you're coming out of there? I don't mean two days later," Koresh replied, "I see no reason not to."

Later that day, a negotiator asked Steve Schneider if there was a chance any Branch Davidians might come out before Koresh finished writing: "It would be a show of good faith." Schneider replied that he hadn't asked anyone if they wanted to go and, besides, people were upset that during the night, a Bradley fighting vehicle had knocked a hole in a Mount Carmel wall some one hundred feet from the front door. The massive new crater was "about as big as a Bradley and about one foot deep." The negotiator said that wasn't supposed to happen.

On April 17, as Koresh took a writing break, he admitted to Clive Doyle that "nothing was going the way he visualized it. . . . God had not shown him this immediate situation, or the way things were going in the siege. Sometimes, prophets don't get to see all that far into the future."

Soon after Reno approved the FBI's CS gas plan, negotiators called in to Mount Carmel to advise that additional "clearing operations" were about to commence in front of the building. The Branch Davidians were warned that while this final cleanup was under way, they must observe "rules of safety"—in particular, coming near windows would be considered making a threat toward federal personnel and agents.

On Sunday morning, April 18, Attorney General Reno informed President Clinton of the CS gas plan to be implemented the next day at Mount Carmel. The president had the authority to call it off. He did not.

On Sunday afternoon, Koresh complained to a negotiator about Saturday's clearing process all around Mount Carmel: "We have done everything we can to communicate in a nice, passionate way. We have told you what our work with God is, and we've been kind. We've not been your everyday kind of cult. We've not been your everyday kind of terrorists, which I'm sure you're familiar with having to deal with." Koresh asked, "What do you men really want?" The negotiator replied, "I think the problem on this thing, David, is that this thing has lasted way too long . . . people just want to see some kind of progress."

Koresh became agitated. He claimed, "You don't realize what progress is being made—there are people all over the world who are going to benefit from this book of the Seven Seals. You don't seem to understand." The negotiator said that he did understand: "What we're trying to do—" and Koresh cut him off, shouting, "It's wrong! You're doing something wrong before God!"

The decision to gas Mount Carmel on Monday was a closely held secret among leaders of the HRT team and operation lead agent Jeff Jamar. Byron Sage, who'd been in Waco since February 28, remembers that "I finally decided, 'To hell with this, I'm going to go home and reintroduce myself to my family.'" His hometown of Round Rock was a few hours' drive south of Waco. "I told Jeff [Jamar] that I was making a speed run home, and would be back in the morning. I was quite literally pulling into my driveway when my phone rang. It was Jeff, asking, 'Where are you? We're going in tomorrow.'"

Not long after Koresh lost his temper with the negotiator on Sunday afternoon, FBI surveillance devices picked up a conversation inside Mount Carmel between Steve Schneider and Scott Sonobe. The two Branch Davidians discussed the FBI assault that they believed could be imminent. Fire, they thought, might result. Schneider joked to Sonobe, "You always wanted to be a charcoal briquette." Sonobe replied, "I told him [Koresh] that there's nothing like a good fire to bring us to the birth."

Later, the same devices recorded an unidentified Branch Davidian woman saying, "There's such a thing as fear. I mean, you read about it, you always think it's far away. But it's here."

To Die in Flames

David Thibodeau was standing guard on the early shift near Mount Carmel's front door on Monday, April 19. About 2 a.m., he saw two tanks and some smaller Bradley fighting vehicles moving closer to the building. Operating tanks under any circumstances is difficult. During the Mount Carmel siege, the FBI had Army tanks, but not Army tank drivers. Agents received minimal instruction, then had to drive the tanks themselves. They rarely demonstrated total control of the massive vehicles. Thibodeau wrote later that the tanks and Bradleys "scurried" into place. Then, after "an interval of silence," the outside public address system began blasting an earsplitting din of animal howls and high-decibel music. Inside Mount Carmel, most of the Branch Davidians still managed uneasy sleep. On the fifty-first day of the siege, they were physically as well as emotionally exhausted. It was cold inside the building, caused as much by howling wind whipping through its many cracks and crevices as the outdoor temperature in the low 40s. The Branch Davidians had stacked hay bales against some walls to serve as insulation, but the wind still whistled in. Coleman lanterns provided minimal heat as well as light. Water and medical supplies were scant, but there was an ample supply of fuel for the lanterns.

Thibodeau was still standing watch when, just before dawn, the phone rang. It was 5:59 a.m., and Byron Sage was calling. Thibodeau picked up the phone. When Sage asked to speak to Steve Schneider, Thibodeau said he was sleeping. Sage said to wake him up: "We have no option. You have to get him."

Thibodeau shook Schneider awake. When he came on the phone, Sage told him that nonlethal gas was about to be inserted into the compound. Everyone was to come out immediately. Schneider yelled to his groggy comrades, "Grab your masks," and, "Everyone, wake up!" Sage demanded, "Come out now," and Schneider hung up. FBI bugs picked up sounds of metal clinking—agents believed the Branch Davidians were gathering weapons.

The cacophony over the outside PA system was replaced by Sage's voice, informing those inside Mount Carmel that "we are in the process of placing tear gas in the building. This is not an assault. Do not fire your weapons. If you fire, fire will be returned. This is not an assault." Sage informed the Branch Davidians that they were going to be placed under arrest: "This standoff is over."

The phone line into the compound was not working. Perhaps Schneider had taken his phone off the hook. Sage announced over the PA, "Send a flag out the front door if you want telephone contact."

The tanks moved in close enough to lob ferret rounds of gas through Mount Carmel's windows. According to Sage, the Branch Davidians immediately responded with gunfire: "They opened up on us at 6:11. We first injected gas around 6:16, when it was still dark out." The FBI's Plan A was to insert CS gas gradually for up to forty-eight hours, so long as the tanks were not fired on. Within the first moments of the tanks' approach, Plan A was abandoned for Plan B.

At 6:25 a.m., the FBI bug revealed Branch Davidians asking, "Are we going to call them back?" and being told that the phone wasn't working. There were "popping sounds," apparently gunshots. The FBI log noted, "We are still taking rounds from the compound." The Branch Davidians' phone came flying out of the building; apparently, a tank had accidentally cut the phone line. The first CS clouds spread inside Mount Carmel. Sage announced over the PA that those inside had two minutes to come out, or more gas would be inserted.

Gas masks were distributed inside Mount Carmel, but as expected none fit the children. Their mothers filled pails with water, soaked rags and towels, and used them to cover the kids' faces. That didn't help much. The CS gas was already affecting even the adults who were wearing masks. Everyone was coughing, and when the gas powder settled on exposed skin, a terrible burning sensation ensued. The ferret rounds were approximately two-thirds the size of Coke cans. By 6:47, thumping sounds as the ferrets whizzed in and smacked off walls and floors were clearly audible to the FBI bugs. One ferret hit a Branch Davidian squarely in the skull, and he dropped unconscious. The FBI log noted that at 6:55 a.m., "Firing at the Bradley's [sic] stopped. Still no firing being returned by the FBI HRT." Clive Doyle wrote later that inside Mount Carmel, "Grown men were almost in tears from the gas getting on their skin." Some instinctively sought shelter in the chapel; women herded panicked, choking children in the general direction of the tunnel leading to the buried school bus. The Branch Davidians were already beaten down.

But the FBI couldn't be sure, and all-out Plan B continued. By just 7:09 a.m., agents already worried that their stock of ferret rounds was running low. They'd begun the assault with four hundred, but after the morning gas attack began, they sent out a plea to local law enforcement agencies for more. One participating agent radioed, "Ferrets not penetrating walls. . . . All windows have been fired into." Some gunfire from Mount Carmel was again directed at the tanks; the bullets bounced off. A PA announcement coaxed, "Come out now, and you won't be harmed. David Koresh no longer directs the compound members. This is not an assault. We will continue to deliver gas until everyone leaves the building. Do not subject yourselves to further discomfort for you and your children. Leave the building now." But tanks ringed Mount Carmel; their protruding gun barrels smoked from expended ferret rounds and CS gas. Many years later, FBI analyst Farris Rookstool III says, "I've never had a warm, fuzzy feeling running toward a tank. Never in my entire life have I encountered any mother who would let her child do that. I don't think that the manner in which the tanks came in created any trust."

The FBI bugs picked up the first Branch Davidian mention of

Koresh: "Don't fire until the last-minute orders by David." The agency's log noted, "They are anticipating, waiting for us to enter." A PA announcement promised, "We are not entering the building. . . . David, this will not come to an end until you are all out of the building. We are ready to meet you and provide appropriate medical attention." The FBI bug picked up, "We don't need to go," and the FBI log noted, "Sounds of guns loading."

Just before 8 a.m., Sage made another PA announcement: "Walk down the driveway and surrender to the guys in the Bradleys. You are now under arrest. This is not an assault. We don't want to hurt anyone."

But moments later, according to the FBI log, its agents became more aggressive. A tank "bre[a]ched [a] hole in 2nd floor and gas being pumped in," though "parts of the building have not been penetrated by gas." Audiotapes later revealed that one tank driver received permission to use combustible "military" rather than non-combustible ferret rounds to insert gas near "the bunker where the [school] bus was." Even these military rounds bounced off. They did not combust.

The news media, penned up two miles from the Branch Davidian property, could see very little of the action. "But you knew what was happening," Carlton Stowers recalls. "We all knew that it wouldn't end pretty."

Some cable and major news networks had long-range cameras on the ground and helicopters hovering on the edges of the Mount Carmel no-fly zone, so Americans all over the country were able to have a relatively unobstructed view of the chaotic proceedings.

About 9 a.m., bugs picked up Steve Schneider saying that he wanted to tell the FBI about Koresh's progress in crafting the Seven Seals manuscript. Even with clouds of gas permeating much of Mount

Carmel, the Branch Davidians still held some hope that if the FBI understood that Koresh was working hard and keeping his promise, agents might relent and keep their promise to wait until his writing was complete.

The FBI began making PA instructions every ten minutes. The Branch Davidians responded by hanging out one of their bedsheet banners: "We want our phone fixed." Koresh, apparently alternating writing about the Seven Seals with checking on his followers, told some of them, "Hold tight. We're trying to establish communication. Maybe we can still work this out." An FBI surveillance device picked up Schneider saying, "The manuscript is almost complete. They were working all night."

A Branch Davidian ran outside, picked up the phone that had been thrown there, and scrambled back into Mount Carmel after yelling, "David's transcript is almost complete!" A PA announcement instructed the besieged to "bring as much [phone] line as you can inside." The FBI would try to resume direct communications.

At 10 a.m., the tanks began knocking down Mount Carmel. It wasn't hard. The fragile walls crumbled when the massive vehicles crashed against them. And as walls collapsed, parts of the building's roof crashed down.

Branch Davidian mothers originally tried to guide their children away from the choking clouds of CS gas by taking an underground tunnel to the buried school bus. But the tunnel was blocked by debris knocked loose in the first few minutes of the assault. They turned around and sought shelter in the concrete-walled gunroom, the former pantry, where cases of ammunition were still stacked high. All the mothers who could pushed their children inside, then crawled in beside them, slamming shut the one door into the room to keep out the gas. But as the tanks slammed into the building, the door was dislodged and the gas wafted in. If the women and children suffered from it, some did so only for moments, because the roof and parts of the walls crashed in on top of them. Many were killed by the impact. Others were pinned where they lay.

Others inside Mount Carmel did not know what happened to those in the gunroom. They were frantically darting from one hallway or room to another, trying to avoid the disintegrating walls and the barrels of the tanks reducing them to rubble. The wind outside grew wilder; Mount Carmel's remaining byzantine corridors provided perfect routes for swirling clouds of CS gas.

Byron Sage got on the PA system at 11:09 a.m. and said, "David, Steve, we're still here. So are you. We're placing tear gas and will continue to do so. You are prolonging the inevitable. . . . Walk out with hands up, no weapons or anything that is construed as a weapon. Your word has been hollow and false. We want you to exit now and submit yourselves to proper authorities." No one came out. The tanks continued smashing into the building. The gymnasium was demolished. Stairways were knocked askew, trapping some Branch Davidians on upper floors. Amid the confusion, the phone line was reconnected and negotiators called in. The phone rang twenty times, but no one answered. For weeks, the FBI had concealed bugs inside milk cartons and medical supplies sent into Mount Carmel. A few still worked. One now confirmed people were still alive inside; their blurted comments included, "The big window, what is that?," "You guys, what's . . . ?," "Right here," "Look out," "Make room," and then the sound of running feet as a tank crunched into a nearby wall. Abruptly, the FBI bugs that remained active stopped transmitting; like the children and mothers in the gunroom, they were crushed by debris.

It was one minute past noon when Byron Sage called out over the PA, "David, we are facilitating you leaving the compound by the front door. David, you have had your fifteen minutes of fame. . . . You're the person that put these people in that condition. Vernon is no longer the Messiah. Leave the building now."

Thibodeau wrote, "By noon, the building is a tinderbox. A thick layer of methylene chloride dust deposited by the CS gas coats the walls, floors, and ceilings, mingling with kerosene and propane vapors from our spilled lanterns and crushed heaters. . . . The whole place is primed like a pot-bellied stove with its damper flung open. Suddenly, someone yells—'Fire!'"

There were, eventually, three popular theories about how Mount Carmel came to burn. The first, and, though beloved by conspiracy theorists, least likely, is that the FBI deliberately set the fire. This theory is often based on the FBI's brief use of "military" rounds during the earliest stage of the gas onslaught. An agent operating a tank radioed in that the noncombustible ferrets couldn't penetrate a corner of Mount Carmel. He requested and received permission to use some more powerful military rounds. These rounds he fired—just two or three—utilized combustible shells. The FBI initially denied they'd been used at all; subsequent discovery of audiotapes and photographs of two spent shells proved otherwise. But these very few combustible rounds did not penetrate the surface they struck, and were fired at least four hours before the Mount Carmel blaze began. The FBI's tactics on April 19, 1993, created the situation that led to the fire, but the agency did not deliberately set the fire itself.

A second, more plausible theory, is that the fire was an accident. Tanks crashing into Mount Carmel caused lit Coleman lanterns and space heaters to fall over and ignite pools of accelerant leaking from other overturned containers. Mount Carmel was mostly constructed of flammable materials, and the hay bales lining walls for rudimentary insulation during the siege were prime kindling for a bonfire. Swirling winds spread highly combustible gas clouds through every cranny of the tottering building. Mount Carmel was engulfed in flames almost before its defenders realized what was happening.

The third, and most popular theory, is that Branch Davidians set the fire themselves, choosing either to die in defiant group suicide or else igniting the blaze as a means of "translating" from mortal flesh to a new life in God's Wave Sheaf. In either instance, it would not have happened by popular vote. Even in the best of times, group communication was difficult when everyone was scattered in different parts of the sprawling building. David might have informed as many followers as possible that the moment had arrived to die in flames and live afterward in glory, but there would still have been dozens who had no idea of what was happening. Afterward, survivor Graeme Craddock would recall hearing someone say, "Light the fire," someone objecting, and then the command repeated: "Light the fire!"

There is a fourth, seldom considered, possibility. Evidence indicates that David Koresh spent some of his time immediately before the conflagration, but after the gas attack began that morning, working on the Seven Seals manuscript. He'd previously finished a poem to precede the main body of work, and his explanation of the First Seal. On April 19, he added something more, an index of specific scriptural passages he'd used as references. This, with Monday's date noted, was preserved on a computer disk along with what he'd written so far. The disk was found in the possession of survivor Ruth Riddle, and subsequently made its way into the possession of scholars James Tabor and J. Phillip Arnold.

Koresh clearly remained in spiritual mode even as the tanks rumbled in and clouds of CS gas engulfed Mount Carmel. Arnold suggests that if, around noon, David ordered fire to be set, his intention may have been not to burn himself and his followers alive, but to create a holy barrier that the FBI's tanks and gas could not penetrate. Zechariah 2:5 tells of a promise that God will save Jerusalem in its peril by surrounding the city with "a wall of fire round about," and that all inside would be safe, while the Lord "will be the glory in the midst." That could be scripturally linked with perhaps David's favorite book of the Bible; Isaiah 43:2 offers God's promise that "when thou walkest through the fire, thou shalt not be burned; neither shall the flame kindle upon thee."

It would not be surprising if, surrounded by what they believed were the forces of Babylon, and with no other escape possible, at Koresh's direction some of the Branch Davidians turned to the Bible for a means of rescuing themselves. With the rest of America watching, it would have been impressive for the TV cameras to record God's fire protecting His loyal servants from the minions of evil.

No matter how or why the fire started, within moments every inch of Mount Carmel was engulfed. Anyone viewing the blaze, on-site, on television, or later in photographs saw something dramatic and unforgettable. Some inside, caught by surprise or else impelled by a last-second sense of self-preservation, tried frantically to escape the burning building. Others chose to stay and die; Clive Doyle recalls Wayne Martin suggesting that everyone pray.

FBI officials watched at their Washington, D.C., headquarters. One muttered, "Holy shit."

Waco Tribune-Herald photographer Rod Aydelotte, stuck with other on-site media almost two miles away, was astonished by the towering flames. He remembers, "The whole place burning didn't take long, really. They didn't have equipment right there to put it out."

Kathy Schroeder, in custody at a Waco hospital, was told by a nurse to come and see what was happening on TV. She watched Mount Carmel burn, and says nearly thirty years later, "Those that died in fire attained a place in the future event [End Time]. They're coming back. While the rest of my friends became Wave Sheaf and translated through fire, I was left behind."

Antigovernment militiaman Timothy McVeigh, watching on television from a farm in Michigan, gaped at the screen and blurted to like-minded friends sitting next to him, "What is this? What has America become?"

At 12:12 p.m., Byron Sage pleaded over the PA, "David, don't put those people through this. Don't lose control. Lead them to safety. David, we need you to bring the people out." One minute later, an

HRT member radioed, "They're torching the place," and from inside Mount Carmel, over the roar and crackle of fire, came the sounds of rounds exploding. The Branch Davidians weren't shooting; their stored ammunition was "cooking off," bursting from the searing heat, all over the building but especially in the gunroom, whose concrete walls were still mostly standing, but portions of whose roof lay in chunks over dead bodies.

People began appearing at different places on the roof, or emerging from holes made by tanks in side walls, nine of the Branch Davidians, all adults—Clive Doyle, Graeme Craddock, David Thibodeau, Jaime Castillo, Derek Lovelock, Misty Ferguson, Renos Avraam, Marjorie Thomas, and Ruth Riddle. FBI agents ordered them to lie on their stomachs and put their hands behind their backs so they could be constrained. Several among the nine were badly burned. A few had traces of accelerant—kerosene, lighter fluid, diesel fuel—on their clothes or shoes. Agents asked repeatedly where the children were—how could they reach them and try to bring them to safety? None of the survivors knew.

It was 12:34 p.m. when county firefighters arrived, the sirens on their trucks echoing along the back country roads to Mount Carmel. But the FBI made them wait about ten more minutes before allowing them to begin extinguishing the blaze; it was possible there were still some Branch Davidians alive inside, armed and ready to shoot at anyone coming near. It took hours to put out the flames, and another day before the smoldering ruins had cooled sufficiently for anyone to begin examining them.

Portions of the building still stood, including parts of the second floor. But inside, there was no sign of life. The only motion came when stored cans of beans, cooking all the while, exploded from pressure, scattering their contents and sounding a great deal like gunfire. Mount Carmel had become a scene of gruesome death, but not yet quiet.

Cyrus Teed, the first Koresh, predicted in the March 25, 1898, edition of *The Flaming Sword* that "the world is mobilizing for its grandest pyrotechnic display." Perhaps he was a prophet after all.

On Tuesday, with the fire put out but the Mount Carmel ruins still sizzling, Texas Department of Public Safety official Mike Cox arrived at the media area and said that six journalists would be taken to view the scene from the road outside the property. Afterward, they would be required to share their notes and photos with everyone else. The half dozen selected complied.

Carlton Stowers was among the six. He remembers, "It was heartbreaking. They were bringing out body bags, laying them side by side. There was still smoke, a lot of it. The place was mostly burned all the way down except for right in the middle, where there had been a room with concrete walls. That was where they'd kept their ammo, and apparently during the fire some of the Davidians tried to get in there. And I said to myself, 'This was so uncalled for.'"

The Texas Rangers were tasked with searching the ruins to discover bodies and collect evidence. It was an unnerving assignment. They were accompanied by FBI analyst Rookstool, remaining on the scene to serve as official crime scene photographer with the FBI's elite Evidence Response Team (ERT), and Dr. Nizam Peerwani, the medical examiner from Tarrant County, where all bodies discovered were to be autopsied and stored.

"Everything was a hot, soupy mess," Rookstool recalls. "There were a lot of people in there over fifty-one days, and, in that time, they accumulated what we estimated at 4,386 pounds of human excrement on that site. The fire department had added water to the debris, and there was a stagnant mess of rotting food, decomposing bodies, and the excrement. The stagnant water was tested, and it contained just about every disease known to man. It got to the point where you would go into one of the porto-johns [placed there by the FBI after the fire] just to get a breath of relatively fresh air."

While the Texas Rangers collected evidence—the 24,000 pounds tagged and stored included "about 300 guns, a few still in firing order, dummy grenades, parts of exploded grenades, about a half-million rounds of 'cooked-off' ammunition . . . homemade, illegal silencers for rifles, and 48 semi-automatic rifles that have been converted to automatic"—Rookstool and Peerwani searched for bodies. They found the remains of David Koresh and Steve Schneider "close together," Rookstool says. "With David, there was nothing left but the upper torso. Steve Schneider shot himself in the mouth." The Tarrant County autopsy noted that David died of "massive cranio-cerebral trauma due to gunshot wound of mid-forehead." The autopsy concluded that "Schneider shot Koresh, then himself."

A few more bodies were quickly located, Rookstool says, but after that "we were wondering, where are the majority of the people? Where the hell did they go?" It was initially believed that many of the Branch Davidians must have tried to escape the fire by using the underground tunnel to the school bus, but "there was nobody on the bus." Then they looked in what was left of the concrete bunker.

What Rookstool and Peerwani found there first was a massive mound of partially melted bullets. "We spent two days, twelve hours a day, shoveling bullets out, and then what I saw was a kid's tennis shoe. I said, 'Guys, I think we've got bodies here.'"

After ten hours of additional digging, Rookstool remembers, "We began to see weapons, feet, arms, and skulls. The roof was collapsing because a Bradley tried to penetrate it with a boom arm and did damage." As each body was uncovered, Rookstool photographed it and the remains were placed in a body bag. He says, "I picked up the body of one little girl and her head came off in my left hand. Her entire intestines came apart over my pants and shoes. The heat in there had gotten up so much [3,000 degrees was the eventual estimation] that it melted the steel shelving, cooked the studs off the walls, and their brains and cranial fluids reached boiling point, so their heads split open." To this day, Rookstool says, "I still have a problem seeing tennis shoes on children."

Some Branch Davidians died of gunshot wounds rather than burning or smoke inhalation. One child was stabbed to death. There would be subsequent speculation that many inside Mount Carmel on April 19 didn't want to stay and die after their leaders set fire to the building, so they were killed rather than being allowed to escape. It is also possible that some Branch Davidians shot others to spare them further suffering from the flames, or to hasten them on their way to join the Wave Sheaf. There is no way to be certain.

Initially, the death toll inside Mount Carmel that day was announced as seventy-four: fifty-three adults and twenty-one children. Twelve of the children had been sired by David Koresh. After body collection and autopsies, it was amended to seventy-six: fifty-three adults and twenty-three children. Nicole Gent and Aisha Gyarfas were in advanced stages of pregnancy. Both spontaneously gave birth during the final assault and fire. These newborns died with their mothers, raising the count of David Koresh's dead children to fourteen. With the addition of the six killed during the initial ATF raid on February 28, the final Branch Davidian death toll was eighty-two.

When Ruth Riddle escaped burning Mount Carmel on April 19, she carried with her the computer disk containing what David Koresh had written so far about the Seven Seals. He'd promised to surrender peacefully when he was done, but the FBI hadn't believed him.

Soon afterward, Riddle was able to convey the disk to James Tabor and J. Phillip Arnold, the two scholars David insisted must have copies of his completed Seven Seals writings before he surrendered. They published "The David Koresh Manuscript: Exposition of the Seven Seals" during the Jewish observation of Rosh Hashanah in September 1993. In their own introduction, Tabor and Arnold wrote that "regardless of one's evaluation of the content, one point is clear—in a short time, under most trying circumstances, David Koresh had produced a rather substantial piece of work."

It can never be known if David planned to abide by his agreement, and surrender to the FBI if he was allowed time to complete his Seven Seals writing project.

On April 20, 1993, President Bill Clinton met with the press at the White House. He said that on February 28, "Four federal agents were killed in the line of duty trying to enforce the law against the Branch Davidian compound, which had illegally stockpiled weaponry and ammunition, and placed innocent children at risk." The president described David Koresh as "dangerous, irrational, and probably insane." The previous day's events were not the fault of the government: "Mr. Koresh's response to demands for his surrender by federal agents was to destroy himself and murder the children who were his captives, as well as all the other people who were there who did not survive. He killed those he controlled, and he bears ultimate responsibility for the carnage that ensued." Clinton defended Attorney General Reno's recommendation that the April 19 assault take place, but added that "I have directed the United States Departments of Justice and Treasury to undertake a rigorous and thorough investigation to uncover what happened and why, and whether anything could have been done differently." The president was offended by one reporter's question regarding whether Reno ought to resign. It was foolish, Clinton said, that "anyone should suggest that the attorney general should resign because some religious fanatics murdered themselves."

On May 12, 1993, what remained of Mount Carmel was leveled by bulldozers. FBI lead agent Jeff Jamar explained, "They're just filling holes so people won't fall in the pits. That's just part of taking care of the scene."

A CNN poll immediately after the deadly fire indicated that 70 percent of Americans approved of the FBI's actions. Three months later, 50 percent disapproved. Americans didn't like what they were learning about the end of the siege in Waco.

After the Siege

On April 28, 1993, Attorney General Janet Reno testified before the House Judiciary Committee. Her appearance was essentially cleanup duty, a means of publicly clearing the FBI from responsibility for the Mount Carmel blaze and the Branch Davidians' deaths. Reno forcefully told the committee that "I wanted, and received, assurances that the [CS] gas and its means of use were not pyrotechnic." Dick Rogers, the head of the FBI's Hostage Rescue Team in Waco, and the man who approved the use of combustible military rounds early on April 19, sat directly behind Reno as she gave her testimony. He did not correct her; for the moment, the attorney general's statement sufficed for committee members regarding the fire. But some also queried Reno about continuing government allegations of child abuse at Mount Carmel. She admitted that, at least for the duration of the fifty-one-day siege, there was no evidence that any child was beaten. Afterward, FBI director William Sessions agreed that his agency had found "no contemporaneous evidence" of child abuse at Mount Carmel.

The press widened that initial crack in the FBI's defense of its performance. On May 3, *Time* devoted a special section to the Mount Carmel operation. While the magazine described David Koresh as "a charismatic leader with a pathological edge," it also quoted Jeff Jamar as acknowledging, "There was never any real negotiations. We stayed in touch to avoid provocation." *Time* also noted that "as the week [after the final assault] progressed, the FBI had to back off certain claims: that they had fresh evidence of child abuse, that they had actually seen a cult member lighting the fire, that some victims were shot by fellow Davidians for trying to flee."

On May 23, 60 *Minutes* rebroadcast its January report about sexual harassment in the ATF; host Mike Wallace added that, in the wake of the recent Mount Carmel tragedy, "almost all" of the participating ATF agents he'd contacted believed that the agency's February 28 raid "was a publicity stunt, the main goal of which was to improve the ATF's tarnished image." None of these agents were identified.

The Treasury Department and Department of Justice launched their promised investigations. The five-hundred-page Treasury report, immediately dubbed "the Blue Book" for the color of its cover, was published in late September. It essentially concluded that the February 28 raid should not have proceeded after the element of surprise was lost, and that Phil Chojnacki and Chuck Sarabyn were involved in altering key documents essential to the subsequent investigation. Both were fired, appealed to a board of labor relations, were ordered reinstated, and reassigned to ATF duties that did not include further participation in field operations. ATF director Stephen Higgins resigned three days before the report was issued. His letter of resignation cited disagreement with "all the conclusions reached, and actions proposed, pursuant to the Waco incident." One of the report's findings was that "ATF's management, perhaps out of a misplaced desire to protect the agency from criticism, offered accounts based on Chojnacki and Sarabyn's statements, disregarding clear evidence that those statements were false."

In the wake of this devasting conclusion, ATF's new focus became pursuing "the worst of the worst" gun law offenders, with less emphasis on monitoring gun dealers and independent gun sales. New agency director John Magaw declared that a disaster like the ATF's raid on Mount Carmel "cannot happen again, because we won't take this kind of operation on. We're not capable of handling it by ourself." The *San Francisco Chronicle* reported, "ATF got the message— investigations of criminal gangs and 'straw purchasers' who buy guns for them are OK; investigations of nonviolent gun owners and dealers, not so much."

In January 2003, ATF was transferred from the Treasury Department to the Department of Justice.

The Department of Justice inquiry, published about ten days after the Treasury Department report, was laudatory regarding the FBI's actions in Waco: "The deaths of Koresh, his followers and their children on April 19th were not the result of a flaw in the gas plan or the negotiation strategy. . . . The FBI exhibited extraordinary restraint and handled the crisis with great professionalism."

But internally, there were consequences. Gary Noesner wrote that "official inquiries and [subsequent] congressional hearings made clear that the negotiation and tactical teams had been at cross-purposes, and those sitting in judgment came to appreciate that the negotiation team had been on the right track, and that Rogers and Jamar had got it wrong. Neither man was dismissed; however, Waco would prove to be the effective end of both men's career advancement."

Farris Rookstool III says, "I don't think Jeff [Jamar] is to blame 100 percent . . . there was this groupthink: 'Yeah, gotta get the bad guys.' Testosterone takes over the mind, and logic is no longer in the equation. You can never have a happy ending when there's this compression of time, feeling that you've got to get this over with."

On August 6, 1993, the Department of Justice obtained grand jury indictments against eleven Branch Davidian survivors (Norman Allison, Renos Avraam, Brad Branch, Jaime Castillo, Graeme Craddock, Clive Doyle, Livingstone Fagan, Paul Fatta, Bob Kendrick, Ruth Riddle, and Kevin Whitecliff) on various charges, including murder and conspiracy to murder federal agents. Kathy Schroeder, credited with turning state's evidence, agreed to plead guilty to impeding a federal officer from executing a warrant and was not charged with murder or conspiracy. She was subsequently sentenced to three years in prison.

The trial in San Antonio commenced on January 10, 1994. U.S.

District Judge Walter Smith presided. Each defendant had his or her own attorney; the lawyers maintained that on February 28, 1993, their clients feared for their lives and acted in self-defense. Judge Smith instructed jurists that, at their discretion, they might consider voluntary manslaughter rather than murder, defining the lesser charge as unlawfully killing "in the sudden heat of passion caused by sufficient provocation."

On February 26, the jury found all eleven innocent of conspiracy to murder federal agents. Seven were found guilty of aiding and abetting voluntary manslaughter, five of carrying a firearm during the commission of a crime of violence, and two of additional arms violations. In June, prior to Smith assessing sentences, jury foreman Sarah Bain sent the judge a letter suggesting that sentences of even five years would be too severe.

But on June 17, Judge Smith set aside the jury's "innocent" verdicts on conspiracy to murder. He then ruled that Renos Avraam, Brad Branch, Jaime Castillo, Livingstone Fagan, and Kevin Whitecliff were guilty of the charge, and sentenced each to forty years' imprisonment. Graeme Craddock was given twenty years. Ruth Riddle was sentenced to five years for possessing a weapon during the ATF shootout. Paul Fatta, who was not at Mount Carmel during the ATF raid, received a fifteen-year sentence for arms violations.

Avraam, Branch, Castillo, Fagan, and Whitecliff appealed their sentences, and in 2000 the U.S. Supreme Court ruled that the penalties imposed by Judge Smith were excessive. Smith then reduced the five men's sentences to fifteen years. Avraam, Branch, Castillo, Whitecliff, Craddock, and Fatta were released from prison in 2006. Fagan was freed in 2007.

ATF agents sued the *Waco Tribune-Herald*, KWTX-TV, and American Medical Transport, the Waco ambulance service, alleging that their employees alerted the Branch Davidians to the pending February 28, 1993, raid. Though none of the companies admitted fault, they settled the case for more than $15 million.

Surviving Branch Davidians and relatives of those who died in the ATF and FBI assaults on Mount Carmel filed a $100 million wrongful-death suit against the government. But in June 2000, the case came before Judge Walter Smith, who ruled three months later that the plaintiffs had no one to blame but themselves: "The law requires each person to act reasonably; the standard is what a reasonable person would do, not what a reasonable Davidian would do. As a matter of law, there was nothing reasonable about the adult Davidians' behavior from February 28, 1993 through April 19, 1993."

In 1995, separate committees in the U.S. Senate and U.S. House of Representatives convened hearings on ATF and FBI actions in Ruby Ridge and Waco. Neither agency emerged unscathed. Treasury Department undersecretary for enforcement Ron Noble declared, "The Treasury review team and six operations experts all concluded that the ATF's [Waco] raid was seriously flawed. We admitted it. We said it." Four FBI agents, including HRT leader Dick Rogers, invoked their Fifth Amendment right against self-incrimination and refused to testify about Ruby Ridge.

Four years later, allegations by filmmaker Michael McNulty and investigative reporting by Lee Hancock of *The Dallas Morning News* resulted in the Department of Justice first denying, then admitting that the FBI's gas assault on Mount Carmel included use of two pyrotechnic rounds. Farris Rookstool's crime scene photos of a spent shell and suggestions where relevant records might be found were also integral to the FBI's terse admission that "pyrotechnic devices may have been used in the early morning of April 19, 1993." The next day, Attorney General Janet Reno raged in *The New York Times* that her credibility was damaged: "I didn't want those [combustible shells] used. I asked for and received assurances that they were not incendiary." Jeff Jamar told a *Times* reporter that no one considered the use of incendiary rounds important "because they were fired hours before the fire." Retired Texas Ranger captain David Byrne, who headed his organization's Waco investigation in 1993, said after the

FBI's deception was exposed that "this affects the credibility of law enforcement. Not only the FBI, but it puts all law enforcement to question."

Next, the FBI faced allegations that, despite agency officials' sworn testimony to the contrary, FBI agents fired guns into Mount Carmel on April 19, 1993, in response to shots fired by the Branch Davidians. On January 25, 2000, 60 Minutes aired a segment titled "What Really Happened in Waco?" Experts identified flashes on videotape as gunfire from agents shooting into the massive building. FBI analysts maintained that these were "just flashes of sunlight." Attorney General Reno appointed former U.S. senator John Danforth as special counsel to conduct an investigation. Three months later, the FBI staged an elaborate reenactment of the FBI's assault on Mount Carmel, using facilities at Fort Hood. Danforth attended, and, on July 21, he issued an "interim report": all federal officials and agents were exonerated. "I give you these conclusions with 100 percent certainty," Danforth wrote. "The blame rests squarely on the shoulders of David Koresh. This is not a close call." But the former senator's final report, issued a few months later, still took the FBI to task for its original claim that no pyrotechnic rounds were used on April 19, 1993, in Waco: "The failure of [Department of Justice investigators] to discover and report that the FBI used pyrotechnic tear gas rounds was the result of initiating the investigation with the assumption that the FBI had done nothing wrong, was inconsistent with the responsibility to conduct a thorough and complete investigation, and was clearly negligent." It has never been definitively resolved whether, on the final day of the siege, the FBI fired guns into Mount Carmel or not.

The Department of Justice issued its own statement after Danforth's interim report: "We join Senator Danforth in wishing that this report begins the process of restoring the faith of the people in their government."

But such faith, once shaken, is not easily restored. In particular, no official confession or contrition could sway those who believed the government proved in Waco that its purpose was to oppress, rather than defend, its citizens. The deaths of Branch Davidians provided justification for them and other like-minded Americans to fight back.

In 1999, asked for comment after the FBI first denied, then confirmed, using incendiary devices in the gas attack at Mount Carmel, retired Texas Rangers captain David Byrnes was blunt about the ongoing Branch Davidian controversy: "I see where this is going to be an endless thing."

Events proved him right.

A Legacy of Rage

A merica was birthed in rebellion. The Revolutionary War is aptly named. Colonists took up arms in response to what they considered oppressive acts by the British government. It wasn't a unanimous uprising. Fully half the population of the original thirteen colonies preferred remaining under British rule.

Conflict over how Americans should be governed didn't end when British general Charles Cornwallis surrendered to George Washington at Yorktown in October 1781. One of the nation's most revered Founding Fathers believed that occasional citizen rebellion remained not only inevitable, but desirable. In 1787, alluding to a failed Massachusetts uprising (Shays' Rebellion, where a disgruntled Revolutionary War veteran led about 1,200 followers in a failed attempt to seize the Springfield, Massachusetts, federal armory and overthrow the fledgling American government), Thomas Jefferson wrote that, "We have had 13 states independent [for] 11 years. That comes to one rebellion in a century and a half for each state. What country before ever existed a century and a half without a rebellion? And what country can preserve its liberties if their rulers are not warned from time to time that their people preserve the spirit of resistance? . . . What signify a few lives lost in a century or two? The tree of liberty must be refreshed from time to time with the blood of patriots and tyrants. It is its natural manure."

The U.S. Constitution, ratified in 1788, addressed the nature and structure of American government. In 1791, a series of constitutional amendments began being added, several of them an attempt to further define the limits of federal control on the rights of citizens. The First Amendment guaranteed freedom of religion, speech, press, and assembly. The Second codified citizens' right to bear arms, though the government retained authority to regulate or place limits on gun ownership. Both amendments presupposed that Americans would exercise these crucial rights with responsible self-restraint, and consideration for those whose opinions differed—and that U.S. citizens should, and would, comply with the laws and taxes passed and enforced by their duly elected government representatives. Disagreement could be freely expressed, but ultimately should be resolved with elections rather than threats or acts of violence.

History proved otherwise. There have always been Americans convinced that their federal government is intent on oppression, rather than protection, of its citizens. Modern technology, especially the advent of television's cable news and, subsequently, the internet and social media, has expanded their means of self-expression: at any hour of every day, it is possible to watch, hear, or read material containing lurid descriptions of federal rascality ranging from basic corruption to exotic perversions, all presented as absolute fact rather than far-fetched allegation. And, in great part because of television and, later, the internet, the 1993 events involving the Branch Davidians became integral in an ongoing proliferation of armed militia movements. That connection began even before the fifty-one-day FBI siege at Mount Carmel commenced.

In the fall of 1992, gun owners were warned repeatedly by the National Rifle Association and Republican presidential candidates that electing a Democrat to the White House was tantamount to abolition of gun rights. A popular saying emerged: "If they want my guns, they'll have to pry them from my cold, dead fingers." Then, a month before voters went to the polls in November, the tragic events at Ruby Ridge occurred. CNN, which began offering all-day news coverage in 1980, and competing electronic media made it possible for audiences to continually observe and judge from outset to conclusion. Many commentators and politicians expressed their outrage: because of arguably excessive government reaction to a missed court appearance following relatively minor gun charges, a woman, a child, and a marshal died.

Only a few months after the Ruby Ridge tragedy and Democrat Bill Clinton's election, the ATF conducted its failed raid on Mount Carmel, followed by more than seven weeks of FBI siege while America looked on. CNN conducted a phone interview with David Koresh on the first night; viewers heard him gasping with pain from his wounds as he described ATF agents leaping out of cattle trailers with guns blazing, wantonly killing several adult Branch Davidians and a small child in the process. ATF initiated the raid based on suspicion of illegal gun possession. To the conspiracy- and antigovernment-minded, this was Ruby Ridge all over again, but with even more victims. The media provided constant coverage; no TV, radio, or print reporter wanted to miss the Big Finish, whatever it was and whenever it finally occurred. Besides the media, gawkers gathered behind every roadblock barring the final mile or so to Mount Carmel. Entrepreneurs sold T-shirts and bumper stickers, many of them touting antigovernment mottos, from the trunks of their cars. Then the macabre festival came to its fatal conclusion.

Like the Kennedy assassination in 1963 and the first moon landing in 1969, Americans were mesmerized by coverage of the horrific fire that consumed Mount Carmel on April 19, 1993. They were able to watch on TV as it happened—besides CNN, then the only widely available cable news network, the conflagration was broadcast live on every major channel. The unforgettable, gigantic flames roared high in the sky; a transfixed nation watched as fifty-three adults and twenty-three children died.

In the weeks immediately following, claims made by FBI and Department of Justice spokesmen during the siege were discredited. There was no proof that children living in Mount Carmel were being beaten. A Branch Davidian hadn't been seen definitively starting the blaze. No evidence confirmed federal claims that some of the Branch Davidians had shot and killed others to prevent them from surrendering. Lead agent Jeff Jamar admitted that there were never any "real negotiations." What remained of Mount Carmel was bulldozed; valuable evidence was lost. In particular, bullet holes in the remaining portions of the roof might have proven whether, as the surviving Branch Davidians claimed, at least one helicopter fired down into Mount Carmel during the raid. 60 *Minutes* quoted anonymous ATF agents as alleging their agency staged the February 28 raid as a publicity stunt.

Radio host Ron Engelman, a vocal Branch Davidian defender during the siege, and who built an audience based on antigovernment broadcasts and commentaries, published the first issue of a newsletter in September 1993. In *The Freedom Report*, Engelman wrote that prosecutors in the upcoming trial of eleven Branch Davidian survivors were filing "a number of ridiculous charges in the hopes that they can get a jury stupid enough to believe that they [the government] wouldn't do anything wrong."

That trial expanded the controversy. One of Mount Carmel's front doors had been preserved. As with the missing portions of the roof, the patterns of bullet holes in it could have provided evidence whether most of the shots through it were fired from inside or outside. But when the trial commenced, authorities announced that the door was missing. The cause might have been simple negligence, but to a growing number of doubters, here was evidence of an obvious government cover-up, or even the latest link in a long-term, widespread federal conspiracy to suppress citizens' rights. These suspicions were heightened further when the judge set aside the jury's "innocent" verdict on conspiracy to murder charges, and assessed maximum sentences to five Branch Davidian defendants.

Throughout, there was no public response from ATF or the FBI beyond general statements that David Koresh alone was responsible for the deaths of his followers and their children. Both agencies placed gag orders on everyone who participated in the initial raid and subsequent siege. This, Byron Sage says now, was "a horrible decision.

We couldn't put out the facts to refute all the rumors that were being spread. So, there were all these allegations, and those making them were offering absolute trash and they knew it. But the response from Washington was deafening in its silence."

Public fascination with the Waco tragedy did not flag. Robert Spoon, a ranch hand who lived across Double Ee Ranch Road from where Mount Carmel once stood, told the *Chicago Tribune* that visitors continued flocking to the death site. Though there was little to see beyond "weed-strewn rubble," Spoon said the crowds often numbered "100 a day on the weekend." Captain Dan Weyenberg of the McLennan County sheriff's department had little respect for the gawkers: "Waco has drawn every nut from all over the world, before, during, and after the siege, and they're still coming."

Mount Carmel–obsessed "nuts" were considered relatively harmless until April 19, 1995, the second anniversary of the fatal blaze. Clive Doyle presided at a memorial service on the Mount Carmel grounds. Branch Davidian survivors who hadn't been imprisoned by Judge Smith planted young crepe myrtle trees, one for each of their dead. But, the *Chicago Tribune* reported, soon "the sect members found themselves taking a back seat to right-wing militia members in camouflage fatigues presenting an honor guard and 21-gun salute." Several of these dissidents made antigovernment speeches. Doyle told the *Tribune* reporter, "I didn't want any government-bashing. I wanted it to be a solemn occasion, but, to be honest, they kind of took over the pulpit."

Two hundred and seventy-three miles away, Timothy McVeigh commemorated the Mount Carmel tragedy's second anniversary by blowing up a federal building in Oklahoma City. The death toll was 168, including 19 children. Subsequent coverage of McVeigh's lengthy preparations, how he accumulated explosive materials, loaded them in a rented truck, and parked the bomb on wheels directly adjacent to a children's day care center on the second floor of his target structure, always mentioned the event that inspired him.

"It's because of Waco," Bill McVeigh explained when asked about his son's deadly actions. "Every time he saw it on TV, he'd go crazy." Timothy McVeigh himself told reporters, "I didn't define the rules of engagement in this conflict. The rules, if not written down, are defined by the aggressor. It was brutal, no holds barred. Women and kids were killed at Waco and Ruby Ridge. You put back in their [the government's] faces exactly what they're giving out."

Surviving Branch Davidians repudiated McVeigh's act. Clive Doyle described the Oklahoma City bombing as "a terrible shame . . . it didn't do us any good. People have likened Waco to the Alamo, and said it was a wake-up call for Americans about their government, but wise people don't go out and rectify that with terrorist acts."

McLennan County sheriff Jack Harwell believed that Mount Carmel was an opportunity, rather than an actual motivation, for the carnage in Oklahoma City: "I don't think that Waco has become a symbol. It's become an excuse for these people to do some things they wanted to do anyway."

Excuse or not, as media and think tank analysts fanned out across the country to find and interview members of antigovernment militias, they found Waco and Mount Carmel to be constantly referenced. According to Mark Pitcavage, senior research fellow at the Anti-Defamation League (ADL) Center on Extremism, the Militia of Montana, formed in late 1993 or early 1994, was modern America's first paramilitary, antigovernment group. But post–Mount Carmel, "militia groups started sprouting up rapidly through 1994, [and] by the spring of 1995, there were over 100 militia groups in the country." Pitcavage believes that "the [influence] of Waco for the far-right in the U.S. was the most important outcome of Waco." Rachel Carroll Rivas, senior research analyst for the Southern Poverty Law Center (SPLC), agrees: "It [Waco] had a very long tail."

These dissidents, whose registered guns and military-style training did not violate the law, were open about what inspired them to prepare for battle. A pamphlet distributed by the Northern Michigan Regional Militia asked, "What force exists to prevent a state or federally orchestrated massacre like the one in Waco from occurring in Michigan?" Ray Southwell, the group's spokesman whose day job was selling real estate, was quoted in an Anti-Defamation League report as predicting, "I'd guess that within the next two years, you will see the Constitution suspended." Gary D. Hunt, active in rousing antigovernment indignation in his home state of Arizona, traveled to Waco during the FBI siege to personally observe events there. He compared the Branch Davidians to heroes of the Revolutionary War: "I understand why they [the Minutemen] were willing to stand and face portions of the greatest military force in the world. And I understand why David Koresh and the other brave defenders of Mount Carmel stand fearlessly defending their home and mine."

The ADL report concluded, "The answer, say these extremists, is ultimately, necessarily, paramilitary resistance. An armed and aroused citizenry must be mobilized and ready for a call to war."

Adapting to what was learned from mistakes made in Waco, the FBI brought a new approach to its siege strategy. In 1996, the agency surrounded a group known as the Montana Freemen for eighty-one days after the paramilitary group refused eviction orders and barricaded itself in its ranch compound outside Jordan, Montana. Eventually, the Freemen wore down and surrendered. FBI director Louis J. Freeh lauded his agency's "fundamentally different approach. . . . I think the American people can take great comfort that the law was enforced and that it was done in a way that did no harm to anyone."

But that success in Montana did not temper the lingering taint of failure in Waco. In an editorial about the Freemen siege, *The New York Times* declared, "The FBI deserved no special commendation for acting in a rational matter. It should have done that before." Soon afterward, *Waco: The Rules of Engagement* debuted at the Sundance Film Festival. The well-received, widely reviewed documentary, which was critical of the FBI, was nominated for an Academy Award and won an Emmy Award for investigative reporting.

• • •

By 1999, Southern Poverty Law Center research indicated the number of "anti-government groups" in America, including militias, had reached 217. But in 2000, that number dropped to 194, then continued dwindling to 131 near the end of George W. Bush's eight years in the White House. Republican Party leaders adopted some of the dissidents' distrust of federal government as their own. Shortly after becoming speaker of the U.S. House of Representatives, Newt Gingrich criticized FBI official Larry Potts's promotion within the agency, because Potts had been involved in planning for both Ruby Ridge and Waco. Gingrich said, "We have to understand that there is, in rural America, a genuine, particularly in the West, a genuine fear of the federal government and of Washington, D.C., as a place that doesn't understand their way of life, and doesn't understand their values."

The terrorist attack on New York and Washington, D.C., on September 11, 2001, also factored into the diminishing number of militias in the United States. Members of paramilitary groups always emphasized their patriotism and loyalty to what they considered fundamental American ideals. Many chose to stand down while their country fought foreign foes.

But rage based in great part on events in Waco still simmered. It was in evidence on April 19, 2000, at the seventh annual memorial program at Mount Carmel. This was an especially auspicious occasion. Branch Davidian supporters had raised almost $100,000 to reconstruct the burned building, though so far, the efforts of an estimated 1,200 volunteers from around the country had only resulted in what *Dallas Morning News* reporter Lee Hancock described as "a simple country sanctuary, one little different in outward appearance from the dozens of churches that line the backroads of McLennan County." An estimated gathering of almost three hundred crowded inside to hear remarks by former U.S. attorney general Ramsey Clark, who told them, "This is an occasion for joy, because from the ashes has risen the church." Clark then warned, "The world must never forget what the United States government did here."

The memorial service itself was led by a man described by

Hancock as "an iconoclastic Austin talk-radio host." Alex Jones, who had recently founded InfoWars, declared, "Never again. No more Wacos in America. The next time a Waco cranks up, if I can get there, we're not going to be building a church."

A bell tolled in memory of the Branch Davidians who died in the 1993 siege. Each deceased's name was reverently announced. Then, Jones presented the new building's keys to Clive Doyle. The *Morning News* reported that "impassioned speeches" were made by "Branch Davidians, militia members, housewives, engineers, and even a retired Air Force general." Mount Carmel survivor Catherine Matteson assured the crowd that "David [Koresh] is coming back to set things straight, and I mean, you have no idea how straight." The biggest applause lines during the program, Lee Hancock wrote, "were the repeated declarations that what happened in Waco was 'our second Alamo,' that the government would be brought to account, and that the standoff that had riveted world attention on this tract of windswept prairie would not be repeated."

Militia enlistments skyrocketed in 2009, when Democrat Barack Obama became president. According to Southern Poverty Law Center research, "antigovernment groups" (which, besides militias, included tax protest and unarmed "sovereign citizens" organizations) in America rose to 542 by year's end, then 824 in 2010, 1,274 in 2011, and, with a surge linked to the rise of the Tea Party movement, peaked at 1,360 in 2012. Obama's second term found these numbers declining slightly, but militant antipathy remained constant, sometimes encouraged by elected officials. During the summer of 2015, the U.S. Army scheduled two months of training exercises in some Southwest states. Across the internet, conspiracy theories abounded regarding the Army's actual intent. *The New York Times* reported that these allegations included confiscating citizens' guns, arresting President Obama's political foes and placing them in concentration camps, and Obama subsequently suspending the Constitution and remaining in office indefinitely. Texas governor Greg Abbott promptly ordered the state's National Guard to shadow all Army activities within the Texas borders so Texans could feel certain that "their safety, constitutional rights, private property rights and civil liberties will not be infringed." The *Times* article concluded, "The specter of Waco has not faded."

The focus of American militias altered after Donald Trump succeeded Obama in the White House. Dissidents still were prepared to use threats of violence, or, sometimes, violence itself, but now its foes were different. A 2020 analysis by the Anti-Defamation League noted that "during the 2015–2016 [presidential] campaign, the greater part of the militia movement became Trump supporters, viewing Trump as an anti-establishment outsider candidate. . . . Trump's victory, though, did pose a threat to the militia movement, because, until Trump took office, the movement had largely sustained and energized itself through its opposition to the federal government."

New enemies were needed. The ADL study stated that "the first substitute enemy to emerge were the left-wing protesters who took to the streets immediately following Trump's election." Next came antifa, "state-level gun control measures, state-level pandemic-related restrictions and Black Lives Matter protests."

Throughout, Southern Poverty Law Center analyst Rachel Carroll Rivas says, "Waco is the one [cause] that has continued. It is still this topic that people talk about. It is still there." Younger militia movement members may not always reference it directly, she points out, but leaders of prominent organizations, such as Stewart Rhodes of Oath Keepers, cut their movement teeth on rage resulting from Mount Carmel.

Rivas believes that the real ongoing tragedy of Waco is how innumerable nonmilitia members have now become caught up in the distrust of government and paranoia that events at Mount Carmel spawned: "It connects to something current, the far-right activity like

January 6 [2021]. Of the seven hundred arrests after January 6, only about eighty [were] members of hate groups. So, how do regular people get pulled in? That's why Waco is notable in this moment."

In a 2010 post on rhe Future of Freedom website, organization founder and president Jacob G. Hornberger postulated that the tragedy at Mount Carmel has had predictable, if regrettable, consequences: "In almost every society, there are certain people with violent propensities who normally remain below the radar screen of life. They go about their everyday affairs from birth to death, without ever calling attention to themselves. But as soon as the government commits a horrific deed, such as massacring dozens of innocent people, those types of people all of a sudden surface. The government's horrible misconduct ignites something within them that drives them to commit some horribly violent act in retaliation. . . . The real solution is: No more Wacos."

But Branch Davidians who survived the Mount Carmel fire regret that the tragedy there spawned a legacy of rage. They do not condone any threats or acts of violence based on "Waco." David Thibodeau says, "What's hard is, our issues were raised by the left and embraced on the right. Radicalism in any form is dangerous. We don't want anyone to do crazy stuff in the name of Mount Carmel. We were never about that. What we did there was more about love than anything else."

Clive Doyle Is Waiting

On a late morning early in June 2021, Clive Doyle sits on the front porch of a small duplex in Waco. The weather is uncomfortably warm and humid; flies buzz around, and Doyle makes occasional attempts to brush them away. He turned eighty a few months earlier, and is in poor health. Respiratory difficulties sometimes reduce Doyle's speaking voice to a near whisper. He clearly would be more comfortable inside, quietly reading or napping, but those are indulgences and duty comes first. Another in a long line of writers sits across from him, ready to begin an interview. Doyle has endured these, patiently answering questions, for nearly thirty years. He's polite, but also certain that this writer, like the others, won't get it.

"Unless you know what we believe, you can't understand what we were doing," Doyle says. "That's the truth of it."

From the moment that the Mount Carmel embers sizzled out in 1993, Clive Doyle stepped up as the most prominent spokesman among surviving Branch Davidians. While others served prison sentences or moved far away from the place where their leader and fellow believers died, Doyle remained in Waco, not only granting interviews to almost anyone who asked, but also organizing and presiding over annual memorial services at the old Mount Carmel site. The personal price he paid there is obvious: Doyle's daughter Shari died in the fire on April 19, 1993. Doyle himself managed to stagger out of the burning building with the skin on his hands bubbling from the intense heat. Doyle even lived on the property until 2006, when disagreements with others claiming ownership (not April 19, 1993, survivors, but Branch Davidians who'd left Mount Carmel rather than follow David Koresh) wore Doyle down, and he moved away.

But not far. As Doyle reminds the visiting writer on this sultry spring morning, "I've become, I think, the oldest remaining who was present throughout." It was 1958 when seventeen-year-old Clive Doyle and his mother, Edna, left Australia, relocating to Mount Carmel while the Branch Davidians living there were led by Ben Roden. Doyle loyally followed Roden, then aligned with Lois Roden when she assumed leadership following her husband's death. Doyle accepted David Koresh as the Lamb promised in Revelation; he has never stopped believing in Koresh and his prophecies, or in the responsibility God has placed on the few surviving faithful to testify to the same message that eighty-two of their fellow believers died for almost thirty years ago.

The greatest misconception, Doyle observes as he waves away a fly, is about what Koresh and the Branch Davidians were trying to do—what they *represented*.

"That came up with particular frequency in 2000," he says. "The press began coming around to interview me about the Millennium. They asked, 'What do you have to say now, what happened to you all predicting the end of the world?' David never taught that, he was never about that. We never predicted the end of the world. It was always about moving past what the world had become, and setting up the Kingdom. There was no specific date. Some of us have been tasked by God to do certain things. We were—it was—never about the end, and always about the beginning. It still is."

This, Doyle says, is why he's remained in Waco and served as surviving Branch Davidians' de facto spokesman for so long. His job isn't over. The beliefs of those who loyally followed David Koresh didn't die with him on April 19, 1993. For survivors, that tragic day fulfilled biblical prophecy. The Lamb and some followers fell at the hands of Babylon. As the Book of Revelation promises, the souls of these heroes are waiting "for a little season," then will return in glory and somewhat altered form to defeat Babylon and bring about the return of Jesus and the advent of a new, sinless Kingdom of God on Earth.

Doyle and other survivors hadn't thought it would take this long. Catherine Wessinger, professor of the history of religions at Loyola University of New Orleans, assisted Doyle in writing his autobiography, *A Journey to Waco*, which was published in 2012. In her own book, *How the Millennium Comes Violently*, Wessinger describes how Branch Davidian survivors believed that "the Mount Carmel events confirmed that Koresh was the Lamb, who will someday be resurrected and return in glory. The anticipated date was December 13, 1996, based on Daniel 12:7–12, which states the power of holy people will be scattered for 1,355 days after the 'daily'—which believers took to mean Koresh's daily morning and evening Bible studies—was taken away. December 13, 1996 was 1,355 days after Koresh's death at Mount Carmel."

Wessinger writes that, when Koresh the Lamb failed to reappear on that much anticipated day, his surviving followers "like Jesus's disciples . . . adjusted their expectations to believe he will return before their generation dies out." In the last few lines of his 2012 memoir, Doyle observes that "if God is going to do something with the people that He trained, or who stepped out in faith and endeavored to do what was required of them, then God needs to do something fairly soon."

A decade later, time is running out for Clive Doyle. Elderly, frail, having waited so long, he still waits. When the great moment comes, he will be ready. Anyone strolling down the street might be who he's waiting for.

"Over the years, people have come around and claimed that they are David Koresh, that they've received his spirit," Doyle says. "Often, they are young people. They come and talk to me, and I listen. So far, I've never thought they are who they claim to be.

"But I always listen, just in case."

Clive Doyle died of pancreatic cancer on June 9, 2022.

Acknowledgments

I owe particular thanks for this book to my agent, Jim Donovan, who suggested the subject. I'm grateful to researchers Anne E. Collier, Jim Fuquay, Andrea Ahles Koos, and Zetta Hamersley, and to photographer Ralph Lauer.

At Simon & Schuster, it's always a privilege to work with Bob Bender, Johanna Li, and Stephen Bedford. Fred Chase's careful copyediting makes my books better and more accurate.

Carlton Stowers, James Ward Lee, Rebecca Moore, and Fielding McGehee read along. As usual, their constructive criticism was helpful.

Individuals interviewed include J. Phillip Arnold, Rod Aydelotte, Blake Boteler, Bill Buford, Robert Champion, Sam Cohen, Keith Constantino, Dick DeGuerin, Dave DiBetta, Clive Doyle, Mike Duncan, Eric Evers, Paul Fatta, Vic Feazell, Guillermo Gallegos, Dudley Goff, Jack Grabowski, Rory Heisch, Phil Lewis, Scott Mabb, Carla Bell Mayfield, Kris Mayfield, Lyn Millner, Jerry Petrilli, Farris Rookstool III, Mike Russell, Byron Sage, Kathy Schroeder, Charlie Short, Carlton Stowers, Sean Sutcliffe, James Tabor, Michael Taylor, David Thibodeau, George Turner, Catherine Wessinger, Bob White, and Tommy Witherspoon.

I had three lengthy long-distance telephone conversations with Branch Davidian and prolific author Livingstone Fagan. He found my questions "problematic." But I appreciate the time he took.

Archivists are the unsung heroes of narrative nonfiction. On this project, I'm grateful to the consummate professionals at the Baylor University Texas Collection in Waco (Benna Vaughn, Paul Fisher,

Sylvia Hernandez, Geoff Hunt, Amie Oliver, Brian Simmons, Darryl Stuhr, and Stephen Bolech) and the Koreshan Collection at Florida Gulf Coast University in Fort Myers (Melissa Minds VandeBurgt, Bailey Rodgers, Vivianna Whalen, and Lexie Velte).

The staff at the Waco-McLennan County Library was both patient and helpful.

Thanks to Cash, who kept me company as I worked.

Everything I write is always for Nora, Adam, Grant, and Harrison.

(And if you find yourself in Fort Worth, Texas, eat at Paris Coffee Shop and Roy Pope Grocery.)

Notes

PROLOGUE: ATF, MORNING, FEBRUARY 28, 1993

As part of my research, I interviewed more than a dozen ATF agents who participated in the February 28, 1993, raid on Mount Carmel. While I cite some individual agents for specific quotes and observations, much here reflects agents' collective memories of what happened that morning. I wish this prologue, and many of the chapters that follow, had direct input from Phil Chojnacki and Chuck Sarabyn, the leaders whose decisions that day remain controversial. But Chojnacki did not return repeated phone messages; Sarabyn declined to be interviewed. Accordingly, I have mostly relied on records of their testimonies to various congressional investigative committees, and details included in reports by those committees, in providing information about their careers and Waco-related acts. I also had access to several internal ATF documents provided to me by sources.

2 *specifically what the Branch Davidians believed:* Rory Heisch, Blake Boteler, Mike Duncan, and Sam Cohen interviews.

2 *After many meetings and drawn-out discussions:* Phil Lewis, Jerry Petrilli, and Bill Buford interviews.

4 *no thought was apparently given:* David DiBetta with Scott Fasnacht, *Plain Old Agent: Reflections on the Siege at Waco and My Career with ATF*, pp. 94–95.

4 *Stacked in three abreast, thirty-seven agents would ride in Trailer #1:* ATF internal document, "Waco Firefight Narrative" (August 10, 1994), obtained from an ATF source.

5 *Typical ATF raids might involve up to twenty participants:* Jerry Petrilli interview.

5 *there was no blueprint on file:* Robert White interview.

5 *masking tape and rope were used to indicate:* Rory Heisch interview.

5 *One hundred and thirty-seven ATF agents:* ATF internal document, "Waco Firefight Narrative."

5 *in the three years previous:* Dick J. Reavis, *The Ashes of Waco: An Investigation*, p. 183.

6 *agents didn't want their bullets plowing:* Kris Mayfield, Mike Russell, and Blake Boteler interviews.

6 *Some of the agents who would lead the way:* Blake Boteler and Kris Mayfield interviews.

7 *ATF hoped to create a family-friendly atmosphere:* Carla Bell Mayfield, Bill Buford, and Jerry Petrilli interviews.

7 *Even the final go-word signaling agents to exit the trailers:* Blake Boteler interview.

8 *There was some concern:* 104th Congress, 2nd Session, House Report 104-749, "Investigation into the Activities of Federal Law Enforcement Agencies Toward the Branch Davidians"; Phil Lewis, Bill Buford, and Jerry Petrilli interviews.

9 *At Fort Hood, the ATF agents were informed:* Kris Mayfield and Jerry Petrilli interviews.

9 *Sarabyn rushed into the room:* "Report of the Department of the Treasury on the Bureau of Alcohol, Tobacco and Firearms Investigation of Vernon Wayne Howell, also known as David Koresh" (September 1993), pp. 171–72; Bill Buford, Robert White, Jerry Petrilli, Kris Mayfield, Rory Heisch, Blake Boteler, and Sam Cohen interviews.

9 *younger ones craving the opportunity:* Guillermo Gallegos interview.

11 *"It's showtime":* Blake Boteler interview.

11 *the driver shouted back to his passengers:* Mike Russell interview.

CHAPTER ONE: THE SHEPHERD'S ROD

For much of the general information throughout the first portion of this chapter, I relied on long interviews about the origin of the Branch Davidians with three distinguished religious scholars and authors who have themselves written on and publicly spoken about the topic—Dr. J. Phillip Arnold of the Reunion Institute in Houston; Dr. James Tabor of the University of North Carolina; and Dr. Catherine Wessinger, professor of Religion Studies at Loyola University of New Orleans. All were extremely generous in sharing their thoughts and opinions with me over a series of long interviews, phone conversations, and exchanges of emails.

Books I consulted for descriptions of the Millerite movement and subsequent emergence of the Seventh-day Adventist Church, then Victor Houteff and the Shepherd's Rod, include *When Time Shall Be No More: Prophecy Belief in Modern American Culture* by Paul Boyer; *Mystics and Messiahs: Cults and New Religions in American History* by Philip Jenkins; *The Ashes of Waco: An Investigation* by Dick J. Reavis; and *How the Millennium Comes Violently: From Jonestown to Heaven's Gate* by Catherine Wessinger. Houteff's statements of belief and warning are taken directly from his book *The Shepherd's Rod: The 144,000 of Revelation 7—Call for Reformation, Vol. 1* (specifically pp. 2, 11, 26, 30, 35, and 41).

Magazine and journal articles providing insightful information included "Sacred and Profane: How Not to Negotiate with Believers" by Malcolm Gladwell, *The New Yorker* (March 31, 2014), and "From Seventh-day Adventism to David Koresh: The British Connection" by Albert A. C. Waite, *Andrews University Seminary Studies* 38, no. 1 (Spring 2000).

Finally, for some descriptions of Victor Houteff, I relied on an interview with ninety-year-old Dudley Goff, who, along with his parents and brother, joined Houteff early on, and was part of the original Mount Carmel community in Waco.

17 *the school effectively banned dancing:* Baylor finally rescinded this ban in April 1996.

17 *its nickname was "Jerusalem on the Brazos":* Carlton Stowers interview.

18 *he stressed that this prophecy would be fulfilled:* Margo Kitts, ed., *Martyrdom, Self-Sacrifice and Self-Immolation: Religious Perspectives on Suicide,* p. 60; J. Phillip Arnold interview.

19 *Mrs. Houteff immediately assumed the role:* Dudley Goff interview.

CHAPTER TWO: THE DAVIDIANS

22 *Florence, who now was divinely inspired:* Catherine Wessinger and J. Phillip Arnold interviews; Kitts, ed., p. 55; Wessinger, *How the Millennium Comes Violently,* p. 87.

22 *Radio would be more effective:* Dudley Goff interview.

22 *if they sold their present property:* Ibid.

23 *No true prophet could make such an error:* Wessinger, *How the Millennium Comes Violently,* p. 87; Reavis, p. 62.

24 *Florence Houteff announced:* J. Phillip Arnold interview.

24 *Ben Roden wrote in one of his frequent letters:* Baylor University Texas Collection, Joe Robert Collection, Box 1, Folder 4.

25 *Ben Roden insisted that she was in error:* Kenneth G. C. Newport, *The Branch Davidians of Waco: The History and Beliefs of an Apocalyptic Sect,* pp. 119–28; Albert A. C. Waite, "From Seventh-day Adventism to David Koresh: The British Connection," *Andrews University Seminar Studies* 38, no. 1 (Spring 2000); Clive Doyle with Catherine Wessinger and Matthew D. Wittmer, *A Journey to Waco: Autobiography of a Branch Davidian,* p. 33.

26 *Recruitment from among Adventists was now solicited:* Doyle, pp. 38–41.

26 *Lois Roden was greatly inquisitive:* James Tabor and J. Phillip Arnold interviews.

26 *Ben and Lois Roden assigned George fine-sounding responsibilities:* Newport, pp. 155–56.

27 *His surviving campaign literature:* Baylor University Texas Collection, Joe Robert Collection, Box 2, Folder 7.

27 *constantly badgered authorities:* Vic Feazell interview.

28 *At about 2 a.m., as she pondered:* Mark Bonokoski, "Our Mother, Who Art in Heaven," *Shekinah* (February 1981).

29 *She used her new station to aggressively proclaim:* Clive Doyle, Catherine Wessinger, J. Phillip Arnold, and James Tabor interviews.

29 *In 1979, he called for a leadership election:* Newport, p. 156.

30 *Ben Roden, faithful to Hebrew traditions in all other things:* Catherine Wessinger interview.

CHAPTER THREE: VERNON WAYNE HOWELL

Sources are scarce for information about Vernon Wayne Howell/David Koresh's early life. He told stories about his childhood to others at Mount Carmel, but many things appear to have been exaggerated (the physical beatings he suffered) or else completely untrue (his mother was a prostitute; his stepfather was connected to organized crime); no official records confirm anything of the sort.

Various biographers disagree on certain events, and there's no clear document trail. While I cite various sources in these chapter notes, in terms of specific key events, I rely on *Memories of the Branch Davidians: The Autobiography of David Koresh's Mother*, written by Bonnie Haldeman with the assistance of Dr. Catherine Wessinger. Bonnie Haldeman was not available for me to interview—she died in 2009 at age sixty-four, stabbed to death by her younger sister, who had a history of mental illness—but I was able to discuss her with Dr. Wessinger and others who knew her. Everyone agrees she was scrupulously honest, including about her own shortcomings as a parent. I believe that the memoir of Koresh's mother, who was sometimes a member of the Branch Davidians in Palestine and Mount Carmel, and who knew and interacted with his wives and children, is the most logical source for dates and events in her oldest son's childhood and early adult life.

31   *The circumstances of Vernon's birth:* Bonnie Haldeman, and Catherine Wessinger, ed., *Memories of the Branch Davidians: The Autobiography of David Koresh's Mother*, pp. 6–20; Catherine Wessinger interview.

33   *he felt the presence of God:* J. Phillip Arnold interview.

33   *Vernon dropped out of school:* Haldeman, pp. 20–22; Reavis, pp. 25, 27–30.

35   *Harriet told Vernon that she knew:* Haldeman, pp. 22–25; Michael Hall, "The Ghosts of Mount Carmel," *Texas Monthly* (April 2003); J. Phillip Arnold interview.

35   *If the twenty-one-year-old expected to be welcomed:* Clive Doyle interview.

35   *someone so befuddled that he constantly stammered:* J. Phillip Arnold interview.

35   *his habit of masturbating too much:* Hall, "The Ghosts of Mount Carmel."

36   *his skill as a handyman:* Wessinger, *How the Millennium Comes Violently*, p. 82.

CHAPTER FOUR: LOIS, VERNON, AND GEORGE

37   *Bonnie Haldeman was curious:* Haldeman, pp. 25–27.

38   *Vernon later confirmed:* Ibid., p. 124; Reavis, p. 75.

39   *George, wearing a holstered gun:* Haldeman, pp. 27–28.

39   *Perry Jones had gradually assumed a place:* Tommy Witherspoon and Kathy Schroeder interviews.

40   *to chat with county sheriff Jack Harwell:* Vic Feazell interview.

40   *Lois called everyone together:* Clive Doyle interview.

42   *surviving Branch Davidians express frustration:* David Thibodeau and Kathy Schroeder interviews.

42 *in particular the publishing of* Shekinah: Doyle, pp. 53–54.

42 *George taught that one of Satan's voices:* Reavis, p. 76.

43 *George sent a telegram:* Baylor University Texas Collection, Joe Robert Collection, Box 2, Folder 8.

43 *Vernon did the unexpected:* Haldeman, pp. 29–30, 124; Doyle, pp. 59–65.

44 *he and a very special companion:* Wessinger, *How the Millennium Comes Violently,* p. 82.

CHAPTER FIVE: THE LAMB

In the course of researching this chapter, I had face-to-face discussions and extensive email exchanges with Catherine Wessinger, James Tabor, and J. Phillip Arnold. I also read and relied on information contained in several excellent books, especially *Why Waco?: Cults and the Battle for Religious Freedom in America* by James D. Tabor and Eugene V. Gallagher; *The Branch Davidians of Waco: The History and Beliefs of an Apocalyptic Sect* by Kenneth G. C. Newport; *The Ashes of Waco: An Investigation* by Dick J. Reavis; and *How the Millennium Comes Violently: From Jonestown to Heaven's Gate* by Catherine Wessinger. Though I cite specific pages from these books in the notes for this and other chapters, I recommend that any reader seeking comprehensive and, sometimes, conflicting analysis of Vernon Wayne Howell/David Koresh's 1985 visionary experience in Israel should read these four books.

45 *Vernon wanted to personally carry out:* James Tabor interview.

45 *Vernon and Rachel lived in a small apartment:* Sometime after April 19, 1993, when Koresh and many of his followers died in the Mount Carmel fire, James Tabor took the latest of several trips to Israel. He previously visited as a scholar and researcher. This time, after becoming involved with events leading up to the catastrophic blaze, he simply wanted to get away for a while. In Jerusalem, he met his old friend Rabbi David Aaron. Rabbi Aaron remembered meeting Vernon and Rachel Howell there in 1985, and my descriptions of their activities are based on what Rabbi Aaron told James Tabor.

46 *He returned to the camp in Palestine, Texas:* J. Phillip Arnold, Clive Doyle, and James Tabor interviews.

46 *Vernon disseminated amazing details by degrees:* Clive Doyle and David Thibodeau interviews.

46 *The facts, as Vernon related them:* J. Phillip Arnold, James Tabor, Clive Doyle, and David Thibodeau interviews; David Thibodeau with Leon Whiteson and Aviva Layton, *Waco: A Survivor's Story—Updated and Revised Edition,* pp. 48–49; Haldeman, pp. 28–29; Doyle, p. 85; James D. Tabor and Eugene V. Gallagher, *Why Waco? Cults and the Battle for Religious Freedom in America,* pp. 54–68; Wessinger, *How the Millennium Comes Violently,* p. 82; Reavis, pp. 93–109; Newport, pp. 180–85, 216–17.

CHAPTER SIX: CYRUS TEED

Florida Gulf Coast University professor Lyn Millner's *The Allure of Immortality: An American Cult, a Florida Swamp, and a Renegade Prophet* is impeccably researched and engagingly written. Besides an interview with the author, I relied mainly on her book in my description of Cyrus Teed's early life, and much of what happened to him afterward.

For readers interested in doing their own research on Teed, I recommend a trip to Fort Myers, Florida, and the extensive Koreshan archives at Florida Gulf Coast University. Besides copies of important documents and copies of most *Flaming Sword* issues, the archive includes many photographs of the Koreshan community at Estero and of Teed/Koresh himself. I can testify from experience that the archives staff is both knowledgeable and helpful.

49 *Cyrus Teed got his childhood education:* Lyn Millner, *The Allure of Immortality: An American Cult, a Florida Swamp, and a Renegade Prophet*, pp. 12–19.

50 *he lay down on a couch:* Ibid., pp. 9, 19–23; Philip Jenkins, *Mystics and Messiahs: Cults and New Religions in American History,* p. 43; Lyn Millner interview.

52 *"One of the supreme factors of the change":* Dr. Cyrus R. Teed (Koresh), "The Clock of Ages Strikes the Hour of Revolution," *The Flaming Sword* (March 25, 1898), Koreshan Collection, Box 17, University Archives and Special Collections, Bradshaw Library, Florida Gulf Coast University.

52 *The Koreshans became prominent:* Adam Morris, *American Messiahs: False Prophets of a Damned Nation,* pp. 179–81.

52 *The Koreshans also engaged:* Lyn Millner interview.

53 *A Koreshan visiting Fort Myers quarreled:* J. Phillip Arnold and Lyn Millner interviews.

53 *From their perspective, everything fit:* J. Phillip Arnold interview.

53 *But Koresh didn't die as quickly:* Lyn Millner interview.

54 *The parallels defy coincidence:* Catherine Wessinger, J. Phillip Arnold, and Lyn Millner interviews.

CHAPTER SEVEN: CONNECTION

Dr. J. Phillip Arnold is the individual who tracked *Koreshanity: The New Age Religion* to the Waco-McLennan County Library. How he heard of the book, recognized its significance, then tried to convince the FBI it would be a useful tool in ending the Mount Carmel siege, will be recounted in a later chapter.

For the moment, the Waco-McLennan County Library copy of the book remains shelved in the library's archive section. Its relative scarcity is indicated by the amount of time it took me to locate another copy available for sale, and what it cost me to purchase it.

I'm grateful for access to the extensive Koreshan Collection, University Archive and Special Collections, Bradshaw Library, Florida Gulf Coast University. Anyone doing research on Cyrus Teed/Koresh and the Koreshans should start there.

CHAPTER EIGHT: PALESTINE AND POINTS WEST AND EAST

60 *He drove to the convention:* Reavis, pp. 97–98.

61 *Someone suggested to Koresh:* Doyle, pp. 63–64.

61 *he still retained aspirations:* David Thibodeau interview.

61 *Koresh rented a house:* San Gabriel Valley (CA) Tribune (April 18, 2003).

62 *Koresh's mother later wrote that she separated from his stepfather:* Haldeman, pp. 31–34.

62 *twenty-two-year-old Marc Breault:* Marc Breault and Martin King, *Inside the Cult: A Member's Chilling, Exclusive Account of Madness and Depravity in David's Koresh's Compound,* pp. 46–51.

62 *They were met at the airport:* Ibid., pp. 53–56.

63 *"I was head deacon there":* Paul Fatta interview.

66 *nineteen-year-old David Thibodeau came to Los Angeles:* David Thibodeau interview; Thibodeau, pp. 13–22.

67 *the new operation turned into something:* Haldeman, p. 50.

68 *enough Adventist elders were concerned about them:* Albert A. C. Waite, "From Seventh-day Adventism to David Koresh: The British Connection," *Andrews University Seminary Studies* 38, no. 1 (Spring 2000).

68 *"Let's face it. We are bad":* "A Letter to Australia, Part B," J. Phillip Arnold Collection.

69 *Koresh always emphasized that nothing about God:* Kathy Schroeder interview.

CHAPTER NINE: SHOOTOUT AT MOUNT CARMEL

70 *George insisted on another election:* Newport, p. 157.

70 *Renters in one house stocked:* Clive Doyle and Paul Fatta interviews.

71 *George disinterred the coffin:* Wessinger, *How the Millennium Comes Violently,* p. 83; Paul Fatta and Vic Feazell interviews.

71 *He drove from Palestine to Waco:* Vic Feazell and Paul Fatta interviews.

73 *"I just can't take much of jail":* Haldeman, p. 58.

73 *Perry Jones took the journalists:* Waco Tribune Herald (January 17, 1988).

74 *"Maybe God will make it up to you":* Reavis, p. 81; Paul Fatta interview.

74 *"Goats were running":* Haldeman, p. 61

75 *he described Koresh and his followers:* Baylor University Texas Collection, Joe Robert Collection, Box 2, Folder 9.

76 *There was a quarrel:* Newport, pp. 195–96.

CHAPTER TEN: NEW ERA AT THE ANTHILL

77 *About sixty followers joined:* Haldeman, pp. 94–95.

77 *newcomers nicknamed their home:* David Thibodeau interview.

78 *Those who stayed did not automatically:* Paul Fatta and Kathy Schroeder interviews.

78 *Many living there found Perry:* Kathy Schroeder interview.

79 *Koresh invited debate:* Malcolm Gladwell, "Sacred and Profane: How Not to Negotiate with Believers," *The New Yorker* (March 31, 2014).

79 *he sometimes alluded to things:* Wessinger, *How the Millennium Comes Violently*, p. 91.

80 *The Fifth Seal, Koresh taught:* J. Phillip Arnold interview.

81 *Three blessed groups would be gathered:* Kathy Schroeder interview.

81 *He might finish, tell everyone to turn in:* Haldeman, p. 64.

82 *even the Lamb couldn't require:* David Thibodeau, Paul Fatta, and Kathy Schroeder interviews.

CHAPTER ELEVEN: THE PRIVILEGES OF THE LAMB

83 *"sometimes you have to use a hook":* Paul Fatta interview.

83 *Koresh and his band rolled:* David Thibodeau interview.

83 *"David Koresh/God Rocks":* Thibodeau, p. 69.

83 *he adopted a more commercial style:* Ibid., pp. 92–94.

85 *"God does not have to present Himself":* Reavis, p. 115.

85 *he picked the movies to be shown:* Kathy Schroeder interview.

85 *He justified this:* Reavis, p. 117.

85 *he banned the sale of Bible study audiotapes:* Ibid., pp. 83–85.

85 *Koresh's original 1987 prophecy:* Wessinger, *How the Millennium Comes Violently*, p. 91.

86 *Rachel wasn't immediately persuaded:* Haldeman, pp. 43–44.

86 *It was Clive Doyle's daughter:* Wessinger, *How the Millennium Comes Violently*, pp. 82–83.

86 *Not all the young women's parents:* Stuart A. Wright, ed., *Armageddon in Waco: Critical Perspectives on the Branch Davidian Conflict*, pp. 59–60.

87 *Koresh enlisted young male followers:* David Thibodeau interview; Thibodeau, pp. 99–101.

88 *"at odds with virtually every social convention":* Malcolm Gladwell, "Sacred and Profane: How Not to Negotiate with Believers," *The New Yorker* (March 31, 2014).

CHAPTER TWELVE: A NEW LIGHT

89 *Mike Schroeder was not a religious man:* Kathy Schroeder interview.

90 *"It was a tough sell":* Thibodeau, pp. 49–50; David Thibodeau interview.

90 *Bonnie, who had reconciled with her husband:* Haldeman, pp. 63–64.

91 *In the evenings after Bible study:* Kathy Schroeder interview.

92 *One night, David Thibodeau encountered:* Thibodeau, pp. 80–84.

93 *He taunted the other men:* Ibid., pp. 107–8.

93 *There was an unspoken pecking order:* Scott Mabb interview.

94 *Mark and Jaydean Wendell left:* Kathy Schroeder interview.

94 *he had absolutely no intention:* Breault, pp. 195–204.

CHAPTER THIRTEEN: RUMBLINGS

95 *Marc Breault couldn't leave the Davidians:* Breault, pp. 194–204.

95 *It was known among other Branch Davidians:* Paul Fatta and Clive Doyle interviews.

96 *Breault wrote to the Gents:* Breault, pp. 205–10.

96 *he took to his bed:* David Thibodeau interview; Thibodeau, p. 33.

96 *Breault held his own:* Breault, pp. 214–16.

97 *she turned to the police in La Verne:* San Gabriel (CA) Valley Tribune (April 18, 2000); Wessinger, *How the Millennium Comes Violently,* p. 96.

97 *Breault contacted U.S. Immigration officials:* Wessinger, *How the Millennium Comes Violently,* pp. 96–97.

98 *"I think he knew down the road":* Haldeman, pp. 67–70.

98 *A Current Affair sent cameras:* David Thibodeau interview; Thibodeau, p. 116; Wessinger, *How the Millennium Comes Violently,* p. 97.

99 *reporters at the Waco Tribune-Herald were tipped:* Clive Doyle interview; *Waco Tribune-Herald* (April 18–19, 1992, February 24, 2018).

CHAPTER FOURTEEN: THE GUNS

101 *from a spiritual rather than secular perspective:* Livingstone Fagan interview.

101 *Mount Carmel's new, single building:* Paul Fatta, David Thibodeau, Livingstone Fagan, Clive Doyle, and Kathy Schroeder interviews; Thibodeau, pp. 37, 72; Haldeman, pp. 143–44; Reavis, pp. 48–49.

102 *except in Koresh's room:* Blake Boteler interview.

102 *Koresh estimated that it cost:* Thibodeau, p. 120; Reavis, pp. 291–92; Paul Fatta interview.

103 *David Thibodeau met a woman:* Thibodeau, pp. 122–23; Wessinger, *How the Millennium Comes Violently,* p. 60; Carlton Stowers interview.

104 *particularly vests with pockets for cartridges:* Clive Doyle and David Thibodeau interviews.

104 *the mailing address they used for it:* Clive Doyle interview.

104 *Henry McMahon had a new suggestion:* Paul Fatta interview; Thibodeau, pp. 122–23.

105 *the Branch Davidians began buying:* The numbers, compiled by ATF agents after months of investigation, are staggering. Legwork involved was prodigious. By law, gun purchase records cannot be computerized. "Paper trail" investigations of who bought what and when must be conducted by contacting sellers and gaining access to their records. Any number of businesses and individuals might be involved in transactions involving a single firearm. In March 1992 alone, the Branch Davidians purchased 17 rifles, six pistols, one shotgun, 10 machine gun conversion kits, 80 cases of assorted ammunition, 100 magazines for 7.62 ammunition, 144 web belts, and four SWG lower receivers for use in converting semiautomatic rifles to M16 fully automatic weapons. Their May 1992 orders totaled 15 rifles, six pistols, 48 cases of steel core ammunition, a case of lower receivers, and 50 combat vests. The numbers cited here are from Wendel E. Frost, *ATF: Sierra One Waco*, pp. 53–54.

CHAPTER FIFTEEN: THE GIRLS

107 *Koresh badgered them not to feel superior:* Clive Doyle interview.

107 *Until their children came of appropriate age:* Kathy Schroeder interview; Kathy Schroeder, Baylor University Texas Collection, Kirk D. Lyons Collection, Box 5, Folder 2.

108 *Secular law in Texas is specific:* Newport, p. 200.

109 *"You often hear them talk":* Livingstone Fagan, *Waco: What Comes Next?*, p. 140.

109 *Some of the additional women:* Thibodeau, p. 106.

109 *In her 1995 testimony to congressional investigators:* Kiri Jewell, Transcript of Joint Hearings, House Subcommittees—Committee of the Judiciary, Subcommittee on Government Reform and Oversight, Subcommittee on National Security, International Affairs and Criminal Justice, July 19–21 and 24, 1995 (hereinafter cited as 1995 Congressional testimony).

111 *David Thibodeau wrote in his memoir:* Thibodeau, pp. 109–11.

111 *David Jewell was contacted by Marc Breault:* Wessinger, *How the Millennium Comes Violently*, p. 97.

112 *"My Mom said I needed to hurry up":* Kiri Jewell, 1995 Congressional testimony.

CHAPTER SIXTEEN: CHILD PROTECTIVE SERVICES

113 *Child Protective Services in McLennan County:* Joyce Sparks, 1995 Congressional testimony.

114 *"I might have whopped him":* Haldeman, p. 20.

114 *but within certain guidelines:* Scott Mabb, Paul Fatta, Clive Doyle, David Thibodeau, and Kathy Schroeder interviews; Haldeman, p. 100.

116 *she'd seen eight-month-old babies:* Kiri Jewell, 1995 Congressional testimony.

116 *Joyce Sparks made her first visit:* Thibodeau, pp. 117–18.

117 *When she called Koresh to explain:* Baylor University Texas Collection, Audiotape, Mark Swett Collection, Box 9 OVZ, Folder 24.

117 *"We knew that babies were being spanked":* Joyce Sparks, 1995 Congressional testimony.

117 *Kiri told the same story:* Ibid.

118 *Sparks replied, "Not at all":* Ibid.

118 *"It looks like persecution is coming":* Doyle, pp. 115–16.

CHAPTER SEVENTEEN: THE MESSAGE EVOLVES

119 *he contacted Steve Schneider's sister Sue:* Wright, ed., p. 217.

119 *"[Koresh] repeatedly told me":* Joyce Sparks, 1995 Congressional testimony.

120 *the tone of Koresh's teaching changed:* Kathy Schroeder interview; Wessinger, *How the Millennium Comes Violently,* pp. 94–95.

120 *Graeme Craddock had visited Mount Carmel:* Haldeman, p. 143.

121 *but not the end of the world:* Clive Doyle interview.

121 *"we should never allow ourselves":* Thibodeau, pp. 121–22.

122 *Some of his followers already had been firing:* David Thibodeau interview.

122 *There was separate target practice:* Kathy Schroeder interview. Paul Fatta is emphatic that nothing of the sort took place: "I was gone a lot, often in town buying things. But I know there was no training [with guns], and anybody who says so is 100 percent false." Because of subsequent events, I believe that Kathy Schroeder is correct about this. But Fatta adds, "Nobody there had even been in the military. There was nothing paramilitary. Nothing." Schroeder is a military veteran, and she served as an observer/instructor whose observations helped David Koresh determine how individual followers were armed. I will add that I do not believe Paul Fatta is being deliberately deceptive. After three decades, he simply remembers things differently.

123 *Koresh leavened the new responsibilities:* Kathy Schroeder interview

123 *the office of U.S. senator Donald Riegle of Michigan received a fax:* FBI records 63-0-113357X-1.

123 *Riegle sent a letter to the FBI:* FBI records 63-0-113357X-2.

124 *FBI agent Byron Sage, who oversaw:* Byron Sage interview.

124 *The final paragraph of the report concluded:* FBI records 50-SA-37281.

125 *"ATF may possibly have a firearms violation":* Ibid.

CHAPTER EIGHTEEN: THE ATF

Unless otherwise noted, all the information about ATF history included in this chapter comes from a comprehensive timeline on the agency's website: https://www.atf .gov/our-history/atf-history-timeline.

126 *"an accident of history"*: Chelsea Parsons and Arkadi Gerney, "The Bureau and the Bureau," Center for American Progress Report (February 19, 2015).

128 *a former NRA lobbyist told* The New York Times: *New York Times* (May 3, 2021).

128 *had just over 4,000 employees*: ATF Public Affairs Division; FBI data from https://www.justice.gov/archive/jmd/1975_2002/html/page 96-99.htm.

128 *instituted agent fines for minor infractions*: Jerry Petrilli interview.

129 *agents in L.A. were mostly tasked*: Mike Russell interview.

130 *In early June, a UPS driver*: Wessinger, *How the Millennium Comes Violently*, p. 60.

CHAPTER NINETEEN: INVESTIGATION

Much of the information in this and subsequent chapters is drawn from a lengthy affidavit submitted by ATF agent Davy Aguilera to the United States District Court, Western Division, in Waco, as he requested an arrest warrant for Vernon Wayne Howell (aka David Koresh) and a search warrant for Mount Carmel and the Branch Davidians' car repair facility. In official records, it is bundled as part of the court documentation for Case W93-17M. For chapter notes purposes, I cite "Affidavit" plus a page number.

131 *Aguilera wrote that he investigated suspects*: Affidavit, p. 1.

131 *Larry Gilbreath had told Barber*: Ibid., pp. 1–3.

132 *Barber contacted Aguilera again*: Ibid., pp. 2–3.

132 *Aguilera began the painstaking process*: Ibid., pp. 4–7.

132 *Aguilera also interviewed Robert Cervenka*: Ibid., p. 4.

133 *Aguilera's records search led him to Hewitt Handguns*: Ibid., p. 6; Henry McMahon and Davy Aguilera, 1995 Congressional testimony.

133 *The agents had bad news for McMahon*: Reavis, pp. 36–38; Newport, p. 240.

134 *He wrote and submitted a report*: Wessinger, *How the Millennium Comes Violently*, pp. 97–98.

134 *an incident occurred at Ruby Ridge, Idaho*: New York Times (August 23, 1992; January 7, 1995; September 3, 1995).

135 *The leader of the HRT team was Dick Rogers*: Gary Noesner, *Stalling for Time: My Life as an FBI Hostage Negotiator*, pp. 89–93.

135 *Weaver was sentenced to eighteen months*: New York Times (September 3, 1995).

136 *He needed something more*: Wessinger, *How the Millennium Comes Violently*, pp. 97–98.

136 *"Randy Weaver was not a man we admired"*: Thibodeau, p. 130.

136 *Ruby Ridge might be Babylon's rehearsal*: Ibid.

CHAPTER TWENTY: THE INVESTIGATION CONTINUES

137 *Some ATF agents from the Dallas office:* Blake Boteler interview.

137 *was tipped by his friend Davy Aguilera:* Keith Constantino interview.

138 *Davy Aguilera turned most of his investigative attention:* Affidavit, pp. 7–14.

142 *ATF erected a "pole camera":* DiBetta, p. 72.

143 *Many adults at Mount Carmel:* Kathy Schroeder interview.

145 *searching for an ideal spot:* DiBetta, p. 72.

CHAPTER TWENTY-ONE: THE UNDERCOVER HOUSE
AND THE HELICOPTERS

146 *its occupants moved out:* Doyle, pp. 117–18.

147 *They believed that the Branch Davidians probably had:* Robert Rodriguez, Baylor University Texas Collection, Kirk D. Lyons Collection, Box 5, Folder 1.

147 *He discovered that the problem:* Dave DiBetta interview.

148 *24/7 observation was mostly reduced:* Jerry Petrilli interview; "Report of the Department of the Treasury on the Bureau of Alcohol, Tobacco and Firearms Investigation of Vernon Wayne Howell, also known as David Koresh" (September 1993).

148 *Their Mount Carmel neighbors figured out:* Kathy Schroeder, Paul Fatta, Clive Doyle, and David Thibodeau interviews.

149 *Vaega grabbed a six-pack of beer:* Doyle, pp. 117–18.

149 *Wayne Martin ran a records check:* David Thibodeau and Paul Fatta interviews; Thibodeau, pp. 136–37; Reavis, p. 67.

149 *The agents were concerned by Perry Jones's regular visits:* Robert Rodriguez, Baylor University Texas Collection, Kirk D. Lyons Collection, Box 5, Folder 1.

150 *she was working out of the ATF office in Lubbock:* Carla Bell Mayfield interview.

150 *reported back to Koresh:* Kathy Schroeder and Paul Fatta interviews.

150 *agency officials' main concern:* 104th Congress, 2nd Session, House Report 104-749, "Investigation into the Activities of Federal Law Enforcement Agencies Toward the Branch Dividians," Committee of Government Reform and Oversight (August 2, 1996); Reavis, pp. 124–25; Bill Buford interview.

151 *compiled a list of eleven Branch Davidians:* Dick Reavis, 1995 Congressional testimony.

151 *The Branch Davidian kids were delighted:* Kathy Schroeder interview.

152 *the January 6 overflight had another result:* House Report 104-749.

152 *Texas-based agent Nathaniel Medrano:* Guillermo Gallegos interview.

153 *Robert Rodriguez, introduced himself as Robert Gonzalez:* Robert Rodriguez, Baylor University Texas Collection, Kirk D. Lyons Collection, Box 5, Folder 1.

154 *"Gonzalez" was permitted to attend a Bible study:* "Report of the Department of the Treasury" (September 1993).

154 *He explained that his followers were hated:* Robert Rodriguez, Baylor University Texas Collection, Kirk D. Lyons Collection, Box 5, Folder 1.

154 *"Gonzalez" visited Mount Carmel several more times:* Ibid.

155 *producers of the popular CBS network news program* 60 Minutes: Timothy Lynch, "No Confidence: An Unofficial Account of the Waco Incident," Cato Institute, Policy Analysis No. 395 (April 9, 2001).

155 *rumors that President-elect Bill Clinton:* Dave DiBetta and Carlton Stowers interviews.

155 *an ATF congressional budget hearing was scheduled:* Reavis, p. 189; Wessinger, *How the Millennium Comes Violently,* p. 61.

CHAPTER TWENTY-TWO: THE PLAN

Almost everything in this chapter is at least partially informed by pages 52–65 of the "Report of the Department of the Treasury on the Bureau of Alcohol, Tobacco and Firearms Investigation of Vernon Wayne Howell, also known as David Koresh," issued in September 1993. Because of the color of its cover, it became widely known as the "Blue Book."

158 *Participants correctly assumed:* Bill Buford, Robert White, Phil Lewis, and Jerry Petrilli interviews.

158 *The presence of women and children inside:* Ibid.

158 *Marc Breault later said:* Wessinger, *How the Millennium Comes Violently,* p. 95.

159 *There was another obvious option:* Vic Feazell and Carlton Stowers interviews.

160 *By mid-December 1992:* DiBetta, p. 72; Chuck Sarabyn, 1995 Congressional testimony; Mike Duncan interview.

160 *a joint ATF/FBI operation in Arkansas:* Bill Buford interview.

164 *For three days prior, most of the ATF agents involved:* Kris Mayfield, Robert White, Phil Lewis, Bill Buford, Jerry Petrilli, Carla Bell Mayfield, Mike Russell, and Sam Cohen interviews.

CHAPTER TWENTY-THREE: "THE SINFUL MESSIAH"

166 *During the months that followed:* Waco Tribune-Herald (February 28, 1998).

166 *McCormick heard rumors that a government investigation:* Waco Tribune-Herald (February 24, 2018); Austin American-Statesman (April 19, 2018).

167 *McCormick called Koresh:* Waco Tribune-Herald (February 24, 2018).

167 *England began a series of telephone interviews:* Thibodeau, p. 140.

168 *The Tribune-Herald series was ready for publication:* "Report of the Department of the Treasury on the Bureau of Alcohol, Tobacco and Firearms Investigation of Vernon Wayne Howell, also known as David Koresh" (September 1993), pp. 67–72, 75–77, 79–80. All subsequent descriptions of meetings and negoti-

ations between ATF and the *Tribune-Herald* in this chapter are based on these pages from this report.

171 *About 8 a.m. on Saturday:* "Report of the Department of the Treasury" (September 1993).

171 *The ATF agent reported afterward:* Robert Rodriguez, Baylor University Texas Collection, Kirk D. Lyons Collection, Box 5, Folder 1.

172 *Steve Schneider called the* Tribune-Herald *newsroom:* "Report of the Department of the Treasury" (September 1993).

172 *Blansett didn't call Schneider back:* Ibid.

173 *Bonnie Haldeman, now living in Chandler:* Haldeman, pp. 76–77.

173 *a cluster of Branch Davidian men speculating:* Thibodeau, pp. 151–54; Kathy Schroeder interview.

CHAPTER TWENTY-FOUR: FORT HOOD

175 *Most of the operation planners arrived:* "Report of the Department of the Treasury on the Bureau of Alcohol, Tobacco and Firearms Investigation of Vernon Wayne Howell, also known as David Koresh" (September 1993).

175 *included a visit from undercover agent:* Blake Boteler interview.

176 *the mock Mount Carmel interior:* Rory Heisch and Robert White interviews.

177 *Chuck Sarabyn had an additional announcement:* Kris Mayfield and Mike Russell interviews; DiBetta, p. 84.

178 *Sharon Wheeler of the Dallas office was told to alert:* Sharon Wheeler, 1995 Congressional testimony; Bill Buford interview.

178 *There were dogs on the Branch Davidian property:* Robert Rodriguez, Baylor University Texas Collection, Kirk D. Lyons Collection, Box 5, Folder 1.

179 *give candy to the kids:* Carla Bell Mayfield interview.

179 *the vital element of surprise was emphasized:* Rory Heisch, Blake Boteler, Mike Russell, Sam Cohen, Mike Duncan, Kris Mayfield, and Guillermo Gallegos interviews.

180 *Pizza Hut was a favorite:* Sam Cohen interview.

181 *many of the agents read and discussed:* Guillermo Gallegos interview.

CHAPTER TWENTY-FIVE: SURPRISE PROMISED

Unless otherwise noted, sources for information in this chapter come from "Report of the Department of the Treasury on the Bureau of Alcohol, Tobacco and Firearms Investigation of Vernon Wayne Howell, also known as David Koresh" (September 1993), pp. 177–79, D12–D15, E-3.

182 *Stephen Higgins remembered that Lloyd Bentsen:* Stephen Higgins, 1995 Congressional testimony.

CHAPTER TWENTY-SIX: SURPRISE LOST

187 *Robert Rodriguez met with ATF operation commander*: "Report of the Department of the Treasury on the Bureau of Alcohol, Tobacco and Firearms Investigation of Vernon Wayne Howell, also known as David Koresh" (September 1993).

187 *Rodriguez returned to Mount Carmel*: Ibid.

188 *His job was to "get everything"*: Phil Lewis interview.

188 *The agency booked 153 hotel and motel rooms*: Austin American-Statesman (April 19, 2008).

189 *"It's not that they didn't want to do it"*: John Magaw, 1995 Congressional testimony.

190 *Kathy Schroeder was out of bed*: Kathy Schroeder interview.

190 *Fatta was supposed to be accompanied*: Paul Fatta interview.

190 *six ATF agents assigned to block*: Jake Grabowski interview.

191 *there was a meeting at Waco's KWTX-TV station*: "Report of the Department of the Treasury" (September 1993).

192 *Peeler became hopelessly lost*: Wessinger, *How the Millennium Comes Violently*, p. 88; Austin Chronicle (June 23, 2000); Austin American-Statesman (April 19, 2008).

192 *Chuck Sarabyn briefly stopped*: "Report of the Department of the Treasury" (September 1993).

192 *He'd told Koresh the night before*: Kathy Schroeder interview.

193 *Koresh had assured everyone*: Ibid.

193 *"I asked him to explain to me"*: Robert Rodriguez, Baylor University Texas Collection, Kirk D. Lyons Collection, Box 5, Folder 1.

193 *Reporters, photographers, and editors gathered*: Tommy Witherspoon and Rod Aydelotte interviews.

194 *Chuck Sarabyn awaited word*: "Report of the Department of the Treasury" (September 1993).

194 *Jones drove out of the compound*: Ibid.; Reavis, p. 45; Doyle, p. 120; Austin Chronicle (June 23, 2000).

195 *he saw David Koresh engaged*: Clive Doyle interview; "Report of the Department of the Treasury" (September 1993); Reavis, pp. 66–67; Robert Rodriguez, Baylor University Texas Collection, Kirk D. Lyons Collection, Box 5, Folder 1.

196 *The ATF undercover agent waited*: Robert Rodriguez, 1995 Congressional testimony; Robert Rodriguez, Baylor University Texas Collection, Kirk D. Lyons Collection, Box 5, Folder 1.

197 *Rodriguez didn't feel safe*: Kris Mayfield interview; Robert Rodriguez, 1995 Congressional testimony.

197 *After hearing Rodriguez's blurted report*: Robert Rodriguez, Baylor University Texas Collection, Kirk D. Lyons Collection, Box 5, Folder 1; Robert Rodriguez, 1995 Congressional testimony.

197 *Phil Lewis was standing:* Phil Lewis interview.

198 *Rodriguez wanted to re-emphasize to Sarabyn:* Robert Rodriguez, Baylor University Texas Collection, Kirk D. Lyons Collection, Box 5, Folder 1; Robert Rodriguez, 1995 Congressional testimony.

198 *Sarabyn consulted with operation commander Phil Chojnacki:* "Report of the Department of the Treasury" (September 1993).

199 *Kathy Schroeder, still in the kitchen:* Kathy Schroeder interview.

200 *They were the only mother and kids:* Ibid.

201 *Robert Rodriguez arrived at the TSTC command center:* Robert Rodriguez, 1995 Congressional testimony; Robert Rodriguez, Baylor University Texas Collection, Kirk D. Lyons Collection, Box 5, Folder 1.

201 *They were surprised:* Rod Aydelotte and Tommy Witherspoon interviews.

201 *Only later would the journalists realize:* Tommy Witherspoon interview.

201 *Dan Mulloney was parked:* Robert Rodriguez, Baylor University Texas Collection, Kirk D. Lyons Collection, Box 5, Folder 1.

202 *Witherspoon climbed out of Aydelotte's car:* Tommy Witherspoon interview.

CHAPTER TWENTY-SEVEN: THE RAID—EARLY MOMENTS

204 *ATF agents agree that the dogs were shot:* Robert Champion, Baylor University Texas Collection, Kirk D. Lyons Collection, Box 3, Folder 4; Jerry Petrilli, Mike Duncan, and Blake Boteler interviews.

204 *grinned "weirdly":* Rory Heisch and Robert White interviews.

204 *vividly recall:* Sam Cohen, Kris Mayfield, and Blake Boteler interviews.

204 *essentially pleaded with the agents:* Malcolm Gladwell, "Sacred and Profane: How Not to Negotiate with Believers," *The New Yorker* (March 31, 2014); Thibodeau, p. 160.

205 *The helicopter fleet consisted of:* ATF internal document, "Waco Firefight Narrative" memo, dated August 10, 1994. This is a stunningly succinct document provided to me by three different sources. In it, three ATF investigators, including Phil Lewis and Davy Aguilera, interviewed all surviving agents who participated in the February 28, 1993, Mount Carmel raid and collected their reminiscences of that event in a chronological report for internal agency use. The memo specifically notes, "The report does not revisit the issues covered by the Treasury Administrative Review [of September 1993]. Instead, this report details for the first time the firefight[s] and related action. Our hope is that this report will enlighten those not there that day and be shared with all employees of ATF, in that events of that day have affected the entire agency." In this and the following chapter describing the events at Mount Carmel, for the ATF perspective I relied on this document as well as my own multiple interviews with agents who participated that day.

206 *When they were still several hundred yards away:* "Report of the Department of

the Treasury on the Bureau of Alcohol, Tobacco and Firearms Investigation of Vernon Wayne Howell, also known as David Koresh" (September 1993); "Waco Firefight Narrative" 104th Congress, 2nd Session, House Report 104-749, "Investigation into the Activities of Federal Law Enforcement Agencies Toward the Branch Dividians," Committee of Government Reform and Oversight (August 2, 1996).

CHAPTER TWENTY-EIGHT: THE PRICE OF PROPHECY

209 *Six had powerful A-15 rifles:* Blake Boteler and Kris Wright interviews.

209 *several agents would say that they never:* Guillermo Gallegos and Mike Duncan interviews.

209 *many of the ATF agents had expended:* Mike Russell and Jerry Petrilli interviews.

209 *It was hard for the agents to hear:* Blake Boteler interview.

210 *Phil Chojnacki and Chuck Sarabyn weren't in any position:* ATF internal document, "Waco Firefight Narrative" (August 10, 1994).

210 *Claire Rayburn leaned from cover:* Ibid.

210 *Clive Doyle, running down a compound hall:* Doyle, pp. 121–23.

211 *Doyle hurried to Blake's room:* Ibid., p. 22. David Thibodeau believes that Blake was shot from above, confirming his belief that a National Guard helicopter strafed the compound.

211 *When the gun battle erupted:* Catherine Wessinger interview.

212 *Wayne Martin used the phone:* Baylor University Texas Collection, Mark Swett Collection, Box 9 OVZ, Folder 36. Listening to the 911 call tapes in the Baylor Collection is a shattering experience.

213 *Teams of agents from ATF's New Orleans division:* Bill Buford, Keith Constantino, and Kris Mayfield described this scene in ghastly detail. Information in this section also comes from "Waco Firefight Narrative."

215 *David Koresh got on the line:* Wessinger, *How the Millennium Comes Violently,* p. 103; Reavis, pp. 174–75.

216 *Finally, Gent was hit:* "Waco Firefight Narrative."

216 *Peter Hipsman, somewhere on an upper floor:* Thibodeau, p. 171; David Thibodeau interview.

217 *two ATF agents, Charles Smith and Charles Giarrusso:* "Waco Firefight Narrative"; Reavis, pp. 154–55.

217 *David Koresh could issue a command:* Kathy Schroeder interview.

218 *When ATF agents stood up:* Robert White, Sam Cohen, and Kathy Schroeder interviews; Doyle, pp. 125–26.

218 *Branch Davidians inside and ATF agents outside:* Blake Boteler interview.

218 *ATF medics gallantly risked their lives:* Bill Buford interview; "Waco Firefight Narrative."

218 *Gabourie, especially, put his life on the line:* Blake Boteler interview.

218 *Gallegos covered Shiver's body with his own:* Shiver survived his wound. After the raid, he presented Gallegos with a watch inscribed with a message thanking him for saving his life.

219 *"This fed jumped up out of the blue":* Reavis, p. 155.

220 *County ambulance drivers refused:* Bill Buford and Guillermo Gallegos interviews.

220 *"There was no leadership at all":* DiBetta, pp. 107–8; Dave DiBetta interview.

221 *That relatively gentle brushoff:* Baylor University Texas Collection, Kirk D. Lyons Collection, Box 5, Folder 1.

221 *Most of the agents thought they'd go back:* Kris Wright and Rory Heisch interviews.

221 *Wade Brown turned to face the building:* "Waco Firefight Narrative."

221 *"Let us know when we can start":* Baylor University Texas Collection, Mark Swett Collection, Box 9 OVZ, Folder 37.

CHAPTER TWENTY-NINE: THE RAID—AFTERMATH

223 *Kathy Schroeder was asked to go to the kitchen:* Kathy Schroeder interview.

223 *It was assumed he was dying:* Clive Doyle and Kathy Schroeder interviews.

224 *"Hello, Mamma. It's your boy":* Wessinger, *How the Millennium Comes Violently,* p. 85.

224 *Koresh said it was the Lord's Will:* Doyle, p. 143.

224 *"All calm, positive negotiations":* Waco FBI transcripts, Box 25i, Folder 1. The FBI transcripts included notes taken by ATF agents and McLennan County sheriff's department Lieutenant Larry Lynch before the FBI arrived on Monday, March 1, to take command of the operation.

224 *Wayne Martin continued his diatribes:* Ibid.

224 *they were helicopters from TV stations:* Reavis, p. 177.

224 *Agent Robert White assigned a few volunteers:* Robert White and Guillermo Gallegos interviews.

225 *they immediately called spouses:* Carla Bell Mayfield and Mike Russell interviews.

225 *As the Mount Carmel battle raged:* Jack Grabowski interview; Doyle, pp. 129–30; Reavis, pp. 190–99; Haldeman, p. 129; "Report of the Department of the Treasury on the Bureau of Alcohol, Tobacco and Firearms Investigation of Vernon Wayne Howell, also known as David Koresh" (September 1993). ATF "Operation Trojan Horse." Afterward, there was considerable controversy about how Mike Schroeder met his death. Surviving Branch Davidians feel that certain bullet holes and trace evidence on his body indicate he was shot at close rather than long range. Schroeder's body, when finally removed from the brush behind the compound several days later, had also been ravaged by coyotes.

229 *reached out to tell his side of the story:* CNN transcript; Thibodeau, p. 186; FBI transcripts, Box 25i, Folder 1.

230 *But the significance wasn't lost:* J. Phillip Arnold and James Tabor interviews.

230 *Young Kiri Jewell saw Koresh on CNN:* Kiri Jewell, 1995 Congressional testimony.

230 *For much of the rest of the night:* Noesner, pp. 98–100; FBI transcripts, Box 25i, Folder 1.

231 *While Koresh and Schneider were on the phone:* David Thibodeau and Kathy Schroeder interviews.

CHAPTER THIRTY: THE FBI TAKES OVER

233 *They were disgusted to hear:* Robert White, Mike Russell, and Mike Duncan interviews.

233 *At a different meeting:* Kris Mayfield, Carla Bell Mayfield, Mike Duncan, Sam Cohen, Blake Boteler, Robert White, and Mike Duncan interviews.

234 *Hartnett sent out an undated memorandum:* I received a copy of this memorandum from a source.

234 *The FBI had been part of the February 28 operation:* Byron Sage interview.

235 *The FBI received a formal request:* "Report of the Department of the Treasury on the Bureau of Alcohol, Tobacco and Firearms Investigation of Vernon Wayne Howell, also known as David Koresh" (September 1993).

235 *They were led by agent Dick Rogers:* Noesner, pp. 94–95.

235 *relegated to a prop plane:* Ibid.

235 *the FBI's immediate goal:* 106th Congress, 2nd Session, House Report 106-1037, "The Tragedy at Waco: New Evidence Examined," Committee on Government Reform (December 28, 2000).

236 *the Branch Davidians weren't charmed:* Doyle, pp. 131–32.

236 *Noesner quickly established:* Noesner, pp. 101–2.

236 *One of their first sources:* Ibid., p. 105.

237 *David Thibodeau recalls that breakfast was:* David Thibodeau interview; Thibodeau, p. viii.

237 *The first evidence that the FBI was ready to fight:* Todd Kerstetter, "'That's Just the American Way,': The Branch Dividian Tragedy and Western Religious History," *Western Historical Quarterly* 35, no. 4 (Winter 2004).

237 *Koresh came on the phone to warn:* FBI transcripts, Box 25i, Folder 2.

237 *Koresh, stating the obvious:* Ibid.

237 *The wound on Koresh's side was seeping:* Kathy Schroeder interview; Reavis, pp. 215–16, 281.

238 *he made an offer:* FBI transcripts, Box 25i, Folder 2.

CHAPTER THIRTY-ONE: LOST IN TRANSLATION

240 *he was upbeat:* FBI transcripts, Box 25i, Folder 2.

240 *By 1:50 a.m., they had two commitments:* FBI transcripts, Box 25i, Folder 1.

240 *"I know I'm in trouble":* FBI transcripts, Box 25i, Folder 2.

240 *for Koresh and his followers:* Kathy Schroeder interview.

241 *the women were arrested:* Wessinger, *How the Millennium Comes Violently*, p. 72.

241 *Carlton Stowers spoke with Matteson:* Carlton Stowers interview.

242 *CBN executives informed the FBI:* FBI transcripts, Box 25i, Folder 1.

242 *Koresh introduced himself:* CBN transcript.

243 *"We gathered in the cafeteria"* Kathy Schroeder, Baylor University Texas Collection, Kirk D. Lyons Collection, Box 5, Folder 2.

243 *an unidentified Branch Davidian woman came on the line:* FBI transcripts, Box 25i, Folder 2.

243 *Koresh informed the negotiators:* Ibid.

243 *he was informing them that he was calling off:* Kathy Schroeder interview; Schroeder, Baylor University Texas Collection, Kirk D. Lyons Collection, Box 5, Folder 2.

244 *Schneider called back and reported:* Noesner, pp. 109–11.

244 *FBI leaders outside Mount Carmel were furious:* Ibid.

245 *"Honestly, we were going to come out":* Ibid.

CHAPTER THIRTY-TWO: SETTLING INTO THE SIEGE

247 *"I did let you down yesterday":* FBI transcripts, Box 25i, Folder 2.

249 *During the first weeks of the siege:* Waco Tribune-Herald (April 1, 1993); Todd Kerstetter, "'That's Just the American Way,': The Branch Dividian Tragedy and Western Religious History," *Western Historical Quarterly* 35, no. 4 (Winter 2004).

249 *"For someone who claimed to be Jesus":* Joe Treen, "The Evil Messiah," WHO (Australia) (March 15, 1993).

250 *By the end of the siege's fifth day:* Thibodeau, p. 213.

251 *From there, they were taken:* Noesner, p. 188.

251 *Rachel Koresh, David Koresh's first wife:* Thibodeau, p. 213.

251 *Koresh sent out $1,000 in cash:* FBI transcripts, Box 25i, Folder 1.

251 *The Branch Davidians believed that their children:* Kathy Schroeder interview.

251 *Joyce Sparks recalled that the kids:* San Antonio Current (March 11, 1993).

251 *Dr. Bruce Perry, an associate professor of psychology and behavioral sciences:* Dr. Bruce Perry, 1995 Congressional testimony.

252 *On March 9, the Texas Department of Protective and Regulatory Services:* Reavis, p. 230.

252 *it might elicit too much sympathy:* Ibid., pp. 227–28.

252 *"You have to understand":* FBI transcripts, Box 25i, Folder 1.

252 *"David is willing to work together":* Ibid.

252 *"When Schneider is on the phone":* Doyle, p. 138.

253 *he'd lost three pints of blood:* FBI transcripts, Box 25i, Folder 2.

253 *planted a listening device in the box:* Reavis, p. 246.

253 *Koresh taught his followers:* FBI transcripts, Box 25i, Folder 2.

254 *"Your talk is becoming vain"*: Ibid.

254 *Jeff Jamar cut electric power*: FBI transcripts, Box 25i, Folder 1.

254 *transmitted a proposed action plan*: 106th Congress, 2nd Session, House Report 106-1037, "The Tragedy at Waco: New Evidence Examined," Committee on Government Reform (December 28, 2000).

CHAPTER THIRTY-THREE: NEGOTIATORS VERSUS TACTICAL

257 *Only a few days into the siege*: Noesner, p. 112.

258 *negotiators sent in copies*: FBI transcripts, Box 25i, Folder 1.

258 *When Rachel Koresh took the phone*: FBI transcripts, Box 25l, Folder 2.

259 *The negotiator admitted*: Ibid.

259 *Koresh asked if the FBI*: Ibid.

259 *Jamar abruptly cut off*: Noesner, p. 117.

259 *He suggested that it could be*: FBI transcripts, Box 25l, Folder 1.

260 *cut Mount Carmel's electricity for good*: Michael Hall, "The Ghosts of Mount Carmel," *Texas Monthly* (April 2003).

260 *One, attempting to turn Schneider*: FBI transcripts, Box 25l, Folder 2.

260 *"I think what Bryan really needs"*: Noesner, p. 120.

261 *"Every day, we check"*: FBI transcripts, Box 25l, Folder 1.

261 *She reported that "they've been super"*: Ibid.

261 *"Kathy sounds like she's becoming"*: Ibid.

262 *The same evening, Jamar ordered*: Noesner, p. 122.

262 *Koresh snapped*: FBI transcripts, Box 25l, Folder 1.

262 *he wrote that a senior agent arriving*: Noesner, pp. 122–23.

262 *"Are you going to kill me?"*: FBI transcripts, Box 25l, Folders 1 and 2.

263 *CEVs knocked down Mount Carmel's*: FBI transcripts, Box 25l, Folder 1.

263 *the FBI began using*: Ibid.

263 *Schneider tried placating*: FBI transcripts, Box 25l, Folders 1 and 2.

263 *"By this time, we knew"*: Doyle, p. 138.

263 *seven more adults did surrender*: Wessinger, *How the Millennium Comes Violently*, p. 74.

263 *the PA system began blasting*: Ibid.

263 *the sound was cranked so high*: Carlton Stowers interview.

264 *Koresh instructed his followers*: Doyle, pp. 142–43.

264 *Livingstone Fagan left Mount Carmel*: FBI transcripts, Box 25l, Folder 1; J. Phillip Arnold interview.

264 *his bosses demanded "significant numbers"*: FBI transcripts, Box 25l, Folder 1.

264 *when outside sympathizers managed to circumvent*: Farris Rookstool III interview.

264 *Noesner was informed*: Noesner, pp. 126–27.

CHAPTER THIRTY-FOUR: ANOTHER WAY

Unless otherwise indicated, the information in this chapter comes from interviews with J. Phillip Arnold, James Tabor, and Dick DeGuerin.

266 *They warmed their gummy MREs:* David Thibodeau interview.

267 *"didn't think they needed to listen":* Joyce Sparks, 1995 Congressional testimony.

268 *Steve Schneider began mentioning:* FBI transcripts, Box 251, Folder 2.

CHAPTER THIRTY-FIVE: A PASSOVER PROMISE

275 *including when Passover officially commenced:* Catherine Wessinger interview; Reavis, p. 255.

275 *Steve Schneider told a negotiator:* FBI transcripts, Box 251, Folder 1.

276 *"We got a long, long statement":* Ibid.

276 *He convened an impromptu Bible study:* Thibodeau, p. 239.

276 *"David studies, contemplates, and waits":* FBI transcripts, Box 251, Folder 1.

276 *"Friends: I offer to you My Wisdom":* Collection of J. Phillip Arnold.

277 *Koresh responded to a negotiator's frantic call:* FBI transcripts, Box 251, Folder 1.

277 *"a work you will not believe":* Collection of J. Phillip Arnold.

277 *during the evening of April 10:* FBI transcripts, Box 251, Folder 1.

278 *Koresh didn't know anything about:* Ibid. Had David Koresh been aware that he was plagiarizing Cyrus Teed, he would not have wanted a book about Teed's teachings sent in to Mount Carmel. It is his reaction to hearing about the book from FBI negotiators that ultimately convinced me he had no idea that there had been another "Koresh" before him.

278 *asked again about "the Koreshian book":* Ibid.

278 *"We'd be interested in seeing it":* Ibid.

278 *Koresh asked a negotiator:* Ibid.

279 *Dick DeGuerin called in:* Dick DeGuerin interview; FBI transcripts, Box 251, Folder 1.

279 *"As far as our progress is concerned":* Collection of J. Phillip Arnold.

280 *Koresh estimated it would take him:* FBI transcripts, Box 251, Folder 1.

281 *"When the word went around":* Doyle, p. 145.

281 *They hung new signs:* FBI transcripts, Box 251, Folder 1.

281 *"We knew we were going to jail":* Doyle, p. 145.

281 *he predicted to a negotiator:* FBI transcripts, Box 251, Folder 1.

281 *"he thought he was the Lamb":* Joyce Sparks, 1995 Congressional testimony.

281 *Koresh was dictating:* J. Phillip Arnold interview; FBI transcripts, Box 251, Folder 1.

281 *he missed Thrifty Maid Hot Sauce:* FBI transcripts, Box 251, Folder 1.

282 *Sixty-two adults and twenty-one children:* Thibodeau, p. viii.

CHAPTER THIRTY-SIX: THE LIMITS OF PATIENCE

284 *Koresh was sometimes refusing:* FBI transcripts, Box 251, Folders 1 and 2.

284 *"What will move this along?":* FBI transcripts, Box 251, Folder 1.

284 *"We need to get some people out ":* FBI transcripts, Box 251, Folder 2.

286 *the Branch Davidians were limiting themselves:* Thibodeau, p. 221; Doyle, pp. 134–35.

286 *agents saw that the kids' hair:* Byron Sage interview.

286 *two Department of Justice officials met:* Department of Justice, "Evaluation of the Handling of the Branch Davidian Stand-off in Waco, Texas, February 28 to April 19, 1993" (October 8, 1993).

286 *The type of gas proposed:* 106th Congress, 2nd Session, House Report 106-1037, "The Tragedy at Waco: New Evidence Examined," Committee on Government Reform (December 28, 2000). Reavis, pp. 264–65.

287 *two addendums typed in all capital letters:* House Report 106-1037.

288 *they attempted "test fittings":* Thibodeau, p. 223.

288 *was considered an additional delaying tactic:* Farris Rookstool III interview.

288 *It included details on gas insertion:* "Briefing for the Attorney General," Department of Justice report, October 8, 1993.

289 *this briefing was "more of a sales pitch":* Noesner, p. 129.

289 *Reno still wasn't convinced:* Reavis, pp. 265–66.

289 *she disapproved the gassing plan: Dallas Morning News* (March 6, 2000). Among all the journalists covering the Mount Carmel siege, *Dallas Morning News* reporter Lee Hancock's reporting was the most insightful. No one then, or since, has done better.

289 *FBI director William Sessions called Reno:* House Report 106-1037.

289 *Koresh closed himself off:* FBI transcripts, Box 251, Folder 1.

290 *Koresh told a negotiator:* Ibid.

290 *"It would be a show of good faith":* Ibid.

290 *The massive new crater:* Ibid.

290 *he admitted to Clive Doyle:* Doyle, p. 146.

290 *Attorney General Reno informed President Clinton:* Wessinger, *How the Millennium Comes Violently,* p. 77.

291 *"We have done everything we can":* Ibid., pp. 106–12.

291 *Koresh became agitated:* Ibid.

291 *FBI surveillance devices picked up:* Kitts, ed., p. 64.

CHAPTER THIRTY-SEVEN: TO DIE IN FLAMES

For the events of April 19, 1993, the FBI created a new transcripts file titled "Major Case 80—WACMUR, Updated Event Log." (WACMUR stands for "Waco Murder." It refers to the violent deaths of four ATF agents on February 28, not the deaths of the Branch Davidians on April 19.) Unless otherwise noted, descriptions and quotes in this chapter are taken from this source.

293 *David Thibodeau was standing guard:* Thibodeau, p. ix.

294 *Thibodeau shook Schneider awake:* Ibid., p. xiii.

294 *"They opened up on us":* Byron Sage interview.

294 *Gas masks were distributed:* Thibodeau, pp. xiv–xv.

295 *"Grown men were almost in tears":* Doyle, p. 147.

296 *The news media, penned up:* Carlton Stowers interview.

297 *Branch Davidian mothers originally tried:* Thibodeau, p. xix.

297 *Many were killed by the impact:* Farris Rookstool III interview; Wessinger, *How the Millennium Comes Violently*, p. 78.

297 *They were frantically darting:* Doyle, p. 150.

297 *The wind outside grew wilder:* Rod Aydelotte and Carlton Stowers interviews.

298 *"By noon, the building is a tinderbox":* Thibodeau, p. xviii.

300 *subsequent discovery of audiotapes and photographs:* Farris Rookstool III interview. Rookstool took the photos, and was instrumental in tracking down crucial evidence afterward.

300 *There is a fourth, seldom considered:* J. Phillip Arnold and James Tabor interviews. After two years of research, and after interviewing surviving Branch Davidians who knew David Koresh, I believe this is what happened. It fits everything we know about what David and his followers believed.

301 *Clive Doyle recalls Wayne Martin:* Doyle, pp. 150–54.

301 *One muttered, "Holy shit!":* 106th Congress, 2nd Session, House Report 106-1037, "The Tragedy at Waco: New Evidence Examined," Committee on Government Reform (December 28, 2000).

301 *Timothy McVeigh, watching on television:* Lou Michel and Dan Herbeck, *American Terrorist: Timothy McVeigh & the Tragedy at Oklahoma City*, p. 161.

302 *People began appearing at different places on the roof:* Major Case 80—WACMUR, Updated Event Log; Clive Doyle and David Thibodeau interviews.

302 *It was 12:34 p.m.:* Wessinger, *How the Millennium Comes Violently*, p. 78.

302 *cans of beans, cooking all the while:* Farris Rookstool III interview.

302 *Cyrus Teed, the first Koresh:* Dr. Cyrus R. Teed, "The Clock of the Ages Strikes the Hour of Revolution," *The Flaming Sword* (March 25, 1898).

303 *six journalists would be taken to view:* Carlton Stowers interview.

303 *The Texas Rangers were tasked:* George Turner interview.

303 *While the Texas Rangers collected evidence:* Reavis, p. 293; Farris Rookstool III and George Turner interviews.

304 *They found the remains of David Koresh and Steve Schneider "close together":* Farris Rookstool III interview.

304 *David died of "massive craniocerebral trauma":* "Non-Jurisdictional Autopsy, Case No. 930009#, Vernon Howell (AKA David Koresh), Office of the Chief Medical Examiner, Tarrant County, Texas.

304 *Some Branch Davidians died of gunshot wounds:* Farris Rookstool III interview.

305 *the death toll inside Mount Carmel that day:* Haldeman, p. 121; James Tabor in-

terview and compiled list of Branch Davidian dead; Wessinger, *How the Millennium Comes Violently*, p. 58; Farris Rookstool III interview.

306 *They published "The David Koresh Manuscript":* James Tabor and J. Phillip Arnold interviews.

306 *President Bill Clinton met with the press:* White House Office of the Press Secretary, April 20, 1993.

306 *what remained of Mount Carmel was leveled:* Wessinger, *How the Millennium Comes Violently*, p. 80.

306 *A CNN poll immediately after:* Ibid.; Dara Linddara, "Waco and Ruby Ridge: The 1990s standoffs Haunting the Oregon Takeover, Explained," vox.com (January 5, 2016).

CHAPTER THIRTY-EIGHT: AFTER THE SIEGE

This chapter only briefly touches on some events that merit full books on their own, in particular the 1994 trial of eleven Branch Davidians (disappearing evidence, especially) and the investigation in 1999 that proved the FBI utilized pyrotechnic shells during the early stages of its April 19, 1993, gas assault on Mount Carmel.

During his 1995 testimony to Congress, Chuck Sarabyn insisted that undercover agent Robert Rodriguez did not specifically tell him on the morning of February 28, 1993, that David Koresh knew the ATF was about to raid Mount Carmel. "I don't think there is a disagreement on the words that Robert has said to me, it's just the interpretation of what those [words] meant to me versus what they meant to him," Sarabyn said.

Rodriguez was devastated, not only by Sarabyn's testimony, but by what he believed was a deliberate attempt by Sarabyn and Phil Chojnacki to place the blame for the catastrophic February 28 raid on him. In 1995, Rodriguez sued his supervisors and ATF, alleging he had been defamed and made a scapegoat. The case was settled out of court for about $2 million. Rodriguez left law enforcement altogether. Several other ATF agents who participated in the Waco raid have stayed in touch with him and report that Rodriguez has never fully recovered emotionally. Robert Rodriguez did not respond to an interview request conveyed to him for me by former ATF agent Keith Constantino.

Again, I regret that Phil Chojnacki, Chuck Sarabyn, and Jeff Jamar did not agree to be interviewed for this book.

307 *Attorney General Janet Reno testified:* 106th Congress, 2nd Session, House Report 106-1037, "The Tragedy at Waco: New Evidence Examined," Committee on Government Reform (December 28, 2000).

307 *He did not correct her:* Ibid.

307 *She admitted that:* Timothy Lynch, "No Confidence: An Unofficial Account of the Waco Incident," Cato Institute, Policy Analysis No. 395 (April 9, 2001).

307 *FBI director William Sessions agreed:* Reavis, p. 229.

307 *the magazine described David Koresh:* Time, Special Section (May 3, 1993).

308 60 Minutes *rebroadcast:* Lynch, "No Confidence."

308 *It essentially concluded:* "Report of the Department of the Treasury on the Bureau of Alcohol, Tobacco and Firearms Investigation of Vernon Wayne Howell, also known as David Koresh" (September 1993).

308 *ATF's new focus became:* San Francisco Chronicle (November 2, 2013).

308 *New agency director John Magaw:* John Magaw, 1995 Congressional testimony.

309 *The Department of Justice inquiry:* Department of Justice, "Evaluation of the Handling of the Branch Davidian Stand-off in Waco, Texas, February 28 to April 19, 1993" (October 8, 1993).

309 *Gary Noesner wrote:* Noesner, p. 131.

309 *Kathy Schroeder, credited with turning state's evidence:* Kathy Schroeder interview; Kathy Schroeder, Baylor University Texas Collection, Kirk D. Lyons Collection, Box 5, Folder 2.

310 *the lawyers maintained:* Lynch, "No Confidence."

310 *Judge Smith instructed jurists:* Haldeman, pp. 163–69.

310 *Jury foreman Sarah Bain:* Lynch, "No Confidence."

310 *Judge Smith set aside:* Wessinger, How the Millennium Comes Violently, p. 59.

310 *in 2000 the U.S. Supreme Court ruled:* Haldeman, pp. 163–69.

310 *ATF agents sued:* Mike Russell and Tommy Witherspoon interviews; Dallas Morning News (February 27, 2018).

310 *Surviving Branch Davidians and relatives:* Lynch, "No Confidence."

311 *But in June 2000:* House Report 106-1037.

311 *"We admitted it. We said it":* John Magaw, 1995 Congressional testimony.

311 *Four FBI agents:* New York Times (September 20, 1995).

311 *allegations by filmmaker Michael McNulty:* House Report 106-1037.

311 *"pyrotechnic devices may have been used":* Lynch, "No Confidence."

311 *Attorney General Janet Reno raged:* New York Times (August 26, 1999).

311 *Jeff Jamar told a* Times *reporter:* Ibid.

312 *"This affects the credibility":* Dallas Morning News (July 28, 1999).

312 *he issued an "interim report":* Lynch, "No Confidence."

312 *the former senator's final report:* House Report 106-1037.

312 *The Department of Justice issued its own statement:* Lynch, "No Confidence."

CHAPTER THIRTY-NINE: A LEGACY OF RAGE

317 *"a number of ridiculous charges":* Ron Engleman, ed., "Randy Weaver Update," and "Ron's Waco Update," The Freedom Report, Vol. 1 (September 1993).

318 *Robert Spoon, a ranch hand:* Chicago Tribune (April 23, 1995).

318 *Clive Doyle presided:* Ibid.

319 *"It's because of Waco":* Michel and Herbeck, p. 318.

319 *"I didn't define the rules"*: Ibid., p. 267.

319 *Clive Doyle described the Oklahoma City bombing*: Chicago Tribune (April 23, 1995).

319 *"It's become an excuse"*: Ibid.

319 *A pamphlet distributed*: Irwin Suall, "Armed and Dangerous: Militias Take Aim at the Federal Government," Anti-Defamation League (1994).

320 *Louis J. Freeh lauded*: CNN broadcast, 6/14/1996.

320 *"The FBI deserved no special commendation"*: New York Times (June 14, 1996).

321 *the number of "anti-government groups"*: Southern Poverty Law Center, "The Year in Hate and Extremism, 2021: Anti-Government Groups 1999–2021."

321 *Gingrich said, "We have to understand"*: New York Times (May 8, 1995).

321 *This was an especially auspicious occasion*: Dallas Morning News (April 20, 2000).

322 *rose to 542 by year's end*: Southern Poverty Law Center, "The Year in Hate and Extremism, 2021."

322 *included confiscating citizens' guns*: New York Times (July 12, 2015).

322 *Texas governor Greg Abbott promptly ordered*: Ibid.

323 *"during the 2015–2016 [presidential] campaign"*: Anti-Defamation League, "The Militia Movement, 2020" (October 19, 2020).

323 *New enemies were needed*: Ibid.

324 *"In almost every society"*: Jacob G. Hornberger, "Bill Clinton's Massacres and Terrorist Blowback," The Future of Freedom Foundation (April 20, 2010).

EPILOGUE: CLIVE DOYLE IS WAITING

Most of this epilogue is based on my interview in Waco with Clive Doyle on June 6, 2021. The two exceptions are noted below.

327 *"the Mount Carmel events confirmed"*: Wessinger, How the Millennium Comes Violently, p. 91.

327 *"If God is going to do something"*: Doyle, p. 179.

Bibliography

Books

Ashcraft, W. Michael. *A Historical Introduction to the Study of New Religious Movements*. Routledge, 2018.

Boyer, Paul. *When Time Shall Be No More: Prophecy Belief in Modern American Culture*. Belknap Press of Harvard University Press, 1992.

Breault, Marc, and Martin King. *Inside the Cult: A Member's Chilling, Exclusive Account of Madness and Depravity in David Koresh's Compound*. Signet, 1993.

Carmer, Carl. *Dark Trees to the Wind*. William Sloane Associates, 1949.

DiBetta, David, with Scott Fasnacht. *Plain Old Agent: Reflections on the Siege at Waco and My Career with ATF*. Acclaim Press, 2015.

Doyle, Clive, with Catherine Wessinger and Matthew D. Wittmer. *A Journey to Waco: Autobiography of a Branch Davidian*. Rowman & Littlefield, 2012.

Fagan, Livingstone. *". . . the Mystery of God Should Be Finished . . ."* Self-published, 2021.

——. *Understanding Waco & Salvation*. Self-published, 2017.

——. *Waco: What Comes Next?* Self-published, 2019.

Frost, Wendel E. *ATF: Sierra One Waco*. PublishAmerica, 2008.

Haldeman, Bonnie, and Catherine Wessinger, ed. *Memories of the Branch Davidians: The Autobiography of David Koresh's Mother*. Baylor University Press, 2007.

Holy Bible: King James Version. Christian Art Publishers, 2019.

Houteff, V. T. *The Shepherd's Rod: The 144,000 of Revelation 7—Call for Reformation, Vol. 1*. Universal Publishing Association, 1930.

Jenkins, Philip. *Mystics and Messiahs: Cults and New Religions in American History*. Oxford University Press, 2000.

Kitts, Margo, ed. *Martyrdom, Self-Sacrifice and Self-Immolation: Religious Perspectives on Suicide*. Oxford University Press, 2018.

Koresh (Teed, Cyrus R.) and U. G. Morrow. *The Cellular Cosmogony; Or, the Earth a Concave Sphere*. Guiding Star Publishing House, 1898.

Lewis, James R., ed. *From the Ashes: Making Sense of Waco*. Rowman & Littlefield, 1994.

Michel, Lou, and Dan Herbeck. *American Terrorist: Timothy McVeigh & the Tragedy at Oklahoma City*. HarperCollins, 2001.

Millner, Lyn. *The Allure of Immortality: An American Cult, a Florida Swamp, and a Renegade Prophet*. University Press of Florida, 2015.

Morris, Adam. *American Messiahs: False Prophets of a Damned Nation*. Liveright, 2019.

Newport, Kenneth G. C. *The Branch Davidians of Waco: The History and Beliefs of an Apocalyptic Sect*. Oxford University Press, 2006.

Nicolson, Adam. *God's Secretaries: The Making of the King James Bible*. Harper, 2003.

Noesner, Gary. *Stalling for Time: My Life as an FBI Hostage Negotiator*. Random House, 2010.

Reavis, Dick J. *The Ashes of Waco: An Investigation*. Simon & Schuster, 1995.

Roden, Ben. *The Flying Roll: Zechariah 5*. Universal Publishing Association, 1969.

Tabor, James D., and Eugene V. Gallagher. *Why Waco? Cults and the Battle for Religious Freedom in America*. University of California Press, 1995.

Thibodeau, David, with Leon Whiteson and Aviva Layton. *Waco: A Survivor's Story—Updated and Revised Edition*. Hachette, 2018.

Weimar, J. Augustus. *Koreshanity: The New Age Religion*. Elizabeth G. Bartosch/The Koreshan Foundation, reprint 1971.

Wessinger, Catherine. *How the Millennium Comes Violently: From Jonestown to Heaven's Gate*. Seven Bridges Press, 2000.

———, ed. *The Oxford Handbook of Millennialism*. Oxford University Press, 2011.

Wright, Stuart A., ed. *Armageddon in Waco: Critical Perspectives on the Branch Davidian Conflict*. University of Chicago Press, 1995.

Periodicals, Journals, and Newsletters

Anti-Defamation League, "The Militia Movement, 2020" (October 19, 2020).

Arnold, J. Phillip, "The Resolution of the Branch Davidian Dilemma," Reunion Institute, Baylor University, Institute for the Studies of Religion (April 18, 2013).

Beran, Dale, "The Boogaloo Tipping Point: What Happens When a Meme Becomes a Terrorist Movement?," *The Atlantic* (July 2020).

Berger, J. M., "What Do the Oregon Ranchers Really Believe?," *Politico* (January 10, 2016).

Cartwright, Dixon,"21 Years Ago This Month: Waco Eyewitness Argues That 1994 Holocaust Was Avoidable," *The Journal: News of the Churches of God* 161 (April 30, 2014).

Catlin, Roger, "The True Story of 'Waco' Is Still One of Contention," *Smithsonian* (January 2018).

Engleman, Ron, "Hot Talk KGBS Radio" (guests: Dr. J. Phillip Arnold and Dr. James Tabor), transcript (April 1, 1993).

———, ed., "Randy Weaver Update" and "Ron's Waco Update," *The Freedom Report* 1 (September 1993).

Firearms Sentinel: Intellectual Ammunition to Destroy "Gun Control," 1, no. 1 (January 1995).

Gladwell, Malcolm, "Sacred and Profane: How Not to Negotiate with Believers," *The New Yorker* (March 31, 2014).

Hall, Michael, "The Ghosts of Mount Carmel," *Texas Monthly* (April 2003).

Hornberger Jacob G., "Bill Clinton's Massacres and Terrorist Blowback," The Future of Freedoms Foundation (April 20, 2010).

Hustmyre, Chuck, "Trojan Horse: Inside the ATF Raid at Waco, Texas," *Close Quarter Combat Magazine* 20 (August/September 2003).

James L. Pate, "Gun Gestapo's Day of Infamy," *Soldier of Fortune* (June 1993).

Kerstetter, Todd, " 'That's Just the American Way': The Branch Davidian Tragedy and Western Religious History," *Western Historical Quarterly* 35, no. 4 (Winter 2004).

Linddara, Dara, "Waco and Ruby Ridge: The 1990s Standoffs Haunting the Oregon Takeover, Explained," vox.com (January 5, 2016).

Lynch, Timothy "No Confidence: An Unofficial Account of the Waco Incident," Cato Institute, Policy Analysis No. 395 (April 9, 2001).

Militia News, "Remember" (February 7, 2019).

Miller, Cassie, and Rachel Carroll Rivas, "The Year in Hate and Extremism, 2021." Southern Poverty Law Center (March 9, 2022).

Moore, James, "What Really Happened at Waco," *Huffington Post* (February 28, 2007).

Moore, Rebecca, "Perspective: Godwin's Law and Jones' Corollary: The Problem of Using Extremes to Make Predictions," *Nova Religio: The Journal of Alternative and Emergent Religions* 22, no. 2 (November 2018).

Parsons, Chelsea and Arkadi Gerney, "The Bureau and the Bureau," Center for American Progress Report (May 19, 2015).

Paul, Ron, "The Lessons of Waco," Ron Paul Institute for Peace and Prosperity (June 14, 2021).

Rainard, R. Lyn, "Conflict Inside the Earth: The Koreshan Unity of Lee County," *Tampa Bay History* (Department of History, University of South Florida) 3, no. 1 (June 1, 1981).

Rathod, Sara, "Patriot Games: A Brief History of Militias in America," *Mother Jones* (November/December 2016).

Roden, Ami (on behalf of George Roden), *The Branch Association* (November 9, 1987).

Shekinah, "Our Mother, Who Art in Heaven" (February 1981).

Simpson, Ian, "Ex-ATF Agents Recall Storm of Gunfire in Deadly 1993 Waco Raid," Reuters U.S. News (February 8, 2013).

Stowers, Carlton, "Show of Force: Was the ATF's Military-Style Assault the Best Way to Flush Out David 'I Am the Lamb' Koresh and the Branch Davidians?," *San Antonio Current* (March 11, 1993).

Suall, Irwin, "Armed and Dangerous: Militias Take Aim at the Federal Government Fact Finding Report," Anti-Defamation League (1994).

Teed, Dr. Cyrus R. (Koresh), "God the Lord Is Alternately Male and Female," *The Flaming Sword* (January 23, 1892).

———, "For Those Who Can Believe," *The Flaming Sword* (January 26, 1900).

———, "The Clock of the Ages Strikes the Hour of Revolution," *The Flaming Sword* (March 25, 1898).

———, "The Possibility of Overcoming Death," *The Flaming Sword* (January 21, 1898).

Thomma, Steven, "'No More Wacos' Becomes Battle Cry for Extremists," *Spokesman-Review* (April 23, 1995).

Time, "Life After the Apocalypse," October 11, 1993.

———, "Waco's False Spring," April 19, 1993.

———, Special Section, May 3, 1993.

Treen, Joe, "The Evil Messiah," *WHO* (Australia) (March 15, 1993).

Waite, Albert A. C., "From Seventh-day Adventism to David Koresh: The British Connection," *Andrews University Seminary Studies* 38, no. 1 (Spring 2000).

Wessinger, Catherine, " 'Cult' Is an Inaccurate, Unhelpful and Dangerous Label for Followers of Trump, QAnon and 1/6," *Religion Dispatches* (July 19, 2021).

White, Robert, as told to Steven Russell, "Ground Zero at Waco: I Was There," *Maxim* (October 2000).

Winsboro, Irvin D. S., "The Koreshan Communitarians' Papers and Publications in Estero, 1894–1963," *Florida Historical Quarterly* 83, no. 2 (Fall 2004).

Wright, Stuart A., "Media Reconstructions of the Federal Siege of the Branch Davidians," *Nova Religio: The Journal of Alternative and Emergent Religions* 22, no. 3 (February 2019).

Newspapers

Austin American Statesman (March 7, 1993; April 19, 2018).

Austin Chronicle (June 23, 2000).

Baltimore Sun (December 26, 1908).

Chicago Tribune (April 24, 1995; July 20, 1995).

Daily Beast (November 26, 2021).

Dallas Morning News (July 28, 1999; August 24, 1999; October 27, 1999; February 27, 2018; March 6, 2000).

Duarte (CA) *Star-Tribune* (March 1, 1993).

The Guardian (April 13, 2014).

Houston Chronicle (March 2, 1993; January 26, 1994; February 8, 1994; March 10, 1994).

Los Angeles Times (July 20, 1995).

New York Times (August 10, 1884; July 27, 1887; June 10, 1892; December 25, 1908;

August 23, 1992; March 28, 1993; April 20, 1993; September 28, 1993; January 17, 1994; January 19, 1994; February 8, 1994; February 12, 1994; February 13, 1994; February 16, 1994; February 17, 1994; March 1, 1994; January 7, 1995; April 23, 1995; May 8, 1995; May 14, 1995; May 15, 1995; August 12, 1995; September 3, 1995; September 4, 1995; September 7, 1995; September 15, 1995; September 20, 1995; October 20, 1995; December 22, 1995; April 14, 1996; October 31, 1996; June 11, 1997; August 27, 1999; June 18, 2000; July 15, 2000; May 13,2001; June 6, 2001; July 17, 2001; October 10, 2001; December 13, 2002; March 30, 2010; July 12, 2015; December 31, 2018; March 7, 2022).

New York Times Magazine (August 19, 2020).

San Francisco Chronicle (November 2, 2013).

San Gabriel Valley (CA) *Tribune* (April 18, 2002).

USA Today (February 28, 1994; June 20, 2002).

Waco Tribune-Herald (January 17, 1988; April 18, 1992; April 19, 1992; February 27, 1993; February 28, 1993; March 1, 1993; March 6, 1993; May 28, 1993; June 10, 1993; September 24, 1993; January 13, 1994; February 28, 1994; February 24, 2018; April 18, 2018; April 19, 2018).

Washington Post (April 8, 1993; February 16, 1994; July 20, 1995; October 6, 1999).

Washington Times (January 26, 1994; February 5, 1994; February 16, 1994; March 10, 1994).

Federal and State Government Sources, Documents, and Reports

104th Congress, 2nd Session, House Report 104–749, "Investigation into the Activities of Federal Law Enforcement Agencies Toward the Branch Davidians," Committee of Government Reform and Oversight (August 2, 1996).

106th Congress, 2nd Session, House Report 106–1037, "The Tragedy at Waco: New Evidence Examined," Committee on Government Reform, December 28, 2000.

ATF Internal Document, "Investigation into Raid Information Source for Journalist Tommy Witherspoon, *Waco Tribune-Herald*" (undated).

———, "Waco Firefight Narrative" (August 10, 1994).

Bureau of Alcohol, Tobacco, Firearms and Explosives (www.atf.gov).

Committee of the Judiciary, Subcommittee on Government Reform and Oversight; Subcommittee on National Security, International Affairs and Criminal Justice, Transcript of Joint Hearings, House Subcommittees (July 19–21 and 24, 1995).

Department of Justice (www.justice.gov/archive).

Department of Justice, "Evaluation of the Handling of the Branch Davidian Standoff in Waco, Texas, February 28 to April 19" (October 8, 1993).

Federal Bureau of Investigation Case Files (obtained through the Freedom of Information Act are identified by file numbers in the chapter notes).

"Non-Jurisdictional Autopsy, Case No. 930009#, Vernon Howell (AKA David Koresh)," Office of the Chief Medical Examiner, Tarrant County, Texas.

"Report of the Department of the Treasury on the Bureau of Alcohol, Tobacco and Firearms Investigation of Vernon Wayne Howell, also known as David Koresh" (September 1993).

Texas Rangers Investigative Report, Branch Davidian Evidence (included in House Report 106–1037) (September 1999).

Texas Rangers Investigative Report #2, Branch Davidian Evidence (included in House Report 106–1037) (January 2000).

U.S. Government Accountability Office, "Department of Defense, Military Assistance Provided at Branch Davidian Incident" (August 26, 1999).

Legal Documents

Affidavit and Search Warrant, United States District Court, Western District of Texas, Waco Division, Case Number W93–15M, for the 77-acre Branch Davidian Compound (filed February 26, 1993).

Criminal Complaint, United States of America v. Vernon Wayne Howell, AKA David Koresh, United States District Court, Western District of Texas, Waco Division, Case Number W93–17M (filed February 26, 1993).

Government's Motion to Seal Complaint, United States of America v. Vernon Wayne Howell, AKA David Koresh, United States District Court, Western District of Texas, Waco Division, Case Number W93–17M (filed February 26, 1993).

Warrant for Arrest, United States of America v. Vernon Wayne Howell, AKA David Koresh, United States District Court, Western District of Texas, Waco Division, Case Number W93–17M (filed February 26, 1993).

Archival Collections

Baylor University Texas Collection (Kirk D. Lyons, Joe Robert, William Smith, and Mark Swett Collections), Waco, Texas.

Koreshan Collection, University Archives and Special Collections, Bradshaw Library, Florida Gulf Coast University, Fort Myers, Florida.

Collection of Dr. J. Phillip Arnold.

"David Koresh as Messiah" by Livingstone Fagan.

Society of Professional Journalists Task Force Report.

Index

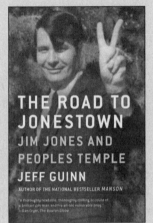

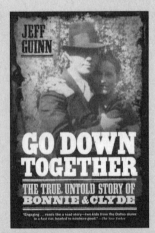